T0312177

Classical Economics, Keynes and Money

Classical Economics, Keynes and Money casts new light on an approach to economic theory and policy that combines the modern classical theory of prices and income distribution with a Keynesian analysis of money and finance.

Structured in four parts, the work considers issues within classical economics, monetary economics, Keynesian and post-Keynesian Economics, rationality and economic methodology. These themes are all central to the work of Carlo Panico, and the chapters both reflect on and build on his key contributions to the field.

This collection is of interest to advanced students and researchers in the history of economic thought, monetary theory, financial economics and heterodox economics.

John Eatwell is Honorary Fellow of Queens' College, Cambridge; Member of House of Lords of the United Kingdom; and Foreign Fellow of Accademia Nazionale dei Lincei, Italy, and was President of Queens' College, Cambridge.

Pasquale Commendatore is Professor of Economics at the University of Naples Federico II, Italy.

Neri Salvadori was Professor of Economics at University of Pisa, Italy, and is Corresponding Fellow of Accademia Nazionale dei Lincei, Italy.

Routledge Studies in the History of Economics

For more information about this series, please visit: www.routledge.com/series/SE0341

Classical Economics, Keynes and Money

Essays in Honour of Carlo Panico

Edited by John Eatwell,
Pasquale Commendatore and
Neri Salvadori

Routledge
Taylor & Francis Group

LONDON AND NEW YORK

First published 2023
by Routledge
4 Park Square, Milton Park, Abingdon, Oxon OX14 4RN

and by Routledge
605 Third Avenue, New York, NY 10158

Routledge is an imprint of the Taylor & Francis Group, an informa business

© 2023 selection and editorial matter, John Eatwell, Pasquale
Commendatore and Neri Salvadori; individual chapters, the contributors

The right of John Eatwell, Pasquale Commendatore and Neri Salvadori to
be identified as the authors of the editorial material, and of the authors for
their individual chapters, has been asserted in accordance with sections 77
and 78 of the Copyright, Designs and Patents Act 1988.

All rights reserved. No part of this book may be reprinted or reproduced or
utilised in any form or by any electronic, mechanical, or other means, now
known or hereafter invented, including photocopying and recording, or in
any information storage or retrieval system, without permission in writing
from the publishers.

Trademark notice: Product or corporate names may be trademarks or
registered trademarks, and are used only for identification and explanation
without intent to infringe.

British Library Cataloguing-in-Publication Data
A catalogue record for this book is available from the British Library

Library of Congress Cataloguing-in-Publication Data
Names: Eatwell, John, editor. | Commendatore, Pasquale, editor. |
Salvadori, Neri, editor.
Title: Classical economics, Keynes and money / John Eatwell, Pasquale
Commendatore and Neri Salvadori.
Description: Abingdon, Oxon ; New York, NY : Routledge, 2022. |
Series: Routledge studies in the history of economics | Includes
bibliographical references and index.
Identifiers: LCCN 2021062454 (print) | LCCN 2021062455 (ebook)
Subjects: LCSH: Economics. | Keynesian economics. | Distribution
(Economic theory)
Classification: LCC HB171 .C62 2022 (print) | LCC HB171 (ebook) |
DDC 330--dc23/eng/20220128
LC record available at https://lccn.loc.gov/2021062454
LC ebook record available at https://lccn.loc.gov/2021062455

ISBN: 978-0-367-61570-3 (hbk)
ISBN: 978-0-367-61571-0 (pbk)
ISBN: 978-1-003-10555-8 (ebk)

DOI: 10.4324/9781003105558

Typeset in Bembo
by MPS Limited, Dehradun

Contents

Contributors

Salvatore Capasso is Professor of Economics at the University of Naples 'Parthenope', Italy and the Director of Institute of Studies on Mediterranean Economy (ISMED), CNR, Naples, Italy.

Santiago Capraro Rodríguez is Professor of Economics at UNAM, Mexico.

Salvatore Ciucci is Scholarship Holder (assegnista di ricerca) at Institute of Studies on Mediterranean Economy (ISMED), CNR, Napoli, Italy.

Pasquale Commendatore is Professor of Economics at the University of Naples Federico II, Italy.

Amitava Krishna Dutt is Professor of Economics at the University of Notre Dame, IN, United States, and Distinguished Professor at FLACSO, Quito, Ecuador.

John Eatwell is Honorary Fellow of Queens' College, Cambridge; Member of House of Lords of the United Kingdom; and Foreign Fellow of Accademia Nazionale dei Lincei, Italy, and was President of Queens' College, Cambridge.

Valerio Filoso is Associate Professor of Economics at the University of Naples Federico II, Italy, and Research Associate at Institute of Studies on Mediterranean Economy (ISMED), CNR, Napoli, Italy.

Giuseppe Freni is Professor of Economics at the University of Naples 'Parthenope', Italy.

Geoff C. Harcourt, who died on 6 December 2021, was Visiting Professorial Fellow at School of Economics, University of New South Wales, Australia; Reader in the Faculty of Economics at the University of Cambridge and Fellow of Jesus College; and Professor of Economics at the University of Adelaide.

Celia Lessa Kerstenetzky is Professor of Economics at the Federal University of Rio de Janeiro, Brazil.

Peter Kriesler is Professor of Economics at the University of New South Wales, Canberra, Australia.

Ingrid Kubin is Professor of Economics at the WU Vienna University of Economics and Business, Vienna, Austria.

Heinz D. Kurz is Professor Emeritus at Graz Schumpeter Centre, University of Graz, Graz, Austria, and was Professor of Economics at the University of Graz.

Michele Limosani is Professor of Economics at the University of Messina, Italy.

Maria Cristina Marcuzzo was Professor of Economics at the University of Rome 'La Sapienza' and is Corresponding Fellow of Accademia Nazionale dei Lincei, Italy.

Giuseppe Mastromatteo was Professor of Economics at the Catholic University of the Sacred Heart of Milan, Italy.

Emanuele Millemaci is Associate Professor of Economics at the University of Messina, Italy.

Fabio Monteforte is Scholarship Holder (assegnista di ricerca) at the University of Messina, Italy.

Juan Carlo Moreno Brid is Professor of Economics at UNAM, Mexico, and was Research Coordinator/Associate Director of ECLAC-MEXICO.

Erasmo Papagni is Professor of Public Economics at the University of Naples Federico II, Italy.

Esteban Pérez Caldentey is Coordinator of the Unit of Finance for Development, United Nations' Economic Commission of Latin America and the Caribbean, Santiago de Chile, Chile.

Cosimo Perrotta was Professor of History of Economic Thought at the University of Salento, Lecce, Italy.

Fabio Petri was Professor of Economics at the Università di Siena, Italy.

Giovanni B. Pittaluga is Emeritus Professor of Economics at Genoa University.

Francesco Purificato is Assistant Professor at the University of Naples Federico II, Italy.

Neri Salvadori was Professor of Economics at the University of Pisa, Italy, and is Corresponding Fellow of Accademia Nazionale dei Lincei, Italy.

Elvira Sapienza is Assistant Professor of Economics at the University of Naples Federico II, Italy.

Rodolfo Signorino is Associate Professor at the University of Palermo, Italy.

Iryna Sushko is Senior Research Fellow of the National Academy of Sciences of Ukraine.

1 Introduction

John Eatwell, Pasquale Commendatore, and Neri Salvadori

This collection of essays is a tribute to Carlo Panico, the pupil, colleague, teacher and friend. But above all the author of important works that develop and evaluate the explanatory power of Classical Economics and Keynesian analysis.

The role of monetary and financial factors in income distribution, development and growth has always been Carlo's main research interest. His intellectual journey began with his PhD dissertation. In that dissertation, he explores the theoretical consequences of Sraffa's hint in *Production of Commodities by Means of Commodities* that it is the rate of interest that is the key to the determination of the distribution of income. The argument was built around a detailed consideration of the evolution of economic thought on the role of the rate of interest in the works of, among others, Marx, Marshall, and Keynes. This set the style for Carlo's later work, approaching analytical questions by first comparing different traditions. For example, he has expanded the study of the impact of monetary factors on income distribution, development and growth by comparing Tobin's and post-Keynesian approaches. Building on this work he later provided a complete analytical framework for financial model building by integrating Tobin's portfolio choice theory and Post-Keynesian theories of income distribution. The monetary theory of distribution hinted at by Sraffa is reconciled with Post-Keynesian theories of growth and income distribution (functional, personal and institutional). These analyses lead Carlo to the debate in the post-Keynesian literature on the 'endogeneity of the money supply'. He supports the Kaldor and Keynes position that monetary authorities do not 'fix' the money supply since to attempt to do so would result in 'undesirable consequences'. His other contributions involved a detailed consideration of Sraffa's early writing on monetary and political matters. Carlo's approach of comparing different economic arguments has been further pursued by integrating in a unified framework various strands of post-Keynesian approaches (Harrod, Kaldor, Pasinetti, and the Steindl-Kalecki), the surplus approach and cumulative causation and evolutionary analyses. He also used this analytical work in applied studies concerned mainly with the coordination of monetary and fiscal policies, the evolution of financial regulation, the institutional organisation of the European Monetary

DOI: 10.4324/9781003105558-1

Union, the impact of the recent financial crisis on income distribution and, more recently, on the economic policy in Mexico. His contribution to the understanding of the analytical approach of, among others, Keynes, Sraffa, Kaldor, Harrod, Kahn, Myrdal, Marx, and Marshall led him to explore some methodological issues concerning rationality in economics.

The editors had close working relationships with Carlo Panico over the past 40 years. John Eatwell was his supervisor in Cambridge when Carlo Panico obtained his PhD, Pasquale Commendatore earned his degrees at the University of Catania and at the University of Naples 'Federico II' under Carlo Panico's supervision, Neri Salvadori has been a close friend since when they were both students at the University of Naples 'Federico II'. All of them have been his co-authors.

The essays in this book have all been freshly written . All the chapters have been reviewed by anonymous referees. The reviewers include many of the contributors to the volume and some other scholars who were not able to contribute to the volume but wanted to honour Carlo by participating in this enterprise as referees. They are Tony Aspromourgos, Roberto Ciccone, Tommaso Luzzati, Martin Puchet, and Marta Vázquez Suárez.

The book is divided into four parts: Classical theory of value and distribution, Keynesian and post-Keynesian theories of growth and distribution, monetary and fiscal policies and the role of institutions, and the problem of rationality in economics. There is also a note by John Eatwell on 'Asking the right questions'. It includes some 'personal reminiscences'and a short analysis of how important is to ask the right questions at the beginning of a career as a preliminary fundamental step in finding correct and meaningful answers.

Classical Economics, as revitalised by Sraffa in the middle of the last century, is the main focus of the papers in the first part. It consists of six chapters. In Chapter 3 Heinz D. Kurz deals with whether and to what extent the exchange ratios of commodities can be explained in terms of 'substances' embodied in, or reflected by, commodities, especially 'labour'. This question has been central in many contributions in the past. Kurz refreshes the issue by exploiting the archive of the unpublished papers by Sraffa deposited at the Wren Library in Cambridge. In Chapter 4 Neri Salvadori and Rodolfo Signorino also use Sraffa's unpublished papers. They bring new light to an issue that Carlo has analysed in the past (with one of the authors of the chapter), namely the links between Sraffa's mid-1920s critique of Marshallian economics and the analysis developed more than 30 years later in *Production of Commodities*. Fabio Petri, in Chapter 5, suggests that Marx's class-conflict perspective is useful in understanding the limited impact of the 2008 financial crisis on academic economics. In Chapter 6 Cosimo Perrotta argues tha today there are all the prerequisites – theoretical and practical – to revive the development experienced during the growth of the welfare state; the only obstacle is the prevalent ideological conviction that the presence of the state in the economy is *always* damaging. Giuseppe Freni and Neri Salvadori provide in Chapter 7 a further analysis of the problem of intensive rent. The chapter identifies the general conditions concerning the distribution of plots of land among landowners that need to be satisfied for Ricardian intensive rent theory to identify a position that is a Nash equilibrium, a problem often neglected. In Chapter 8 Giuseppe Mastromatteo and Battista Pittaluga investigate the crucial role attributed by Sraffa to institutions, which calls for an analysis of his thinking on aspects inherent in the origin and development of institutions.

Sraffa's contribution of 1960 has been often connected with the Keynesian revolution of a few decades earlier. This is the main focus of the second part. It consists of four chapters. In Chapter 9 Geoff Harcourt and Peter Kriesler deal with the importance of institutions and political forces in shaping economic events, and the central role of effective demand and of money and finance in post-Keynesian Economics. In Chapter 10 Amitava Krishna Dutt compares recent heterodox theories of growth and distribution with classical theories of wages and suggests how the former can usefully employ elements contained in the latter. In Chapter 11 Maria Cristina Marcuzzo compares Joan Robinson and Sraffa on the distinction between changes and differences. This issue is important in the interpretation of the concept of equilibrium, and in the interpretation of Sraffa's work. In Chapter 12 Pasquale Commendatore, Ingrid Kubin, and Iryna Sushko present a two-class Pasinetti-Solow model of income distribution, introducing behavioural features into workers' saving. This causes shifts in growth regimes and has a profound impact on the income and wealth distribution between workers and capitalists.

The third part places particular emphasis on monetary institutions. The chapters are generally more empirical. They relate not only to issues analysed by Carlo but also to the areas of the world (Europe and Latin America) with which he was concerned. It consists of five chapters. In Chapter 13 Salvatore Capasso and Salvatore Ciucci address the two-way relationship between financial development and the scale of the underground economy. A two-way causality is explored first by modelling the case in which the level of financial development, which affects firms' access to credit and the cost of their external financing, determines the level of the underground economy; and then the case in which it is the level of the underground economy that determines the working of the financial system by influencing banks' lending procedures. In Chapter 14 Juan Carlo Moreno Brid, Esteban Pérez Caldentey, and Santiago Capraro Rodríguez investigate the causes of Latin America's economic slowdown in the last two decades, approaching the issue from the point of view of both the structuralist approach and the Keynesian tradition. They investigate both the impact of the balance-of-payments constraint, which becomes tighter with the intensification of commercial and financial globalisation processes, and, in this context, suitable macroeconomic policies to spur economic growth. Michele Limosani, Emanuele Millemaci, and Fabio Monteforte discuss in Chapter 15 the political budget cycle, finding empirical evidence of its existence in Italy, including at the regional level. Their results hold notwithstanding that the reference period covered a time when strict fiscal discipline was enforced in Europe. In Chapter 16 Erasmo Papagni and

Francesco Purificato address the problem of coordination of monetary and fiscal policies in the Economic and Monetary Union. Two important recent factors are considered: the reform of the EMU national fiscal framework and the implementation of expansionary monetary policy by the European Central Bank (ECB). Theoretical modelling suggests that more indebted countries should pursue an expansionary fiscal policy in response to an accommodating monetary policy, independently of the interest rate level fixed by the ECB. However, their empirical findings show a U-shaped relationship between fiscal and monetary policies. In Chapter 17 Francesco Purificato and Elvira Sapienza provide a theoretical and empirical assessment of the Single Supervisory Mechanism (SSM), a reform of institutions for the supervision of the European banking system. This reform better satisfies Tinbergen's principle by introducing a further tool targeted at financial stability, while monetary policy can be dedicated to macroeconomic stability.

The fourth part analyses the problem of rationality in economics, an issue that Carlo has dealt with mainly in connection with Keynes and his *Treatise on Probability*. He suggested that the contributions of Keynes, Sraffa and Myrdal during the 1920s and 1930s are fundamental to developing adequate and competent answers. In Chapter 18 Celia Lessa Kerstenetzky identifies a common methodological element that allows the inclusion of the economic and sociological explanations under the broader umbrella of the social sciences, the notion of situational logic. This methodological element can also offer an encompassing principle of economic rationality within which the concept of rationality as maximisation of an objective function features only as a particular case. In Chapter 19 Valerio Filoso discusses and expands some crucial nodes of the debate on the concept of rationality as discussed by Carlo in his history of rationality in economics.

We take this opportunity to thank all contributors for their fine work and the colleagues we involved in assessing early versions of the chapters for their help in improving them.

Last but not least, we thank Carlo Panico for his generosity, kindness, support and friendship over many years.

2 Asking the right questions

John Eatwell

Intellectual progress requires two steps: first, asking the right questions, and, second, finding the right answers.

In his Cambridge PhD dissertation, later published as Panico (1988a), Carlo Panico took up Sraffa's suggestion that in the analysis of distribution it might be that a 'given' real wage is not the variable that completes a surplus theory of value and distribution, but instead that the rate of profits might be 'susceptible of being determined from outside the system of production, in particular by the level of the money rates of interest' (Sraffa, 1960, p. 33). A large part of Panico's subsequent work has been devoted to developing the questions posed by the integration of money and finance into the surplus approach, stimulated not just by Sraffa's aside in *Production of Commodities by Means of Commodities* but also by Sraffa's earlier monetary studies. The insights that emerge are summed-up by Panico as follows:

Sraffa's approach to money and banking was thus characterised by four elements:

i the analyses of monetary events and income distribution are closely related;
ii monetary legislation and policy measures are part of the distributive conflicts among economic and social groups;
iii lobbying activities and the relations of power among firms, technical authorities and governments are relevant in the formation of legislation and policy measures;
iv the level of distributive variables is influenced by the historical evolution of society and by the choices of the authorities and of the financial sector.

(Panico, Pinto and Puchet Anyul, 2012; see also Panico, 1988b, 2001; Eatwell and Panico, 1987)

At the very core of these theses is the first: Sraffa's neglected proposition that the operation of the financial and monetary system and the distribution of income are inter-related phenomena. Taking up this proposition Panico argued that if Sraffa's conclusions on the relationship between money, finance and distribution, and, in particular, his suggestion of a determination of

DOI: 10.4324/9781003105558-2

distribution by the level of money interest rates, are to be well-founded, then two questions need to be answered:

1   What is the theory of the interest rate on money that 'does not depend upon variations in the rate of profits'?
2   How do competitive market forces ensure that 'variations in the [interest] rate ... lead to a change in the [profit] rate'?

In his dissertation, Panico analysed the answers to these two questions proposed by Marx and by Keynes.

Marx identified the system of credit as the powerful means by which competition operates to enforce the gravitation towards a general rate of profit. He also emphasised the role of bankers as producers of financial services, earning profit from their activities. (The term 'bankers' stands for what today we would identify as the financial sector as a whole.) As producers of the financial services required to set production in motion, financial sector firms are as much a part of the overall circulation process as are other services (such as transportation) and of course as is the production of commodities.

Marx characterised the relationship between interest and profit as a competitive struggle between different capitalists for shares of the surplus, the real wage being given. It was Keynes, in the elaboration of his theory of interest in the *General Theory* who argued that the rate of interest was not determined by the rate of profit. Instead, 'It may be more accurate, perhaps, to say that the rate of interest is a highly conventional, rather than a highly psychological, phenomenon' (Keynes, 1936, pp. 202–3). In Keynes's analysis causation flowed from interest rate to profit rate. As is now well known, his characterisation of the relationship between the rate of interest and the rate of profit was flawed by his adoption of the marginal efficiency of capital schedule as a demand function for investment (Garegnani, 1978). Eliminating this flaw leaves the causal relationship between the rate of interest and the rate of profit unresolved.

Nonetheless, Panico makes clear that in answer to his first question both Marx and Keynes 'proposed a method of analysis which puts together historical and economic elements, underlying the need for a conventional determination of the interest rate in terms of factors operating in the money market ...' (Panico, 1988a, p. 141).

Relating the analysis of money and finance and the determination of the interest rate to the analysis of production and the distribution of income must form the core of a monetary theory of production, the core of the theory of the operation of a market economy. This was Panico's next step.

Panico combined the standard surplus approach of Part I of *Production of Commodities* with a Keynesian monetary analysis based on an institutionally determined structure of interest rates. He derived a simple linear model incorporating both the production of commodities and the production of credit, in which the rate of interest, via the risk premium, determined the rate of profit (Panico, 1988a, chapter 6). Monetary policy has an exogenous impact on distribution and prices by operating on the risk premia along the yield curve, and, crucially, the risk premium as between the rate of interest and the rate of profit.

An empirical assessment of Panico's analysis was attempted by Valle Baeza and Muñoz (2012). Using US data from 1869 to 2009 on the profit rate, the short-term interest rate and the long-term interest rate they found that (1) the rate of profit was an upper bound to both short and long real rates of interest consistent with Marx's argument, and (2) that Grainger causality tests suggested that variations in real interest rates preceded variations in the rate of profit. These results are suggestive, but far from conclusive. As Kaldor pointed out in debates on monetarism, changes in product markets will always tend to be preceded by complementary changes in money markets (Kaldor, 1970). Timing alone is not sufficient to establish causation.

What is lacking is an analysis of how competition might tend to bring the rate of profit into equality with the rate of interest – the second question posed by Panico.

While the past decade's experience of quantitative easing, during which central banks have intervened in bond markets to keep interest rates at persistently low levels has reinforced the view that 'historical and institutional factors' are the key determinants of conventional interest rates (while liquidity preference impacts on the shape of the yield curve) Panico's second question remains largely unanswered. It might seem obvious that competition will tend to equalise rates of return (subject to risk premia) as between real and financial assets. But in fact, the mechanism is not as apparent as might be expected. For example, while quantitative easing has had a clear impact on the valuation of existing assets – real estate and stocks and shares – officials of the Bank of England concede that, a decade after the introduction of the policy, there is little understanding of the 'transmission mechanisms' into the real economy (House of Lords, Economic Affairs Committee, 2021, p. 20).

An obvious place to look for a link between financial and real returns should be the equity market, i.e. to understand how competition might operate as between the financial market evaluation of a firm and the return on real capital invested. This is the motivation behind analyses of investment based on Tobin's Q (Tobin and Brainard, 1968). Q, the valuation ratio, is the ratio of the equity value of a company to the replacement value of the capital stock of that company. In a competitive environment, it might be expected that once the risk premium is taken into account, the ratio would tend towards 1. Typically, the valuation ratio is less than 1, with an average value over the period 1900–2014 of 0.68, with pronounced secular swings. These secular swings of Q around its mean have been cited as foundations of a theory of investment and hence the competitive link between the rate of interest and the rate of profit (Smithers and Wright, 2000). However, Blanchard, Rhee and Summers (1993) using a US time series on Q from 1900 to 1988 found a larger role in investment decisions for fundamentals (the expected real rate of profit) than for the ratio of stock market valuation to fundamentals, suggesting a lack of a consistent competitive process linking the rate of interest in financial markets to the rate of profit. Simply stating that the relationship between the rate of interest and the rate of profit is defined by the risk premium is an empty statement, a definition not a proposition about the competitive process.

A related approach to the competitive linkages between financial markets and the real rate of return is to be found in analyses of the takeover mechanism. Marris (1964) suggested that takeovers constitute a market for corporate control that would select the fittest companies for survival and secure economic efficiency (a view subsequently championed by Jensen (1988) and many others; see Romano (1992)). Marris is implicitly assuming that a competitive financial mechanism, namely takeovers, establishes a relationship between the rate of interest (the return to financial assets) and the rate of profit.

Singh (1971) demonstrated conclusively that this assumption is not supported by the data. By detailed empirical study of takeovers, he revealed that it is not possible to distinguish between the characteristics of acquired and non-acquired firms, other than that there is a tendency for smaller firms to be taken over. The valuation ratio is not a discriminatory variable. Equally, both the short- and long-run impacts of takeovers on share prices suggest that, on average, takeovers lead to substantial loss of wealth for shareholders of the acquiring company. Firms seeking to avoid takeover were better off pursuing increased size rather than increases in long-term profitability.

While Singh's research was focussed on the failure of the takeover mechanism to secure market efficiency, his analysis of the relationship between financial valuation and real performance provides, as a joint product, an insight into the competitive relationship between the rate of interest and the rate of profit. No causal process is identified.

The puzzle of the competitive process linking financial and real returns is heightened by the fact that, as Farhi and Gourio have demonstrated, while

> during the past 30 years, most developed economies have experienced large declines in risk-free interest rates and increases in asset prices such as housing or stock prices, with occasional sudden crashes. At the same time … earnings growth of corporations has been strong … leading in most countries to an increase in the capital share and to stable or slightly rising profitability ratios.

Hence creating, in their words, 'an increasing wedge with safe interest rates' (Farhi and Gourio, 2018, p. 147).

Following extensive data analysis, Farhi and Gourio conclude that 'about half the increase in the spread between the return on private capital and the risk-free rate is due to rising market power, and half is due to rising risk premia' (p. 217).

This 'historical and institutional' argument concerning the role of market power in the determination of the distribution of income, is also to be found in an analysis of 'declining worker power' by Stansbury and Summers (2020) and in detailed studies of the 50 years of 'wage suppression' during which real wages have grown more slowly than the rate of growth of productivity (Mishel, Gould and Bivens, 2015; Mishel and Bivens, 2021).

Mishel and Bivens argue that the factors determining the real wage are: austerity macroeconomics, corporate-driven globalisation that undercuts wages and job security; purposely eroded collective bargaining; weaker labour standards, including a declining minimum wage; new employer-imposed contract terms; and shifts in corporate structures, resulting (among other factors) in buyer dominance affecting entire supply chains, and increases in the concentration of employers (2021, p. 3). They also reject the proposition that 'apolitical forces' such as technological change and automation explain wage trends and wage inequality, especially in the period since 1995 (2021, Appendix A). They conclude that the

> wedge between pay and productivity growth was driven by two facets of inequality: the *decline in labor's share of income* (particularly in the 2000s) and the growth of *inequality of compensation*, such that compensation grew far faster at the very top. (2021, p. 12; emphasis in original)

Strangely, missing in the comprehensive study by Michel and Bivens is any consideration of the impact on income distribution of the liberalisation of the financial sector in the 1970s, and the subsequent growth of that sector in western economies (other than its role in the growth of earnings of the 'top 0.1%'). This is particularly surprising since financial liberalisation and the growth of the financial sector as a share of GDP coincides with the era of wage suppression.

A major characteristic of the post-liberalisation growth of the financial sector has been the development of long chains of financial intermediaries involved in channelling funds from the ultimate creditors to the ultimate borrowers (Shin, 2010). The inevitable consequence is the growth of the gross assets of the financial sector as a whole (the sum of gross assets of each link in the chain) relative to GDP. The ratio of bank assets to GDP in advanced countries has risen from around 0.4 in 1970 to 2.0 today, i.e. five times over. At constant interest rates (or even lower rates), the financial sector must therefore command a higher volume of profits, and hence contribute to an increased profit share in the economy as a whole.

The impact of this growth of the financial sector on the distribution of income have been analysed by Panico, Pinto and Puchet Anyul (2012):

> Summing up, the data on income distribution and the financial sector show that after 1980 [income] inequality and the turnover of financial firms increased. The profit share rose at the expense of the wage share. … The wage rate was stagnant and benefited little from the rise in labour productivity. Consumption was supported by loans to low- and middle-income groups. Lending activities and other financial transactions to foreign and domestic sectors grew at higher rates than international trade

and GDP. The 'explosion' of financial activities occurred through traditional and innovative instruments and offered opportunities to borrow to all income groups. (Panico, Pinto and Puchet Anyul, 2012, pp. 1462–3)

Panico, Pinto and Puchet Anyul combine these factors into a model that incorporates both real and financial sectors and includes the role of the supply of credit in funding the effective demand necessary to realise the profit share of the financial sector – in effect integrating the surplus approach and the distributional consequences of the funding of effective demand. They conclude that:

> the income shares of capitalists and workers change when the banking industry expands its activity, even if the rates of wage and of profits remain constant … when the percentage variation of the rate of growth of the loans to workers is higher than the rate of growth of total wages, the profit share rises at the expense of the wage share, and when the rate of growth of total loans is higher than the percentage variation of the rate of growth of the loans to workers, the share of income of the bankers rises more than that of the other capitalists. (2012, p. 1473)

Panico, Pinto and Puchet Anyul provide the missing element in the explanation of the increase in the share of profits, namely the institutional and historical changes in the provision of financial services that enable the realisation of increased share of profits, an increased share itself inherent in part in the changed structure of intermediation. The expansion of credit sustains demand from wage earners, even though real wages are lagging behind productivity.

Returning to the two questions that Panico posed in his PhD dissertation, it may, at this stage in the development of his analysis, be concluded that:

1   It is clear that 'historical and institutional' factors, in both labour markets and financial markets, and in economic policy-making are major determinants of the distribution of income between wages and profits. 'A-political' economic answers will not suffice. The weight of evidence would seem to suggest that these factors bear more heavily on the side of real wages, rather than the rate of profit (as distinct from the profit share). Yet at the same time, the institutional determination of the rate of interest is clear. From Panico's search for the answer to his first question two different insights ultimately emerge: first, the multi-faceted character of the institutional determination of the rate of interest; second, the relationship between the development of the financial sector and the share of profit in income.

2   The major unresolved issue is the answer to Panico's second question, what is the competitive relationship between the rate of interest and the

rate of profit? What is the source of the increasing wedge between the two in the recent past? The decision to invest in financial instruments is quite different from the decision to invest in real capital – the former is typically liquid, the latter typically illiquid. Nonetheless, given that in a monetary economy it is access to finance that is the underpinning of real investment, competition would be expected to establish a persistent relationship between the two. In the long run such a persistent relationship does exist, as demonstrated by Valle Baeza and Mendieta Muñoz, with the rate of profit being an upper bound to the money rate of interest. The problem is determining the direction of causation between them.

What emerges from this brief review is that Carlo Panico has certainly asked the right questions. The integration of the surplus approach and money and finance to create a monetary theory of production is fundamental to the understanding of the determinants of the distribution of income. He has also provided some of the answers. There is more to be done.

References

Blanchard, O., Rhee, C. and Summers, L. (1993). The stock market, profit, and investment. *Quarterly Journal of Economics* 108(1): 115–136.

Eatwell, J. and Panico, C. (1987). *Piero Sraffa*. In J. Eatwell, M. Milgate and P. Newman (eds), *The New Palgrave Dictionary of Economics*, vol. 4. London: Macmillan.

Farhi, E. and Gourio, F. (2018). Accounting for macro-finance trends: market power, intangibles, and risk premia. *Brookings Papers on Economic Activity* (Fall).

Garegnani, P. (1978). Notes on consumption, investment and effective demand: part 1. *Cambridge Journal of Economics* 2(4): 335–353.

House of Lords, Economic Affairs Committee. (2021). *Quantitative Easing: A Dangerous Addiction?* HL Paper 42, London.

Jensen, M. C. (1988). Takeovers: Their causes and consequences. *Journal of Economic Perspectives* 2(1): 21–48.

Kaldor, N. (1970). The new monetarism, reprinted in *Further Essays in Applied Economics*. New York: Holmes & Meier, 1978.

Keynes, J. M. (1936). *The General Theory of Employment, Interest and Money*. London: Macmillan.

Marris, R. (1964). *The Economic Theory of 'Managerial Capitalism'*. London: Macmillan.

Mishel, L. and Bivens, J. (2021). *Identifying the Policy Levers Generating Wage Suppression and Wage Inequality*. Washington, DC: Economic Policy Institute.

Mishel, L., Gould, E. and Bivens, J. (2015). *Wage Stagnation in Nine Charts*. Washington, DC: Economic Policy Institute.

Panico, C. (1988a). *Interest and Profit in the Theories of Value and Distribution*. London: Macmillan.

Panico, C. (1988b). Sraffa on money and banking. *Cambridge Journal of Economics* 12(1): 7–28.

Panico, C. (2001). Monetary analysis in Sraffa's writings. In T. Cozzi and R. Marchionatti (eds), *Piero Sraffa's Political Economy: A Centenary Estimate*. London: Routledge.

Panico, C., Pinto, A. and Puchet Anyul, M. (2012). Income distribution and the size of the financial sector: a Sraffian analysis. *Cambridge Journal of Economics* 36(6): 1455–1477.

Romano, R. A. (1992). Guide to takeovers: theory, evidence, and regulation. *Yale Journal on Regulation* 9:119–179.

Shin, H. S. (2010). Financial intermediation and the post-crisis financial system. *BIS Working Papers*, No. 304. Basel: Bank for International Settlements.

Singh, A. (1971). *Take-Overs: Their Relevance to the Stock Market and the Theory of the Firm.* Cambridge, UK: Cambridge University Press.

Smithers, A. and Wright, S. (2000). *Valuing Wall Street: Protecting Wealth in Turbulent Markets*. New York: McGraw-Hill.

Sraffa, P. (1960). *Production of Commodities by Means of Commodities*. Cambridge, UK: Cambridge University Press.

Stansbury, A. and Summers, L. (2020). Declining worker power and American economic performance. *Brooking Papers on Economic Activity*: BPEA Conference Drafts.

Tobin, J. and Brainard, W. C. (1968). Pitfalls in financial modelling. *Papers and Proceedings of the Eightieth Annual Meeting of the American Economic Association* 58(2): 99–122.

Valle Baeza, A. and Muñoz, I. M. (2012). What is the relationship between the rates of interest and profit? An empirical note for the U.S. economy, 1869–2009. *Investigación Económica*. Universidad Nacional Autónoma de México (UNAM).

Part I

Classical theory of value and distribution

3 On physical real cost, labour and metaphysics

Sraffa on alternative theories of value and distribution and on Pareto's distinction between 'literary' and 'mathematical economists'[1]

Heinz D. Kurz

1 Introduction

This chapter deals with some closely intertwined problems regarding alternative approaches to the problem of value and distribution in systems in which commodities are produced by means of commodities. The attention focuses on contributions of the classical economists and Marx; on whether and to what extent the exchange ratios of commodities can be explained in terms of 'substances' embodied in, or reflected by, commodities, especially 'labour'; the objections Vilfredo Pareto levelled at the approaches of what he called 'literary' as opposed to 'mathematical' economists; the necessity to treat the problem of value and distribution in terms of simultaneous equations; and Piero Sraffa's reflections upon and responses to views on these matters in his early papers written in the late 1920s.

A special problem concerns the question whether the British classical political economists, especially Adam Smith, David Ricardo and James Mill, on the one hand, and Karl Marx, on the other, advocated the same concept of 'labour' or whether there are noteworthy differences between them. Another one concerns the relationship between the classical economists' search for an 'ultimate measure of value' and Marx's concept of a 'common third' or 'tertium comparationis' of commodities. This latter problem had haunted many authors. Marx was arguably the most prominent advocate of an essentialist concept of value, but, interestingly enough, also some of his marginalist critics, such as Eugen von Böhm-Bawerk, with their cardinal concept of utility defended a variant of it. Vilfredo Pareto, on the other hand, attacked indiscriminately the classical, the socialist and the marginalist economists and insisted that there was no such common substance of whichever kind. He also insisted that the problem of value and distribution had of necessity to be tackled in terms of simultaneous equations and the mathematics needed to deal with them, which, however, was not at the disposal of the authors mentioned. They therefore are said to have sought refuge in metaphysics.

DOI: 10.4324/9781003105558-4

Piero Sraffa commented on the writings of all the authors mentioned in his interpretive and constructive work on which he embarked in the second half of the 1920s and which culminated some three decades later in his book (Sraffa, 1960). What did he have to say on the problems mentioned and the authors referred to in the first period of his respective work, which extended roughly from 1927 to the beginning of the 1930s? What is the unique significance of the contributions of the classical authors, which distinguishes them both from Marx and the early marginalists? What can we learn from Pareto's attack on the 'literary' economists and does his contribution to mathematical economics keep what he promised? Is his analysis devoid of any metaphysical influences, or are these buried and hidden in the concepts and tools he uses?

In this chapter, I deal briefly with the issues under consideration, focusing attention on what I consider to be the bare essentials that deserve to be mentioned. The composition of the chapter is as follows: Section 2 describes the surprise by which several scholars, including the author of the present chapter, were struck when they first had access to Sraffa's hitherto unpublished papers kept in the Wren Library of Trinity College, Cambridge, in the late 1990s. The material they were confronted with did often not correspond to what they had expected. In particular, Sraffa's claim that the labour-value-based reasoning of the classical authors and Marx implied a 'corruption' of the true concept of cost and that 'the fatal error of Smith, Ricardo, Marx had been to regard "labour" as a quantity, to be measured in hours or in kilowatts of human energy, and thus commensurate to value' (D3/12/11: 36), came as a huge surprise.[2] Why did Sraffa take a critical stance in this regard? And didn't this contradict the proclaimed intention of his 1960 book to return to the 'standpoint' of the old classical economists from Smith to Ricardo (Sraffa, 1960, p. v)? Section 3 turns to Smith, Ricardo and Mill and shows that these authors advocated a concept of 'labour' that was not limited to human labour, but also included the labour of working animals, machines and nature. What mattered according to these economists in the theory of value and distribution were 'physical real costs', to use Sraffa's concept, that is, all the means of subsistence in support of workers and working animals, the fuel for the engines and the means of production employed and used up in the course of the production process. Labour came into the picture only via the second problem mentioned, more precisely, the classical economists' concern with an 'ultimate measure of value'. This was supposed to allow them to reduce the value of each and every commodity unequivocally to the unit of measurement, thereby rendering heterogeneous physical real costs homogenous and commensurate with one another. Section 4 turns to Karl Marx, who explicitly rejected the broad classical concept of labour and replaced it by one that covers exclusively 'human labour' and 'energy'. He did so on the ground that in bourgeois society the notion of 'human equality' had acquired the fixity of a 'popular prejudice'. His focus of attention therefore was exclusively on human labour. From this, he also derived his answer to the second problem. He insisted that what is really equal in different commodities is 'abstract' human labour expended in their production. It is said to provide the sought *tertium comparationis* and therefore the scale according to which commodities are exchanged for one another. Vilfredo Pareto, to whom we turn briefly in Section 5, rejected this view and traced the root of what we may, for short, call 'essentialist' thinking back to the fact that its advocates lacked the proper tools to deal with the analytical challenge they were facing: the determination of relative prices and income distribution in a system of interdependent industries. This challenge requires the use of simultaneous equations and the mathematics of how to solve them, which had not been at the disposal of these authors. In Pareto's view, they had instead recourse to 'metaphysics' when tackling the issue under consideration. It will be argued that things are invariably more complex. It will be shown that Pareto's criticism applies only partly, confounds the different approaches of the classical authors and Marx, and is vastly exaggerated. Section 6 summarizes the argument and concludes that reducing the values of commodities to some ultimate measure of value is no attempt to identify *the* cause of value, but to render heterogeneous commodities commensurate. Much of the reasoning refers to Sraffa's 'First Equations', that is, systems of production without a surplus.

2 Physical real cost

2.1 The background of Sraffa's early work

Readers of Sraffa's papers will notice that much of his argument in the period from 1927 to 1932 revolves around the concept of 'physical real cost' and traces of it he encountered in the literature – old, recent and then contemporary. He discerned this concept in many authors, from William Petty via the Physiocrats to the classical economists and beyond (Section 3). The break came essentially with the marginalists, who replaced it with the subjectivist concept of costs, including disutility, waiting, abstinence and the like. Alfred Marshall tried to patch over the gulf separating the two in terms of his concept of 'real cost', which was supposed to collect both objectivist and subjectivist elements under a single umbrella. His move reflects inter alia the fact that by the time of the last third of the nineteenth century at the latest, the classical approach to the theory of value and distribution was widely perceived as having got into a cul-de-sac. Failing to escape from it was seen as a clear sign that it had exhausted its explanatory potential and needed either to be entirely abandoned, as Young Turks like William Stanley Jevons pressed for, or completely overhauled. Many but far from all interpreters of the situation on both sides of the fence saw the cul-de-sac to consist in the labour theory of value. It did not provide a convincing explanation of income distribution and relative prices but was stuck in inconsistencies and contradictions. Its critics insisted in particular that focusing attention only on the production or supply side of the problem missed the consumption or demand side and therefore provided at best an incomplete picture of the story. What was badly needed, marginalist authors opined, was a reformulation of the supply side and complementing it with a coherent analysis of the demand side. Marginal productivity theory in combination with its Siamese twin, marginal utility theory, was said to have accomplished the task.

Even scholars not prepared to abandon what they considered to be the classical approach to value and distribution had to admit that the theory was in bad shape. In the Marxist camp, the (in)famous 'transformation problem' caused a lot of headache, and since the classical economists, who were taken to have started from labour values, were also increasingly read through a Marxian lens, their followers, too, faced essentially the same problem. With the attention now strictly focused on labour-value-based reasoning, the proper roots of the classical approach had largely fallen into oblivion and the approach itself clouded in uncertainty.

In several respects, Sraffa felt highly uncomfortable with this state of affairs. He had already expressed his critical stance towards the partial equilibrium version of the marginalist doctrine championed by Alfred Marshall (Sraffa, 1925, 1926). It was clear to him that he could not leave things at that, but had to scrutinize also general equilibrium theory in its then most advanced form put forward by Vilfredo Pareto. This he actually began to do in the late 1920s. And, most importantly, he was not convinced by Pareto's claim that the classical approach to the theory of value and distribution was irremediable. His intuition rather told him that the approach was fundamentally sound, but that something had gone wrong in the course of its elaboration. The question then was: (i) what precisely was sound and (ii) what precisely had gone wrong and why, and (iii) how what was sound could be coherently developed and what was wrong to be replaced? In his investigation of the changing meanings of the concept of 'cost' from the beginnings of systematic economic analysis up until the time in which he wrote, he came naturally across the idea that value was closely connected with cost and that cost expressed the 'difficulty of production', as especially Ricardo had insisted. The difficulty of production was reflected by the amounts of necessary means of subsistence in the support of workers and means of production 'productively consumed', or 'destroyed', in the course of the process of production by means of which the product in effectual demand was generated: in short, the difficulty of production was reflected by physical real cost. This, Sraffa was convinced, was the right starting point into a probing of the factors determining cost and ultimately value alias price. Such a starting point had been assumed by authors such as William Petty and the Physiocrats, but thereafter physical real cost was increasingly displaced by cost in terms of hours of labour worked – with the labour theory of value beginning to dominate the discourse. This was, so to speak, the 'original sin' committed by the classical authors, which had far-reaching consequences: it eventually landed the classical approach in a stalemate, which in turn prepared the ground for an alternative to it, marginal theory.

It is against this background that Sraffa composed several of his notes and manuscripts especially in the first, but also in the second period of his interpretive and constructive work. Here, we provide some evidence concerning three intimately intertwined aspects of the problem under consideration: (a) the abandonment of the concept of physical real cost and its replacement with labour; (b) the limitation of the concept of labour exclusively to human labour, a criticism that applied especially to Marx, as we shall see in Section 4 (but interestingly enough it also applies, for example, to Marshall); and (c) the inability of the classical authors and Marx to deal with the concept of simultaneous determination of variables and thus the need to redefine the concepts of cause and effect. Since Christian Gehrke, Neri Salvadori and I, alone or together, have published on these issues several papers, I will limit myself here to the bare essentials and ask readers wishing to see the full argument and evidence in its support to consult, for example, Gehrke and Kurz (2006, 2018), Kurz (2006, 2012), Kurz and Salvadori (2005, 2009, 2021) and Gehrke, Kurz and Salvadori (2019).

2.2 Physical real cost vs labour

In Sraffa's papers, there is a document entitled 'Degeneration of cost and value' that was in all probability written in November 1927. In it, Sraffa argued: 'A. Smith and Ricardo and Marx indeed began to corrupt the old idea of cost –, from food to labour. But their notion was still near enough to be in many cases equivalent' (D3/12/4: 2(1)). Towards the end of 1927, he stressed that 'the sort of "costs" which determines values is the collection of material things used up in production' (D3/12/7: 106). In another note, we read:

> The fatal error of Smith, Ricardo, Marx has been to regard "labour" as a quantity, to be measured in hours or in kilowatts of human energy, and thus commensurate to value … . All trouble seems to have been caused by small initial errors, which have cumulated in deductions (e.g. food of worker = quantity of labour, is nearly true). Petty had foreseen the possibility of being misunderstood (D3/12/11: 36; similarly D3/12/4: 4)

Sraffa's formulation is reminiscent of the famous story of the tailors of Laputa in Jonathan Swift's satirical novel *Gulliver's Travels*. Each single error committed may be small, but if errors do not compensate one another, they pile up and, in the extreme, may result in plain nonsense. In the case of the labour theory of value, things were not that bad, but the error committed got the classical approach into serious trouble. As Sraffa clarified later in his work, the close relationship between the labour theory of value and a coherent reformulation of the classical approach to the theory of value and distribution can be seen by noticing that the two started from the same set of data, or givens, namely, the gross output levels of the various industries; the methods of production available to cost-minimising producers; and the real wages rates (or the share of wages in net national income). This distinguished the two from (long-period) marginalist theory, which starts, in addition to given technical alternatives, from given preferences and given endowments of the economy of factors of production, including a factor called 'capital', whose quantity is taken to be knowable independently of prices and the rate of profits.

2.3 Which labour?

Sraffa in his early manuscripts was therefore opposed to the use of 'labour' as a quantity in his production equations, an opposition that extended well into 1929. In a document stemming from November 1927, he wrote:

> It is the whole process of production that must be called "human labour", and thus causes all product and all value. Marx and Ricardo used "labour" in two different senses: the above, and that of one of the factors of production ("hours of labour" or "quantity of labour" has a meaning only in the latter sense). It is by confusing the two senses that they got mixed up and said that value is proportional to quantity of labour (in second sense) whereas they ought to have said that it is due to human labour (in first sense: a non measurable quantity, or rather not a quantity at all). (D3/12/11: 64)

Sraffa was particularly critical of the narrow concept of labour many authors advocated, who focused attention exclusively on *human* labour. In an undated manuscript contained in a folder 'After 1927', he insisted that 'we have no reason to attach such a peculiar importance to human labour' (D3/12/7: 27). And in a related note, he was even more explicit and insisted:

> There appears to be no objective difference between the labour of a wage earner and that of a slave; of a slave and of a horse; of a horse and of a machine; of a machine and of an element of nature (? this does not eat) It is a purely mystical conception that attributes to human labour a special gift of determining value. Does the capitalist entrepreneur, who is the real "subject" of valuation and exchange, make a great difference whether he employs men or animals? Does the slave-owner? (D3/12/9: 89)

As we will see in Section 3, the classical authors, in particular Smith and Ricardo, held a broader concept of labour and therefore this criticism does not really apply to them, although it applies to passages in their writings in which only human labour played a role. It applies, however, to Marx (Section 4) and to marginalist authors such as Francis Y. Edgeworth and especially Marshall (D3/12/42: 36). Marshall ([1890] 1977, p. 504) had in fact qualified as a 'key note' of his *Principles* 'that free human beings are not brought up to their work on the same principles as a machine, a horse, or a slave'. Sraffa's above passage can be interpreted as containing a direct response to Marshall's keynote, but its message is, of course, of much wider applicability.

2.4 Trying to cope with heterogeneity

Values, we have heard, reflect the difficulties of production of the various commodities available in an economic system. These difficulties are in turn reflected by the real physical costs of their production, that is, in a given system of production by the quantities of means of subsistence and means of production used up per unit of output. As Sraffa stressed repeatedly in his early manuscripts in a way that is bound to perplex the modern reader: the value of a commodity 'is' the amounts of commodities used up in its production. And when he jotted down his First Equations he appeared to add together the quantities of different commodities. Was not one of the first lessons taught in political economy: 'never add up apples and oranges'? Heterogeneous things had first to be rendered homogeneous and thus commensurate, before they could be summed up. But how could this be accomplished? The early authors approached this problem by asking: What was indiscriminately common to all commodities, which commodities were needed in their production, what was the universal building material from which they were made and to which they could all be reduced? They were on the lookout for what was variously called 'ultimate measure of value'.

Petty had suggested 'bread', conceived as a *compositum mixtum* of means of sustenance, to be the sought measure, because it fed workers in all processes of production operated in the economy, from the processes' early beginnings up until their termination, when the products were made available. Petty therefore opted in favour of a physical real cost element in terms of which all commodities could be expressed. Alas, soon bread gave way to labour because in all processes of production labour had to be employed and there was assumed a strict proportionality between the amount of labour put to work and the amount of wages paid. As we have heard, it was this move that according to Sraffa involved a corruption of the original concept of cost.

The difficulties the classical economists faced and were unable to tackle effectively can be exemplified with respect to Robert Torrens. In the context of a discussion of interpretations of Torrens' argument in the literature, Sraffa pointed out:

> Torrens knew that the (absolute)[3] value of the product is determined by (in fact, *is*) the amount of things that have been destroyed for its production. But he did not see his way through without finding a "common measure" of them: he probably felt a repulsion to, or thought that *it could not be done, to sum together quantities of heterogeneous things measured in different units*. This was of course fatal: he started to find something common in them, upon which to base his measurement: the labour theory was ready at hand, all those things had been "made by labour", and he therefore regarded them simply as quantities of "accumulated labour". The result was of course absurd. He proceeded to say that the "exchangeable value" was determined entirely by "the

amount of capital, or *quantity of accumulated labour*", and not the sum of accumulated and immediate labour expended on production…

Sraffa continued:

> This meant, the labour spent in raw materials, plus the labour spent in machinery used up, plus the labour spent in producing the subsistence of direct labour – but *not* direct labour itself! The notion that labour, in order to determine value, must be, not fresh, but seasoned, is so preposterous that no sensible man can have held it without a serious provocation. (D3/12/5: 26-7; Sraffa's emphasis)

Other classical economists, especially Ricardo, did not commit the same error by ignoring direct labour, but they all seem to have felt, in Sraffa's words, 'a repulsion, or thought that it could not be done, to sum together quantities of heterogeneous things measured in different units', to use Sraffa's words. This was indeed the case, and for good reasons heterogeneous things cannot possibly be summed up. After a fruitful discussion with Frank Ramsey in mid-1928, Sraffa wrote his First and Second equations by multiplying quantities of commodities by their respective prices. Ascertaining the values of commodities (and in the case of a system with a surplus the corresponding general rate of profits) that allows for a self-replacing state of the economic system requires solving a system of simultaneous equations or using some other device that accomplishes the same task.

2.5 Physical real cost vindicated

This convinced Sraffa that the problem of value and distribution can indeed be coherently approached and solved from a physical real cost perspective, which confirmed that the intuition of Petty and the classical economists was sound. It also showed, as Sraffa emphasized in the third period of his constructive work, that there was no 'need of [the various commodities] being first reduced to some uniform substance' (D3/12/52: 2), before their exchange ratios could be determined. The identification of such a substance – the 'ultimate measure of value' or Marx's *tertium comparationis* – was not something that had to be accomplished first; it could rather be a by-product of the determination of relative prices. To be sure, labour was a candidate in this respect, but how could one know the amounts of labour 'embodied' in the various commodities prior to solving a system of simultaneous equations in which wages exhausted the entire net product and there were no profits? It was then also clear which other substances were potentially eligible in the regard under consideration, namely all those commodities that entered directly or indirectly in the production of all commodities and combinations of such commodities, or what Sraffa was to call 'basic' products (Kurz and Salvadori, 2021). (One such combination is the real wage rate, if paid ante factum, that is, out of capital.)

Finally, as regards the question of cause and effect, it was clear that the values of commodities depend on the system of production in use and in the case of a system with a surplus product in addition to the rule according to which the surplus is distributed between various claimants, that is, workers and capitalists.

In the above, we insisted with Sraffa that the classical economists' theory of value and distribution, despite the predominance of labour value-based reasoning in their works, was essentially rooted in a physical real cost approach. We also drew the attention to the broad concept of 'labour' they entertained. In the following section, we will exemplify this with regard to Smith, Ricardo and James Mill in terms of evidence Sraffa had collected in his papers.

3 Smith, Ricardo and James Mill on physical real cost and 'labour'

We deal with the three economists one after the other in chronological order.

3.1 Adam Smith

In the *Wealth of Nations* (1776), and putting on one side what he wrote about 'the early and rude state of society', prior to the appropriation of the land and the accumulation of capital (produced means of production), the Scotsman did not see the source of value creation confined to the labour performed by 'free' human beings. He called an ox a productive worker and saw slaves as also performing productive labour.[4] In his (mistaken) theory of rent he even traced the rent of land landlords obtained back to the labour performed by nature, which in his view was a 'free gift'. Smith stressed that when a businessman or a farmer has to decide which kind of labour to employ – that of a wage earner, a slave, a horse, an ox or a machine – it is the cost of production associated with its use per unit of output that matters, that is, the cost in terms of food, shelter and clothing, of fodder and stable, of fuel and building, and so on. In competitive conditions, he insisted, the choice is decided by cheapness. However, Smith saw that in certain social circumstances the profit motive could be thwarted and together with it the principle of cost minimization. Otherwise, it would be difficult to understand why slavery was able to survive despite the fact that the labour of a free man generally costs his master 'much less than that of a slave' (WN I.viii.41). However, Smith observed: 'The pride of man makes him love to domineer, and nothing mortifies him so much as to be obliged to condescend to persuade his inferiors. Wherever the law allows it, and the nature of the work can afford it, therefore, he will generally prefer the service of slaves to that of freemen' (WN III.ii.10). Profits on the one hand and power and domination on the other may, but need not, always work in the same direction.[5]

As is well known, one of Smith's main objections to what he called the 'mercantile system' was that it was based on a false idea about the relative productivities of the different sectors of the economy – agriculture, manufacturing, domestic trade and foreign trade. Reflecting his Physiocratic prejudice, Smith maintained that agriculture exhibits the highest surplus generating capacity per unit of capital employed because in it nature co-operates with man for free. The 'natural course of things' would therefore consist in developing and promoting agriculture first and industry, the towns and foreign trade only later, whereas the mercantile system had reversed this order and thus forsaken opportunities to grow. Nature is taken to perform labour alongside man, domesticated animals and machines, but it does so not equally across all sectors of the economy: it is taken to privilege agriculture with its free gifts. Humans are at any rate not the only source of labour and also for this reason not the only source of value.

The problematic points in Smith's analysis were spotted soon after the publication of *The Wealth of Nations*. Critics pointed out that nature's 'co-operation' is not restricted to agriculture: the steam engine of his colleague James Watt in Edinburgh uses the powers of nature no less than the ships of the merchant fleet. And, as David Ricardo showed, Smith's explanation of rent in terms of the generosity of nature was flawed – it is nature's niggard-liness in combination with private property of lands that is the source of rent: the fact that land of the best quality (and location) is available in a limited amount only and less favourable qualities of land have to be cultivated in order to meet the demand for corn and other agricultural products cause differential rent to be paid to the owners of the more favourable qualities. Rent reflects the scarcity of the (best qualities of) land and of other natural resources.

Smith's flawed view on labour and productivity can also be seen with re-spect to another aspect of his doctrine according to which agriculture was of special importance compared with other trades and sectors. He insisted that it produced the only (composite) commodity, corn (wheat), needed directly and indirectly in the production of *all* commodities, including itself. Manufactured commodities on the other hand were taken to be either luxury goods ('trin-kets' and trumpery) or means of production employed in their own produc-tion or in that of other luxuries. 'Nature', Smith insisted, has established a 'great and essential difference … between corn and almost every other sort of goods' (WN IV.v.a.23): corn is needed everywhere as a means of subsistence of workers, whose wages are paid out of the capital advanced at the beginning of the production period. In terms of Sraffa's (1960, p. 6) distinction between basic and non-basic commodities, corn was the only basic product in the system, whereas manufactures were non-basics. This involved an important analytical step forward as regards the discrimination between different types of commodities and their different roles in the process of production and income distribution and foreshadowed Ricardo's concept of the corn-ratio theory of profits (Vianello, 1999). But empirically and historically, it totally missed the manufacturing sector's role as an 'engine of growth' deriving from its re-markable capability to put the results of modern science and technology to productive use and employ the powers slumbering in nature. It also erro-neously relegated the labour performed in industry to the set of 'unproductive labour', which was seen to be useless with regard to the development and growth of the economy. Smith appears to have vaguely glimpsed the role of the manufacturing sector as the powerhouse of the Industrial Revolution by entertaining the view that it allows for a much deeper division of labour and thus dynamically increasing returns to scale than any other sector. But by treating the sector as non-basic he totally misconceived its dynamic role for the economy as a whole.

3.2 David Ricardo

In the third edition of the *Principles of Political Economy*, published in 1821, David Ricardo famously added a chapter on the employment effect of the introduction and diffusion of improved machinery. In this chapter, he discussed not only the substitution of machines but also that of horses for workers. He wrote:

> There is one other case that should be noticed of the possibility of an increase in the amount of the net revenue of a country, and even of its gross revenue, with a diminution of the demand for labour, and that is, when the *labour of horses* is substituted for that of man. If I employed one hundred men on my farm, and if I found that the food bestowed on fifty of those men, could be diverted to the support of horses, and afford me a greater return of raw produce, after allowing for the interest of the capital which the purchase of the horses would absorb, it would be advantageous to me to substitute the horses for the men, and I should accordingly do so; but this would not be for the interest of the men, and unless the income I obtained, was so much increased as to enable me to employ the men as well as the horses, it is evident that the population would become redundant, and the labourers' condition would sink in the general scale. It is evident he could not, under any circumstances, be employed in agriculture; but if the produce of the land were increased by the substitution of horses for men, he might be employed in manufactures, or as menial servant. (*Works* I, pp. 394-5; emphasis added)

What is of interest to us here is that Ricardo saw the labour of men explicitly to be on a par and competing with the labour performed by working animals and machines. What mattered, and what mattered exclusively from the point of view of the classical authors, were the costs at which the different kinds of labour were available to the producer in given circumstances. These costs consist of the real wages of human labour, of the fodder of horses (and other working animals) plus, as we have just heard, the interest on the value of the animals,[6] and of the annuity of machines, covering replacement costs and interest. A knowledge of the set of alternative methods of production available to producers, employing men, animals or machines, and about the costs of their employment, were all that was needed to decide on the involved choice of technique problem. In conditions of free competition, which the authors under consideration typically assumed, this choice led to the adoption of the cost-minimising system of production or technique. This system together with the given real (or share of) wages then decided on the values or prices of the various commodities. The latter therefore reflected data describing (i) the chosen technique, including the cost-minimising treatment of working animals and the utilization, maintenance and repair of machines, tools and buildings, and (ii) the remuneration of workers.

In a long footnote, Ricardo in the *Principles* takes issue with Smith, who singled out agriculture as the only sector of the economy in which nature labours along with man at zero cost and yet contended that the value this labour generates is reflected in the rent paid to landlords. Ricardo asks: 'Does nature nothing for man in manufactures? Are the powers of wind and water, which move our machinery, and assist navigation, nothing? ... There is not a manufacture which can be mentioned, in which nature does not give her assistance to man, and gives it too, generously and gratuitously' (*Works* I, p. 76, fn). Smith's view was fundamentally mistaken: his false perception of the origin of rent carried over to his theory of value.

It is interesting to note that Sraffa, in the preparatory work on his book and in his work on the Ricardo edition was keen to clarify the concept of labour in Ricardo and other economists. In Sraffa's papers and notes, his annotations in books in his huge library and on fly-leafs of some of those books and elsewhere there are numerous references to the concepts of 'cost' and 'labour' in several authors. Some of the relevant references have been mentioned in Gehrke and Kurz (2006), Kurz and Salvadori (2009) and Kurz (2012). Here it suffices to note that in the 'General Index' to the Ricardo edition, there is an entry 'Labour of horses', which directs the readers' attention also to references to 'labour of machines' and 'labour of nature' in the edition (*Works* XI, p. 46). And in a sub-entry of the entry 'Machinery', Sraffa refers to the 'labour of' (*Works* XI, p. 53).

There are two further aspects that deserve to be mentioned. First, in the theory of value and distribution, Ricardo insisted, human labour as well as the other kinds of labour matter to the extent to which they give rise to physical real costs. Interestingly, in all three editions of the *Principles* we encounter a numerical example, which is formulated exclusively in terms of commodities, not labour, and whose specificity consists in transposing the concept of the 'corn model' to a three-dimensional level. In the corn model, the rate of profits can be ascertained simply by relating the surplus product in terms of corn to the capital employed also in terms of corn: no prices are needed, a comparison of two corn magnitudes is all that matters. In the numerical example referred to (Ricardo, *Works* I, pp. 50 and 64–6) the homogeneity condition between aggregate and surplus output, on the one hand, and aggregate capital, on the other, is also met, but now in terms of two bundles consisting of amounts of three commodities each that are linearly dependent. The three commodities are hats, coats and corn; they constitute the substrate of the real wage rate and are therefore 'necessaries' or capital goods needed in the production of the three commodities themselves (and possibly also in that of other commodities, about which nothing is being said). As in much of his argument, Ricardo for simplicity assumes that capital consists exclusively of real wages (or can be reduced to them). He compares two situations with one another. In one of them, of the 100 units produced of each of the three commodities workers and landlords get 25 units each, in the other one they get 22 units each. In the former situation, profits consist accordingly of 50 units of each commodity, in the latter of 56 units. With capital consisting only of the real wages bill, the rate of profits can again be ascertained independently of values and amounts to $(50/25) = 2$ or 200% in the first situation and $(56/22) = (28/11)$ or just under 255% in the second.

Seen against the background of Ricardo's more general argument, the importance of this exceedingly simple and special numerical example lies in this: first, it shows that the general rate of profits in the economy can be ascertained in purely material terms. Second, for a given system of production, the rate of profits is inversely related to real wages, which confirms Ricardo's 'fundamental law of distribution'. Third, (human) labour and labour values are not mentioned in all of this; the entire reasoning is conducted exclusively in physical terms, and costs of production are physical real costs.

The second observation concerns Ricardo contemplating a futuristic situation in which human (and all other kinds of) labour except that of machines are needed no longer: the reference is to a fully automated system of production in which machines and other products are produced by machines alone. In a letter to John Ramsay McCulloch of 30 June 1821 he wrote: 'If machinery could do all the work that labour now does, there would be no demand for labour. Nobody would be entitled to consume anything who was not a capitalist, and who could not buy or hire a machine' (*Works* VIII, pp. 399–400). Riches and values are being produced, but human labour plays no longer any role in it.

3.3 James Mill

In an undated document entitled 'Notes from James Mill' contained in a file 'May–July 1928, May 1932', Sraffa excerpted a number of passages from the third edition of James Mill's *Elements of Political Economy*, published in 1826 (see D3/12/9: 106–118). The passages refer to the concepts of production, cost, labour and fixed capital. We focus attention on those that are pertinent to the theme under consideration here.

Mill stated:

> It is found that the agency of man can be traced to very simple elements. He does nothing but produce motion …. In strictness of speech, *it is matter itself which produces the effects*. All that man can do is to place the objects of nature in a certain position … (Mill, 1826, pp. 5–6; emphasis added)

Especially the remark that matter itself produces the effects appears to have attracted Sraffa's attention. This becomes clear when we turn to the second passage Sraffa excerpted:

> Whenever we say that such and such effects are produced by pure labour, we mean the consumption and operations of the labourer, taken conjunctly. There can be no labour, without the consumption of the labourer. ... [I]n all these cases, equally, whenever we speak of his labour, as a thing by itself, a detached, independent, instrument of production, the idea of subsistence is included in it. (Ibid, p. 9)

And on the following page, Mill argued: 'If wages be taken as synonymous with the consumption of the labourer, the labour cannot be taken, as an item of an aggregate, and its wages as another. As often as this is done, an error is the necessary consequence' (ibid, p. 10). This remark may be said to foreshadow Sraffa's above criticism of the move from physical real cost to labour values. Mill called 'error' what Sraffa was to qualify as the 'corruption' of a concept – that of physical real cost.

Finally, there is the following remarkable proposition by Mill that appears to have left a deep impression upon Sraffa: 'The agents of production are the commodities themselves ... They are the food of the labourer, the tools and the machinery with which he works, and the raw materials which he works upon' (ibid, p. 165). Interestingly, up until the last moment before he sent the final manuscript of his book to the publisher, Sraffa tinkered with the idea of giving it the title 'Production of Commodities by Commodities', significantly dropping the two words 'by Means'. As the classical economists had insisted, the agent of production, the worker, can be seen as being enabled to perform his productive task via the intake of commodities that keep his labour power intact.[7]

Sraffa stressed, however, that explaining the value of commodities in terms of the value of commodities used up in their production would imply arguing in a circle, as already James Mill had argued and as Samuel Bailey had 'ably' criticised in his *Critical Dissertation on Value* (D3/12/9: 112). What matters is the 'quantity of capital', that is, the amounts of commodities it represents, not its value (ibid). The value of commodities had to be explained with reference to the various 'agents of production' – that is, the commodities employed and totally or partly used up: food, tools, machinery and raw materials.

We now come to Marx who, despite all appearances to the contrary, advocated a rather different concept of labour and its role in the formation of value.

4 Marx on Aristotle, human labour and a 'popular prejudice'

Marx's oeuvre is peppered with references to Greek philosophers, especially Aristotle. This is hardly surprising, given the fact that in his doctoral dissertation he discussed the differences between the philosophies of nature of

Democritus and Epicurus, with Aristotle as an omnipresent towering figure. Marx had studied intensively Aristotle's *Politics* and *Nicomachean Ethics* and referred to them repeatedly in *A Contribution to the Critique of Political Economy* and in volume I of *Capital*. To Marx, Aristotle was a 'great thinker' and in fact the 'greatest thinker of antiquity' (1954, pp. 64 and 383). Marx in fact elaborated his labour value-based approach to the theory of value in direct contestation with the Greek philosopher's propositions on the subject.

4.1 Relying on the 'fixity of popular prejudice'

Aristotle, Marx insisted, was 'the first to analyse so many forms, whether of thought, society, or Nature, and amongst them also the form of value' (1954, pp. 64–5). However, he accused Aristotle of having failed to see the 'substance of value' – *abstract labour*. Aristotle is said to have been right in maintaining in the fifth book of the *Nicomachean Ethics* that exchange

> "cannot take place without equality, and equality not without commensurability"... Here, however, he comes to a stop, and gives up the further analysis of the form of value. "It is, however, in reality, impossible ... that such unlike things [as different commodities] can be commensurable" – *i.e.*, qualitatively equal. Such an equalisation can only be something foreign to their real nature, consequently only "a makeshift for practical purposes". (Ibid, p. 65)[8]

What was it that caused Aristotle's sudden 'stop'? According to Marx, 'it was the absence of any concept of value', a lack of understanding that 'what is really equal' in different commodities *is* 'human labour' (ibid). Why had the greatest thinker of antiquity failed to see what to Marx seemed to be obvious? It was the fact that attributing value to commodities 'is merely a mode of expressing *all labour as equal human*, and consequently as *labour of equal quality*'. Aristotle could not see this because 'Greek society was founded upon slavery, and had, therefore, for its natural basis, the inequality of men and of their labour-powers'. Consequently,

> The secret of the expression of value, namely, that all kinds of labour are equal and equivalent, because, and so far as they are human labour in general, cannot be deciphered, until the notion of *human equality* has already acquired the *fixity of popular prejudice*. This, however, is possible only in a society in which the great mass of the produce of labour takes the form of commodities, in which, consequently, the dominant relation between man and man, is that of owners of commodities. (Ibid, p. 65)

Marx concluded:

> The brilliancy of Aristotle's genius is shown by this alone, that he discovered, in the expression of the value of commodities, a relation of

equality. *The peculiar conditions of the society in which he lived, alone prevented him from discovering what, "in truth", was at the bottom of this equality.* (Ibid, pp. 65–6; emphases added)

With commodity production and exchange firmly established at the time when Marx lived, he could discover what was still hidden before Aristotle's eyes. Marx, we might put it, benefitted from the mercy of a late birth. At his time, the socioeconomic features mentioned had 'already acquired the stability of natural, self-understood forms of social life', in which 'the labour-time socially necessary for [the production of commodities] forcibly asserts itself like an over-riding law of Nature' (Ibid, p. 80).

4.2 Only 'human' labour matters

As the evidence from *Capital* and the *Theories of Surplus Value* shows, Marx reserved the concept of labour strictly for *human* labour only. No other types of labour are comprised as in the classical authors. Marx's concept and his 'law of value' are explicitly rooted in the said 'popular prejudice', namely that all humans are 'equal'. However, as he kept stressing in other parts of his analysis, in capitalist society humans are substantially highly unequal and at best only formally equal. The clearest expression of this inequality is the 'exploitation' of some humans by others – in capitalism no less than in feudalism or other modes of production. Nevertheless, the said 'prejudice' becomes the salient point ('Springpunkt') of Marx's entire construction when defining the substance of value. No such transfiguration is to be found in the classical authors. While Marx developed his theory of value from a perverted popular perception of humans in contemporary bourgeois society, the classical authors started from the material metabolism of modern society. The difference is striking and it is remarkable that Marx nevertheless thought that authors like Ricardo had embarked on an intellectual trajectory that of necessity was to converge on his, Marx's, construction.

Judging the propositions on value contained in the writings of the classical authors in terms of his own doctrine, it must not come as a surprise that Marx was not pleased. A few examples Sraffa spotted suffice to confirm this. In the French edition of the *Theories of Surplus Value*, the eight volumes of the *Histoire*, which Sraffa used at the time, he came across a criticism Marx had levelled at an observation by John Ramsay McCulloch. The latter had insisted that it was not only human labour that mattered, a view Marx repudiated strongly (Marx, 1925, vol. VII, pp. 22 and 24). Sraffa in turn rejected the criticism: in his own index of the volume he jotted down: 'Sbagliata critica c.[ontra] McCulloch [Mistaken criticism of McCulloch] 22, 24'. He also noted: 'Smith appelle un boef [sic] un ouvrier productif [Smith calls an ox a productive worker] 23'. In the context under consideration, Smith considered the work performed by an ox to be on a par with the work performed by a labourer. Sraffa sided with Smith and not with Marx in this regard.[9]

4.3 Where do labour values come from?

Marx bases his reasoning on the following two highly suggestive and intimately intertwined contentions: first, when two commodities exchange for one another in a given proportion this expresses the relative embodiment of a common substance in them; second, this substance is of necessity abstract labour. Numerous readers of *Capital* have fallen victim to the purported logic of these propositions. However, closer scrutiny shows that their meaning is far from self-evident, as Marx appears to think , and that therefore their explanatory power, if any, is not clear. How precisely is the concept of abstract labour defined and how are the quantities of it embodied in the various commodities ascertained? Under which circumstances is the exchange ratio of two commodities equal to the ratio of the amounts of abstract labour embodied in them?

As regards the concept of abstract labour, an obvious question is how it deals with heterogeneous labour. A careful examination of Marx's works shows that he followed the classical economists by rendering different kinds of concrete labour uniform by means of actually given relative wage rates.[10] If the wage paid per hour of labour *s* happens to be 2 shillings and the wage per hour of labour *t* 4 shillings, and if abstract labour is expressed in terms of labour *s*, then one hour of labour *t* would count as the equivalent of two hours of labour *s*. This implies, however, that the resulting concept of abstract labour is not totally independent of income distribution. And since nominal wage rates are supposed to allow workers to buy the commodities needed in order to re-produce the different kinds of labour power, that is, to buy the bundles of commodities defining the corresponding real wages rates, prices play a role in this, which means that labour values are not entirely independent of prices. To claim that labour values are magnitudes that are not 'contaminated' by being dependent on prices cannot be sustained.

But how do we know how much abstract labour is needed altogether in the production of one unit of a particular commodity? Marx simply assumes that this is already known, but he does not tell the reader what is the source of this knowledge. Obviously, in a system in which commodities are produced by means of commodities, as in the one Marx contemplated, labour values can be ascertained only by solving a system of simultaneous equations (or by using a device that makes use of all the information offered by such a system; see later) With $\mathbf{v}$ as the vector of (abstract) labour values, $\mathbf{A}$ as the matrix of material inputs and $\mathbf{l}$ as the vector of direct inputs of abstract labour, we have

$$\mathbf{v} = \mathbf{A}\mathbf{v} + \mathbf{l}$$

If we now look at a system of 'prices of production' satisfying Marx's requests, we have

$$\mathbf{p} = (1 + r)(\mathbf{A}\mathbf{p} + w\mathbf{l}),$$

with r as the general rate of profits and w the real wage rate of that kind of labour that defines abstract labour. In the case in which $r = 0$ and w therefore is at its maximum level, exhausting the net product, one sees at a glance that relative prices of production equal relative labour values. Hence, labour values are nothing else than a particular solution of a system of simultaneous production equations: they are a special price system. Sraffa expressed this fact by aptly speaking of a 'Value Theory of Labour' rather than a labour theory of value. (A 'Value Theory of Capital' would obtain in the hypothetical case of $w = 0$ and $r = R$, where R is the maximum rate of profits compatible with non-negative wages.)

We now turn briefly to Vilfredo Pareto's view on some of the issues under consideration and Sraffa's response in his early manuscripts. It is remarkable that Pareto dealt with almost all the problems discussed in the above and put forward specific views on them, which, interestingly, Sraffa right at the beginning of his interpretive and re-constructive work scrutinised critically. The problems concern: How are the exchange ratios of commodities in circular (as opposed to linear or 'Austrian') systems of production ascertained? Are exchange ratios of commodities reflecting amounts of a common substance 'embodied' in the latter or does the very idea of a common substance imply a retreat into metaphysics? What are the 'forces' shaping relative prices? Is a purely objectivist explanation possible?

5 Sraffa on Pareto

5.1 Pareto on the non-mathematical economists

Similar to Aristotle, Pareto disputed the claim that the exchange of two commodities at a given rate expresses the fact that they represent a common third, whose quantitative embodiments in the two commodities determines their rate of exchange or relative price. He did so in his two volumes *Les systèmes socialistes* (1902–1903), in the *Manuale di economia politica* (1906) and in articles he published at around the same time.[11] There are numerous references to Pareto in Sraffa's early notes and manuscripts. We can even be more precise in this regard: we know from Sraffa's papers and from his *Cambridge Pocket Diary* that he significantly consulted the *Manuale* in November 1927 and *Les systèmes socialistes* in early 1928 respectively.[12] Sraffa was intrigued by Pareto's conception of economics as a 'natural science', founded upon facts, his notion of general equilibrium, and his attack on the older, non-mathematical economists. How did in Pareto's view the classical economists and the socialist writers attempt to come to grips with the intricate problem of interdependence in the theory of value and distribution. Sraffa had to make up his mind on all this and, more generally, on the merits and demerits of general equilibrium theory. In particular, was it true that the theory of value and distribution could not do without simultaneous equations and the mathematics how to solve them, and did the concepts of cause and effect have to be reinterpreted vis-à-vis relations of mutual dependence?

Sraffa was both surprised and pleased to see Pareto argue that with regard to states of equilibrium of the economic system as a whole no reference what-soever to utility or disutility was needed. Sraffa therefore scrutinised carefully whether Pareto did in fact manage to establish this for good or whether his thinking brought back into the picture subjectivist concepts in a covert way. As Sraffa discerned, this was in fact the case without Pareto noticing it. This led immediately to the question, whether attempts at elaborating a concept of economic equilibrium in entirely objectivist terms was necessarily doomed to failure, as Pareto's case seemed to demonstrate? Sraffa did not think so and was keen to establish what Pareto had promised, but had failed to deliver.[13]

When Sraffa in late 1927 put down his first systems of simultaneous equations, he insisted in a document contained in a folder entitled 'London Summer 1927': 'How useless the notions of utility and disutility are in the study of equilibrium … Explain the notion of *equilibrium*, and its relation to *causes*: much to be found in Pareto' (D3/12/3:1; Sraffa's emphases). The said uselessness, which Pareto had failed to demonstrate convincingly, Sraffa established in terms of his 'First' and 'Second Equations' referring to systems without and with a surplus. When in 1942 he resumed his work on his book, looking back at his notes stemming from the first period of his constructive work, he stressed that it consisted in '[1] as-certaining the conditions of equilibrium of a system of prices and the rate of profits, independently of [2] the study of the forces which may bring about such a state of equilibrium'. In his view, the 'forces' the marginalist authors, including Pareto, invoked could not bear the brunt of the argument put on them: the subjectivist forces, Sraffa insisted in several notes and comments, played a much smaller role than other forces, especially those that determined wage rates or the share of wages in the social product. The properties of equilibrium, he was convinced, could be investigated quite independently of the forces that were supposed to bring equilibrium about. He explained:

> Since a solution of the second problem carries with it a solution of the first, that is the course usually adopted in modern theory. The first problem however is susceptible of a more general treatment, independent of the particular forces assumed for the second; and in view of the unsatisfactory character of the latter, there is advantage in maintaining its independence. (D3/12/15: 2)

In the *Manuale* Pareto had insisted: 'the mutual dependence of economic phenomena … makes the use of mathematics indispensable for studying these phenomena' since 'relations of mutual dependence' defy being investigated in terms of 'ordinary logic' (1971, p. 180).[14] Sraffa agreed to this part of Pareto's criticism. However, he did not subscribe to the particular kinds of simulta-neous equations the Lausanne economist had put forward, also because con-trary to the latter's contention they did not establish the unimportance of ophelimité, etc. in characterizing states of equilibrium. The systems of equa-tions Sraffa elaborated succeeded on the contrary in establishing precisely this.

Pareto went on to maintain that the 'literary economists' tried to cope with the difficult situation in which they found themselves as best as they could by using the analytical methods at their disposition, which, however, were inadequate. They 'make *superhuman efforts*', Pareto maintained,

> to treat separately phenomena which they do not know to consider in their state of mutual dependence. This is the reason why they have conceived vaguely *metaphysical theories* of *value* ... [and] continue to propound a mass of erroneous propositions. (1971, 241, n. 7; the last emphasis is Sraffa's)

5.2 Sraffa's reaction to Pareto

There is compelling reason to presume that the passages just quoted from the *Manuale* (Sraffa used, of course, the Italian edition) were a point of reference in the notes Sraffa jotted down on the day that saw the breakthrough in his constructive work, that is, 26 November 1927. On that day he managed to see clearly the possibility of determining relative prices in the case of a system without a surplus independently of any subjectivist elements, or 'forces'.[15] In a document drafted on that day entitled 'Metaphysics' (D3/12/4: 14–17), he took up Pareto's argument and commented on it. While the latter's name is not mentioned, content, circumstantial evidence and Sraffa's formulations speak strongly in favour of his engagement with Pareto: the title of the document echoes Pareto's reference to 'metaphysical theories'; Sraffa adopts Pareto's term 'superhuman efforts'; he discusses what could be meant by 'metaphysics' in the context under consideration and departs from Pareto's respective point of view; and both authors are concerned with the problem of mutual dependence of economic variables and opt in favour of approaching it in terms of simultaneous equations.

In the document, Sraffa critically scrutinises Pareto's antinomy of metaphysics and mathematical economics. Things are invariably more complex than Pareto was inclined to think. First, it is naïve to assume that mathematical economists are not also under the spell of some metaphysics or other. Second, differences in metaphysics 'can make to us absolutely unintelligible an otherwise perfectly sound theory' (D3/12/4: 15). However, third, such differences may also affect very little 'the truth of our conclusions', where the same truths can be expressed using widely different forms (ibid). With regard to the analytical techniques employed, Sraffa stressed: 'Our metaphysics is in fact embodied in our techniques; the danger lies in this, that *when we have succeeded in thoroughly mastering a technique, we are very liable to be mastered by her*' (ibid; emphasis added).

Sraffa disagreed with important elements of Pareto's criticism of the classical economists and Marx. First, Pareto had not done justice to Marx, whose main achievement consisted in having rediscovered from under thick layers of (mis) interpretation what he, Sraffa, considered to be a basically 'sound theory' – the classical theory of value and distribution. Marx had accomplished this, Sraffa insisted (adopting Pareto's expression), 'either by accident or by *superhuman effort*' (D3/12/4: 17; emphasis added).

Second, Sraffa's First Equations showed that the values of commodities were fully determined by physical real costs of production.[16] That is, they confirmed the fundamental hypothesis from which the classical economists had originally started their analyses. What is more, they also confirmed Pareto's intuition, which, alas, he had failed to establish, namely that in equilibrium subjectivist elements play no role. The fact that Pareto had come up with this intuition, Sraffa took as exemplifying his conviction that scholars advocating different orientations in economics may nevertheless share similar metaphysical notions. The paucity of Pareto's understanding of the classical economists' doctrine, Sraffa took as an illustration of the fact that even small differences in metaphysics may block the comprehension of theories despite their basic correctness.

Third, Pareto's dismissal of some earlier authors' search for a common substance reflected by, or embodied in, commodities that are exchanged for one another, was difficult to sustain for the following reasons. First, and most importantly, Sraffa showed by means of his First Equations (no-surplus economy) that Pareto was wrong in contending against the classical economists that 'the consideration of certain obstacles to production [alone is not] enough to give [value] existence' (Pareto, 1971, p. 179). Information about the means of production and means of subsistence needed to overcome such obstacles is all that is needed in order to ascertain the (relative) values of commodities. Second, the classical economists' search for an 'ultimate measure of value' was not chasing a will-o'-the-wisp. Starting from his First Equations, Sraffa employed what he later called the 'Reduction method' by means of which the commodity inputs in all industries were gradually reduced to some given commodity – the ('ultimate') measure of value – by replacing these inputs by amounts of the measure needed directly and indirectly in their production. This led to a set of infinite series, which, however, converged to some finite value each. The result was that in the case of a system without a surplus, in which each and every commodity is needed directly or indirectly in the production of each and every commodity, that is, is a 'basic' product, *any* commodity (and a fortiori any bundle of commodities) could be used as such a measure. The exchange rates of commodities ascertained by solving the system of simultaneous production equations would then turn out to be equal to the relative amounts of the commodity chosen as measure embodied in the various commodities. Therefore, in the case under consideration, and contrary to Pareto's contention, there was not only one common third, there were rather multiple single and compound substances that could be seen in the role of an ultimate measure or *tertium comparationis*.

Sraffa did also not agree with Pareto's following views in the *Manuale*: reducing the value of any commodity to quantities needed directly and indirectly of some other commodity (or labour) in its production did not mean, as Pareto had misleadingly insinuated, that value is taken to have only '*one* cause'. Therefore, Pareto's excommunication of the 'literary economists' was undeserved: 'it can be declared henceforth that any economist who looks for *the cause* of value shows thereby that he has understood nothing about the synthetic phenomenon of economic equilibrium' (1971, p. 179; emphasis in the original). To reduce the value of commodities to one particular substance does not (pace Marx) mean that this substance is supposed to be *the* (only) cause of value. The classical economists' reduction to some such substance was rather designed to render heterogeneous 'things' homogeneous and therefore commensurate. In the context of Sraffa's First Equations, this follows strictly from the fact that the role of measure of value can be attributed to any particular commodity in the system: there are as many such substances as there are basic products. We may add that Sraffa's concept of Standard commodity derives from the set of basic commodities and thus a multiplicity of what Pareto misleadingly called 'causes'. It is also worth mentioning that reducing the value of a commodity to amounts of some other commodity needed directly or indirectly in its production implies moving from the production equation of the first commodity to the production equations of all the other commodities and then back again, and so on and so forth. The reduction method is therefore nothing else than a particular way of solving the system of simultaneous equations via convergent series. Immediately after Sraffa had composed his First Equations he began to reduce commodities to some other commodities using simple numerical examples. He concluded with respect to some such illustration: 'The series is infinite, but the sum is finite' (D3/12/7: 31).

Hence, while Pareto was right to observe that the 'literary economists' failed to provide a fully coherent solution to the problem of value and distribution, he grossly overstated their failure. He overlooked in particular that the reduction method proposed by authors such as Adam Smith and Ricardo was essentially an attempt to come to grips with the problem of the heterogeneity of commodities in a system of production characterized by a sophisticated social division of labour and the production of commodities by means of commodities. The method may be said to express their understanding of the interconnectedness of the various industries of the economy and the need of a simultaneous solution of the equations of production.

6 Concluding observations

In this chapter, I have argued, first, that the concept of 'labour' entertained by the classical economists (as opposed to that entertained by Marx) included not only human labour but also the labour of working animals, machines and even nature. The focus of attention of these authors was therefore on how much it cost in given competitive conditions to employ one labour or another to produce a particular commodity. This involved a choice of technique perspective that revolves around alternative costs of production. The concept of cost advocated was that of 'physical real cost' and included the food, shelter, etc. of a worker (and his family), given his or her real wage rate, the fodder, etc. needed to support a working animal and the fuel and maintenance and repair costs to operate a machine. Working animals and machines, the classical economists insisted, ought to be treated like fixed capital items; the costs incurred by employing them included also wear and tear and interest. The classical authors did not argue that the 'cause' of value was exclusively human labour, as Marx did. To them, the labour theory of value, focusing on human labour, was a makeshift solution to a problem, the complexity of which they did not yet master fully. The labour theory of value was taken to provide an approximately correct solution to the problem of value. Ricardo significantly opined that while labour was 'the foundation of all value', obviously referring to the labour process, he surmised that the relative quantity of labour was only 'almost exclusively determining the relative value of commodities' (*Works* I, p. 20).

A closely related problem concerns the question of whether and when commodities can be understood as 'embodying' certain substances (some other commodity or labour) that explain their exchange rates. This is reflected by the classical economists' search for an 'ultimate measure of value' by means of which they attempted to come to grips with the heterogeneity of commodities and render them homogeneous and therefore commensurate. For this purpose, they reduced all commodities to amounts needed directly and indirectly of the chosen measure used as an input in production, where the proposed measure was typically conceived of as a *compositum mixtum* of commodities; viz, for example, William Petty's 'bread' (i.e. means of sustenance in general). Critics of the classical economists like Pareto, probably misled by Marx's essentialist approach, mistook the search for an ultimate measure of value for a search for *the* cause of value. Pareto also failed to see that commodities may be understood as 'embodying' (or reflecting) certain amounts of the measure of value that can explain their exchange rates or relative prices. Sraffa demonstrated this in late 1927 and early 1928 in terms of his First Equations dealing with a system of production that does not generate a surplus product and in which all commodities are therefore basic products. In such a system there is not only a single commodity or substance that can serve as such a measure – there are (infinitely) many. Against this background, Pareto's attack on what he dubbed the 'literary' as distinct from the mathematical economists turns out to be vastly exaggerated, since the method of reduction of the values of commodities to dated amounts of commodities (or labour) is nothing but a device to reveal the properties of a system of simultaneous equations.

Notes

1 With this chapter, I wish to pay tribute to Carlo Panico, a close friend and highly esteemed colleague. While his work on Sraffa focuses on the monetary side of the latter's contribution and his cooperation especially with John Maynard Keynes, I focus on the real side and the inspiration Sraffa drew from the classical authors, especially Ricardo. Over the years, I benefited tremendously from closely collaborating with Christian Gehrke and Neri Salvadori on the problems under consideration. Christian and Hans-Walter Lorenz have kindly commented on an earlier version of the

manuscript and made valuable suggestions. I am also grateful to an anonymous referee for useful remarks and observations and to Neri Salvadori for a fruitful conversation about the chapter. I tried to incorporate the suggestions as best as I could. All remaining errors and misinterpretations are of course exclusively my responsibility.

2 References to Sraffa's papers follow the catalogue prepared by Jonathan Smith. Unless otherwise stated, all emphases are in the original.

3 Sraffa appended a footnote here that need not interest us in the present context.

4 According to Smith, skilled workers and animals also share some similarities with machines. Sraffa developed his analysis of fixed capital against the background of the classical economists' views on the matter; see Kurz and Salvadori (2005). Working animals, for example, Sraffa observed, are like fixed capital items, which are gradually worn out. From the mortality table of the kind of animal in question, one can infer how many animals have to be employed in each age segment of a stock with an even age distribution that will maintain the population constant, when the number employed in the segment that uses freshly born animals are added every year (see D3/12/30: 6).

5 It is perhaps worth noting that in an essay on the political element of business cycles, Michal Kalecki argued that a successful employment policy tends to undermine the power of business leaders and therefore is 'a first class political issue' (Kalecki, 1943, p. 324). He explained: '*maintenance* of full employment would cause social and political changes which would give a new impetus to the opposition of the business leaders. Indeed, under a regime of permanent full employment, "the sack" would cease to play its role as a disciplinary measure' (ibid, p. 326; emphasis in the original). Worse than lower profits would be to business leaders the erosion of the 'discipline in the factories' and 'political stability'.

6 Ricardo in the passage quoted above does not mention the wear and tear of this kind of particular fixed capital item presumably because of the natural self-reproduction of horses. Hence, instead of the annuity, it suffices to mention only the interest on the price paid when the animal was bought. Men also reproduce naturally, but other than under slavery they cannot be bought and sold and thus do not constitute durable means of production.

7 Sraffa also copied a passage in which Mill argued that the non-consumed part of a durable capital good 'may be always taken, as an additional commodity, the result of the productive process' (ibid, p. 81). This foreshadows the treatment of used capital goods as joint products of the main product.

8 We might say that Aristotle's position and that of Ricardo bear some resemblance to one another in the following respect. As we have seen (Section 3), Ricardo considered the labour theory of value a sufficiently good approximation to a coherent explanation of value in competitive conditions, which he was desirous to elaborate up until the end of his life; see the fragments of his essay on 'Absolute and Exchangeable Value' in *Works* IV. However, in general, there is no exact equality between the ratio of the labour embodied in two commodities that are exchanged for one another and the actual exchange rate of the two commodities. Yet Ricardo was clear that with vanishing profits and wages absorbing the entire net product, the exchange ratio of two commodities would reflect their 'absolute values' by which he meant the amounts of labour embodied in them. We might perhaps say that while Marx was a dyed-in-the-wool essentialist, Ricardo was a pragmatist with some essentialist sprinkles.

9 Among other things, Sraffa took excerpts from the 'Report of the Meeting' of the Committee of the British Association in 1878 on 'a common measure of value in Direct Taxation' (see D3/12/2: 24–5). There it is argued that as regards the 'cost of labour', workers should not be looked upon differently from horses: 'As the horse has to be clothed and stabled, so the productive labourer has to be clothed and housed', etc. Hence, what matters are in all cases physical real costs or 'food' and not whether these costs pertain to a wage earner, a slave, a horse or a machine.

10 See the evidence and the references to the secondary literature provided in Kurz and Salvadori (1995, 336–7).

11 Pareto's criticism was directed at what we have, for short, called 'essentialist' doctrines of value and not only at the labour value-based reasoning of socialist economists (Pareto, 1971, pp. 178–9). Eugen von Böhm-Bawerk, for example, who advocated a cardinal concept of (marginal) utility, had put against Marx's concept of abstract labour that of abstract use value, according to which the various commodities represented nothing but masses of a kind of utility 'gelatine', 'utility in abstracto'.

12 Up until now this fact has hardly received the attention it deserves. For an exception, see Kurz (2020). Early hints at what may, for short, be called the 'Pareto connection' can be found in Kurz (1998) and more recently in Gehrke and Kurz (2006, p. 99; 2018, p. 433, fn. 11), Kurz (2012, pp. 1545, 1547, fn. 16), and Gehrke, Kurz and Salvadori (2019, pp. 102–3, fn. 4).

13 For a more comprehensive treatment of Sraffa's remarks on Pareto, see Kurz (2020).

14 In a paper published in German in 1902, Pareto had argued:

> Economists who do not know mathematics are in the situation of people, who wish to solve a system of equations without knowing what a system of equations or even a single equation is. Basically the procedure to which they have recourse consists in assuming that all equations except one are met and then study the changes in the quantities, which are connected to these equations. In this way one arrives occasionally at useful studies of some detail, but not at an *understanding of the system as a whole*. (1902, p. 1114; my translation; emphasis added)

15 Apparently on the same day, Sraffa informed Keynes about his breakthrough, with Keynes 'approving' Sraffa's equations. Two days later Keynes informed his wife, Lydia Lopokova, in a letter about Sraffa's excitement, which made him walk up and down in his study room all the time and prevented him from sitting down.

16 Sraffa reached fully clarity in this regard only in the course of a meeting with Frank Ramsey on 26 June 1928, mentioned above; see Kurz and Salvadori (2000).

References

Gehrke, C. and Kurz, H. D. (2006). Sraffa on von Bortkiewicz: reconstructing the classical theory of value and distribution. *History of Political Economy* 38(1): 91–149.

Gehrke, C. and Kurz, H. D. (2018). Sraffa's constructive and interpretive work, and Marx. *Review of Political Economy* 30(3): 428–442.

Gehrke, C., Kurz, H. D. and Salvadori, N. (2019). On the 'origins' of Sraffa's production equations: a reply to de Vivo. *Review of Political Economy* 31(1): 100–114.

Kalecki, M. (1943). Political aspects of full employment. *The Political Quarterly* 14(4): 322–331.

Kurz, H. D. (1998). Against the current: Sraffa's unpublished manuscripts and the history of economic thought. *The European Journal of the History of Economic Thought* 5(3): 437–451.

Kurz, H. D. (2006). The agents of production are the commodities themselves: on the classical theory of production, distribution and value. *Structural Change and Economic Dynamics* 17(1): 1–26. Reprinted in Kurz, H. D. and Salvadori, N. (2007). *Interpreting Classical Economics: Studies in Long-period Analysis*. London: Routledge, pp. 131–158.

Kurz, H. D. (2012). Don't treat too ill my Piero! Interpreting Sraffa's Papers. *Cambridge Journal of Economics* 36(6): 1535–1569.

Kurz, H. D. (2020). 'Superhuman efforts' and the theory of value and distribution. Sraffa on Pareto. In D. Basu and D. Das (eds), *Conflict, Demand and Economic Development. Essays in Honour of Amit Bhaduri*. London: Routledge, pp. 171–190.

Kurz, H. D. and Salvadori, N. (1995). *Theory of Production: A Long-Period Analysis.* Cambridge: Cambridge University Press.

Kurz, H. D. and Salvadori, N. (2000). Sraffa and the mathematicians: Frank Ramsey and Alister Watson. In T. Cozzi and R. Marchionatti (eds), *Piero Sraffa's Political Economy: A Centenary Estimate.* London and New York: Routledge. Reprinted in Kurz, H. D. and Salvadori, N. (2003). *Classical Economics and Modern Theory: Studies in Long-Period Analysis.* London and New York: Routledge.

Kurz, H. D. and Salvadori, N. (2005). Removing an 'insuperable obstacle' in the way of an objectivist analysis: Sraffa's attempts at fixed capital. *The European Journal of the History of Economic Thought* 12(3): 493–523.

Kurz, H. D. and Salvadori, N. (2009). Sraffa and the labour theory of value: a few observations. In J. Vint, J. S. Metcalfe, H. D. Kurz, N. Salvadori and P. A. Samuelson (eds), *Economic Theory and Economic Thought: Festschrift in Honour of Ian Steedman.* London: Routledge, pp. 187–213.

Kurz, H. D. and Salvadori, N. (2021). White elephants and other non-basic commodities: Piero Sraffa and Krishna Bharadwaj on the role and significance of the distinction between basics and non-basics. *Indian Economic Journal* 2021: 1–23. doi:10.1177/00194 662211017261

Marshall, A. ([1890] 1977). *Principles of Economics.* London: Macmillan. Reprint of the 8th edition (1920).

Marx, K. (1925). *Oeuvres complètes de Karl Marx: Histoire des doctrines économiques*, vol. VII. Paris: Alfred Costes.

Marx, K. (1954). *Capital*, vol. I. London: Lawrence & Wishart.

Mill, J. (1826). *Elements of Political Economy.* London: Baldwin, Cradock and Joy. 3rd revised and corrected edition.

Pareto, V. (1902). Anwendungen der Mathematik auf Nationalökonomie. *Encyklopädie der mathematischen Wissenschaften* I(7): 1094–1120.

Pareto, V. (1902–1903). *Les systèmes socialistes.* Two vols, vol. I (1902), vol. II (1903). Paris: Giard & Brière.

Pareto, V. (1906). *Manuale di economia politica con una introduzione alla scienza sociale.* Milan: Società editrice libraria.

Pareto, V. (1971). *Manual of Political Economy.* New York: Augustus M. Kelley. Translated from the French edition of 1927.

Ricardo, D. (1951–1973). *The Works and Correspondence of David Ricardo*, 11 vols. Edited by P. Sraffa with the collaboration of M. H. Dobb. Cambridge, UK: Cambridge University Press. In the text referred to as *Works*, volume number, page number.

Smith, A. ([1776] 1976). *An Inquiry into the Nature and Causes of the Wealth of Nations*, two vols. In R. H. Campbell and A. S. Skinner (eds), *The Glasgow Edition of the Works and Correspondence of Adam Smith*, vol. II. Oxford: Oxford University Press.

Sraffa, P. (1925). Sulle relazioni fra costo e quantità prodotta. *Annali di Economia* 2: 277–328.

Sraffa, P. (1926). The laws of returns under competitive conditions. *Economic Journal* 36(144): 535–550.

Sraffa, P. (1960). *Production of Commodities by Means of Commodities.* Cambridge, UK: Cambridge University Press.

Vianello, F. (1999). Social accounting with Adam Smith. In G. Mongiovi and F. Petri (eds), *Value, Distribution and Capital: Essays in Honour of Pierangelo Garegnani.* London: Routledge, pp. 165–180.

4 Sraffa and the problem of returns

A view from the Sraffa archive

Neri Salvadori and Rodolfo Signorino[1]

1 Introduction

About a quarter of a century ago, Carlo Panico and one of the authors of this chapter published a paper on 'Sraffa, Marshall and the problem of returns' (*EJHET* 1994) in which they explored links between Sraffa's mid-1920s critique of Marshallian economics and the analysis developed some 35 years later in *Production of Commodities*. The 1994 contribution focused exclusively on Sraffa's published works since his unpublished manuscripts were not yet freely accessible. With the benefit of hindsight, it may be claimed that Sraffa was a scholar who, during his lifetime, published little but wrote a lot (Kurz, 2008). Hence, when in December 1994 Trinity College Cambridge, UK, opened the Sraffa Archive, a huge amount of hitherto unknown material became available to the scientific community. Our aim in this chapter is to reconsider some of the results achieved in the 1994 contribution in the light of the new evidence provided by Sraffa's manuscripts.

The 1994 paper investigated four issues: (i) the chronological development of Sraffa's thought in the second half of the 1920s, (ii) the analysis of the firm in the 1920s and in 1960, (iii) the determinants of variable returns in the 1920s and in 1960 and, finally, (iv) interdependence among sectors and the assumption of given quantities. In this chapter, we focus on the last two issues since, as regards item (ii), we were not able to find elements of interest in the Sraffa Archive while Garegnani (2005) and Kurz and Salvadori (2005a) have provided a thorough scrutiny of unpublished material related to item (i).

2 Determinants of variable returns in the 1920s and in 1960

The main aim of this section in the 1994 paper was to clarify that 'in spite of the limited space devoted to this subject, … in 1960 Sraffa maintained, on the determinants of both kinds of returns, the same view as that held in his 1920s critique of Marshall's supply functions' (Panico and Salvadori, 1994, pp. 332–3). In the 1925 article, Sraffa pointed out that variable costs are determined either by '(a) a modification in the *proportion* between the quantities of the two factors [employed by a given industry]' or '(b) an increase in the *size*

DOI: 10.4324/9781003105558-5

of the industry' (Sraffa, 1925 [1998], p. 327, Sraffa's emphasis). Moreover, he clarified that decreasing productivity is caused only by circumstance *sub* (a), *notwithstanding* the potential contrary effect entailed by circumstance *sub* (b), while increasing productivity is caused only by circumstance *sub* (b), *notwithstanding* the contrary effect entailed by circumstance *sub* (a) (*ibidem*). For Sraffa (1925), the definition of a 'constant' factor as a factor whose amount available to the producer cannot be increased is somewhat ambiguous as this definition does not specify whether and to what extent the producer is free to let a portion of the available amount of the 'constant' factor stay idle. If the producer is free to employ *less* than the available amount of the 'constant' factor and if he/she does not make mistakes in the choice of the cost-minimizing technique, i.e. in the proportion of the constant and the variable factor, then, Sraffa concludes, it would only be possible to observe a constant productivity of the variable factor up to the point in which the available amount of the 'constant' factor is fully employed and a decreasing productivity afterwards. Such an analysis of the productivity pattern of a variable factor applied to a constant factor allows Sraffa to dispose of the (then and now) standard textbook explanation of diminishing factor productivity in terms of (presumed) technical laws of production unfailingly governing each and any production sector. By contrast, Sraffa's explanation of the phenomenon of diminishing marginal productivity of a variable factor runs in terms of cost-minimizing choices knowingly made by any rational producer. The clearest statement is worth quoting in full:

> This explanation presupposes two conditions: (1) the application of the principle of substitution, that is to say the criterion by which economic choice is made; (2) the existence of a certain degree of variety and of independence among those elements that make up the variable factor, or between those parts that make up the constant factor, or between the methods by which two factors can be combined (that is, between the ways in which the variable factor can be used). Given these conditions, diminishing returns must of necessity occur because it will be the producer himself who, for his own benefit, will arrange the doses of the factors and the methods of use in a descending order, going from the most favourable ones to the most ineffective, and he will start production with the best combinations, resorting little by little, as these are exhausted, to the worst ones. (Sraffa, 1925 [1998], p. 332)

Panico and Salvadori (1994, p. 329) provide a diagram to summarize the main content of the above passage and show how this procedure can be related to the analysis of land provided in Chapter XI of *Production of Commodities*.

In the Preface of *Production of Commodities*, Sraffa explicitly confirmed that variable returns are linked either to changes in the 'scale of an industry' or to changes in the proportions in which different 'factors of production' are employed by a given industry. Moreover, an echo of the two elements stressed above, i.e. a plurality of production techniques are typically available and entrepreneurs choose the technique that minimizes production costs, may be found in §88 of *Production of Commodities*, where Sraffa analysed intensive diminishing returns. Sraffa claimed that land scarcity is the necessary condition for rent to arise, but it is something that economists cannot *directly* observe. The only observable fact is the contemporaneous employment of more than one method of production, which may happen either by chance, in a switch point, or because the use of more than one method is required. Accordingly, switch points between two methods aside, if an economist observes the employment of two methods side by side, then he or she can safely conclude that land is scarce since, whenever land is non-scarce, a cost-minimizing farmer would employ just one method.

Scrutiny of the relevant material in the Sraffa Papers at the Wren Library shows that immediately after Sraffa had elaborated the first versions of his 'equations' in November 1927, he began to investigate the 'twin' problems of land and land-rent. At first Sraffa, and for a considerable time, thought that, unlike extensive rent, intensive rent could not be dealt with. He felt that intensive rent had to be set aside because it involved a dynamic issue which was incompatible with his method of analysis. As regards the problem of extensive rent, it appears that Sraffa succeeded in integrating different qualities of land into his equations with a surplus as early as the second half of 1928: see D3/12/7: 131–2. The document is entitled 'Man from the Moon'.[2] In this document, Sraffa investigated the problem of the 'significance of the equations'. This document has been extensively analysed by Kurz and Salvadori (2004, 2005b). Here we focus on the question of diminishing returns. The relevant passage is the following:

> We consider here only differential rents arising from differences in the quality of land used by different farms.
>
> In the first representation[3] we had an equation for every industry: this means lumping together all the materials used by different farms in an industry, on one side, and all their products on the other.
>
> We now have to represent separately the conditions of prod of the several farms in the industry, regarding the fertility of the land used as the basis of their differences. We do not assume that they use all the same means of production and in the same proportions: we make no assumptions whatever on this point – different farms may use materials as different as those used by different industries. We therefore do not know a priori (i.e. before solving the equations) which are producing at lower and which at higher costs, in fact we do not even know whether the costs per unit produced (measured in value) of two firms {sic} are equal or different, since they may use altogether different kinds of materials, which are therefore incomparable, except in value. We had *n* equations for *n* industries. Let us now take one industry, composed of m farms, and let us split up its

equation into m equations representing the conditions of its m firms {sic}. We thus have $m - 1$ new equations and we have to add an equal number of unknowns. If we knew a priori which is the marginal farm, all would be plain sailing; since the rents of the other $m - 1$ farms would be the required unknowns. But we simply know that one farm must have zero rent (this is implied in the definition of the differential rent) although we do not know which. This however provides us with an additional equation, which expresses the fact that the product of all the rents of all the farms in an industry must be equal to zero, i.e.: $R_I R_{II} R_{III} \ldots R_m = 0$. (Rent is introduced as an unknown fractional factor multiplied by the product of the farm: this term is added on the side of costs of production). Thus we have m − 1 new equations from the farms, and with this one we have m equations which determine the m unknown rents.

The last equation however does not involve (as we must) that all the rents we shall find are positive. In fact, being an equation of the mth degree, it will have m sets of solutions; the differences between the solutions will be equal in all sets, but absolute values will be different; in fact, every set of solution will give the rent of a different farm as equal to zero, and all those greater than it as positives, those smaller as negatives. The only significant set of solutions will be the one in which the smallest rent is zero, and all the others positive. (D3/12/7: 131–2)

This argument corresponds almost *verbatim* to what Sraffa wrote in §86 of *Production of Commodities*, which Panico and Salvadori (1994) connected to the analysis of Sraffa (1925). Yet a criticism may be levelled both at this unpublished 1928 document and at the definitive text of the 1960 book: it is not true that '[t]he only significant set of solutions will be the one in which the smallest rent is zero, and all the others positive'. All sets of solutions have an economic meaning. What is different among the various sets is the list of the qualities of lands (in the 1960 book) or the farms (in the 1928 document) that are cultivated since a quality of land can be cultivated only if its rent is non-negative. Therefore, the different sets of solutions correspond to different amounts of the product. It goes without saying that Sraffa's argument is correct *if and only if* the qualities of land that are cultivated are known and all qualities of land that are not cultivated are ignored as well as all the processes that employ them. Hence, if we follow the metaphor of the 'Man from the Moon' or that of the 'photograph' (Kurz and Salvadori, 2018), the above criticism may be eschewed.

In a document entitled 'Puzzles on the Theory of Rent' (D3/12/13: 23(1–16)), drafted in the summer of 1929, Sraffa studied intensive rent and became aware of the fact that two processes are needed to produce a commodity, but he linked the question to dynamic issues and therefore time. At the time, this outcome left him unsatisfied and perplexed:

Another point that has puzzled me often is this: There may very well be two methods of cultivating a given piece of land, which yield the same rent and have the same marginal product (qui è il busillis {here is the difficulty}: how measured? is it one or two commodities that are produced?) but employing different amounts of other factors. The point is not so much to find how the choice is determined.

The real difficulty is the apparent contradiction of the above, which is certainly possible, with the ordinary presentation of the theory of rent, by means of a "marginal product (or cost)" diagram. This necessarily assumes that, as more doses of other factors are employed, the marginal product falls (or – as more is produced the marg. cost rises) and the rent falls {sic}. The three variations must thus be strictly connected; to an increase of the first, a fall in the second and a rise in the third must always follow/ (accompany it)/. But from the above it appears that a higher rent may correspond to a smaller amount of other factors employed (or of gross product). How can these two things be reconciled? (D3/12/13:23(2))

The third puzzle is the enormous difference in the nature of the assumptions underlying extensive and intensive diminishing returns …

The fundamental difference is that the extensive (different qualities of land) is truly a purely timeless, or geometrical representation: all the different lands exist simultaneously, ᶦat one instant,ᶦ they and their products can be ascertained, distinguished and measured at one instant, without changing anything in the present arrangements.

On the contrary, the intensive (successive doses of c. and l. on a piece of land) dim. ret. do not exist at any one instant: the "doses" are (supposed to be) all identical, and since there is not a different location in space of each of them (each is applied on all the surface of land) we have no knowledge of (and there is no meaning in the expression) the product of a separate dose: we know only the product of all together, and if we like we may deduce an average. We can only find these dim. ret. by change, or movement: that is to say, we require time. (D3/12/13: 23(1bis))

In the document quoted above, Sraffa distinguishes two possible representations of the phenomenon of rent. The former is a timeless, 'geometrical' representation, to use his own wording, while the latter is related to change. Sraffa links the former representation to extensive rent and the latter to intensive rent. Yet already a year and half before, in November 1927, he had admitted the possibility that extensive rent could be tackled by means of the former representation:

Dim. ret is a dynamic assumption and therefore must be ignored (depends upon incr. pop.{ulation}, etc.). We must consider only the different fertility of different plots of land: but not in the dynamic sense, of the order in which they are brought under cultivation. It is simply the fact that lands of different fertility are *simultaneously* cultivated by *independent producers* … and that at the same time the market price for wheat must be *one* and the same, whatever the land each bushel comes from. (D3/12/11: 33)

What appears to have escaped Sraffa's attention at that moment is the fact that the same argument holds for intensive rent too: the question of change is connected to the distinction between which processes are operated and which are not. On the contrary, if the operated processes are known (irrespective of the reason why this is so), then the analysis can be performed without any reference to time. In our view, a plausible explanation of Sraffa's insistence on the issue of the time dimension in the analysis of intensive rent is the following. Whereas in the case of extensive rent, to postulate the existence of a process for each quality of land appears to be an obvious assumption, in the case of intensive rent the assumption of the existence of two processes operated at the same time may sound *arbitrary*, to make use of one of Sraffa's favourite expressions.[4] Granted our explanation, it may be argued that Sraffa's reference to a dynamic process in the case of intensive rent aims to convince the reader that the presence of two processes to produce the same commodity is not an *arbitrary* assumption. (By the way, this is exactly the position expressed by Sraffa in §88 of *Production of Commodities*.)

Sraffa came back to the issue of land and land-rent in the second period of his reconstructive work (1940–1944). In November 1942, he confronted himself with the problem of the order of fertility of various plots of land and discovered that such an order depends on distribution: see D3/12/25: 1–2. Nevertheless, Sraffa did not insert this result into *Production of Commodities* and indeed it was (re)discovered several years after the publication of his book (Quadrio Curzio, 1967; see also Kurz and Salvadori, 1995, chapter 10, §1.3 and the literature referred to in §6 of the same chapter). In our view, the most plausible interpretation is that Sraffa did not deal with the issue of the order of fertility since he avoided considering the dynamic process and considered the assumption of the existence of a number of processes equal to the number of cultivated qualities of land as unproblematic.

In October 1943, in an attempt to re-interpret the concept of marginal product within his own framework (D3/12/35: 15–25), and then in several other manuscripts, Sraffa began to discuss the case of intensive diminishing returns in terms of a change in the proportion in which two equi-profitable methods of production are employed side by side on a given plot of land:

The similarity of the "two methods" cases with Joint Products is evident. The degree of freedom, which is there supplied by the variability of the relative price, is here supplied by the variability in the relative extension of the two methods, i.e. the variability of the ratio of constant to variable capital; while here the relative price of the "products of the two methods" is invariable, since the "two products" are identical. (D3/12/35, p. 15 f.8 recto)

The comparison, suggested by Sraffa himself, between joint production and land is interesting. In chapter VII of *Production of Commodities* on 'Joint Production', Sraffa assumed that in a system of production, or a technique, the number of processes is equal to the number of commodities involved. The subsequent literature has criticized this assumption, but what is important here is the motivation that Sraffa supplied in a footnote:

> considering that the proportions in which the two commodities are produced by any one method will in general be different from those in which they are required for use, the existence of two methods of producing them in different proportions will be necessary for obtaining the required proportion of the two products through an appropriate combination of the two methods. (Sraffa, 1960, p. 43f2)

Indeed, it is possible to use exactly the same argument to justify the assumption of two methods in the case of intensive rent. And this is what Sraffa did in 1943 while in 1960 he preferred to refer to the dynamic process described in §88.

In a document entitled 'Margins and margins' (D3/12/46, pp. 50 recto–53 recto, probably composed in 1958), Sraffa envisaged an asymmetry between 'extensive' diminishing returns and 'intensive' diminishing returns: in a stationary economy an observer could immediately discover the existence of the first kind of diminishing returns since there is no need to conduct any experiment with factor proportions, while the second kind may be observed if and only if the observer is allowed to perform such an experiment. The relevant passage is the following:

> A man who was in a position to observe the methods of production of a stationary society (but not to make experiments) would be able by observation to discover all about the returns from lands of different fertility, but could never find out *by observation alone* the "marginal product" on one and the same land: this is not a visible object, for the reason that it has no existence. The "experiment" of the successive doses, described in the textbooks, does not merely ascertain or measure the marginal product, it brings it into existence. (D3/12/46: 50 recto–51 recto, Sraffa's emphasis)

This is clearly an echo of the distinction made in 1929 between timeless 'geometrical' representation and 'mechanical' representation related to change. The logic of Sraffa's argument implies that in a non-stationary economy nothing prevents an economist from observing marginal magnitudes: in such an economy an experiment concerning factor proportions may be devised, at least ideally, to bring marginal magnitudes into actual existence.[5] By contrast, the existence of two processes operated simultaneously is clear and unambiguous evidence of the fact that intensive rent is at work: no experiment needs to be performed.

Be that as it may, in October 1943 also the problem of intensive rent was solved and, what is more, it was done so by following the lead of the main analytical intuition of the 1925 Italian paper: diminishing returns derive from the producer's cost-minimizing choices and not from alleged natural-technological laws.

3 Interdependence and the assumption of given quantities

The main aim of this section in the 1994 paper was to clarify that it is 'possible to think that some origins of the method based on the assumption of "given quantities" can also be found in the Marshallian tradition and in the 1920s critique that Sraffa presented against it' (Panico and Salvadori, 1994, p. 336). This was also obtained by a comparison between the dynamic process described in §88 of *Production of Commodities* on one side and the 1920s criticism of the typical Marshallian method that starts from the assumption of an *ad hoc* variation in the gross produced quantity of an industry, leaving all the other gross produced quantities as constant (thus ignoring the interdependence between the effects of this variation on the costs of production of that industry as well as of all other industries), on the other.

While Sraffa's manuscripts provide many elements that contribute to clarifying Sraffa's thought concerning the assumption of given quantities, we were not able to find much about the relationship between the assumption of given quantities and Marshall's partial equilibrium method. Yet scrutiny of Sraffa's manuscripts allowed us to recognize elements that are present in *Production of Commodities*, but went somewhat unrecognized.

Let us consider the path from the 'abstract' to the 'concrete' followed by Sraffa in *Production of Commodities*.[6] The starting point is production for subsistence, i.e. an 'extremely simple society which produces just enough to maintain itself'. It is worth noting that in such an economy the Marshallian method of analysis would involve a logical contradiction. Put differently, the theorist is not allowed to introduce any assumption concerning an *ad hoc* variation in the gross produced quantity of an industry, leaving all the other gross products unchanged. The obvious reason is that any variation in the gross produced quantity of an industry would prevent the economy reproducing itself. In this set-up, it is self-evident that the marginal product of a factor (or, by the same token, the marginal cost of a product) 'would not be there to be found' (p. v).

The role of the assumption of given quantities becomes manifest in the second step of Sraffa's path from the abstract to the concrete where the object under investigation becomes an economy able to produce a surplus. In such a set-up, a change in factor proportion or in the scale of an industry is materially possible. Hence, there is no theoretical reason for denying that, when a surplus is produced, the marginal productivity of a factor and the marginal cost of a product may be *at least ideally* calculated without jeopardizing the possibility of the economy reproducing itself. But the assumption of given quantities – 'No

changes in output and (at any rate in Parts I and II) no changes in the proportions in which different means of production are used by an industry are
considered' (*ibidem*) − prevents the theorist from following this route. Put
differently, whenever a surplus obtains, the theorist can calculate a marginal
magnitude only by violating the assumption of given quantities.[7] The simple
fact that there are circumstances in which marginal magnitudes are not simply
un-observable but plainly non-existent and whose existence cannot be 'generated' by an experiment by the economist/observer or, to stick to Sraffa's
metaphor, the man fallen from the Moon, suggests that there are interesting
economic problems that may be investigated without making use of marginal
magnitudes. According to Sraffa, Smith and Ricardo were perfectly aware of
this 'fact' but the subsequent advent of the marginal method has condemned
this awareness to oblivion.

Let us now consider the elements that we consider important for an assessment of the assumption of given quantities in the Sraffa Papers, which were
the central elements of two other papers by one of the authors (Kurz and
Salvadori, 2004, 2005b). Accordingly, here just a few remarks suffice. We start
from a quotation from a document entitled 'Man from the Moon', probably
written in the late 1920s. (The document is not dated but is contained in a
folder with material most of which was written, and some even dated, from
1927 to 1931.) In this document, Sraffa clarified the significance of the
equations of production he had begun to develop in the second half of 1927:

> The significance of the equations is simply this: that if a man fell from
> the moon on the earth, and noted the amount of things consumed in
> each factory and the amount produced by each factory during a year,
> he could deduce at which values the commodities must be sold, if
> the rate of interest must be uniform and the process of production
> repeated. In short, the equations show that the conditions of exchange
> are entirely determined by the conditions of production. (D3/12/7: 87)

An echo of this argument can be found in a note of 1942 in which Sraffa
sought to clarify his aims:

> This paper deals with an extremely elementary problem; so elementary
> indeed that its solution is generally taken for granted. The problem is that
> of ascertaining the conditions of equilibrium of a system of prices + the
> rate of profits, independently of the study of the forces which may bring
> about such a state of equilibrium. Since a solution of the second problem
> carries with it a solution of the first, that is the course usually adopted in
> modern Theory. The first problem however is susceptible of a more
> general treatment, independent of the particular forces assumed for the
> second; + in view of the unsatisfactory character of the latter, there is
> advantage in maintaining its independence. (D3/12/15: 2)

These two quotations show the way Sraffa intended to circumscribe the problem under investigation in order to determine prices independently of the specific forces at work, whether such forces are demand and supply or any other causal mechanism. The treatment of this problem is much more general and independent of the specific causal mechanism investigated by the theorist in any given model. Indeed, the first problem can be solved. Sraffa's awareness of the nature of the solution becomes even clearer when we turn to the 1950s when, as his manuscripts reveal, Sraffa started drafting the preface to his book. In a draft dated 2 April 1957, he explained:

> This is not proposed as a complete system of equilibrium. The data assumed are not sufficient to determine either distribution or values. Only the effects of hypothetical, arbitrarily assumed extra data (such as the wage, or the rate of profits) are discussed. (D3/12/46: 32a)

This 'preliminary' Sraffa explicitly designed for the purpose of finding out 'whether there is room enough for the marginal system' (ibid.). Or, as he had emphasized in a note dated 16 September 1956, the book was meant to accomplish two tasks: (i) 'to facilitate the interpretation of some/certain theories of the classical economists and of Marx which seem puzzling/to puzzle the present-day/modern student'; (ii) 'to supply a platform (base, formulation) for a critique/re-examination of the marginal theory of production and distribution' (ibid.: 32b). For task (i), the assumption of 'given quantities' may be appropriate, but for task (ii) its use may be debatable. Indeed, if quantities are given, then no assumption on returns is needed. However, we acknowledge that the assumption of 'given quantities' stands in the way of a proper analysis of a few problems that have a genuine economic content. Therefore, different assumptions about returns must be adopted. (Sraffa appears to be conscious of this fact when he mentions that to deal with the problem of choice of techniques, in Part III, changes in the proportions in which different means of production are used by an industry may be considered.)

4 Final remarks

In this chapter, we have investigated the treatment of decreasing returns and the role of given quantities in *Production of Commodities by Means of Commodities* in the light of the unpublished material made available after the opening of Sraffa's archive in the Wren Library. Attention has been given to the distinction between extensive and intensive rents and how they can be analysed either in a timeless representation or in relation to change and how this distinction evolves in Sraffa's intellectual journey. The assumption of given quantities is explicitly related by Sraffa to the problem of returns, but also plays a separate role. This is investigated both with respect to the path from the 'abstract' to the 'concrete' followed by Sraffa in *Production of Commodities* and with regard to documents available in the archive related to the significance of the equations. The chapter updates a previous analysis of the same issues by Panico and Salvadori (1994), who made no reference to the unpublished documents, unavailable at that time.

Notes

1 We wish to thank without implicating Heinz D. Kurz, Christian Gehrke and an anonymous referee for their comments on a previous version of this chapter.
2 Kurz and Salvadori (2018, p. 120) argue that the title was probably added at a later date, in the 1940s, when Sraffa revised his old manuscript.
3 The reference is to his 'second equations'.
4 In a private conversation, Christian Gehrke suggested that in the late 1920s Sraffa had some difficulties realizing that intensive rent could be analysed in terms of the co-existence of two methods since he still was, at least partially, under the spell of the marginal method. In Gehrke's opinion, this could be a plausible explanation for Sraffa's failure to realize, at that time, that also intensive rent can be treated 'geometrically'.
5 As stressed by Rosselli and Trabucchi (2019), the analysis of intensive rent by means of the coexistence of two different methods of production is a remarkable result from the standpoint of Sraffa's logic of scientific research since the two different methods are visible objects and not the outcome of a mental experiment by the economist/observer. For a comprehensive reconstruction of Sraffa's dissatisfaction with the marginal method, see Marcuzzo and Rosselli (2011).
6 On the recent philosophical debate concerning the process of de-idealization in economics, see Mäki (2011) and the literature cited therein.
7 The use of marginal magnitudes is related to optimal choices and therefore, in the context of the 1960 book, to the choice of technique. Indeed, the arguments supplied by Sraffa in §93 could be completed by the use of inequalities that are equivalent to using marginal magnitudes, as the subsequent literature has actually done, but Sraffa preferred to complete the arguments of §93 by means of the arguments of §94, based on the continuity of the w-r relationships. Note that in pure subsistence economies no choice of technique is allowed: otherwise a surplus would arise. This fact had been known to Sraffa since 1927 (we thank Christian Gehrke for this observation). Indeed, in a document titled 'Physical real costs' (D3/12/3: 44–7), Sraffa discussed the issue of substitution among different commodities within the workers' consumption basket and highlighted the theoretical difficulties involved by workers' choices concerning their consumption pattern. In the left margin of the sheet (p. 44), Sraffa added a note where he stated 'in a community that produces just what is sufficient to keep it going would there not be only one combination which satisfies the above condition? it would be "the cheapest"'. Note that from this document it may be inferred that, for Sraffa, besides choice of technique, also workers' consumption choices cannot be allowed in a pure subsistence economy.

References

Garegnani, P. (2005). On a turning point in Sraffa's theoretical and interpretative position in the late 1920s. *The European Journal of the History of Economic Thought* 12(3): 453–492.

Kurz, H. D. (2008). Preface. In H. D. Kurz, L. L. Pasinetti and N. Salvadori (eds), *Piero Sraffa: The Man and the Scholar. Exploring His Unpublished Papers*. London and New York: Routledge.

Kurz, H. D. and Salvadori, N. (1995). *Theory of Production: A Long-Period Analysis*. Cambridge, New York and Melbourne: Cambridge University Press.

Kurz, H. D. and Salvadori, N. (2004). 'Man from the Moon': on Sraffa's objectivism. *Économies et Sociétés* 38(8–9): 1545–1557. Reprinted in Heinz D. Kurz and N. Salvadori (eds) (2007). *Interpreting Classical Economics: Studies in Long-Period Analysis*. London: Routledge, pp. 134–144.

Kurz, H. D. and Salvadori, N. (2005a). Removing an 'insuperable obstacle' in the way of an objectivist analysis: Sraffa's attempts at fixed capital. *The European Journal of the History of Economic Thought* 12(3): 493–523.

Kurz, H. D. and Salvadori, N. (2005b). Representing the production and circulation of commodities in material terms: on Sraffa's objectivism. *Review of Political Economy* 17(3): 413–441.

Kurz, H. D. and Salvadori, N. (2018). On the "photograph" interpretation of Piero Sraffa's production equations: a view from the Sraffa archive. In M. Corsi, J. Kregel and C. D'Ippoliti (eds), *Classical Economics Today: Essays in Honor of Alessandro Roncaglia*. London and New York: Anthem Press, pp. 113–128.

Mäki, U. (2011). Models and the locus of their truth. *Synthese* 180(1): 47–63.

Marcuzzo, M. C. and Rosselli, A. (2011). Sraffa and his arguments against 'marginism'. *Cambridge Journal of Economics* 35(1): 219–231.

Panico, C. and Salvadori, N. (1994). Sraffa, Marshall and the problem of returns. *The European Journal of the History of Economic Thought* 1(2): 323–343.

Quadrio Curzio, A. (1967). *Rendita e distribuzione in un modello economico plurisettoriale*. Milan: Giuffrè.

Rosselli, A. and Trabucchi, P. (2019). Sraffa, the 'marginal' method and change. *Structural Change and Economic Dynamics* 51: 334–340.

Sraffa, P. (1925 [1998]). Sulle relazioni fra costo e quantità prodotta. *Annali di Economia* 2: 277–328. English translation by John Eatwell and A. Roncaglia (1998). On the relations between cost and quantity produced. In Luigi L. Pasinetti (ed), *Italian Economic Papers*, vol. III. Bologna: Il Mulino and Oxford: Oxford University Press, pp. 323–363.

Sraffa, P. (1960). *Production of Commodities by Means of Commodities: Prelude to a Critique of Economic Theory*. Cambridge: Cambridge University Press.

5 Class struggle and hired prize-fighters

A Marx-inspired perspective on the present state of economic theory and its social causes[1]

Fabio Petri

1 The question: why so little effect of the 2008 crisis on economic theory

The crisis that started in 2007–2008 blocked economic growth and in less than two years caused a fall of industrial production by 15% or more in Germany and other nations and an increase in the rate of unemployment by at least 5 points on average in the USA and Western Europe; and no doubt without the massive government interventions the fall in production and increase in unemployment would have been much greater. Therefore, we have lived through a historical episode as important as the crisis that followed the first oil price increase in 1973 (and put an end to the Golden Age), or even as the Great Depression of the 1930s. But, differently from what happened in these two episodes (the 1930s crisis favoured the success of Keynesian theory and opened the way to Keynesian policies; the 1970s crisis saw the rise of monetarism and of its developments that at present dominate mainstream macroeconomics), the recent crisis – in spite of being clearly not attributable to pro-wage-labour policies and therefore radically questioning the optimistic post-monetarist vision – does not seem to have significantly affected the dominant political discourses on the nature of capitalism and the tasks of governments, nor academic mainstream scientific production. There has been, it is true, the birth of a few new 'heterodox' journals (but owing to initiatives that had started before the 2008 crisis), but there seems to be no change in the teaching of advanced macroeconomic theory (at least, this is what I gather from recent textbooks and from an Internet examination of teaching programs in a number of those, of the economics departments of prestigious universities, that permit access to this information), and certainly no change in the theories and models utilised by the Research Offices of central banks. The prevalent, indeed unique, theoretical basis of the macroeconomic elaborations that find room in the so-called 'top' journals and in the research papers of central banks continues to be the Dynamic Stochastic General Equilibrium approach, in which the existence of neoclassical decreasing demand curves for factors is accepted without discussion, Say's Law is taken for granted and justifies intertemporal optimisation by consumers, and unemployment is exclusively

DOI: 10.4324/9781003105558-6

voluntary even in the very short period, although perhaps in some cases only indirectly voluntary in that it depends on trade union policy, which however is able to influence wage bargaining because it enjoys the union members' support. The initial admissions by Greenspan, Acemoglu and others of erroneousness of some of the dominant macroeconomic ideas do not seem to have left significant traces.[2] An external observer might conclude that the dominant theories must be scientifically solid, which is the opposite of the truth as I will briefly remember. But then how come they resist?

I want to argue that Marx is useful in the search for an answer.

2 Marx's perspective on economic theory as politically conditioned

In the Preface to the first edition of *Das Kapital*, Marx stresses that:

> In the domain of political economy, free scientific inquiry does not merely meet the same enemies as in all other domains. The peculiar nature of the material it deals with summons into the fray on the opposing side the most violent, sordid and malignant passion of the human breast, the Furies of private interest. (Marx, 1976; Preface to the first edition, p. 92)

The thesis is clarified and expanded upon in the Postface to the second edition, where Marx argues that

> In so far as political economy is bourgeois, i.e. in so far as it views the capitalist order as the absolute and ultimate form of social production, instead of as a historically transient stage of development, it can only remain a science while the class struggle remains latent or manifests itself only in isolated and sporadic phenomena (ibid., p.96.)

Marx illustrates the argument with the well-known passage quoted here at the end of this paragraph, where the social situation after Ricardo's death – with the victory of the bourgeoisie in Western Europe, and the beginning of workers' organised struggles – is depicted as leaving room in economic discussion almost only for 'hired prize-fighters', for 'the bad conscience and evil intent of apologetics'. The implicit message is that when the ruling class is strong but some initial danger for its social control appears, in the disciplines whose doctrines have political implications the search for truth takes second place to the defense and justification of the status quo. However, if the oppressed classes show some strength, then their claims are 'no longer to be ignored', the official scientific discourse is obliged to concede something.

> Let us take England. Its classical political economy belongs to a period in which the class struggle was as yet undeveloped. Its last great

representative, Ricardo, ultimately (and consciously) made the antag-onism of class interests, of wages and profits, of profits and rent, the starting-point of his investigations, naïvely taking this antagonism for a social law of nature. But with this contribution the bourgeois science of economics had reached the limits beyond which it could not pass. Already in Ricardo's lifetime, and in opposition to him, it was met by criticism in the person of Sismondi.

The succeeding period, from 1820 to 1830, was notable in England for the lively scientific activity which took place in the field of political economy. It was the period of both the vulgarizing and the extending of Ricardo's theory, and of the contest of that theory with the old school. Splendid tournaments were held. What was achieved at that time is little known on the European Continent, because the polemic is for the most part scattered over articles in reviews, *pièces d'occasion* and pamphlets. The unprejudiced character of this polemic – although Ricardo's theory already serves, in exceptional cases, as a weapon with which to attack the bourgeois economic system – is explained by the circumstances of the time. On the one hand, large-scale industry itself was only just emerging from its childhood, as is shown by the fact that the periodic cycle of its modern life opens for the first time with the crisis of 1825. On the other hand, the class strugge between capital and labour was forced into the background, politically by the discord between the governments and the feudal aristocracy gathered around the Holy Alliance, assembled in one camp, and the mass of the people, led by the bourgeoisie, in the other camp, and economically by the quarrel between industrial capital and aristocratic landed property .... With the year 1830 there came the crisis which was to be decisive, once and for all.

In France and England the bourgeoisie had conquered political power. From that time on, the class struggle took on more and more explicit and threatening forms, both in practice and in theory. It sounded the knell of scientific bourgeois economics. It was thenceforth no longer a question whether this or that theorem was true, but whether it was useful to capital or harmful, expedient or inexpedient, in accordance with police regula-tions or contrary to them. In place of disinterested inquirers there stepped hired prize-fighters, in place of genuine scientific research, the bad conscience and evil intent of apologetics ....

The Continental revolution of 1848 also had its reaction in England. Men who still claimed some scientific standing and aspired to be something more than mere sophists and sycophants of the ruling classes tried to harmonize the political economy of capital with the claims, no longer to be ignored, of the proletariat. Hence a shallow syncretism, of which John Stuart Mill is the best representative. This is a declaration of bankruptcy by 'bourgeois' economics (*Capital*, vol. I, cit., *Postface* to the second edition, pp. 96–98).

I will argue that this perspective appears confirmed by the evolution of economic theory.

3 Political conditionings on the subsequent evolution of economic theory: a quick overview

Few would deny that the birth and the success of the marginal or neoclassical approach to value and distribution was greatly motivated by the need to counter the socialist criticisms of capitalism. There are very clear sentences by, for example, Carl Menger or J. B. Clark on the importance of the new doctrine as a weapon to refute the socialist arguments. What is less widely perceived is that a disenchanted look at the robustness of the theories of Jevons, Carl Menger, Walras, J. B. Clark, Böhm-Bawerk, Wicksell, Marshall reveals grave weaknesses in them, which would have permitted merciless criticisms if these theories had been immediately analysed with the same competence and the same desire to find them wrong as manifested vis-à-vis Marx's theory. Let me remember (Petri, 2016; Dvoskin and Petri, 2017) that:

- Wicksell admitted the grave incompleteness of Jevons' theory.
- Carl Menger was unable to solve the 'imputation' problem, and admitted in particular that he was unable to supply a theory of capital, declaring he could only hope that Böhm-Bawerk would supply it.
- Böhm-Bawerk's period of production was rejected by Wicksell already in 1900, and Wicksell came extremely close to admitting the illegitimacy – later openly admitted by Lindahl, Hayek, Lutz – of a given endowment of value capital.
- Veblen explicitly criticised J. B. Clark's theory of capital and distribution precisely because, capital being a quantity of exchange value, that theory had to treat relative prices as given while it should have determined them.
- Marshall, although less openly, ultimately based his analyses on the same conception of capital as a value factor as J. B. Clark.
- Walras in the 4th edition of the *Eléments* admitted that his system of equations was actually wrong, and furthermore introduced the absurd tâtonnement based on 'bons', thus implicitly admitting the inability of his theory to supply a plausible account of the tendency towards equilibrium.
- Pareto in his *Manuel* completely dropped Walras's theory of capitalisation, leaving his approach devoid of a theory of value and distribution for economies with capital goods.
- Hicks in 1932 and 1934 expressed very serious reservations on Walras' specification of the capital endowment as a given vector, but in those same years was obliged by Gerald Shove's lashes to admit grave mistakes in his own traditional treatment of capital as a single factor, to the point of refusing to allow reprints of his *Theory of Wages* for thirty years.
- Irving Fisher's approach to capital and investment was later found logically circular by Armen Alchian because it treated relative prices as given in

order to determine the rate of interest while in fact relative prices depend on the rate of interest.

It would seem therefore that the picture generally transmitted by textbooks, of a triumphant advance of economic science brought about by the new insights of marginalism, should be modified into that of a marginal theory aprioristically accepted because of the rosy picture of capitalism it supplied, in spite of its evident incompleteness and weaknesses, in particular in the treatment of capital, weaknesses which – it was fideistically believed – would be surmounted by further theoretical progress.

Nor can it be argued that no alternative was available: in 1906, Bortkiewicz, utilising Dmitriev, had shown (in German, a language read by most economists) that in Ricardo and Marx the defective labour theory of value could be replaced by a more correct theory of the rate of profit and relative prices; which implied that there was little obstacle to resuming their approach. One cannot but wonder whether it would have taken so long for this discovery, if there had not been after 1830 precisely the anti-Ricardian reaction noted by Marx, motivated by its political implications as made clear, for example, by an author Marx does not mention, George Poulet(te) Scrope (1797–1876):

> Surely the publication of opinions taken up hastily upon weak, narrow and imperfect evidence – opinions which, overthrowing as they did the fundamental principles of sympathy and common interest that knit society together, would not but be deeply injurious even if true – does amount to a crime… In their theory of rent, they [the Ricardians, F.P.] have insisted that landlords can thrive only at the expense of the public at large, and especially of the capitalists; in their theory of profits, they have declared that capitalists can only improve their circumstances by depressing those of the labouring and numerous class; … In one and all of their arguments they have studiously exhibited the interests of every class in society as necessarily at perpetual variance with every other class! (1831; quoted in Blaug, 1958, pp. 149–50)

But Dmitriev and Bortkiewicz remained neglected for decades: no one was interested in strengthening Ricardo or, even worse, Marx.

One must wait for the Great Depression of the 1930s coupled with the danger of communism to see the hold of marginal theory and policy partly shaken: Keynes candidly admitted he wanted to save capitalism from itself in order to save it from communism, and here we have a strong reason for the general acceptance of his theory in spite of the immediate wave of criticisms, not entirely unjustified, moved against it by Henderson, Hicks, Meade and others. And the beautiful book by Armstrong, Glyn and Harrison, *Capitalism since 1945*, convincingly shows how at the end of WW2 the fear that the working class would turn communist was the reason for the concession of the welfare state in

Western Europe and for a general acceptance, in the USA too, of the inter-ventionist Keynesian state with a duty to maintain unemployment low.[3]

There was also an opening of theory to many non-marginalist views, for example, Kaleckian views, multiplier-accelerator theories of growth. When in the second half of the 1960s this situation was coupled with student protests, anti-Vietnam war demonstrations and a wave of workers' politicisation and activism culminating in May 1968 in France and in the Hot Autumn of 1969 in Italy, the circulation of radical and Marxist views was unparalleled. In Italy an impressive number – perhaps even a majority – of young economists turned to study Sraffa, Garegnani, Sylos Labini, Pasinetti, and ultimately Marx.

But this political climate did not last. The 1970s witnessed the end of the Golden Age. Palma (2009, p. 837) reports a declaration by Sir Alan Budd (a top civil servant at the British Treasury under Thatcher, and later Provost of Queen's College, Oxford) on the real reasonings behind the Thatcher government's use of neoclassical monetarist arguments to justify its brutal restrictive monetary policy:

> The Thatcher government never believed for a moment that [mone-tarism] was the correct way to bring down inflation. They did however see that this would be a very good way to raise unemployment. And raising unemployment was an extremely desirable way of reducing the strength of the working classes .... What was engineered – in Marxist terms – was a crisis of capitalism which re-created the reserve army of labour, and has allowed the capitalists to make high profits ever since.

This and other evidence strongly suggests that the Golden Age ended above all because of a conscious decision by the dominant classes to weaken wage labour through an increase in unemployment. This decision is exactly what Marx (or Kalecki, 1943) would have expected after the increase in the share of wages and the political turmoil at the end of the 1960s, and I would suggest it was made possible by the disappearance of the fear that the working class would turn communist. The latter fear must have decreased when the restrictive fiscal po-licies adopted after the first oil price increase (1973) caused increases in un-employment which however did not cause a shift of votes to the left but rather the opposite. The explanation is probably that the attractiveness of communism had decreased with the increasing information on the realities of the Stalinist period and on the increasing difficulties of the USSR economy; and that the dislike of capitalism among the lower and intermediate social strata had decreased too because of the low unemployment and high growth in the 1950s and 1960s and, in Western Europe, the creation of the welfare state.[4] In this situation, it would seem that the slowdown of growth and the acceleration of inflation in the 1970s pushed the median voter to prefer more conservative political programs, aided ideologically in this by the crisis of Keynesian theory, which for the causes referred to in the next section was rapidly losing ground to monetarism.

4 The scientific weakness of monetarism and of its developments

The victory of monetarism too deserves reconsideration from the perspective suggested by Marx. True, the ground for that victory was prepared by the neoclassical synthesis: the latter, favoured by Keynes's acceptance of the marginalist decreasing demand curves for labour and for capital,[5] used the 'Keynes effect' against Keynes, arguing that although perhaps it would take a long time (and therefore government intervention was preferable), still according to Keynes's own theory a downward flexibility of money wages would bring about an increase in employment because the lower money wages would cause a decrease in the price level which, by reducing the demand for money, would reduce the rate of interest, thus stimulating investment. But this argument needed not to bring to the monetarist conclusion that the economy was always very close to full employment (i.e. to only frictional unemployment) and fiscal policy was to be avoided; it suffices to mention Modigliani, Samuelson, Tobin as examples of economists who accepted the 'neoclassical synthesis' but continued to believe in the need for an interventionist state. In fact, the argument supporting the tendency toward full employment on the basis of the 'Keynes effect' was rather weak; it needed:

- no serious and lasting trouble deriving from expectations, for example, a decrease in money wages must not induce a repeated postponement of investment decisions in the expectation of further decreases of wages;
- an exogenous supply of money not decreased by a reduced demand for money;
- that investment is not reduced by financial difficulties of firms caused by the increased real burden of debts owing to the decreasing price level;
- that the reduction of real wages, during the interval between the decrease in money wages and the decrease in prices, does not cause a reduction of consumption expenditure that discourages investment;
- that the negative rate of inflation during the price decrease does not cause the *real* rate of interest not to decrease or even increase, in spite of a decrease in the nominal rate of interest;
- a significant negative interest elasticity of investment, which was not confirmed by the empirical evidence; the latter clearly showed, from the first studies in the 1940s onwards,[6] a zero or extremely low interest elasticity of investment (apart perhaps from residential investment), and on the other hand a clear role of the accelerator, with connected potential instabilities.

The convergence of the process based on the 'Keynes effect' to a full-employment equilibrium was therefore uncertain, and the likelihood was high that the process, even if converging, was so slow as to undermine the right to take the supply of capital as given during the adjustment, rather than endogenously determined by an investment path considerably different from the full-employment path. It was possible to use this kind of considerations to develop Keynes's insight that investment determines savings via variations of aggregate income, into views on growth such as the ones of Kaldor or Joan Robinson, where capital growth was no longer determined by the full-employment supply of savings, even without a fully reasoned out rejection of the marginalist mechanisms and conception of capital.[7] After Sraffa's 1960 book, there was a quick convergence of further economists to his rejection of the marginal approach (e.g. Pasinetti, Bhaduri, Harcourt, Garegnani, Nell); it became even clearer that it was possible to develop Keynes's theory in directions different from the neoclassical synthesis and the neoclassical approach more generally, and that there were theoretical reasons supporting such a different approach.

I will not take sides here on the complex question whether scientific arguments are sufficient to explain the limited success of these anti-neoclassical developments vis-à-vis the 'neoclassical synthesis' in the debate on Keynes. Possibly they are sufficient; certainly, the incomprehensions in the debate on capital theory, which were frequent among critical economists too, can be largely explained without recourse to extra-scientific pressures, as due to the loss of understanding of the logic of the marginal approach among the generality of economists after the shift to neo-Walrasian formulations with Hicks and Arrow-Debreu,[8] a loss of understanding that for many years was insufficiently contrasted by the critical economists (Garegnani, 2012; Petri 2020). For example, Garegnani's 'Sraffian' interpretation of the debate on Keynes and of the relevance of reswitching for Keynes's theory was made available in English only in 1978–1979. One must also take into account the difficulty with thinking differently for economists exclusively steeped in marginalist ways of thinking.

But things change when one comes to monetarism proper and its subsequent developments: rational expectations, real business cycle theory. The dogmatism and weakness of their microfoundations are indisputable and make it inevitable to admit political-ideological influences behind their success.

Let us take Friedman's 1968 Presidential Address to the American Economic Association, 'The Role of Monetary Policy', where the thesis of a gravitation towards the natural rate of unemployment and the vertical long-run Phillips curve were first expounded. One basic element of the paper is well grasped in the following commentary:

> The central idea was that aggregate demand management would have only temporary effects – an expansionary monetary policy could cause unemployment to fall below its 'natural rate' at which the labour market was cleared, but in the medium term it would return to this level, which Friedman described as that 'which would be ground out by a Walrasian system of general equilibrium equations' …. Employers are fully aware of what wages and prices are doing, whereas employees can be fooled by the

actions of the monetary authorities. Indeed this is the only reason why output deviates from its full employment level. Keynesian ideas of effective demand have disappeared out of the window; it is never suggested that lack of demand could constrain output. We are back in a completely neoclassical world, where it is assumed that if the real wage is such as to equalise the demand and supply of labour, full employment follows automatically. But none of this is argued out; *it is simply assumed.* (Bleaney, 1985, pp. 139–140, italics in the original)

This description of Friedman's paper is fully correct; indeed, the only argument Friedman advances against Keynes is that Pigou's real-balance effect undermines

Keynes' key theoretical proposition, namely, that even in a world of flexible prices, a position of equilibrium at full employment might not exist. Henceforth, unemployment had again to be explained by rigidities or imperfections, not as the natural outcome of a fully operative market process. (Friedman, 1968, p. 3)

But even granting the neoclassical mechanisms, the existence of a full-employment equilibrium based on the real-balance effect had not been proved (nor has since) because of the possibility of bankruptcies if debts fixed in nominal terms are included among the data of equilibrium and the reaching of equilibrium requires a lowering of the price level; and even if this equilibrium existed, it would be irrelevant if the convergence towards it were highly doubtful or too slow owing to the problems mentioned earlier; in which case a reluctance of nominal wages to decrease could not be accused of irrationality, which was Keynes's point when arguing that nominal wage decreases were more likely than not to make things worse; then persistent unemployment would indeed appear to be 'the natural outcome of a fully operative market process' because that's how a 'fully operative market process' works.

Friedman's low theoretical rigour is also evidenced by his assuming against all good sense (as stressed by many commentators) that employers understand what is happening while employees are too dumb to realise it, and by his taking for granted the stability of general equilibrium in spite of the negative results of general equilibrium specialists on the issue; and clearly, probably out of incompetence on the historical development of general equilibrium theory and its new versions, Friedman does not worry about the fact that 'Walrasian' general equilibrium theory is now intertemporal general equilibrium theory, that needs the absurdities of complete futures markets or perfect foresight, and instantaneous adjustments.

But even if one leaves aside this last weakness of Friedman's position, whose criticism would have entailed a questioning of the entire neoclassical approach, it seems clear that there weren't strong theoretical reasons for preferring monetarism to the 'neoclassical synthesis'. The empirical support for the monetarist theses was also very weak. I have remembered the anti-neoclassical empirical results on investment theory. Friedman and Schwartz's thesis of a causal role of monetary policy in the birth of the Great Depression was – as far as I am able to judge – totally refuted by Peter Temin, *Did Monetary Forces Cause the Great Depression?* (1976), a careful book that for mysterious reasons is never mentioned when assessing Friedman's contribution. Blinder (1988) has convincingly argued that it is false that 'the demise of Keynesian economics was due to the doctrine's poor empirical predictions' concerning inflation.

> It is, of course, true that pre-1972 Phillips curves were ill-equipped to handle the food and energy shocks that dominated the period from 1972 to 1981 and, in consequence, badly underestimated inflation. But it is also true that Keynesians quickly added supply-side variables (like oil or import prices) to what had up to then been an entirely demand-oriented theory. Soon thereafter supply shocks were also appended to empirical Phillips curves. By the early 1980s, numerous studies had documented the fact that a conventional Phillips curve equation with a supply shock variable (any one of several will do) fits the US data of the 1970s and 1980s extremely well. The charge that empirical Keynesian models were, in Lucas and Sargent's (1978) words, 'wildly incorrect' is, well, wildly incorrect. (Blinder, 1988, p. 282)

The natural rate of unemployment, in particular, the thesis that, at a lower unemployment rate, inflation will continuously accelerate, was denied by numerous empirical studies, even for example by Ray Fair, professor at Yale, not a 'heterodox' economist (Petri, 2003). Coming to the subsequent theoretical developments, it will suffice to note that the empirical foundations of the rational expectations assumption are non-existent: the assumption requires that everybody agrees on one theory of how the economy functions, which is ridiculous in view of the incontrovertible evidence of ample disagreements among economists. And real business cycle theory was immediately found by a majority of commentators to be in contradiction with the evidence.

5 The current situation: the dominance of neoclassical theory is scientifically unjustified

But now let us discuss the issue whether scientific reasons justify the continuing dominance up to now of the monetarist approach with its later developments such as Dynamic Stochastic General Equilibrium models and New Keynesian models (recently also called, and more correctly, New Neoclassical models), vis-à-vis the non-mainstream alternatives consisting of one version or other of a Keynesian-Kaleckian approach where output is determined by aggregate demand, the marginalist/neoclassical factor substitution mechanisms are absent, and income distribution is conflictually determined by the relative bargaining power of wage labour vs 'captains of industry' (Kalecki, 1943).

The discussion is made easier by the increasing acceptance, in the mainstream, of Lucas' argument that macroeconomic theory must be consistent with the sole rigorous microeconomic theory around (according to him), Arrow-Debreu general equilibrium theory. The whole of mainstream macroeconomics has followed him on this: 'it is now widely agreed that macroeconomic analysis should employ models with coherent intertemporal general-equilibrium foundations' (Woodford, 2009, p. 269). The result is the absence of any defensible microfoundation for applied macro analyses; this is easily proved, the problem is rather how come this is so little recognised.

A macro analysis concerns the entire economy; therefore, it cannot be based on partial-equilibrium *ceteris paribus* assumptions. It must endogenously determine income distribution and labour employment. Since actual economies do not have an auctioneer-based instantaneous adjustment mechanism nor perfect foresight, a theory of the functioning of an actual economy must include time-consuming adjustment processes which make room for mistakes and error corrections. Modern, neo-Walrasian general equilibrium theory has no room for such processes. It determines the equilibrium(s) corresponding to given data, assuming the equilibrium is instantaneously reached. But some of the data it relies upon in order to determine the equilibrium have no persistence: the initial endowments of the several capital goods will be quickly altered by production, so unless the equilibrium is reached instantaneously the initial behaviour of the economy will not correspond to the equilibrium behaviour, and as a result the endowments of the several capital goods will be, one period later, different from how the equilibrium would have determined them if instantaneously realised; then the original intertemporal equilibrium path can no longer be followed, the economy's equilibrium is now a different one; but again the economy cannot instantaneously reach it, again the endowments of capital goods will change differently from how the new equilibrium would have them change; a cumulation of divergences of the actual path of the economy from the initial intertemporal equilibrium path cannot be excluded. In fact, even on the extent of the *initial-period* divergence of the behaviour of the economy from a full-employment equilibrium, for an economy without the auctioneer (and perfect foresight) neo-Walrasian general equilibrium theory is simply silent; for example, it does not tell us whether, in an economy without auctioneer, in a situation that starts at $t = 0$ with unemployment a reduction of real wages will increase or reduce employment because it does not tell us whether the investment will be encouraged or discouraged: general equilibrium theory simply *assumes* that investment will be equal to savings in equilibrium because the definition of equilibrium entails it, but it has no argument that this equality will be really brought about by disequilibrium adjustments in an actual economy; so it cannot exclude that by $t = 1$ unemployment has not decreased or has even increased. On what happens when one admits time-consuming disequilibrium the theory tells us *nothing at all*.

This claim may appear too strong, but it will not appear so when one realises that all applied neoclassical analyses concerning actual economies and time-consuming adjustments traditionally relied (and continue to rely!) on factor substitution mechanisms which include among the factors a factor 'capital' of variable 'form', a quantity of exchange value,[9] and it is the long-period substitutability between this 'capital' and labour (I leave land aside for simplicity) that allows deriving a decreasing demand curve for labour, and a decreasing demand curve for 'capital' that implies an interest-elastic investment function. Now, modern neo-Walrasian general equilibrium theory originates in the decision to drop this notion of 'capital' recognised by Lindahl, Hayek and Hicks to be untenable already in the 1930s, and to return to a Walrasian treatment of each capital good as a distinct factor with its given endowment. But this rejection of 'capital' undermines the two fundamental pillars of neoclassical analyses, the demand curve for labour, and the investment function. Here, it will suffice to comment on the former: if the real wage changes, the change in the composition of consumption and in the technical choices of firms will quickly change the composition of the economy's stock of capital goods: since the conception has been dropped of this change as only a change of the 'form' of a factor 'capital' unchanged in amount (assuming negligible net savings), the theory no longer can argue that the demand for labour will increase. Analogous considerations hold for the investment function. That is, the rejection of 'capital' in favour of neo-Walrasian equilibria causes both an insufficient persistence of the equilibrium and the loss of the decreasing demand curves for factors without which the theory knows nothing on the tendencies of time-consuming disequilibrium adjustments.

Although without clarity about the root cause of this state of affairs, the difficulty with deriving from modern general equilibrium theory inferences about actual economies does transpire in many statements of esteemed specialists in general equilibrium theory, for example, in the frequent description of general equilibrium as only an ideal 'benchmark' – which of course leaves the theory of how actual economies operate totally to be specified. Franklin Fisher has been particularly explicit:

> In a real economy, however, trading, as well as production and consumption, goes on out of equilibrium … [I]n the course of convergence to equilibrium (assuming that occurs), endowments change. In turn this changes the set of equilibria. Put more succinctly, the set of equilibria is path dependent … . [This path dependence] makes the calculation of equilibria corresponding to the initial state of the system essentially irrelevant. (Fisher, 1983, p. 14)[10]

In the same direction go the frequent expressions of dissatisfaction with the assumption of perfect foresight, indispensable to intertemporal equilibria since complete futures markets would require the presence at the initial date of yet-to-be-born consumers. Michael Mandler, one of the best younger general equilibrium specialists, has declared: 'Perfect foresight models are not designed to deliver descriptive accuracy' (Mandler, 2005, p. 487). But since in intertemporal equilibrium theory there is no alternative to perfect foresight, and temporary equilibrium theory has been abandoned, the implication is that *the whole* of the neoclassical 'rigorous' theory of value and distribution is 'not designed to deliver descriptive accuracy'. That is, at present, there is *no* descriptive disaggregate neoclassical theory of value and distribution. The pretence of Lucas and Woodford and more generally DSGE authors to find in general equilibrium theory the microfoundation of their descriptive macroeconomic models is un-founded, and they have been told so several times by many general equilibrium specialists – without ever attempting to face the criticism.

A question spontaneously arises: How can these macroeconomists continue to refer to general equilibrium theory as the microfoundation of their mac-roeconomic models? How can they not realise that a general equilibrium theory, which cannot even *define* the equilibrium without absurd assumptions such as perfect foresight, cannot say anything about the behaviour of economies characterised by continuous errors and error-correction, discovery of novelties, and discrepancies between supply and demand on the several markets? My suggestion is that these economists are of course conscious of these aspects of real economies, but continue to believe in the existence of the persistent forces postulated by traditional marginalist theory – the tendency of the demand for labour to increase if real wages decrease, the tendency of investment to increase if the rate of interest decreases – without understanding that those tendencies were based on 'capital'-labour substitution and can no longer be postulated if the factor 'capital' is truly rejected as officially claimed. It is only because general equilibrium paths are qualitatively similar to the average paths determined by traditional theory (full employment, savings determining investment, income distribution determined by marginal pro-ducts) and nowadays represented in simplified form by one-good Solow-type growth models, that the claim can be advanced that general equilibrium paths too have some descriptive value. It is not the persuasiveness of modern general equilibrium theory but its accord with a previous dogmatic certainty as to the correctness of the supply-and-demand approach, that explains the continuing reference to general equilibrium theory as the rigorous microfoundation of macro analyses which in fact that theory does not support.

But the hidden continuing reliance on an officially abandoned conception of capital and on traditional time-consuming adjustments cannot be made explicit; the solution is to borrow from modern general equilibrium theory the trick to concentrate on equilibrium and neglect how the economy can converge to it, that is, to assume a continuous perfect-foresight (in the sto-chastic sense) optimising equilibrium, and completely to stop mentioning the stability-of-equilibrium issue. This has prompted, in many universities, student protests against the sterility of the economic theory they were asked to learn – a phenomenon unheard of in other scientific disciplines.

Given this incredible weakness of the microfoundations of the post-monetarist developments in mainstream theory, it seems difficult to avoid a conclusion of scientific superiority of the classical-Keynesian-Kaleckian broad approach. This approach is free of inconsistent notions of capital and of capital-labour substitution; it has no need for absurd assumptions such as the auctioneer or perfect foresight because it has no problem with admitting mistakes and time-consuming adjustments; it accepts the role – strongly confirmed by the empirical evidence – of aggregate demand in the determination of aggregate output and of investment; it does not posit a spontaneous tendency of market economies toward full employment, again in agreement with the empirical evidence of unemployment and crises; it is open to the conflictual approach to income distribution that the first unprejudiced observer of the functioning of capitalism, Adam Smith, found obvious and subsequent historical developments have amply confirmed. Let me single out, as just one example of the lesser difficulty this approach has than the neoclassical approach with explaining observations, the downward rigidity of wages in the presence of unemployment. This rigidity is not viewed as irrational in this approach – as it was not by the classical authors – because in order for a market economy to work there *must* be social mechanisms preventing an indefinite downward flexibility of wages if the latter flexibility would not eliminate unemployment: the neoclassical approach can neglect this need only because it argues that unemployment will be quickly eliminated by the fall in wages. But once one rejects – together with the conception of capital as a single factor that justified them – the neoclassical decreasing labour demand curve and the assumed capacity of the interest rate to adjust investment to savings, a fall in wages offers no guarantee of an increase in employment, more probably the effect is the opposite because of the fall in consumption; then an indefinite fall in wages as long as there is unemployment would destroy the possibility of a continuation of orderly economic activity; it is then only to be expected that social conventions will have developed which cause a resistance of wages to fall, and which cannot be considered irrational nor an obstacle to the good functioning of markets.[11]

My teaching experience to PhD students confirms the above assessment: when exposed to both mainstream teachings and to a clearly explained classical-Keynesian approach, students near unanimously find the latter more persuasive.

Therefore, extra-scientific reasons seem indispensable to explain the dominance achieved by the DSGE approach from the 1980s in spite of its unrealistic assumptions and in spite of the existence of a strong alternative. Then, Marx's perspective immediately draws attention to the coincidence of this situation in economic theory with a period of weakness of wage labour (including the middle classes) since Reagan and Thatcher, testified by the higher unemployment, the impressive income redistribution, and the generalised legal modifications against job security in more or less all advanced capitalist nations (although less so in the Scandinavian countries).

6 Marx's perspective appears confirmed, and supplies the answer to the original question

The reasonings I have presented show that Marx's perspective, which he based on the anti-Ricardian reaction caused by the first labour protests, is not refuted by subsequent developments in economic theory; on the contrary, it appears supported by the probable importance of extra-scientific, political influences in:

- the success of the marginal approach, in spite of its incompleteness and weaknesses, because useful as a counter to socialist arguments;
- the success of Keynesian economics and policies, as a counter to the danger that the working class might turn communist;
- the opening to more radical theories when there was a general radicalisation of grassroots politics in the 1960s;
- the return to anti-Keynesian theories (monetarism), in spite of their dogmatism and implausibility, as a support to the need to re-establish control over labour in the second half of the 1970s;
- the nearly total dominance of a scientifically extremely weak post-Lucas 'paradigm' from the 1980s onwards, in a situation of weakened labour and middle classes.

What do we learn from these five episodes (six, if we add the anti-Ricardian reaction), which may help to explain from the same Marxian perspective the lack of a change in economic theory after the 2008 crisis, differently from the changes after the Great Depression of 1928 and following years, and from the changes after the end of the Golden Age in the 1970s? They suggest that officially accepted economic theory comes to include relevant elements of criticism of capitalism only when there is a strong left-wing political pressure (as in the second and third episodes). I submit that here we find our answer. This political pressure has been absent in recent decades, including after 2008, as confirmed by electoral results. In the European Parliament, conservative parties had and have maintained a clear majority; in the USA, neither party reflects any strength of left-wing pressures; the Democratic Party is very moderate too, as shown by its preference for Hillary Clinton first, and then Joe Biden, over more left wing candidates like Sanders; paradoxically, Trump seems to give more importance to the fight against unemployment than the Democratic Party. To explain this weakness of the Left since the 1980s (its swan song was Mitterrand's Union of the Left in France in 1982) would take us to discuss how much Marx's views on the evolution of class struggle under capitalism are being borne out by history, and there is no room for this here (see Petri, 2012, pp. 111–23, for a brief exposition of my own views; also Gallino, 2012). Let it suffice to add, to what was said in Section 3 on the end of the Golden Age, that in recent decades in the advanced nations the working class is weakened not only by the crisis of its traditional utopian perspective and by unemployment but also by free financial capital mobility, globalisation (that makes it easier for firms to threaten transferring production to other nations), and immigration. Little wonder, then, that the policies adopted after 2008 have shown very little willingness really to reduce the power of financial capital. Keynes wanted considerably to limit this power because he wanted to save capitalism from communism. Now, this need no longer exists.

7 Five causes of the persistence of neoclassical theory

Still, one may ask how this capacity of the political situation to determine to such an extent the dominant economic theory concretely operates. Here, as far as I am aware, Marx does not help us, he does not analyse the issue. Nor am I aware of other analyses of the issue, although I confess I have not done much search on this. I wish to share here my first, rather unorganised thoughts on the issue. I pose the question in the following form (motivated by the current situation): if for many years now the arguments in favour of the classical-Keynesian approach have really been so strong scientifically, how come this approach remains minoritarian? What permits such a strong 'hysteresis' of neoclassical economic theory? I will list five causes.

The first cause is the ideology of the social strata from which in their majority university professors come and in which university salaries allow them to remain. University teachers, even middle-level ones, earn better salaries than the median, and mostly come from analogously placed families; in the nineteenth century and first half of the twentieth century, the thing was even more evident. Just as one does not expect a majority of the rich to be left-wing, so although to a lesser degree the same expectation must be held for university professors. One must therefore expect from them an inclination to share the ideology of the relatively privileged social strata from which in their majority they come and in which their social role confirms them. The neoclassical approach presents a much rosier picture of capitalism than a classical-Keynesian approach; it agrees better with a justification of the status-quo with its privileges. One must therefore expect, on average, a reluctance of university professors to abandon the neoclassical approach in favour of approaches that come close to considering their high salaries as sharing to some degree in the exploitation of workers.

The second cause, the most important one, is the social, political and economic pressures in order that economic theory not be critical of the status quo. Private funds to economic research centres come from large firms, or from ultra-rich individuals, and it is then obvious that, apart from isolated exceptions (George Soros), they will go to conservative think-tanks. The Koch scandal in all likelihood is only the tip of the iceberg, it finally made evident a thing that should have been obvious from the start: privately funded university chairs in politically delicate fields cannot be insulated from the donor's preferences, the donor will discontinue the financial support if dissatisfied with the appointment.[12] Central banks, whose boards are expressions of the world of banking and finance, cannot be expected to prefer hiring persons who try to prove that banks and financial institutions operate against the best interests of society. The same holds for the selection of experts to sit on the boards of private firms. As to public funds, they risk being decreased to those institutions which hire and support scholars who strongly criticise the government's economic policies. McCarthyism is a very evident example of political pressures on hirings, but these pressures although less evident are always present. The selection is obviously political for the consultants to Ministries and other politically selected committees. Since one cannot exclude some opportunism among researchers, the awareness of which scientific choices increase the possibility to reach politically assigned privileged positions will influence scientific production too.

With the third cause, I start considering phenomena of 'hysteresis' common to other disciplines too. Consider the sociology of the functioning of academia. When there are scientifically competing schools of thought in a field, and one school has majority support, on average in the committees that select new professors the members of the dominant school will be more numerous than those of other schools, and their pupils will therefore be in a more advantageous position in the competition for jobs. A dominant school will also dominate journals, both in the sense that its journals will receive more submissions and can therefore claim to be more highly considered, and in the sense that it will have greater influence in the editorial board of those journals which by statute should be open to all viewpoints in the field.[13] Opportunism then may add itself to the first cause, and young pupils may choose to adhere to the dominant school even when not really convinced, because it helps their career. Note also that academic power is based on the support of others, in particular of one's pupils; therefore, if a professor has succeeded in placing pupils in important positions, he/she will not wish to argue that the scientific work done by them (not to speak of his own) was a waste of time, this would weaken his academic power. Therefore, one must expect a great reluctance even by tenured professors to admit doubts on the validity of what they and their pupils have produced, even apart from a human tendency to resist admitting that one's entire scientific career may have been wasted on a wrong theory. Of course, this slows down the admission of weaknesses in the dominant theories.

The fourth cause is the difficulty with abandoning interpretative frameworks that have been adopted for decades. It is from the natural sciences, where one can presume an interest in the choice of the best theory less conditioned by non-scientific pressures, that the well-known observation has come (Max Plank) that a new theory replaces the old one not because the advocates of the old theory change their mind but because they get old and disappear, while the young accept the new theory.[14] Which implies an admission of an enormous difficulty on the part of mature scholars with abandoning long-accepted theoretical frameworks, evidently for reasons connected with how the human brain works, independently of opportunistic motives.

The fifth cause (really an extension of the first and third one) is the difficulty with becoming acquainted with theories different from the dominant one if the latter monopolises teaching to the point that alternative theories are considered unworthy of teaching, and are excluded from textbooks and from teaching programmes. This is what has been going on for decades now in both microeconomics and macroeconomics. In microeconomics, there isn't yet an advanced textbook that presents (or even only mentions) any approach to income distribution other than the neoclassical general equilibrium one. In macroeconomics, a representative example is the 1998 textbook on growth theory by Charles Jones, very well done in the presentation of what it discusses but including *no mention at all* of the existence of schools of thought (Keynesian, Post-Keynesian, Kaleckian, Marxian, Sraffian, evolutionist) that deny the validity of the neoclassical approach as a foundation for the theory of growth, as if the numerous holders of university chairs adhering to these schools of thought – presumably people of some intelligence – did not exist, nor their journals, associations, conferences. And we know from the experience with pseudoreligious sects how difficult it is to escape worldviews that everybody around you is obsessively repeating.

These fourth and fifth causes seem to have a very important role in this period. Paul Krugman on 27 January 2009 in his *New York Times* blog, and then in his intervention in the *New York Times Magazine* on 2 September 2009, showed that several economists in Chicago and Minnesota seemed unable to conceive that the economy might *not* be continuously at full employment. And I frequently meet PhD students who have at most a very vague idea of the interaction between accelerator and multiplier, or of the paradox of savings. In Siena, we correct this ignorance, but elsewhere? Certainly, a macro-textbook like Wickens (2008), which does not even explain the multiplier or discuss the investment function because it directly assumes[15] that investment is all the time determined by full-employment savings along a Ramsey path, is not going to help.

8 A glimmer of hope?

However, this state of affairs is also indicative of a significant weakness of orthodoxy: there must be fear, behind the refusal by the orthodox to engage in debate with the critics. For the last three decades, the choice has been not to mention the unorthodox schools at all, to maintain the young ignorant of their existence – the same choice as frequently made by churches vis-à-vis heresies, evidently in the conviction that it would not be easy to persuade the young, in fair debate, that orthodoxy is more solid than the heretical views. It is unclear how often in economics this is due to a conscious choice, and how often to the fifth cause, i.e. to ignorance. But for a large part of scholars ignorance does not appear plausible unless as the fruit of a conscious *decision* to remain ignorant, not very commendable as a scientific attitude. I feel compelled to conclude that at least for a number of scholars this refusal of debate is a conscious choice. This means that, however persuaded these scholars may be that their theory is correct, since they are consciously hampering scientific debate they cannot be entirely absolved from 'the bad conscience and evil intent of apologetics'.

This bad conscience, I suggest, reveals fear, and indicates a consciousness of weakness. Perhaps there is here a glimmer of hope. My argument appears to imply that one cannot expect a crisis of the dominance of neoclassical economics in the absence of a significant shift of political preferences and of parties in power to the left. However, so evident has become the scientific weakness of the foundations of the neoclassical approach, that perhaps this time Marx will be shown wrong. The birth of protests among students, and of initiatives like Rethinking Economics, might be symptoms that something is going to change.

Notes

1 Revised version (March 2021) of the paper with the same title presented at the Conference 'Marx, 1818–2018. New Developments on Karl Marx's Thought and Writings', Lyon, 27–29 September 2017. I thank an anonymous reviewer for the acute useful comments.

2 Same absence of change in advanced microeconomics, as testified by recent textbooks: Kreps (2013) and Muñoz-Garcia (2017).

3 Cavalieri, Garegnani and Lucii (2004) argue along the same line.

4 Cavalieri, Garegnani and Lucii (2004).

5 Evidenced by the presence in his theory of the decreasing marginal product of labour, and of the decreasing marginal efficiency of investment admitted by Keynes himself to be essentially the same as what other economists were calling the marginal productivity of capital.

6 See e.g. Junankar (1972).

7 This rejection is indeed only partial in the writings of these two authors before Sraffa's 1960 book; on the limits of Joan Robinson's 1953 article that starts the Cambridge controversy, see Petri (2004, pp. 227–33), Petri (2020) and Garegnani (1989); Kaldor (1955–1956) is clearer but stops short of a total rejection of the notion of a 'quantity of capital'.

8 However, extra-scientific pressures or, to put it more bluntly, a dogmatism about the correctness of a supply-and-demand approach to income distribution which sends us back to the reasons for the success of the marginal approach, appear necessary to explain the faith of Lindah, Hayek, Hicks that the abandonment of the conception of capital as a single factor of variable 'form' did not question the marginalist forces originally based on that conception (Dvoskin and Petri, 2017).

9 This factor had to be of variable 'form' in order to allow an endogenous determination of its composition, as required for the equilibrium to be persistent; it had to be a quantity of exchange value because the normal rewards earned by capital goods are proportional to their values (because the rate of interest is tendentially uniform) and therefore if one wants to see those rewards as paying for the service of a common factor 'capital' embodied in the different capital goods, the amount of this common factor 'capital' embodied in each one of them must be proportional to their value. The endowment of this factor 'capital' could be conceived as only slowly altered by net savings, therefore as persistent as the supply of labour and not suffering from the impermanence problem that undermines the data of neo-Walrasian general equilibria; so it allowed the determination of a persistent general equilibrium which could be conceived as a centre of gravitation of time-consuming disequilibria. This is what traditional marginalist theory assumed (Petri, 2004, 2016).

10 Fisher's attempt to surmount the problem is shown to have been a failure in Petri (2004, pp. 67–71).

11 Which does not prevent one from admitting that in particular situations of weakness, or conflict with immigrants, or convincing proof that only a wage decrease can save jobs (e.g. by avoiding the bankruptcy of a firm), wage decreases may well happen.

12 Paul Baran, the sole self-confessed Marxist economist teaching in a US university in the 1950s, obtained tenure at Stanford University before McCarthyism was in full swing, so in the absence of law infringements Stanford University could not get rid of him, but it took care to inform all its potential donors that Baran's salary had been frozen and he was being harshly treated in other respects too.

13 Citation indices and journal rankings will then inevitably favour the majority school of thought, reinforcing the advantage of its pupils. In recent years, the tendency in economics to use these as selection criteria has acquired strength, no doubt as part of a struggle to marginalise 'heterodox' schools. Recently, I have seen a committee assign a professorial chair in Italy exclusively on the basis of the *number* of articles published by the candidates in so-called 'top' journals, without entering at all into an assessment of the scientific contribution of those articles (not to speak of the zero consideration of books, papers in collective volumes, etc.). As university professors know the effects of these selection criteria, the reason for their acceptance in a field like economics where schools of thought are in harsh conflict can only be to privilege the dominant school.

14 But in the natural sciences one can presume a readiness of the young to accept the new theory if scientifically persuasive because in these disciplines the social pressure is towards increasing control *over nature*; generally (although there are exceptions) society has little interest in boycotting a better theory, the young improve their chances of getting a good job by accepting the better theory. In the social sciences, the aim is a better control over *social* processes, and the direction in which the control is desired will differ depending on the interests involved; the selection processes may make it extremely hard for the young to get a good job if they follow a theory disliked by the dominant social forces because of its political implications.

15 With no justification except the unsupported statement that one must assume intertemporal equilibrium.

References

Armstrong, P., Glyn, A. and Harrison, J. (1991). *Capitalism since 1945*. Oxford: Basil Blackwell.

Blaug, M. (1958). *Ricardian Economics*. New Haven: Yale University Press.

Bleaney, M. (1985). *The Rise and Fall of Keynesian Economics*. London: Macmillan.

Blinder, A. S. (1988). The fall and rise of Keynesian economics. *Economic Record* 64(4): 278–294.

Cavalieri, T., Garegnani, P. and Lucii, M. (2004). La sinistra e il problema dell'occupazione. Anatomia di una sconfitta. *La rivista del Manifesto*, No. 48.

Dvoskin, A. and Petri, F. (2017). Again on the relevance of reswitching and reverse capital deepening. *Metroeconomica*. doi: 10.1111/meca.12137

Fisher, F. M. (1983). *Disequilibrium Foundations of Equilibrium Economics*. Cambridge: Cambridge University Press.

Friedman, M. (1968). The role of monetary policy. *American Economic Review* 58(2): 1–17.

Gallino, L. (2012). *La lotta di classe dopo la lotta di classe*. Bari: Laterza.

Garegnani, P. (1989). Some notes on capital, expectations and the analysis of changes. In G. R. Feiwel (ed), *Joan Robinson and Modern Economic Theory*. London: Macmillan, pp. 344–367.

Garegnani, P. (2012). On the present state of the capital controversy. *Cambridge Journal of Economics* 36: 1417–1432.

Jones, C. I. (1998). *Introduction to Economic Growth*. New York and London: W. W. Norton.

Junankar, P. N. (1972). *Investment: Theories and Evidence*. London: Macmillan.

Kaldor, N. (1955–1956). Alternative theories of distribution. *Review of Economic Studies* 23(2): 83–100.

Kalecki, M. (1943). Political aspects of full employment. *Political Quarterly*. Cambridge: Cambridge University Press, 1971, pp. 138–145. Reprinted in M. Kalecki, Selected Essays on the Dynamics of the Capitalist Economy, 1933–1970.

Kreps, D. M. (2013). *Microeconomic Foundations I. Choice and Competitive Markets*. Princeton and Oxford: Princeton University Press.

Mandler, M. (2005). Well-behaved production economies. *Metroeconomica* 56(4): 477–494.

Marx, K. (1976). *Capital*, vol. I. Translated by B. Fowkes. Harmondsworth: Penguin.

Muñoz-Garcia, F. (2017). *Advanced Microeconomic Theory: An Intuitive Approach with Examples*. Cambridge, Mass:MIT Press.

Palma, J. G. (2009). The revenge of the market on the rentiers. Why neo-liberal reports of the end of history turned out to be premature. *Cambridge Journal of Economics* 33(4): 829–869.

Petri, F. (1999). Professor Hahn on the Neo-Ricardian criticism of neoclassical economics. In G. Mongiovi and F. Petri (eds), *Value, Distribution and Capital: Essays in Honour of Pierangelo Garegnani*. London: Routledge.

Petri, F. (2003). Should the theory of endogenous growth be based on Say's Law and the full employment of resources? In N. Salvadori (ed), *The Theory of Economic Growth: A 'Classical' Perspective*. Cheltenham: Edward Elgar, pp. 139–160.

Petri, F. (2004). *General Equilibrium, Capital and Macroeconomics*. Cheltenham, UK: Edward Elgar.

Petri, F. (2012). Una prospettiva disincantata sulla crisi economica contemporanea e sulla teoria economica contemporanea. In P. D. Posta (ed), *Crisi dell'Economia e Crisi della Teoria Economica*. Napoli: Liguori Editore, pp. 85–130.

Petri, F. (2015). Neglected implications of neoclassical capital-labour substitution for investment theory: another criticism of Say's Law. *Review of Political Economy* 27(3): 308–340.

Petri, F. (2016). Capital theory. In G. Faccarello and H. D. Kurz (eds), *Handbook on the History of Economic Analysis*, vol. III. Cheltenham (UK) and Northampton, MA (USA): Edward Elgar, pp. 40–69.

Petri, F. (2017). The passage of time, capital, and investment in traditional and in recent neoclassical value theory. *OEconomia. History, Methodology, Philosophy*. Online since 1 March 2017. http://oeconomia.revues.org/2596; doi:10.4000/oeconomia.2596

Petri, F. (2020). Capital theory 1873–2019 and the state of macroeconomics. *History of Economics Review* 74(1): 1–24. doi:10.1080/10370196.2020.1722411

Temin, P. (1976). *Did Monetary Forces Cause the Great Depression?* New York: W. W. Norton.

Wickens, M. (2008). *Macroeconomic Theory: A General Equilibrium Approach*. Princeton: Princeton University Press.

Woodford, M. (2009). Convergence in macroeconomics: elements of the new synthesis. *American Economic Journal: Macroeconomics* 1(1): 267–279.

6 On the productiveness of welfare expenditures[1]

Cosimo Perrotta

1 The question

This chapter in a sense continues on a specific issue the analysis of my 2018 book about the theories of unproductive labour.[2] In that book, among other things, we have tried to show that in the 1970s all the traditional economic streams (classical, neo-classical and Marxist) considered welfare expenditures as due to the necessity to meet the basic needs of the lower classes or to the need to avoid overproduction (by employing part of the surplus outside investment). In both cases, those expenditures were seen as a burden on profit, due either to higher taxes or to less infrastructures and less support to production. Only a few heterodox authors of the three schools admitted that those expenditures were conducive to economic development (Chapters 16 and 19).

The Post-Keynesians were the only defenders on the theoretical level of the welfare state and implicitly assumed its productiveness. Still, now they uphold it against the neoliberal attacks. Carlo Panico has always shared the Post-Keynesian view of the welfare state, and I hope this chapter can support his approach.

However, usually the Post-Keynesians – like Keynes himself – do not consider the long run, although in general only in the long run the returns of public investments appear. Thus, the doubts about the productiveness of public services remain unsolved. We are still trapped in the vicious circle of 'austerity'. According to the neoliberal approach, public services make the resources they employ unavailable to the investment for private profit; thus, they hinder development and must be minimised. But actually, the reduction of public services impoverishes workers and depresses both demand and human capital growth; then, it hinders development. The knowledge of past thought should help us to avoid this vicious circle.

2 The classical approach

The great increase in social expenditures undertaken for implementation of the welfare state was, as we know, contrary to traditional economic theory. Both in the classical and in the neo-classical approaches, public expenditures

DOI: 10.4324/9781003105558-7

are considered unproductive, although necessary to some extent. Thus, they have to be kept at the lowest possible level, since they are subtracted to investment for profit. Wealth only derives from the production of profit.

The tendency to reduce the production of wealth to the production of profit – although very rarely expressed as such – has always vitiated economics since the times of Adam Smith. In the first phase of modern economic thought, this actual identification was in a sense justified by the polemics against the huge proportions of parasitic rent. The early economists implicitly championed investment and the production of profit in opposition to land rent. The former increased social wealth, while the latter consumed it unproductively. This opposition was theorised during the Enlightenment. Not only Smith, but a great number of Enlightenment authors embraced this view.[3]

Their attitude was perfectly reasonable given that in the early classical period many authors – like Lauderdale, Dugald Stewart, Spence and Chalmers, for example – were still defending rent against the prevalence of investment for profit.[4] However, the defence of investment and profit – conducted by Charles Sismondi, Jean-Baptiste Say, David Ricardo, James Mill, Destutt de Tracy and Karl Heinrich Rau, among others[5] – led authors to greatly underrate the importance of public spending in economic development.

Smith stood as the reference point for the classical debate on this subject. He had used the distinction between productive and unproductive labour as the main criterion to defend the economy based on investment and profit. According to Smith, labour is productive only if it adds value to the product. But that is not all. To be productive, labour must also be material labour, i.e. it must add value to the product by transforming materials.[6] Consequently, Smith's approach excludes public workers doubly, so to say, from the field of productive labour: first, because they do not yield profit; and, second, because their labour is usually non-material. Thus, the state expenditures which pay for public labour and do not yield a profit are unproductive as well.

However, some authors – although agreeing with Smith's productive/unproductive labour distinction – rejected this conclusion and stated that public employees, or some of them, are indirectly productive insofar as they increase the private workers' productivity.[7]

Other authors – John Ramsey McCulloch above all – explicitly stated that public employees are productive. But they wisely noted that these workers must be strictly controlled in both number and efficiency because, unlike the other workers, they are not subject to market control.[8] Here, we find an important implicit distinction between state expenditures that are necessary and productive and those which are unnecessary and unproductive. But this distinction was eventually lost. Most classical and neo-classical economists adhered to the radical view that the state economic function (and its expenditures) must be confined to those of a 'night watchman'.

Thus, in the end, even among the classical authors who supported Smith's distinction between productive and unproductive labour, the most rigid line of thought prevailed. Marx, the last great representative of the classical school, stated that all public expenditures and all sorts of public labour are unproductive, deeming that in the capitalist system only the direct production of surplus value, later transformed into profit, can be productive.[9]

In the classical authors, there is an implicit view of public work as work which escapes the productivity control guaranteed by the market. This is the question raised by McCulloch, and it is a real one. But while it holds on the empirical level, it does not touch on the principles. McCulloch was able to avoid this confusion, while the overwhelming majority of classical economists was not.

3   The neo-classical approach

During the nineteenth century, various authors simply rejected Smith's division between productive and unproductive labour. They took a subjective approach, and considered not only labour but also nature and capital as the three sources of wealth and the value of goods.[10] From this viewpoint, production and productiveness could not be credited only to labour. Consequently, Smith's main criterion for development policy, namely the distinction productive/unproductive labour, lost its significance. These authors considered all labours productive,[11] insofar as they yield an income.

After the 1830s, this approach gained momentum, until – as we well know – it served as the basis for the rise of the new economics, with the neo-classical school. One might have expected that according to these economists public work should be productive, like all the other work. But this is not the case. The income public workers receive does not derive from the market but from the state, i.e. from taxes. This means that it is ultimately paid for with the other economic activities.

It was only in the 1940s that some neo-classical authors affirmed the productiveness of public expenditures. Alvin Hansen provided an outstanding analysis, maintaining that public expenditures can generate utilities like private investments or increase the investment efficiency. They can also create income because they boost employment. Hansen notes: they say that private expenses are self-sustaining, while public spending is not. But no private business could sell without a flow of public expense. The 'private sector is not self-sustaining either'. During depressions, only the government is able to support income.

Hansen adds that those who state that public expenses are fed by private income are like the physiocrats, who affirmed that industry is maintained by agriculture. Nowadays we can satisfy many needs thanks only to public activities. It is wrong to say that some sectors of the economy maintain certain other sectors with their surplus. Every sector contributes to the general flow of revenue. Agricultural products are essential, but this priority is paramount only in the primitive economies, when society is so poor that nearly all labour must be devoted to the production of food. When material productivity increases, it allows for other types of consumption, satisfying artistic or intellectual needs, for example.[12]

Some authors followed Hansen, notably with contributions by Simon Kuznets, Lekachman, Kapp and Sleeman.[13] But the vast majority of neo-classical authors held on to the traditional position, incoherent as it was. The book by Bacon and Eltis maintained that public expenditures hindered the British economy because they subtracted wealth from the profit private sector, which is the only producer of social wealth.[14]

4 The Marxist approach

Marx saw state expenditures as one of the unproductive expenses (*faux frais de production*) borne by profit.[15] However there is a contradiction in Marx on this issue: in a few points in his very extensive notes, he writes of the parasitic bourgeoisie growing more and more, and absorbing a large part of the growing surplus.[16] Thus, while Marx confirms the classical assumption that normally the surplus goes to investment, he also admits the increase in the 'unproductive' middle classes.[17] The two statements are incompatible.

In contrast, Loria, and later Paul Sweezy maintained that capitalism had a strong tendency to overproduction, and that the only remedy was to employ an increasing part of it unproductively, the most important part of such un-productive use being represented by the expenditure of the state. This is channelled in very different and numerous directions, but – apart from the channel devoted to public enterprises – all of them are, by definition, un-productive.[18]

Sweezy's analysis was the main basis of later Marxist theories of accumu-lation. It was followed by, among others, Maurice Dobb, Gillman, Baran, then set out in an organic form in *Monopoly Capital*, by Baran and Sweezy.[19] Thus, the majority of Marxist authors interpreted the expenditures for im-plementation of the welfare state as an intensification of the process of waste to avoid overproduction and the consequent crisis; see, for example, Mandel, Offe, Altvater, Balibar, Bravermann and Fine and Harris.[20] Note that the orthodox Marxists were influenced by Sweezy only with regard to the ab-sorption of the surplus while, as to the unproductiveness of the public sector, they were inspired directly by Marx.

These authors appear somewhat indifferent to the great social revolution of the welfare state. For the first time in history, even the lowest classes were involved in welfare and comfort. Houses, roads, railways, infrastructures, schools, hospitals and public offices were built. National social security and the health care system were organised. Education and research received ample funding. The incomes of the lower categories and the unemployed were guaranteed at a decent level.

Besides bringing about great improvement in the welfare of people, all these policies increased labour productivity enormously. Thus, the welfare state was actually the greatest investment that capitalist accumulation ever made.

However, a certain number of Marxist authors did recognise that welfare expenditure was not unproductive parasitism but real investment in favour of both the lower classes and accumulation. Some of these authors – Barratt Brown, Gough and Nagels,[21] for instance – saw in it a twofold nature, containing both unproductive and productive elements, while others – for example, Joseph Steindl, Negri, Rowthorn and Desai[22] – were definitely in favour of social expenditures as favouring productivity and as investment.

5 Keynes' view

John Maynard Keynes, with his empirical approach, was not particularly interested in the productive/unproductive labour distinction, and even less in the question as to whether public work was productive. This is well illustrated with his famous paradox, creating employment by digging holes and filling them in. He simply wanted to raise demand in the short run, mainly through an increase in employment, as Hicks noted.[23] He was confident that, once demand was sufficiently raised, the usual working of accumulation would be restored. This is why he tenaciously refused to get involved in the long-run questions.

Keynes brilliantly demolished the neo-classical analysis of the causes of crisis, which was not due to excessively high levels of wages, deriving from their rigidity, but rather to excessively low wages. However, he embraced the dominant idea that crises in general, even the most deep-reaching and devastating, were due to the business cycle. On this issue, he was simply repeating the tradition, never questioned, which started with John Stuart Mill and arrived up to Gottfried Haberler.[24] Even Marx had in fact bowed to this identification of crises with the business cycle. Having stated that the final crisis of capitalism has nothing to do with the periodical crises, he reduced the latter to simple fluctuations.[25] They too derive from the basic 'contradiction' of capitalism between the production of use values and of surplus value. But they do not really hinder the advance of capitalist accumulation.

Things, however, were more complex. In the 1930s, the crisis was not, of course, an episode of the business cycle, nor did it last like a business cycle. Indeed, it lasted not only up to World War II, but even after. To consolidate the post-war boom, besides the public huge expenditures for reconstruction there was also a great need for large-scale social interventions in favour of the lower classes.

All this was necessary to reverse the tendency to economic depression, opening the way to fast accumulation and progress. The Post-Keynesians did in fact support these innovative policies, but even then they – like their master – did not concern themselves with whether these expenditures were productive or not.[26] They strived for full employment while assuming that in the short run all new employments are productive since, by raising demand, they make production restart. However, the proper dimension of the welfare state boom lays in the long run. In the long run, there is constant growth in productivity. Increased productivity stimulates demand for new goods, and this new demand absorbs the increase in production. But no policy for implementing such a virtuous spiral in the long run was planned, and the result was the crisis of the welfare state boom.

6 Unlimited needs and investment in human capital

On the other hand, there is a long tradition which points to the prospect of production growth supported by variation in consumption. When discussing the periodical crises of their times, both Say and Ricardo maintained, against Malthus, that accumulation has no limits. It can proceed indefinitely because – as the Enlightenment authors, Smith included, had already stated – human needs are unlimited.[27] But this can only happen on one condition, namely that goods constantly vary in nature to satisfy ever new needs.[28] The progress of accumulation allows production to supply ever new goods, which meet people's increasingly refined needs.[29]

Similar views were later advanced by Friedrich List, J.S. Mill, Alfred Marshall and various other authors. Even Karl Marx, in the *Grundrisse* (which he then put aside in the 'official' theory of *Capital*), suggests a prospect of indefinite variation of needs which, he says, are generated by capitalist accumulation itself.[30]

It is hard to say whether the *Grundrisse* influenced the critical Marxists of the socialist countries. As a matter of fact, while the vast majority of western Marxists repeated the official Marx in a scholastic way, a suggestive new stream of thought was flourishing in the socialist countries, theorising development based on progress in science, innovations and a potentially infinite multiplication of needs.

Ossowski described the economic progress of his time as based on the new middle classes (public employees, technicians and functionaries). Löbl acutely noted that every good contains innumerable contributions involving different activities, ranging from the materials and their sources to distribution and even the public administration. Thus, we cannot say how much labour is contained in a certain good. But certainly, the major public services, like education, research or health care, have increasing importance in the production of society's wealth, because they increase workers' efficiency and productivity. Richta and his large team depicted an alluring prospect of a new economy based on culture, science and constant innovation.[31]

However, we also find some very interesting authors who envisage similar prospects in western countries. Mallet, e.g. enthusiastically described the growth of the new middle classes. The latter, being highly educated and skilled, increase the general productivity of the economy. Roman Rosdolsky – again following in the footsteps of the *Grundrisse* – insightfully describes the welfare state boom as fully developing all the potentialities of human labour thanks to permanent technological innovation and the prevalence of creative labour.[32]

Of the authors following the same line of thought, mention should be made at least of Daniel Bell, Thomas Bottomore, Cazzaniga and Cerroni, the latter two showing particularly keen appreciation of the *Grundrisse*.[33]

Finally complete theorisation of development based on unlimited needs was provided with three brilliant analyses. Tibor Scitovsky underlined the need for consumers to receive ceaseless new stimulation through ever different goods. Luigi Pasinetti built up a model of indefinite development based on increase in refined consumption, recalling Engel's law. Charles Kindleberger, too, commented on Engel's law. With the increasing income – he notes – new goods initially acquired as luxury consumption gradually become ordinary and lose their income elasticity. Kindleberger unwittingly repeated the principle of the Enlightenment authors that there is no distinction between necessary and superfluous goods. The driving force of accumulation is innovation in the production sectors and consumption.[34] Both Pasinetti and Kindleberger underline that the private economy is not always able to satisfy the need for continual innovations, often calling for state intervention.

This precious legacy was soon dispersed, and the issue of the welfare state was reduced to inane debate on the need for more or less state intervention.

7 Conclusion

As we have tried to show, today there are all the requisites – theoretical and practical – for reviving and continuing, *mutatis mutandis*, the development experienced during the welfare state boom. The only obstacle is the ideological conviction that the presence of the state in the economy is *always* a damage. This chapter is a modest attempt to show that such a conviction is unfounded.

Notes

1 I presented this analysis at the ESHET Conference 2018 in Madrid. I thank the discussant and the participants in the discussion.
2 Perrotta (2018).
3 Hume (1752: 326–30), Genovesi (1765–67: I.11.6), Smith (1776: b. II, Ch. 3) and many others.
4 Lauderdale (1804: Ch. I, pp. 12–3), Stewart (1809–10: 261–5), Spence (1807) and Chalmers (1832).
5 Sismondi (1819: 49–51, 85, 90), Say (1803: 36–40), Ricardo (1951–73: vol. 1, pp. 150–1), Mill (1808: pp. 68–74), Destutt de Tracy (1817: 168–74) and Rau (1826–27: 148–9).
6 Smith (1776: I.I.6, II.3.1-2).
7 Jakob (1805: §§ 486–96). The author of the entry *Political Economy* of *Encyclopaedia Britannica* (1810: 120b). Malthus (1820: 37–8), Rau (1826–27: I, §§ 94–5 and 332–9), etc.
8 McCulloch (1824: 275b–78b), Read (1829: 38–9, 40-1fn) and Sanfilippo (1828: 130–1).
9 See e.g. Marx, *Grundrisse*: 208. *Theories*, I, IV.1.
10 Say (1803: I, chs. 3, 4, 7; 1820: 32–8).
11 Gray (1815: I.2: 5; see also II.3: 47–69).
12 Hansen (1941: 144–52).
13 Kuznets (1966: 224–34), Lekachman (1966: 104–6), Kapp (1950: 28–30) and Sleeman (1979: 2–3, 38–9).
14 Bacon and Eltis (1978).
15 Marx (*Theories*, IV.7.a, 348; IV.17).

16 Marx (*Theories*, part II, Ch. 18, B.1.d: 745–6).
17 Marx (*Capital I*, IV.XV.168-169; VII.XXV.46; Ch. 30. *Capital III*, Ch. 15).
18 Loria (1889, I, Ch. 4) and Sweezy (1942: 226–36).
19 Dobb (1946: 321–37), Gillman (1957), Baran (1957: Ch. 2) and Baran and Sweezy (1966).
20 Mandel (1972: 404–6), Offe (1971–77: 67–76), Altvater and Huisken (1970: 43–65), Balibar (1974: 154), Bravermann (1974: 284–93) and Fine and Harris (1979: 49–53).
21 Barratt Brown (1969: 31–68), Gough (1975) and Nagels (1974: 190ff, 208, 308).
22 Steindl (1952: 355–77), Negri (1974: 239–40), Rowthorn (1979) and Desai (1979).
23 Hicks (1974: 57).
24 Mill (1844, II essay), Keynes (2013: Ch. 22, 313–15) and Haberler (1937: 118–22).
25 Marx (*Theories*, Ch. 17. *Capital III*, Ch.s. IV.XVIII, V.XXX).
26 Eichner (1979: 179).
27 Smith (1776: I.11.59), Malthus (1820: II.1.9, 401–5), Say (1828–29: VII.4, tome 2, 210–13) and Ricardo (1821: 21.7).
28 Say (1803: I, XV, 92) and Ricardo (1821: 21.5).
29 Perrotta (2004: Ch. 11, 231–37).
30 Marx, *Grundrisse*, notebook VI: 639–40.
31 Ossowski (1957: 202–4), Löbl (1967: 190–92, 201) and Richta (1967, 1968).
32 Mallet (1969: 15–27, 94–8), Bell (1973: 148–54) and Rosdolsky (1968: Ch. 28.2).
33 Bottomore (1973: 21–7), Formenti (1980: 18–29), Cazzaniga (1981: 235–6) and Cerroni (1983: 304–5).
34 Scitovsky (1976), see at least chs. 4, 6 and 12; Pasinetti (1981), see at least chs. 4 and 11; Kindleberger (1990: 5–21).

References

Altvater, E. and Huisken, F. (1970). *Lavoro produttivo e improduttivo*. Trans. from German. Milano: Feltrinelli, 1975.

Bacon, R. and Eltis, W. (1978). Marketed output – yes, luxury – no. A reply to Mrs. Ietto Gillies. *British Review of Economic Issues* 1978: 47–54.

Balibar, É. (1974). *Cinque studi di materialismo storico*. Trans. from French. Bari: De Donato, 1976.

Baran, P. (1957). *The Political Economy of Growth*. New York: Monthly Review Press.

Baran, P. and Sweezy, P. (1966). *Monopoly Capitalism*. New York and London: Modern Reader, 1968. Online: scribd.com.

Barratt Brown, M. (1969). Il marxismo e lo sviluppo economico del capitalismo. Trans. from English. In F. Aymone et al. (eds), *Sviluppo economico e rivoluzione*. Bari: De Donato, pp. 23–76.

Bell, D. (1973). *The Coming of Post-Industrial Society*. New York: Basic Books.

Bottomore, T. (ed.). (1973). *Introduction* to *Karl Marx*. Oxford: B. Blackwell.

Bravermann, H. (1974). *Labor and Monopoly Capital*. New York: Monthly Review, 1998.

Cazzaniga, G. M. (1981). *Funzione e conflitto*. Napoli: Liguori.

Cerroni, U. (1983). *Teoria della società di massa*. Roma: Editori Riuniti.

Chalmers, T. (1832). *On Political Economy* ... Glasgow: Collins and New York: Appleton.

Desai, M. (1979). *Marxian Economics*. Oxford: B. Blackwell.

Destutt de Tracy, A. (1817). *A Treatise on Political Economy*. Trans. from unpublished French original. New York: Kelley, 1970.

Dobb, M. (1946). *Studies in the Development of Capitalism*. London: Routledge & Kegan Paul, 1950.

Eichner, A. (1979). A look ahead. In F. Eichner (ed.), *A Guide to Post-Keynesian Economics*. London and Basingstoke: Macmillan.

Fine, B. and Harris, L. (1979). *Rereading 'Capital'*. London: Macmillan.

Formenti, C. (1980). *La fine del valore d'uso*. Milano: Feltrinelli.

Genovesi, A. (1765–1767). *Lezioni di commercio*. Revised ed., 1768–1770. Milano: Vita e Pensiero, 2013.

Gillman, J. (1957). *Il saggio di profitto*. Trans. from English. Roma: Editori Riuniti, 1961.

Gough, I. (1975). State expenditures in advanced capitalism. *New Left Review* 1975: 53–92.

Gray, S. (George Purves). (1815). *The Happiness of States*. London: Hatchard.

Haberler, G. (1937). *Prosperity and Depression*. Geneva: League of Nations, 1939.

Hansen, A. (1941). *Fiscal Policy and Business Cycle*. London: Allen & Unwin.

Hicks, J. (1974). *The Crisis of Keynesian Economics*. New York: Basic Books.

Hume, D. (1752). *Of interest*. In Id. *Philosophical Works. Vol. III: Essays Moral, Political and Literary*. Aalen: Scientia, 1964, pp. 320–330.

Jakob, L. H. (1805). *National-Oeconomie oder National-Wirtschaftslehre*. 2nd ed. Charcow etc. printed for the Author, 1809.

Kapp, W. (1950). *The Social Cost of Private Enterprise*. Cambridge, MA: Harvard University Press.

Keynes, J. M.(2013). *General Theory of Employment, Interest and Money*, Vol. VII of *The Collected Writings of J.M. Keynes* edited by A. Robinson and D. Moggridge, London: Macmillan. Original date of publication, 1936.

Kindleberger, C. (1990). *Leggi economiche e storia dell'economia*. Trans. from English. Roma-Bari: Laterza.

Kuznets, S. (1966). *Modern Economic Growth*. New Haven: Yale University Press.

Lauderdale, J. (1804). *An Inquiry into the Nature and Origin of Public Wealth ...* New York: Kelley, 1962. Hathi Trust, online.

Lekachman, R. (1966). *The Age of Keynes*. New York: Random House.

Löbl, E. (1967). *Geistige Arbeit. Die wahre Quelle des Reichtums*. Trans. from Slovak. Wien-Düsseldorf: Econ, 1968.

Loria, A. (1889). *Analisi della proprietà capitalista*. 2 vols. In Id. *Opere*. Vol. 1, Torino: UTET, 1957. Vol. 2, Torino: Bocca.

Mallet, S. (1969). *La nouvelle classe ouvrière*. 5th ed. Enlarged. Paris: Éditions du Seuil.

Malthus, T. R. (1820). *Principles of Political Economy*. 2nd ed. London: Pickering, 1836. https://oll.libertyfund.org/title/malthus-principles-of-political-economy

Mandel, E. (1972). *Late Capitalism*. Trans. from German. London: New Left Books, 1975.

Marx, K. (1857–61). *Grundrisse*. Harmondsworth: Penguin, 1973. Trans. from German

Marx, K. (1861–63). *Theories of Surplus-Value*. Trans. from German. Moscow: Progress Publishers. https://www.google.com/search?client=firefox-b-d&q=Marx%2C+Karl.+%5B1861-63%5D.+Theories+of+Surplus-Value

Marx, K. (1867). *Capital I*. Trans. from German. Library of Economics & Liberty. https://oll.libertyfund.org/title/marx-capital-a-critique-of-political-economy-volume-i

Marx, K. (1864–65). *Capital III*. Trans. from German. Library of Economics & Liberty, online.

McCulloch, J. R. (1824). Political economy. *Supplement of Encyclopaedia Britannica* 6: 216–278.

Mill, J. (1808). *Commerce Defended*. London: Baldwin, Online Library of Liberty.

Mill, J. S. (1844). *Essays on Some Unsettled Questions ...* 2nd ed. London: Longmans etc., 1874, online, Library of Economics & Liberty.

Nagels, J. (1974). *Travail collectif et travail productif ...* Bruxelles: Univ. de Bruxelles.

Negri, A. (1974). Stato, spesa pubblica, … In Id. *La Forma-Stato*. Milano: Feltrinelli, 1977.

Offe, C. (1971–77). *Lo stato nel capitalismo maturo*. Trans. from German. Milano: Etas Libri, 1977.

Ossowski, S. (1957). *Struttura di classe e coscienza di classe*. Trans. from Polish. Torino: Einaudi.

Pasinetti, L. (1981). *Dinamica strutturale e sviluppo economico*. Torino: UTET, 1984.

Perrotta, C. (2004). *Consumption as an Investment. The Fear of Goods from Hesiod to Adam Smith*. London-New York: Routledge.

Perrotta, C. (2018). *Unproductive Labour in Political Economy. The History of an Idea*. London-New York: Routledge.

Political Economy. (1810). *Encyclopaedia Britannica*. 4th ed. Edinburgh: Constable, pp. 106–123.

Rau, K. H. (1826–27). *Corso di economia politica*. Trans. from German (vol. 1). Genova: Monni, 1855.

Read, S. (1829). *Political Economy*. Edinburgh, printed for the Author.

Ricardo, D. (1821). *Principles of Political Economy* … Library of Economics & Liberty, online.

Ricardo, D. (1951–73). *Works and Correspondence*. Edited by P. Sraffa. Cambridge, UK: Cambridge University Press.

Richta, R. (1967). *Civilization at the Crossroads*. Trans. from Czech. 3rd ed. White Plains, NY: International Arts & Sciences, 1969.

Richta, R. (ed.). (1968). *Progresso tecnico e società industriale*. Trans. from German. Milano: Jaca Book, 1975.

Rosdolsky, R. (1968). *The Making of Marx's 'Capital'*. Trans. from German. London: Pluto Press, 1977.

Rowthorn, B. (1979). Skilled labour in the Marxist system. In Id. *Capitalism, Conflict and Inflation*. London: Lawrence & Wishart, 1980, pp. 231–245.

Sanfilippo, I. (1828). *Sposizione dei principj di economia politica*. 2nd ed. Palermo: Reale Stamperia, 1839.

Say, J.-B. (1803). *Traité d'économie politique*. 6th ed. Paris: Guillaumin, 1841.

Say, J.-B. (1820). *Lettres à M. Malthus*. Paris: Bossange. https://fr.wikisource.org/wiki/Lettres_%C3%A0_M._Malthus_sur_l%E2%80%99%C3%A9conomie_politique_et_la_stagnation_du_commerce

Say, J.-B. (1828–29). *Cours complet d'économie politique pratique*. 2nd ed. Paris: Guillaumin, 1840.

Scitovsky, T. (1976). *L'economia senza gioia*. Trans. from English. 2nd ed. Roma: Città Nuova, 1992.

Sismondi, J. C. (1819). *Nouveaux principes d'économie politiques*. 2nd ed. Paris: Delaunay, 1827. https://openlibrary.org/books/OL23322235M/ Nouveaux_principes_d%27%C3%A9conomie_politique

Sleeman, J. (1979). *Resources for the Welfare State*. London and New York: Longman.

Smith, A. (1776). *Wealth of Nations*. Cannan ed. Library of Economics & Liberty, online.

Spence, W. (1807). Britain independent of commerce. In Id. *Tracts on Political Economy*. London: Longman, pp. 1–92.

Steindl, J. (1952). *Maturità e Ristagno nel Capitalismo Americano*. Trans. from English. Torino: Boringhieri, 1960.

Stewart, D. (1809–10). Lectures on political economy. In Id. *Collected Works*, vols. 8 (1855) and 9 (1856). Edinburgh: Constable.

Sweezy, P. (1942). *The Theory of Capitalist Development*. London: Dobson, 1962.

7   Is Ricardian intensive rent a Nash equilibrium?

Giuseppe Freni and Neri Salvadori

1 Introduction

The intellectual journey of Piero Sraffa has been at the centre of Carlo's research interests. Even if he mainly focussed on the monetary writings of Sraffa, he also analysed Sraffa's participation in the debate on the Marshallian cost curves of the 1920s and the role that these contributions had in developing the ideas that were later aired in his book of 1960 (Panico, 1991; Panico and Salvadori, 1994). An important part of Sraffa's contribution in the 1920s concerns the determinants of variable returns, aspects that are also mentioned in 1960. Sraffa's explanation of the phenomenon of diminishing returns runs in terms of cost-minimising choices knowingly made by any rational producer: the problem of diminishing returns is indissolubly related to the problem of rent.

   This chapter is devoted to further analysis of the problem of intensive rent. The chapter 'On Rent' in Ricardo's *Principles* is undoubtedly the *locus classicus* of the Ricardian theory of rent. More recently, the issue was investigated by Samuelson (1959) and Sraffa (1960, pp. 74–8); see also Kurz and Salvadori (1995, pp. 277–320) and the literature referred to therein. Following Ricardo and the other Classical authors, the majority of modern contributors do not investigate the possibility that agents may try to limit competition or strategically take advantage of special conditions. In particular, it is supposed that landowners do not collude or take advantage of the distribution of plots of land in order to obtain an extra rent. Hence, the distribution of plots of land among landowners is ignored. An exception, among others, is a paper by Salvadori (2004) which considers only extensive rent, and no attempt is made to extend the same reasoning to intensive rent. In this chapter, on the contrary, we will argue that if the demand for agricultural commodities and the distribution of marginal land ownership are such that demand can be satisfied only if the owner of the largest plot of land rents out at least part of his or her plots of land, then a positive extra rent is possible (if landowners behave in a strategic way). This chapter is not devoted to a complete analysis of the case under consideration. More precisely, we will not determine the Nash equilibria that exist if landowners behave strategically and a positive extra rent is possible, nor

DOI: 10.4324/9781003105558-8

whether or not such equilibrium exists. To do so, further assumptions may be required, which could well be the topic of another paper by the authors.

2 Preliminaries: Ricardian intensive rent theory

In this section, we will give a presentation of intensive rent in the simplest case, that is when a commodity is produced by labour and land. The aim is just to introduce the language that will be used in the rest of the chapter. Thus, the reader familiar with the literature on rent referred to by Kurz and Salvadori (1995, pp. 305–11) can skip this section.

Consider an economy which produces only 'corn'. At the beginning of the production period, farmers cultivate the land and at its end they harvest the crop. There is no commodity input in production, i.e. there are no produced means of production. Corn is the only means of subsistence to support the population. Cultivation of the land does not alter its quality. Labour is of uniform quality. There is no use of land other than employing it in corn production. As a consequence, the reservation price of the use of land is zero. By contrast, the reservation price of labour in terms of corn is positive and equals $\bar{w}$. Production is taken to be a time-consuming process. The length of the production period is assumed to be uniform across all available processes of production; that period is here called a 'year'. Wages and rents will be paid to workers and landlords respectively at the end of the year.[1] The production technology can be represented, in abstract terms, as a set of processes. Returns to scale with regard to each process are assumed to be constant. There is a single quality of land and n processes producing corn by means of land and labour. Each process can be described as follows:

t_i acres of land $\oplus$ l_i hours of labour $\to$ 1 bushel of corn

or, for short,

$t_i \oplus l_i \to 1.$

The symbol '$\to$' stands for the 'black box' in which farmers working for l hours at a given intensity of work on t acres of land generate 1 bushel of corn during a yearly production cycle. Hence, a process is well defined by an amount of land and an amount of labour, i.e. it may be indicated by the pair (t_i, l_i). We will exclude all dominated processes. A process is dominated if it uses more inputs than a convex combination of some other processes. The existing (non-dominated) processes using land i can be numbered in such a way that

$$l_1 < l_2 < \ldots < l_n \qquad (7.1)$$

Indeed, if $l_i = l_{i+1}$, then at least one of the two processes (t_i, l_i) and (t_{i+1}, l_{i+1}) is dominated. For the same reason,

$$t_1 > t_2 > \ldots > t_n \tag{7.2}$$

Indeed, if $t_i \leqslant t_{i+1}$, then process (t_{i+1}, l_{i+1}) is dominated by process (t_i, l_i).
   If process (t_i, l_i) is operated, then

$$t_i q + w l_i = 1 \tag{7.3}$$

where $q \geqslant 0$ is the rent per acre (or rate of rent) and $w \geqslant \bar{w}$ is the wage rate. Moreover, in equilibrium no process can yield a surplus; otherwise, farmers would prefer to operate the surplus-yielding process. Therefore,

$$t_j q + w l_j \geqslant 1 \tag{7.4}$$

for each process (t_j, l_j), whether or not it is operated. Whether or not a process is operated depends on the amount of corn produced G and the existing amount of land T. In the following we will use G as a parameter. The Ricardian intensive rent will be presented using the following propositions.[2]

Proposition 2.1. *In any equilibrium, if land is not fully cultivated, then $q = 0$, only process (t_1, l_1) is operated, $w = w_1 := \frac{1}{l_1}$, and $G \leqslant \frac{T}{t_1}$.*

Proof. If $q > 0$, then owners of uncultivated plots of land would offer them at a lower rent. If a process different from (t_1, l_1) is operated, then Equation (7.3) and inequalities (7.4) are violated. The wage rate is determined by Equation (7.3). The last claim is obvious since $\frac{T}{t_1}$ is the maximum amount of corn which can be produced on T acres of land with process (t_1, l_1). □

Proposition 2.2. *In any equilibrium, if land is fully cultivated and the two non-dominated processes (t_i, l_i) and (t_{i+h}, l_{i+h}) are operated, then $h = 1$,*

$$w = w_{i+1} := \frac{t_i - t_{i+1}}{l_{i+1} t_i - l_i t_{i+1}} \tag{7.5}$$

$$q = q_{i+1} := \frac{l_{i+1} - l_i}{l_{i+1} t_i - l_i t_{i+1}} \tag{7.6}$$

and $\frac{T}{t_i} \leqslant G \leqslant \frac{T}{t_{i+1}}$.

Proof. Let us first prove that process (t_{j+u}, l_{j+u}) is not dominated by processes $(t_j, l_j), (t_{j+v}, l_{j+v})$, with $0 < u < v$, if and only if

$$(l_{j+u} - l_j) t_{j+v} + (l_{j+v} - l_{j+u}) t_j > (l_{j+v} - l_j) t_{j+u} \tag{7.7}$$

By definition process (t_{j+u}, l_{j+u}) is not dominated by processes (t_j, l_j) and (t_{j+v}, l_{j+v}) if and only if there is no β such that

$$\beta l_{j+v} + (1 - \beta)l_j \geqslant l_{j+u} \text{ and } \beta t_{j+v} + (1 - \beta)t_j \geqslant t_{j+u} \tag{7.8}$$

Because of inequalities (7.1) there is a single λ, $0 < \lambda < 1$, such that $\lambda l_{j+v} + (1 - \lambda)l_j = l_{j+u}$ and therefore the first inequality (7.8) is satisfied if and only if $\beta \geqslant \lambda$. Similarly, the second inequality (7.8) is satisfied if and only if $\beta \leqslant \eta$, where $0 < \eta < 1$ is the single solution to the equation $\eta t_{j+v} + (1 - \eta)t_j = t_{j+u}$. Hence, inequalities (7.8) cannot be both satisfied if and only if $\lambda > \eta$, that is

$$\frac{l_{j+u} - l_j}{l_{j+v} - l_j} > \frac{t_{j+u} - t_j}{t_{j+v} - t_j}$$

which is equivalent to inequality (7.7).

Now we prove the proposition. If $h > 1$, then

$$w = \frac{t_i - t_{i+h}}{l_{i+h}t_i - l_i t_{i+h}}$$

$$q = \frac{l_{i+h} - l_i}{l_{i+h}t_i - l_i t_{i+h}}$$

because of Equations (7.3) and process (t_{j+1}, l_{j+1}) cannot satisfy inequality (7.4):

$$qt_{i+1} + wl_{i+1} = \frac{l_{i+h} - l_i}{l_{i+h}t_i - l_i t_{i+h}}t_{i+1} + \frac{t_i - t_{i+h}}{l_{i+h}t_i - l_i t_{i+h}}l_{i+1} < 1$$

The inequality is a consequence of the fact that process (t_{j+1}, l_{j+1}) is not dominated, and therefore inequality (7.7) holds with $j = i$, $u = 1$, and $v = h$. The last claim is obvious. $\qquad\square$

Proposition 2.3. *In any equilibrium, if land is fully cultivated and only process* (t_i, l_i) *is operated, then* $G = \dfrac{T}{t_i}$, $\max \{w_{i+1}, \overline{w}\} \leqslant w \leqslant w_i$, *and* $q_i \leqslant q \leqslant \min\left\{q_{i+1}, \dfrac{1 - \overline{w}l_i}{t_i}\right\}$, *with the convention that* $\max \{w_{n+1}, \overline{w}\} = \overline{w}$ *and* $\min\left\{q_{n+1}, \dfrac{1 - \overline{w}l_i}{t_i}\right\} = \dfrac{1 - \overline{w}l_i}{t_i}$.

Proof. Obviously $G \leqslant \frac{T}{t_i}$. If $G < \frac{T}{t_i}$, then owners of uncultivated plots of land would offer them at a lower rent. The wage rate and the rent are then constrained by inequalities (7.4) and by the constraint on the reservation price of labour. □

Propositions 2.1–2.3 allow the following to be maintained:

1   If $G \in [0, \frac{T}{t_1})$, then $w = w_1$ and $q = 0$ (provided that $w_1 \geqslant \overline{w}$), and only Gt_1 units of land are cultivated.

2   If $G \in \left(\frac{T}{t_i}, \frac{T}{t_{i+1}}\right)$, then $w = w_{i+1}$ and $q = q_{i+1}$ (provided that $w_{i+1} \geqslant \overline{w}$), and land is fully cultivated.

3   If $w_n < \overline{w}$, then only m processes can really be operated; processes (t_{m+1}, l_{m+1}), (t_{m+2}, l_{m+2}), ..., (t_n, l_n) cannot sustain the reservation wage rate $\overline{w}$, where $w_m \geqslant \overline{w}$ and $w_{m+1} < \overline{w}$.

4   if $G = \frac{T}{t_i}$ $(i \leqslant m)$, then w and q vary in specified ranges; if $i < m$, $w_i \geqslant w \geqslant w_{i+1}$ and $q_i \leqslant q \leqslant q_{i+1}$; if $i = m$, $w_i \geqslant w \geqslant \overline{w}$ and $q_i \leqslant q \leqslant q_{max}$, where $q_{max} = \frac{1 - l_m \overline{w}}{t_m}$.

The aforementioned points and intervals constitute a partition of the range $[0, \frac{T}{t_m}]$ and G cannot be produced if it is not in this range.

3 The distribution of land ownership

No attention to the distribution of land ownership was paid in the previous section. Nevertheless, it was argued that if land is not fully cultivated, rent must equal zero since otherwise 'owners of uncultivated plots of land would offer them at a lower rent'. Could the same principle, typical of Nash equilibrium, be extended to other cases, such that an equilibrium can be defined as a position from which no owner of land is interested in deviating? In order to analyse this, we need to know the distribution of land ownership. Let us assume, then, that there exist s landowners; landowner j owns T_j units of land and, with no loss of generality, $T_1 \geqslant T_2 \geqslant ... \geqslant T_s$, and $T_1 + T_2 + ... + T_s = T$. Each landowner announces the rate of rent at which they undertake to lease their land up to availability.

3.1 The residual demand

In order to assess whether the claims of the Ricardian theory of intensive rent is a Nash equilibrium, we have to investigate the case in which all landowners but one claim the rent rate predicted by the Ricardian theory of intensive rent and only one landowner claims a higher rent rate. This allows us to limit the analysis of the residual demand to the investigation of the problem in which a set of landowners claim the rent rate $q_A \geqslant 0$ and all the others claim the rent rate $q_B > q_A$. We will refer to the plots of land that are offered at the rent rates q_A and q_B as plots A and B, respectively. We will refer to the total area of all plots A as T_A.

Let us first assume that $q_A \in (q_i, q_{i+1})$. The demand for plots A is clearly equal to Gt_i. If $T_A \geqslant Gt_i$, then the residual demand for plots B is nought; whereas if $T_A < Gt_i$ *and* $q_B < q_{i+1}$, then the residual demand for plots B equals $Gt_i - T_A$. On the contrary, if $T_A < Gt_i$ *and* $q_B > q_{i+1}$, the farmers prefer to use plots A more intensively instead of using any land B. Note that if the farmers intensify the use of plots A, then the holders of plots A, whether they are the owners or just farmers who obtained permission to use them because of the payment of the rent rate q_A to the owners, are able to get an extra rent on the use of plots A. We will call this extra rent rate η_A.

In order to calculate the residual demand for plots B, we have to find non-negative intensities of operation of processes on plots A, $x_j, x_{j+1}, \ldots, x_m$ ($j \geqslant i$); non-negative intensities of operation of processes on plots B, $y_j, y_{j+1}, \ldots, y_m$ ($j \geqslant i$); and prices $w \geqslant \overline{w}$ and $\eta_A \geqslant 0$ such that

$$\sum_{j=1}^{m} x_j + \sum_{j=i}^{m} y_j = G \tag{7.9}$$

$$\sum_{j=i}^{m} x_j t_j \leqslant T_A \tag{7.10}$$

$$1 - l_j w - t_j(q_A + \eta_A) \leqslant 0 \quad j = i, \ldots, m \tag{7.11}$$

$$1 - l_j w - t_j q_B \leqslant 0 \quad j = i, \ldots, m \tag{7.12}$$

$$\eta_A \sum_{j=i}^{m} x_j t_j = \eta_A T_A \tag{7.13}$$

$$x_j[1 - l_j w - t_j(q_A + \eta_A)] = 0 \quad j = i, \ldots, m \tag{7.14}$$

$$y_j[1 - l_j \overline{w} - t_j q_B] = 0 \quad j = i, \ldots, m \tag{7.15}$$

Then the residual demand for plots B is $\sum_{j=i}^{m} t_j y_j$, provided that $w \geqslant \overline{w}$. Equation (7.9) has an obvious meaning: the amount of corn demanded by consumers must be satisfied (and the price of corn cannot be nought). Inequality (7.10) also has an obvious meaning: processes operated on plots A cannot use more than the available plots A. Equation (7.13) adds that if plots A are not fully cultivated, then $\eta_A = 0$. Inequalities (7.11) and (7.12) imply that no tenant can get extraprofits from the operation of the processes either on plots A or on plots B, and equations (7.14) and (7.15) add that processes that require extra costs cannot be operated.

The following is easily established:

1   If $Gt_i < T_A$, then the residual demand for plots B is 0: Equation (7.9) is satisfied with all $y_j = 0$ and all $x_j = 0$ but $x_i > 0$; inequality (7.10) is satisfied as a strict inequality; inequalities (7.11) and Equations (7.14) are satisfied with $w = \frac{1 - t_i q_A}{l_i}$; inequalities (7.12) are satisfied as strict inequalities.

2   If $Gt_i = T_A$, then the residual demand for plots B is 0: Equation (7.9) is satisfied with all $y_j = 0$ and all $x_j = 0$ apart from $x_i > 0$; inequality (7.10) is satisfied as an equality; inequalities (7.11) and Equations (7.14) are satisfied with $w = \frac{1 - t_i(q_A + \eta_A)}{l_i}$ and $0 \leqslant \eta_A \leqslant$ min $\{q_{i+1} - q_A, q_B - q_A\}$; inequalities (7.12) are all satisfied as strict inequalities when $\eta_A < q_B - q_A$ whereas all but one (two) are satisfied as strict inequalities when $\eta_A = q_B - q_A \neq q_{i+1} - q_A$ ($\eta_A = q_B - q_A = q_{i+1} - q_A$).

3   If $\frac{T_A}{t_{h-1}} < G \leqslant \frac{T_A}{t_h}$ ($h > i$) and $q_B > q_h$, then the residual demand for plots B is 0: Equation (7.9) is satisfied with all $y_j = 0$ and all $x_j = 0$ apart from $x_{h-1} \geqslant 0$ and $x_h > 0$; inequality (7.10) is satisfied as an equality; inequalities (7.11) and Equations (7.14) are satisfied with $w = w_h$ and $\eta_A = q_h - q_A$; inequalities (7.12) are satisfied as strict inequalities.

4   If $\frac{T_A}{t_{h-1}} < G \leqslant \frac{T_A}{t_h}$ ($h > i$) and $q_B = q_h$, then the residual demand for plots B may be positive: Equation (7.9) is satisfied with all $y_j = 0$ and all $x_j = 0$ apart from $y_{h-1} \geqslant 0$, $y_h \geqslant 0$, $x_{h-1} \geqslant 0$ and $x_h \geqslant 0$; inequality (7.10) is satisfied as an equality; inequalities (7.11) and (7.12) and Equations (7.14) and (7.15) are satisfied with $w = w_h$ and $\eta_A = q_h - q_A = q_B - q_A$; all inequalities (7.11) except two and all inequalities (7.12) except two are satisfied as strict inequalities. Plots B are demanded if x_{h-1} is sufficiently high (and x_h is sufficiently low): residual demand is in the range $[0, Gt_{h-1} - T_A]$.

5   If $\frac{T_A}{t_{h-1}} < G \leqslant \frac{T_A}{t_h}$ ($h > i$) and $q_B < q_h$, then the residual demand for plots B is $Gt_{h-1} - T_A$;

$$w = \max_{j} \frac{1 - t_j q_B}{l_j} = \frac{1 - t_{h-1} q_B}{l_{h-1}} \tag{7.16}$$

and all inequalities (7.12) but one are satisfied as strict inequalities, and one of them is satisfied as an equality; $\eta_A = q_B - q_A$, such that all inequalities (7.11) but one are satisfied as strict inequalities and one of them is satisfied as an equality; Equation (7.9) is satisfied with all $y_j = 0$ and all $x_j = 0$ except $x_{h-1} > 0$ and $y_{h-1} > 0$; inequality (7.10) is satisfied as an equality.

If $q_A = q_1 = 0$, then the same results are easily obtained. If, on the contrary, $q_A = q_i$ and $i > 1$, then the demand for plots A is in the range $[Gt_{i-1}, Gt_i]$. Residual demand is calculated again by means of systems (7.9)–(7.15). Moreover, points 3, 4, and 5 are confirmed, whereas points 1 and 2 need to be modified. Residual demand is confirmed to be nought, but if $Gt_{i-1} \leqslant T_A$, then all $x_j = 0$ apart from $x_i > 0$, and inequality (7.10) is satisfied as a strict inequality (except in the case in which $T_A = Gt_i$); whereas if $\frac{T_A}{t_{i-1}} < G \leqslant \frac{T_A}{t_i}$, then all $x_j = 0$ apart from $x_{i-1} \geqslant 0$ and $x_i > 0$ and inequality (7.10) is satisfied as an equality.

Note that if some plots B are cultivated, then plots A and B are cultivated at the same intensity.

3.2 When the claims of the Ricardian theory of intensive rent constitute a Nash equilibrium

Let us assume that G is at the level at which the Ricardian intensive rent theory, explored in the previous section, predicts that $w = w_i$ and $q = q_i$, that is $G \leqslant \frac{T}{t_1}$, if $i = 1$, or $\frac{T}{t_{i-1}} < G \leqslant \frac{T}{t_i}$, if $i > 1$. If all landowners but one charge a rent rate equal to q_i and one landowner charges a higher rent rate, will this cunning landowner be able to get a higher rent? As we will see, the landowners who stand a greater chance of obtaining a higher rent by deviating from the propositions of the Ricardian theory of intensive rent are those with the largest plots of land. Hence, in order to simplify the notation, we will assume that the landowner charging a higher rent rate is landowner 1. Therefore, we assume that the area $T - T_1$ of land is offered at rate q_i, whereas the area T_1 is offered at a higher rent rate, which we will refer to as q_B.

If $\frac{T - T_1}{t_{h-1}} < G \leqslant \frac{T - T_1}{t_h}$, then the residual demand may be positive only if $q_B \leqslant q_h$; otherwise, the residual demand equals 0. If $q_B < q_h$, then the residual demand is $t_{h-1} G + T_1 - T$; if $q_B = q_h$, then the residual demand is in the range $[0, t_{h-1} G + T_1 - T]$. If, further, $(t_{h-1} G + T_1 - T)q_h > T_1 q_i$, it is certainly possible to find a $q_B \leqslant q_h$ for which landowner 1 finds it worth deviating from the propositions of the Ricardian intensive rent theory. (If $q_B = q_h$, this may require a tie-breaking rule that maximises the deviator's payoff.)[3] Hence, the claims of the Ricardian theory of intensive rent $w = w_i$ and $q = q_i$ constitute a Nash equilibrium if and only if

$$G \leqslant \frac{T}{t_{h-1}} - \frac{T_1}{t_{h-1}} \frac{q_h - q_i}{q_h} \tag{7.17}$$

Note that if

$$T_1 \frac{q_h - q_i}{q_h} \geqslant T \frac{t_{i-1} - t_{h-1}}{t_{i-1}}$$

no $G > \frac{T}{t_{i-1}}$ may satisfy inequality (7.17). Hence, the range in which the claims of the Ricardian theory of intensive rent $w = w_i$ and $q = q_i$ constitute a Nash equilibrium may be empty if T_1 is sufficiently large with respect to T. On the contrary, if T_1 is sufficiently small with respect to T, the claims of the Ricardian theory of intensive rent are confirmed in large part of the levels of corn production within the feasible range. This means that if the land property is highly fractionated such that the owner of the largest estate owns a small portion of the existing land, then the Ricardian theory of intensive rent is confirmed.

4 Concluding remarks

This chapter identified the general conditions concerning the distribution of plots of land among landowners that need to be satisfied in order for the Ricardian intensive rent theory to identify a position that is a Nash equilibrium. These conditions basically amount to determining a threshold that the plot of land owned by the owner(s) with the largest area must have. Below such a threshold the Ricardian intensive rent theory identifies a position that is a Nash equilibrium. Above such a threshold the theory identifies a position that is not a Nash equilibrium. The chapter did not attempt to determine a general analysis of the Nash equilibria that may prevail. Indeed, a general analysis of this type is very difficult and given the present knowledge only a number of cases can be determined. This will be attempted in other papers, but the condition stated in this chapter concerning the claims of the Ricardian intensive rent theory is absolutely general.

Notes

1 Alternatively, *ante factum* wages can be considered as paid at the beginning of the production period by capitalists; accordingly, profits are calculated only on advanced wages. In this interpretation, the *post factum* wage rate w equals $(1 + r)\overline{w}$, where r is the rate of profit: *ante factum* wages are the only 'capital' advanced at the beginning of the production period by capitalists.
2 We will use the material presented in Salvadori (2020, chapter 1).
3 In Bertrand-like games, tie-breaking rules (or sharing rules) specify how agents share total demand in the event of a tie. In some cases, specific sharing rules are required for the existence of an equilibrium. See e.g. Simon and Zame (1990) and Hoernig (2007).

References

Hoernig, S. (2007). Bertrand games and sharing rules. *Economic Theory* 31(3): 573–585.
Kurz, H. D. and Salvadori, N. (1995). *Theory of Production: A Long-Period Analysis*. Cambridge, Melbourne and New York: Cambridge University Press.
Panico, C. (1991). Some notes on Marshallian supply functions. *Economic Journal* 101(406): 557–569.

Panico, C. and Salvadori, N. (1994). Sraffa on returns. *The European Journal of the History of Economic Thought* 1: 2. Reprinted in Kurz, H. and Salvadori, N. (1998). *Understanding Classical Economics*. Abingdon and New York: Routledge.

Salvadori, N. (2004). Is Ricardian extensive rent a Nash equilibrium? in Richard, Arena and Neri, Salvadori (Eds.) *Money Credit and the Role of the State: Essays in honour of Augusto Graziani*. Aldershot: Ashgate, pp. 349–360. Reprinted in Kurz, H. and Salvadori, N., Interpreting Classical Economics, Abingdon and New York: Routledge, 2007.

Salvadori, N. (2020). Ricardo's theory of growth and accumulation. *A Modern View (The Graz Schumpeter Lectures)*. Abingdon and New York: Routledge.

Samuelson, P. A. (1959). A modern treatment of the Ricardian economy: I. The pricing of goods and of labor and land services; II. Capital and interest aspects of the pricing process. *Quarterly Journal of Economics* 73: 1–35; 79: 217–231.

Simon, L. K. and Zame, W. R. (1990). Discontinuous games and endogenous sharing rules. *Econometrica* 58(4): 861–872.

Sraffa, P. (1960). *Production of Commodities by Means of Commodities: Prelude to a Critique of Economic Theory*. Cambridge: Cambridge University Press.

8 Organisations and institutions in Sraffa's thinking[1]

Giuseppe Mastromatteo and Giovanni B. Pittaluga

1 Introduction

In contrast to the neoclassical–Marshallian theory, in Sraffa's theory the production of goods and income distribution are not determined simultaneously. In fact, in Sraffa, companies' choice of the production process depends not only on technology but also on the wages and profits, that is, income distribution. As Garegnani (1960, p. 3) writes:

> Sraffa's essential research concern is 'the study of the "surplus product" [that] is the true object of economics'... Consequently, the system of production prices that receives most attention in PCMC – in which capitalist producers and workers share a variable part of the surplus – is simply one example of a specific societal configuration and not in itself the 'true object of economics'. ...

It is not surprising, therefore, the solicitation of various scholars to deepen Sraffa's thought on the role of economic and political institutions in a capitalist system.[2] As it is known, in such a system while economic institutions define a system of property rights that regulate economic exchanges, political institutions consist of the legislative and procedural framework that establishes how policy choices are adopted.

The main explanations of the origin and change of institutions can be categorised into two schools of thought.[3] A first conception emphasises the benefits of institutions for the whole community. The second conception, mainly attributable to Marx, emphasises the benefits of institutions in favour of certain segments of society. Sraffa refers to this second school of thought. His analysis of the origin and change of institutions is concentrated above all in the first phase of his scientific career. It is in the writings of this period that Sraffa stresses the fact that the level of wages and profits is determined, rather than by market mechanisms, by the institutional context.

Given the crucial role of institutions in the distribution of income, the social classes struggle to exert control or influence them. Sraffa, while sharing the above with classical Marxism, departs from this ideology in some respects. In

DOI: 10.4324/9781003105558-9

particular, he does not accept the determinism of classical Marxism, believing that cultural values and ideals are not simply a superstructure, but rather that they have their own autonomy and can, therefore, affect the structure. In his view, cultural values and ideals are not only functional to acquiring or maintaining power, but can translate into actual changes in institutions. The crucial role attributed by Sraffa to institutions calls for an analysis of his thought on aspects inherent to their origin and their changes.

This contribution aims to clarify these aspects. It is divided into three sections. In Section 2, we attempt to explain the link between production and income distribution in the neoclassical-Marshallian economy and in Sraffa. Section 3 is dedicated to an analysis of how, according to the Turin economist, institutions affect the distribution of income, while Section 4 illustrates his view on the determinants of institutional change and the role of changes within organisations.

2 Production and distribution in the neoclassical approach and in Sraffa

As it has been made clear by an extensive literature, the connecting thread of Sraffa's intellectual path is a closely reasoned critique of the neoclassical-Marshallian economy and a re-proposal of the classical circular economics.

At the root of the neoclassic or Marshallian economy is exchange. Each individual is endowed with a certain quantity of goods. And, based on their preferences, they exchange these goods on the market, aiming to maximise their utility. In this context, the production of output and its distribution reflects this exchange and depends on the prices at which goods are exchanged. In equilibrium, the prices of the factors of production, wages and profits are equal to their marginal productivity.

In the neoclassical-Marshallian model, the market is the institution that allows the efficient allocation of resources and distributes income in a manner consistent with the contribution of inputs to the final output. Any imbalance between supply and demand in the market for goods or that of production factors is cleaned through changes in prices. Hence, the supply and demand's adjustments bring the market back to equilibrium. In this context, not only is there full employment of the productive factors, but the distribution of income, depending on the marginal productivity of the productive factors, essentially responds to a principle of 'social harmony'. The neoclassical theory of distribution, making reference to the concept of capital's marginal productivity, requires that the value of capital is measured regardless of the distribution of income.[4]

This last aspect is the subject to severe criticism by Sraffa who, in PCMC – but also in various earlier texts – observes that capital, unlike labour and land, is not a natural factor that can be measured, since production is a circular process, characterised by complex interdependencies.[5] These interdependencies take on importance since the economic system produces various commodities which are characterised by different relationships between capital and labour. In such a context, the relative prices of commodities depend on the rate of wages and on the rate of profit. Changes in the distribution of income, therefore, affect the relative prices of goods. Even with respect to the same production techniques, the value of capital changes as the distribution of income varies.[6] This being the case, the relationship between the prices of the factors of production and the quantity of them used as the basis of the neoclassical theory is broken.[7]

Moving from the critique of this theory, Sraffa (1960) comes to elaborate a theory that takes up the circular theory of production, proposed by classical economics. According to Roncaglia (1978):

> it would seem more correct to say that Sraffa's analysis is not static, but rather that it represents a "photograph" of a particular moment in a system's development … time is taken into account by the fact that any particular moment of time is determined by its past history, and serves as the determining factor of the next moment in time.[8]

Therefore, in Sraffa's economic theory, social relations play an important role in at least three aspects.[9] In the first place, social conditions are reflected in the level of wages and, in this way, on the methods of production and the distribution of the surplus. Second, production methods, precisely because they depend on social conditions, are determined before prices. Therefore, the interdependencies and interactions between output levels of different sectors must be analysed taking into account their social and historical specificities. Third, the above implies a separation of the analysis of quantity and prices.

As for the previous points, in Sraffa the production of commodities is broken down into two stages: the determination of the prices of the productive factors and the choice of their combinations on the basis of the existing technology and the prices of the factors fixed at the distribution level.

This is in stark contrast to the neoclassical theory, where the prices of goods, their quantities and the distribution of income are, given a certain technology and certain preference structure of individuals, determined simultaneously.

It follows that in Sraffa, the social factors which regulate income distribution are upstream of the production process and affect its outcome. These factors consist of institutions, that is, formal and informal constraints on the behaviour of individuals, and organisations, that is, groups of individuals pursuing common goals. Sraffa's main reflections on these issues are found above all in his unpublished papers conserved at the Wern Library of Trinity College of Cambridge.[10]

Taking up this aspect of Sraffian thought and referring to the neoclassical approach prevalent in the early 1990s, Eatwell (1994, p. 36) writes: 'economics is failing today … it is failing because economics today is built upon theoretical foundations which exclude the very substance of economic policy, namely the economic institutions through which economic life is actually lived'.

However, at the very beginning of the 1990s, North[11] highlighted the role of institutions in the development of economies and how the level of development depended on the quality of the institutions, on their ability to reduce transaction costs, that is: 'the costs involved in protecting property rights, measuring what is being exchanged, and in enforcing agreements'.[12] Given that the goal of individuals is to maximise their utility and that this goal is achievable through the exchange of goods and services, it is necessary to use resources to meet the transaction costs. Efficient institutions, protecting property rights and reducing transaction costs, allow for the growth of trade and therefore higher levels of productivity and individual satisfaction. From the above, it is clear that in North, but more generally in neo-institutionalist scholars,[13] institutions increase the benefits of cooperation between individuals and the cost of 'defection' and conflict. In this sense, they facilitate the functioning of the market economy as designed in the neoclassical–Marshallian analysis.

The Sraffian vision of institutions and their role is placed in a completely different context. Indeed, it can be traced back to Marx and explains institutions in terms of the benefits they bring, not to society as a whole, but only to segments of it. In this perspective, institutions play a crucial role in determining the distribution of income and the institutional set-up is the result of conflict between the different social classes.

Referring to the Gramscian distinction between 'state' and 'civil society', Sraffa distinguishes between political and economic institutions. Political institutions are the result of the conflict between different social classes to acquire power and influence the distribution of income. This outcome can consist of a negotiated division of power, as occurs in democracies, or in the absolute domination of one or more classes over the rest, as occurs in dictatorial regimes. An example of the latter is given by the prevalence of fascism in Italy in the early 1920s.

> In post-war Italy the struggle between labour and capital had reached a critical stage. The capitalist and the working classes had come to be firmly consolidated into two opposing and exclusive parties which made a definite bid for the control of the state … The opposing interests did no longer fight on the merits of particular points of contention … It was to all practical effects a state of war, in which each of the parties was little concerned with the immediate advantages to be gained or the temporary hardships to be suffered, concentrating for the time being all its energies in securing the final victory. Later, it was thought, when one of the two classes had got the supremacy, it would have been easy for it to settle all the particular questions according to its own views and interests.[14]

In the context just outlined political institutions are the result of a deliberate design. Emblematic in this sense is what Sraffa wrote in 1923 regarding the construction in Italy of the so-called state corporatism by the fascist regime.

The latter undertook in their first two years in power to destroy the institutions and reforms of the democratic regime.

> When this work [of destruction] was completed, the need was felt for something more original and constructive, for a new conception of the state to be substituted both to the liberal and to the socialist conceptions and for a machinery which would both justify and ensure the permanency and stability of the fascist regime. ...[15]

The institutional architecture of the corporate state was constructed to ensure the dominance of the bourgeoisie in the distribution of income.

While political institutions are the outcome of a deliberate project, economic institutions are usually the outcome of an 'unintended' evolutionary process. This does not mean that there are no interconnections between these two types of institutions. Indeed, on the one hand, economic institutions and organisations have a significant influence on the ability of social classes to exert pressure on the political elite or even to express it; on the other hand, political institutions can influence economic institutions and organisations.

3 The role of institutions and interest groups in the distribution of income

It is plausible to believe that in his vision of social reality Sraffa was mainly influenced by the Turin economic school of the early twentieth century and by the Gramscian version of Marxism. From the Turin economic school, he receives the idea that policy choices are strongly influenced by the pressures of the various interest groups, which aim to seize as large a share of national income as possible.[16]

The influence of Gramsci's thought on Sraffa concerns aspects of both method and interpretation of political and social reality. Several scholars have analysed the first aspect. Davis (1993, 2002), for example, has highlighted how Sraffa takes from Gramsci the concept of 'emergence' and that of 'catastrophe'. Ginzburg (2015) has shown how in both scholars emerges the issue of 'translability', or 'the reconstruction of the conception of the world, dictated by unit of theory and practice'.[17] Sen (2003) underlines the importance that Gramsci attributed to language as an expression of the conception of the values of a given social group and sees in it a link between Sraffa, Wittgenstein and the Italian philosopher.

Here we try, instead, to highlight the influence exerted by Gramsci on Sraffa's vision of social and institutional dynamics. As is well known, in the Marxist conception the state is seen as the apparatus, the instrument, through which the ruling class exercises power. The state therefore constitutes a superstructure with respect to the structure constituted by civil society and the economic relations that characterise it. Gramsci goes beyond this vision and 'identifies' a separation between state and civil society. The latter is the 'space' where the classes compete, also on an ideological level, to win power or 'hegemony'. From manuscripts preserved at the Wren Library of Trinity College, it emerges that in Sraffa the distinction between politics and society is always present. The political elite does not slavishly reflect the interests of the main social groups who support it, but seeks to preserve and consolidate its power through policy choices aimed at acquiring the consent of other social groups. This aspect emerges clearly in two letters from Sraffa to Tasca published in 'Lo Stato Operaio' (official monthly magazine of the Communist Party of Italy) in November–December 1927. They were a response to an article published in the same magazine in March–April 1927 in which Tasca argued that the revaluation of the lira after Mussolini's Pesaro speech of 18 August 1926 was an offensive against workers' wages. In the letter to Tasca on 17 September 1927, Sraffa argued that in revaluing the lira,

> … fascism has voluntarily made a policy contrary to the interest of financiers and industrialists. My explanation is … that this revaluation …, is part of an attempt by fascism to acquire the support of the middle classes and some layers of workers since it is undeniable that the only ones truly advantaged by the revaluation are in those classes.[18]

As is well known, Gramsci (1971) departs from the classical view of Marxism in believing that the political elite and the interest groups it represents make use of ideological propaganda as well as coercion to maintain power.

> The historical unity of the ruling class is realized in the state, and their history is essentially the history of states. But it would be wrong to think that this unity, concretely results from the organic relations between state or political society.[19]

Propaganda contributes crucially to the latter's support of the regime, that is to say the 'inoculation' in it of values and ideals consistent with the economic and social order that the elite aims to achieve. 'It is true that the conquest of power and achievement of a new social world are inseparable, and that propaganda for one is also propaganda for the other …'.[20]

Sraffa in several of his writings shows that he attaches great importance to ideological propaganda as an instrument of power. Emblematic, for example, is what he writes regarding the representation of the corporative state at the basis of the stability of the fascist regime. According to the propaganda in this type of state:

> the interests of labour and capital are identical, and also of the nation at large are identical so far as production is concerned: the larger the product, the larger the share that will fall to each, and the greater the national power.[21]

According to Sraffa, these

> base outlines may give the impression that the dictatorship is independent
> of sectional interests, that it is a well meaning attempt to govern paternally
> a backward people which is unfit for democratic government or at least
> that, if it is oppressive, its burden falls equally upon the different sections
> of the community.[22]

The propaganda of the ruling elite, its need to inculcate certain values in
society and rationally justify the existing economic and political equilibrium
tends to influence theoretical explanations of economic facts. It is not un-
common for economic theory to satisfy the need of political elite for propaganda.[23]

Political power allows the elite, that is, the dominant interest group or
groups, to make decisions that determine the distribution of income. These
decisions relate mainly to choices regarding legislation and regulation, fiscal
policy and the management of monetary and exchange rates.

For example, with reference to the first type of instruments, Sraffa shows
how in Italy, in the period immediately following the First World War,
powerful industrial groups exerted pressure on the political class to realise

> large "groups" of companies of the most varied kinds concentrated round
> one or more banks … Within these "groups" the various interests are all
> equally subject to the interests of a few individuals who control the whole
> group … Each group keeps several press organs which support its policy,
> and some of the accusations made against certain Ministry of being
> actuated by the interests not of a class, but of private concerns, and of
> favouring one financial group against another, have no doubt a basis of
> truth.[24]

Another example of regulation used to redistribute income is given by Sraffa
with reference to the fascist ideology of the state corporatism. In fact, behind
the cover of this ideology and in the name of the pursuit of the general interest, the relations between labour and capital were regulated by the fascist
government to the disadvantage of the workers. The strike, in fact, was
considered a crime and punished accordingly; on the other hand, lock-outs
were punished only if without 'adequate reason'.[25] Besides, in negotiations,
the workers' unions were almost always strictly controlled by the fascist regime
and this made them weak and compliant with respect to their counterparts (the
employers). This was the result of the procedures for choosing the leadership
of the employer associations and the trade unions.

> The employers associations are genuine voluntary organizations, which
> have freely been established long before fascism existed: they have simply
> been included in the general system … In the trade unions the members

are not entitled to take part in decisions on matters of policy or in regard to wages agreements, nor they elect the officials and the executive committees. The President of the General Confederation of fascist unions (who has been in the first instance nominated by the Prime Minister) nominates the officers of the big Confederations. ...[26]

The attention to the redistributive implications of monetary policy can be found in his own degree thesis.

In it, Sraffa gives an explanation of the reasons of war and post-war inflation slightly different from that of other economists of the time, like Cabiati (1925) and Einaudi (1933). In fact, while the latter scholars trace that inflation to a tug of war, or to the resistance of the various interest groups to accept tax increases, Sraffa sees in it a largely deliberate choice, an outcome of the social conflict that typifies capitalistic economies.[27] Indeed,

> [d]uring the war, ... producing money was left totally to arbitrary decisions of banks and the governments ... industrialists could avoid subordination to banks and, from being their debtors, they became creditors. The reason for this was the large profits the industrialists made due to war supplies and the fact that the state, their most important customer, itself financed raw materials imports and production.[28]

In this view, therefore, inflation does not always and in all cases derive from the monetary coverage of public deficits. It may be caused by an excessive increase in bank money as a result of high corporate demand and the accommodative behaviour of ordinary banks and the central bank. In this context, money creation is largely endogenous.

It is by taking into account the redistributive effects of inflation that Sraffa criticises the concept of forced saving in his review of Hayek's 'Prices and Production'[29] published in the *Economic Journal* in 1932. For the Austrian economist, in fact, an excessive monetary expansion, which is associated with a market interest rate lower than the 'equilibrium interest rate', has distorting effects on the capital structure of production. However, these effects are subsequently reabsorbed to the earlier capital structure when, with a monetary tightening, the market interest rate is brought back to the level of the natural interest rate. On the contrary, Sraffa shows that the distorting effects on the capital structure are not induced by monetary expansion, but by the redistribution of income that derives from the inflation connected to it. This leads him to exclude that even when the excess of money creation is reabsorbed, the capital structure returns to its initial level. In fact, due to inflation:

> one class has, for a time, robbed another class of a part of their incomes, and has saved the plunder. When the robbery come to an end, it is clear that the victims cannot possibly consume the capital, which is now well out of their reach.[30]

Inflation and the excess money creation with their redistributive effects are the way in which, according to Sraffa (1922a, 1922b), the Italian authorities tried to resolve the crises that afflicted the Italian banking system, starting with the crisis of the Discount Bank in the early 1920s. On that occasion, the issuing banks released a large amount of liquidity to support the banks in crisis. This form of intervention was possible for the issuing banks

> owing to the extreme super-elasticity of Italian circulation due to the right they have of issuing uncovered loans to commerce in unlimited quantity ... if ... bank notes are issued in great quantity it is because of the great influence which the Government exercises over the banks of issue.[31]

In this way, through the inflationary tax, a large part of the costs of the errors of management of the banks and in particular of the discount bank fell on fixed income earners and workers.[32]

As we have just seen, the political elite tends to use a variety of tools to achieve an almost always capitalist-friendly redistribution of income. In some cases, however, the political elite may pursue a redistribution of income solely aimed at their preservation of power. This aspect is dealt with by Sraffa, as well as in the aforementioned analysis of the effects of the revaluation of the lira, also in the manuscripts of 1923 in which he analyses the economic policy of the early years of the fascist regime.[33] In fact, in these manuscripts Sraffa distinguishes between the liberal approach supported by the capitalist class, in particular by the industrialists, and the 'interventionist' approach in favour of an expansion of the state budget supported by the leadership of the fascist party.[34] As regards the possibility of conflict within the economic elite, we have already seen how Sraffa believed that the re-valuation of the lira benefited rentiers and landowners at the expense of industrialists and how this choice corresponded to the need of the political elite to consolidate its power.

The idea that social and political conflict is not limited to the opposition between employers and workers, but affects wider and more articulated areas, leads Sraffa to a different vision of institutional change from classical Marxism but also from Gramsci, in which the focus is almost exclusively on the conflict of capital and labour. This aspect is developed in the next section.

4 Changes in economic organisations and institutions

As already mentioned, in Marx institutional changes occur as a result of changes in the relations of production. In this interpretation, therefore, institutions proceed in 'leaps': there are no incremental changes, but rather we pass from one institutional system to another.

Sraffa disagrees with this vision, believing, as did Hayek (1973), that changes in institutions occur gradually through an unintentional process.

> What usually happens is that new institutions gradually grow out of the old state of things, without any conscious plan being made to bring them about, and in part without anybody noticing that big change is taking place, and much less understanding the significance.[35]

However, Sraffa, unlike Hayek, does not believe that the evolution of institutions is the result of a competition between different institutional arrangements, the outcome of which is the prevalence and survival of the most efficient ones. Indeed, his opinion is that, left to their own spontaneous evolution, institutional changes often have outcomes that do not ensure the optimal allocation of resources.

Sraffa offers two examples of this in his 1929 Lectures on Continental Banking and 1941–43 Lectures on Industry. In the latter, he shows how over time in industry, with the transition from sole proprietorships to joint stock companies, a separation of ownership from control has occurred. The latter now being exercised by managers, who tend to have as their objective, rather than maximising the firm's profit, maximising their personal 'profit', their prestige, their social position, their power. If 'the desire for personal profit is the main motive, we must conclude that the interests of control are different, and often opposed, to those of the shareholders'.[36] In contrast to what had happened in the past when property and control coincided, the interest of joint stock companies tends to coincide with the interests of control, rather than with that of the shareholders. In extreme cases, the contrast between control and ownership can lead to the bankruptcy of the company.

It follows that the laissez-faire ideology, referring to a society composed of individual firms competing with each other and based on the assumption that such competition ensures the efficient allocation of resources, can no longer be accepted. The 'golden rule' advocated by Robertson (1923) in 'Control of industry', according to which net profits are appropriated by the owners, is no longer valid because they control the company and take risk.[37]

With the advent of joint stock companies, the monitoring role of ownership was furtherly undermined by the fact that the shareholders in their choices essentially consider the performance of a stock on the Stock Exchange. This trend is affected by speculation rather than by the actual value of the company.[38] Indeed, the shareholders

> constantly look at the Stock Exchange list and the value of his shares fluctuates violently from day to day, quite independently of the state of the business in which the investment is effected, but according to an extremely unstable speculative situation.[39]

Even the changes in the organisation of companies that are at the root of the institutional changes described are the result of an unintended evolutionary process. The origin of these changes

> has been almost invariably the accumulation of large surplus stocks, which brought down the price of the product. And in most cases these were due to technical improvements either in the form of cheaper methods of production or of a new and richer source of supply.[40]

The fact that the changes in the relationship between ownership and control of companies have affected the functioning of the 'institution-market' shows that in Sraffa the causal link underlying institutional changes goes from organisations to institutions. It is the changes that for various reasons occur in the former that favour changes in the economic institutional framework. In this context, neither the quality of the institutions nor that of the organisations tend spontaneously towards efficiency, as happens instead in Hayek and in neo–institutionalism, where the efficiency of institutions leads to the creation of efficient organisations.

Another example both of the fact that the spontaneous evolution of institutions leads to an inefficient allocation of resources and of the fact that changes in organisations determine different institutional arrangements is offered by Sraffa in his Lectures on Continental Banking held in 1929 and is represented by the spontaneous evolution of the English banking system. This evolution can be traced back to the Bank Act of 1844 with which the Bank of England was subjected to limits on the issue of bank notes. However, in the presence of a constant quantity of money, the growth of trade would have been possible only at the cost of an enormous fall in prices. The latter, in turn, would have negatively affected the growth of trade. The introduction of cheques made it possible to satisfy the increased demand for money due to the growth of trade. The banking system thus became the hub of the British payment system. The institutional change just described took place without there being a preordained design and without anyone realising what was happening.[41]

The introduction of cheques as a means of payment brought about changes in banking organisations and a cascade of the financial system as a whole. In it, the role of the central bank compared to ordinary banks was limited to support interventions in critical situations.

The English banking system, seen as the result of the spontaneous evolutionary process just described, is compared with the German banking system based on the universal bank and considered as the result of a deliberate design.

Sraffa illustrates how the first attempt to carry out the project of an industrial banking as envisaged by Saint Simon was the establishment of the Crédit Mobilier by the Pereire brothers in 1852. This bank, after having financed rebuilding Paris and the start of various industrial enterprises, went bankrupt 15 years later. Its failure was due both to management errors (primarily the financing of long-term loans with short-term deposits) and to the hostility to it of the Bank of France and the French government, worried about losing political control over credit to the economy.

According to Sraffa, the Pereire brothers' project was ahead of its time. The project was fully implemented in Germany. In fact, the German universal banks took the form of an imitation of the Crédit Mobilier.[42] It was their constitution and the institutional framework that made them a success and are considered by Sraffa as an example of planned institution building. In fact, '[i]n the half century that followed their establishments, up to the war, the German banks have very closely followed their initial program'.[43]

The main reason for the industrial banks' possible difficulties lies in the different liquidity of the assets and liabilities of these banks. In fact, Sraffa explains that the liquidity of an asset does not consist in the fact that it is payable at an early date, but in the fact that it is readily marketable.[44]

> Therefore, … the relevant quality of assets, in order to be liquid, is not that they should be payable at an early date, but that they should be readily marketable. By selling these assets a bank can change them into cash immediately; whereas if it has to wait till maturity, this involves a more or less prolonged delay.[45]

The main trouble of industrial banks arose from the low liquidity of their assets.[46]

Given the low liquidity of their assets, industrial banks need constant support from the central bank and not episodic as in the case of the Bank of England.[47] The role played in the German banking system in the decades preceding WWI by the Reichsbank is emblematic. This institution was called upon to perform the role of planning officer. In this role, the Reichsbank helped to allocate credit efficiently.

The German banking system, centred on universal banks and the Reichsbank, was the basis for Germany's intense industrial development in the pre-WWI period, after which this system dissolved. Consequently, on the one hand, the German banks highlighted the tendency to converge towards the English model, but on the other, following the Dawes Plan, the Reichsbank was made independent from the government and transformed into an institution similar to the Bank of England.

As De Cecco (2005) observes, the comparison between the English and the German banking systems (which Sraffa considers to be more efficient) must be contextualised to the period in which the Lectures on Continental banking were held. In those years, in fact, explanations were sought for the reasons why, before WWI, Germany had significantly higher output growth rates than those of England. On a more general level, Sraffa, taking the example of the German banking system, wants to demonstrate that the deliberate creation of certain institutions leads to a more efficient allocation of resources than that resulting from institutions that emerges spontaneously and unintentionally. By taking this position, he departs from classical Marxism.[48] In fact, in his view, economic institutions are a superstructure deeply conditioned by social relations of production when left to their spontaneous evolution, but they can also be the result of a deliberate design. Sraffa's conclusion stems from a re-reading of the thought of Saint Simon on banks and his proposals for reform of the banking system.[49] The French philosopher's project arose from his critical analysis of the inefficiencies deriving from production under competition, typical of the capitalist system. In fact, in this system, given the impossibility of individuals to predict what was required, overproduction of some commodities and underproduction of other commodities inevitably resulted.

For Saint Simon, banks, given the information they had at their disposal, were better able than individuals to know and satisfy the needs of the manufacturing industry. They could have fulfilled these functions either by specialising in credit to particular industrial sectors or by re-organising the banking system as a whole. At the top of the latter, there should have been 'a single bank of a general character, managed by the best bankers available, from which specialised banks, for particular industries or localities, would depend'.[50] It is easy to recognise in the latter bank characteristics similar to those of a central bank considered as an economic planner.

This role of central banks is stressed in some of Sraffa's manuscripts of the late 1950s and of the 1960s. In these manuscripts, he shows that, in some circumstances, in the circular production system it is preferable to take the rate of profits, and therefore the money interest rate, as the independent variable instead of the wage rate.[51]

> I am convinced that the maintenance of the interest rate by the bank and (or) the stock exchange has had its part in the determination of income distribution among social classes … I do not see any difficulty in the determination of the rate of profit through a controlled or conventional interest rate, provided that the rate of profit will not be assumed to be determined by external unchangeable circumstances. …[52]

Since the interest rate is a conventional variable,[53] the central bank can direct resources towards the most efficient allocation. However, due to its conventional nature, the policy interest rate can be managed by central banks to implement redistributive policies according to the wishes of the elite.

5 Conclusions

The reading of Sraffa's manuscripts allows us to ascertain that in his vision of social reality and its dynamics there is a substantial continuity with respect to his early writings. As in these writings, also in the manuscripts, the institutions are considered the fruit of the conflict between social classes with differing interests. Their nature expresses the interests of the prevailing classes and ensures their privileged role in the distribution of income. The latter is mainly the result of laws, regulations, monetary and fiscal policies favourable to the ruling classes. In this perspective, inflation is a way, in some respects deliberate, of transferring income and wealth from certain classes to others. Sraffa makes similar considerations regarding the choices to deflate the economy such as those adopted by Mussolini with the revaluation of the lira in 1926.

Probably influenced by the Gramscian distinction between state and civil society, Sraffa distinguishes between the political and the socio-economic elite. The first aims to maintain power and, therefore, in certain contexts it is willing to pursue policies that differ from those suggested by the socio-economic elite. Emblematic is the case of the economic policy of the early years of fascism, initially inspired by the industrial and liberal sector and, then shortly after, under pressure from the upper echelons of the fascist party, or-iented towards a significant expansion of public spending.

While political institutions are shaped by the ruling classes, economic in-stitutions generally evolve spontaneously. This evolution is the result of changes taking place in organisations. Thus, for example, the Bank Act of 1844 in England favoured the issuance by banks of cheques, or monetary innovation. This innovation transformed the banking business. It also led to a redefinition of the Bank of England's role as lender of last resort. Therefore, unlike new institutionalism, in Sraffa the causal link goes from organisations to economic institutions and not vice-versa. Spontaneous changes in organisa-tions and institutions often have a disordered outcome for market functioning mechanisms and, therefore, unlike Hayek's contention, there is no sponta-neous selection process in favour of the most efficient institutions. This is highlighted in the Lectures on Continental Banking through the comparison between the English banking system, which arose spontaneously, and the German one, the result of a deliberate choice, and also in the Lectures on Industry with reference to the transformation of companies from individual to joint stock companies.

Hence, the need to build a framework of efficient institutions through a deliberate plan. Sraffa sees such an accomplishment in the pre-WWI German banking system in which the Reichsbank played the role of planner. Although he is convinced that the capitalist economy when left to market mechanisms does not favour an efficient allocation of resources, he is nonetheless far from the determinism of classical Marxism. Indeed, Sraffa pays great attention to Saint Simon's utopian socialism and believes that organisational and institutional changes can derive from an intellectual project. In this, he seems very close to Keynes's view that, as he writes in Chapter 24 of the General Theory:

> The ideas of economists and political philosophers, both when they are right and when they are wrong, are more powerful than is commonly understood. Indeed the world is ruled by little else ... I am sure that the power of vested interests is vastly exaggerated compared with the gradual encroachment of ideas.[54]

Notes

1 We would like to thank the anonymous referee for his comments and advices.
2 See among others Blankenburg, Arena and Wilkinson (2012) and Cesaratto and Di Bucchianico (2020).
3 See Knight (1992, p. 4).
4 On this aspect, see Robinson (1953) and Garegnani (1960).
5 The problem was already known to Wicksell (1934, vol. I, p. 149) and to several authors of the 1920s. Subsequently, Robinson (1953) raised the problem again. However, the most thorough discussion of this topic can be found in Garegnani (1960).
6 Harcourt (1972).
7 It may happen that high interest rates are associated with a high value of the capital employed but also that vice versa low interest rates are associated with a low value of the capital employed (Sraffa, 1960, p. 37). On this aspect, see Garegnani (1966).
8 See Roncaglia (1978, p. 219). This view is not shared by Pasinetti according to whom

> [i]n Production of Commodities ... [Sraffa] does not rely on any institutional set-up, he does not make reference to any historical context, he does not mention any kind of 'economic agent'. He carefully avoids making any assumptions on human behavior, on market structure, on competition, on returns to scale. He even avoids taking a specific stand on distribution. ...

See Pasinetti (2007, pp. 192–3). However, contrary to Pasinetti's claim, Sraffa in his book refers to 'producers' that is to a social class concerned with cost minimisation. See Sraffa (1960, p. 81, 83).
9 See Bharadwaj (1975, 1978); see also Garegnani (1960, 1984).
10 On Internet available at the Janus website of Trinity College Library of Cambridge University, which we have used in this chapter.
11 See in particular North (1990).
12 North (1996, p. 7).
13 Acemoglu, Johnson and Robinson (2001) and Greif (2006).
14 See Sraffa Archive D2.2 p. 1 recto.
15 See Sraffa Archive D2.2 p. 3 recto.
16 The attention of the Turin economic school to the distribution conflict emerges, for example, with evidence in the positions taken by economists belonging to it, such as Cabiati (1926) and Einaudi (1925), on the social implications of the return of the lira to the gold standard and the consequent indications on the modalities with which to implement this decision. On the links between Sraffa and the Turin economic school, see Naldi (2009).
17 Ginzburg (2015).
18 Sraffa and Tasca ([1927] 1992, p. 181).
19 Gramsci (1971, p.52)
20 Gramsci (1971, p. 116).
21 See Sraffa Archive, D2.2 p. 1.f.4.
22 Sraffa Archive, D2.2 p. 1.f.11. The same fascist propaganda in favour of the territorial expansion of Italy is considered by Sraffa as a way to distract the masses from internal problems of the country and at the same time make sense of colonial expansion. 'Moral of the last lesson: the mirage of conquests has always been presented to the Italian people as a diversion to distract attention from internal problems. We have always been told that it is not worth looking into our homes, there are no lands, there are no riches, we must go and get them abroad'. See Sraffa Archive D2.7 p. 4 recto.
23 'A second difficulty of economic theories derives from the interests with which they are connected! Whether the earth revolves around the sun, or the sun around the earth, does not affect the personal interests of astronomers. But for economic theories it is very

different ... Therefore, very often the different economic theories are supported by the various interested in this ...'. See Sraffa Archive D2.1 p. 2 verso.

24 Sraffa (1922a, p. 196). For an analysis referring to recent years of the effects of banking and financial regulation on income distribution, see Panico, Pinto and Puchet Anyul (2012).

25 See Sraffa Archive, D2.2 p. 1.f.12 recto.

26 See Sraffa Archive, D2.2 p. 1.f.12 recto and p. 1.f.14 recto.

27 On this aspect, see Panico (1988), De Cecco (1993) and Arena (2014).

28 Sraffa (1920, p. 14).

29 Hayek (1931).

30 Sraffa (1932, p. 48).

31 Sraffa (1922a, p. 187).

32 By insisting that inflation and the resulting redistribution are often a deliberate target, Sraffa departs from other post-Keynesian scholars who, while considering inflation as the outcome of a social conflict, underline its unintentional character. See, for example, Robinson (1938) and Rowthorn (1977).

33 See Sraffa Archive D2.3.

34 'In the economic policy of fascism in power, two currents of interests have manifested themselves... Of these tendencies, one is an expression of the real capitalist class which has given fascism the means to conquer power, but always intending to use it in their own interest; the other, the new fascist oligarchy which, having come to power, has made itself financially independent and is not suited to serve as an instrument for others. The first dominates the Council of Ministers ... The governing body of the second is the Grand Fascist Council'. See Sraffa Archive D3.3 p. 1.f.1.

35 See Sraffa Archive D2.5 p. 1.f.8 recto.

36 See Sraffa Archive D2.8 p. 6.f.4 recto.

37 See Sraffa Archive, D2.8 p. 8.f.8 recto.

38 Sraffa's analysis of the changes that took place in capitalism in the early part of the twentieth century, with particular reference to the emergence of financial capitalism, presents relevant similarities with that of Hilferding (1910). On this aspect, see Mastromatteo (2019).

39 Sraffa Archive D2.8 p.8.f.8 recto. On this aspect, see Blankenburg, Arena and Wilkinson (2012).

40 See Sraffa Archive D2.8 p. 28.f.3. On this aspect of Sraffa's thought, see Arena (2010).

41 In continental Europe the institutional change just described did not occur. 'Since in most countries there were no rigidly fixed limits to the issue of notes, additional quantities of banknotes could readily be supplied whenever they were required by trade, and no demand arose for a substitute for them'. See Sraffa Archive D2.5 p. 14.f.1 recto.

42 In retracing the characteristics and history of these banks, Sraffa relied on the fundamental work of Riesser (1905).

43 See Sraffa Archive, D2.5 p. 15.f.7 recto.

44 According to De Cecco (2005), this view anticipates the Sraffa's analysis in the debate with Hayek, where he introduced the concept of 'own interest rate'.

45 See Sraffa Archive D2.5 p. 1.f.12 recto.

46 'In most cases in which this sort of banks have got into trouble, including the CM [Crédit Mobilier], it has been not owing to their having lost their own capital and the money of their creditors, but owing to their inability to transform their assets into cash as fast as depositors were withdrawn their deposits'. See Sraffa Archive D2.5 p. 14.f.1 recto.

47 Whose interventions as lender of last resort were limited to banks' liquidity crises.

48 For different views about the influence of classical economists, in particular of Marx, on Sraffa's thinking, see among others De Vivo (2003, 2016), Gilibert (2001), Garegnani (2005), Kurz and Salvadori (2004, 2005), Kurz (2012), Bellofiore (2012), Porta (2012) and Gehrke and Kurz (2018).

49 See, in particular, Bellet and Lutz (2020).
50 See Sraffa Archive D2.5 p. 1.f.12 recto.
51 On this point, see Panico (2021).
52 Quoted in Panico (2001, pp. 301–2).
53 This view can be seen as the outcome of his critique of the concept of the natural rate of interest in Hayek's 1932 essay on Prices and Production. The manuscripts of the Sraffa Archive D3.12.68 p. 2 recto and D3.12.80 p. 9 recto can help to clarify whether and in what way with his theory of the conventional interest rate Sraffa influenced Chapter 17 of the General Theory. On the latter aspect, see Barens and Caspari (1997), Kurz (2007) and Grieve (2012).
54 Keynes (1936, p. 383). On the difference between Keynes and Marx about this aspect, see Skidelsky (2010).

References

Acemoglu, D., Johnson, S. and Robinson, J. A. (2001). The colonial origins of comparative development. *American Economic Review* 91: 1369–1401.

Arena, R. (2010). Corporate limited liability and Cambridge economics in the inter-war period: Robertson, Keynes and Sraffa. *Cambridge Journal of Economics* 34: 869–884.

Arena, R. (2014). On the importance of institutions and forms of organization in Piero Sraffa's economics: the case of business cycles, money and economic policy. *European Journal of History of Economic Thought* 21: 775–800.

Barens, I. and Caspari, V. (1997). Own-rates of interest and their relevance for the existence of unemployment equilibrium positions. In G. C. Harcourt and P. A. Riach (eds), *A Second Edition of the General Theory*. London: Routledge.

Bellet, M. and Lutz, A. (2020). Piero Sraffa's St Simonian temptations. An examination of the Sraffa's Papers. *European Journal of the History of Economic Thought* 27: 428–459.

Bellofiore, R. (2012). The 'tiresome objector' and Old Moor: a renewal of the debate on Marx after Sraffa based on the unpublished material at the Wren library. *Cambridge Journal of Economics* 36: 1385–1399.

Bharadwaj, K. (1975). Valore e distribuzione esogena. In G. Lunghini (ed.), *Produzione, capitale e distribuzione*. Milano: Isedi.

Bharadwaj, K. (1978). *Classical Political Economy and the Rise to Dominance of Supply and Demand Theories*. New Delhi: Orient Longman.

Blankenburg, S., Arena, R., and Wilkinson, F. (2012). Piero Sraffa and 'the true object of economics': the role of the unpublished manuscripts. *Cambridge Journal of Economics* 36: 1267–1290.

Cabiati, A. (1925). La lotta di interessi attorno al problema monetario. *La Stampa*, 9 June.

Cabiati, A. (1926). *Il ritorno all'oro*. Milano: Corbaccio.

Cesaratto, S. and Di Bucchianico, S. (2020). From the core to the cores: surplus approach. Institutions and economic formations. *Centro Sraffa Working Papers*, No. 45.

Davis, J. B., (1993). Sraffa, interdependence and demand: the Gramsci influence. *Review of Political Economy* 5: 22–39.

Davis, J. B. (2002). Gramsci, Sraffa, Wittgenstein: philosophical linkages. *European Journal of Economic Thought* 9: 384–401.

De Cecco, M. (1993). Piero Sraffa's "Monetary inflation in Italy during and after the war: an introduction". *Cambridge Journal of Economics* 17: 1–5.

De Cecco, M. (2005). Sraffa's lectures on continental banking: a preliminary appraisal. *Review of Political Economy* 17: 349–358.

De Vivo, G. (2003). Sraffa's path to production of commodities by means of commodities. An interpretation. *Contributions to Political Economy* 22: 1–25.

De Vivo, G. (2016). Some notes on Marx's role in the development of Sraffa's thought. *Contributions to Political Economy* 35: 57–70.

Eatwell, J. (1994). Institutions, efficiency and the theory of economic policy. *Social Research* 61: 35–53.

Einaudi, L. (1925). L'assurdità del ritorno immediato alla lira-oro. *Corriere della Sera*, 12 March 1925. Reprinted in Einaudi, L. (ed.), *Cronache Economiche e Politiche di un Trentennio(1893–1925)*. Torino: Einaudi.

Einaudi, L. (1933). *La condotta economica e gli effetti sociali della guerra italiana*. Bari: Laterza.

Garegnani, P. (1960). *Il capitale nelle teorie della distribuzione*. Milano: Giuffrè.

Garegnani, P. (1966). Switching of techniques. *Quarterly Journal of Economics* 80: 554–567.

Garegnani, P. (1984). Value and distribution in the classical economists and Marx. *Oxford Economic Papers* 36: 291–325.

Garegnani, P. (2005). On a turning point in Sraffa's theoretical and interpretative position in the late 1920s. *European Journal of the History of Economic Thought* 12: 453–492.

Gehrke, C. and Kurz, H. D. (2018). Sraffa's constructive and interpretative work, and Marx. *Review of Political Economy* 30: 438–442.

Gilibert, G. (2001). Gramsci, Sraffa and the second book of Capital. In G. Petronius and M. P. Musitelli (eds), *Marx and Gramsci: Memory and Actuality*. Rome: Manifestolibri.

Ginzburg, A. (2015). Two translators: Gramsci and Sraffa. Mimeo, University of Modena and Reggio Emilia.

Gramsci, A. (1971). *Selection from Prison Notebooks*. London: Lawrence and Wishart.

Greif, A. (2006). *Institutions and Path to the Modern Economy*. New York: Cambridge University Press.

Grieve, R. H. (2012). Keynes, Sraffa and the emergence of the General Theory. *Review of Political Economy* 24: 51–67.

Harcourt, G. C. (1972). *Some Cambridge Controversies in the Theory of Capital*. Cambridge: Cambridge University Press.

Hayek, F. A. (1931). *Prices and Production*. London: Routledge.

Hayek, F. A. (1973). *Law, Legislation and Liberty*. Chicago: University of Chicago Press.

Hilferding, R. (1910). *Das Finanzkapital*. Vienna: Wiener Volksbuchhandlung. English Edition: *Finance Capital*. London: Routledge and Kegan, 1981.

Keynes, J. M. (1936). *The General Theory of Employment, Interest and Money*. London: MacMillan.

Knight, J. (1992). *Institutions and Social Conflict*. Cambridge: Cambridge University Press.

Kurz, H. D. (2007). Keynes, Sraffa and the latter's secret scepticism. In B. Bateman, T. Hirai and M. C. Marcuzzo (eds), *The Return to Keynes*. Cambridge: Harvard University Press.

Kurz, H. D. (2012). Don't treat too ill my Piero! Interpreting Sraffa's papers. *Cambridge Journal of Economics* 36: 1535–1569.

Kurz, H. D. and Salvadori, N. (2004). Man from the moon: on Sraffa's objectivism. *Economies et Societés* 35: 1545–1557.

Kurz, H. D. and Salvadori, N. (2005). Representing the production and circulation of commodities in material terms: on Sraffa's objectivism. *Review of Political Economy* 17: 69–97.

Mastromatteo, G. (2019). Financial capital and banks in Hilferding and Sraffa: lessons for today. *European Journal of the History of Economic Thought* 26: 51–80.

Naldi, N. (2009). Piero Sraffa e gli economisti torinesi. In R. Marchionatti (ed.), *La scuola di economia di Torino*. Florence: Leo S. Olshki.

North D. C. (1990). *Institutions, Institutional Change, and Economic Performance*. Cambridge: Cambridge University Press.

North, D. C. (1996). *Institutions, Organizations and Market Competition*. Germany: University Library of Munich. Economic History 9612005.

Panico, C. (1988). Sraffa on money and banking. *Cambridge Journal of Economics* 12: 7–28.

Panico, C. (2001). Monetary analysis in Sraffa's writings. In T. Cozzi and R. Marchionatti (eds), *Piero Sraffa's Political Economy*. London: Routledge.

Panico C. (2021). Sraffa's monetary writings, objectivism and the Cambridge tradition. In A. Sinha (ed.), *A Reflection on Sraffa's Revolution in Economic Theory*. New York: Palgrave Macmillan.

Panico, C., Pinto, A. and Puchet Anyul, M. (2012). Income distribution and the size of the financial sector: a Sraffian analysis. *Cambridge Journal of Economics* 36: 1455–1477.

Pasinetti, L. (2007). *Keynes and the Cambridge Keynesians: A 'Revolution in Economics' to be Accomplished*. Cambridge: Cambridge University Press.

Porta, P. L. (2012). Piero Sraffa's early views on classical political economy. *Cambridge Journal of Economics* 36: 1357–1383.

Riesser, J. (1905). *The German Great Banks and Their Concentration*. Washington: National Monetary Commission.

Robertson, D. H. (1923). *Control of Industry*. London: Nisbet.

Robinson, J. (1938). Review of "The Economics of Inflation", by C. Bresciani-Turroni. *Economic Journal* 48: 307–313.

Robinson, J. (1953). The production function and the theory of capital. *Review of Economic Studies* 21: 81–106.

Roncaglia, A. (1978). *Sraffa and the Theory of Prices*. New York: John Wiley and Sons.

Roncaglia, A. (2009). *Piero Sraffa*. Basingstoke: Palgrave Macmillan.

Rowthorn, R. E. (1977). Conflict, inflation and money. *Cambridge Journal of Economics* 1: 215–239.

Sen, A. (2003). Sraffa, Witgenstein, and Gramsci. *Journal of Economic Literature* 41: 1240–1255.

Skidelsky, R. (2010). The crisis of capitalism: Keynes versus Marx. *Indian Journal of Industrial Relations* 45: 321–335.

Sraffa, P. (1920). *L'inflazione monetaria in Italia durante e dopo la guerra*. Turin, University dissertation. Published in the same year in Milan with the Premiata Scuola Tipografica Salesiana. Translated in English by W. J. Harcourt and C. Sardoni and published in 1993 as P. Sraffa: Monetary inflation in Italy during and after the war. *Cambridge Journal of Economics* 17: 7–24.

Sraffa, P. (1922a). The bank crisis in Italy. *Economic Journal* 32: 178–197.

Sraffa, P. (1922b). Italian banking today. *The Manchester Guardian Commercial - Reconstruction in Europe*, 7 December: 675–676.

Sraffa, P. (1932). Dr. Hayek on money and capital. *Economic Journal* 42: 42–53.

Sraffa, P. (1960). *Production of Commodities by Means of Commodities*. Cambridge: Cambridge University Press.

Sraffa, P. and Tasca A. (1927). Politica monetaria. *Lo Stato Operaio*, November-December, 1089–1095. Reprinted in Villari, L. (ed.), *Il capitalismo italiano del Novecento*. Bari: Laterza, 1992.

Wicksell, K. (1934). *Lectures on Political Economy*, vol. I. London: George Routledge and Sons, 1946.

Part II

Keynesian and Post-Keynesian theories of growth and distribution

9 Key elements of post-Keynesian economics

Geoff C. Harcourt and Peter Kriesler

1 Introduction

The editors asked us to write on key elements of post-Keynesian economics for this volume celebrating Carlo Panico's 70th birthday and his many contributions to the heterodox literature. We are both privileged and delighted to do so; having known Carlo for many years, indeed decades, and having learnt much from his approaches to analysis, application and policy.

In 2013, Oxford University Press published *The Oxford Handbook of Post-Keynesian Economics*, two volumes, which we jointly edited. We tried to cover all aspects of post-Keynesian economics. From these, we concentrate on what we believe to be the key elements, which we devoutly hope will continue to influence theory, application and policy.

By its very nature, post-Keynesian economics is not a homogeneous analysis. It is inherent in the view of method that, unlike modern neoclassical theory, post-Keynesians do not try to present a mathematically elegant general abstract model with no relation to reality. Post-Keynesians are interested in trying to understand the dynamics of actual economies. They follow Keynes's dictum, best known from his *Introduction to the Cambridge Handbooks*, that economics is not a set of answers, but rather a way of thinking:

> The theory of economics does not furnish a body of settled conclusions immediately applicable to policy. It is a method rather than a doctrine, an apparatus of the mind, a technique of thinking, which helps its possessor to draw correct conclusions. (Keynes, 1922: 856)

Joan Robinson summarised this by likening economics to a box of tools – the art of being a good economist is choosing the appropriate one for the problem at hand. Keynes, Kalecki and Joan Robinson are especially associated with the 'horses for courses' approach as are their modern counterparts, Victoria Chick and Sheila Dow, and the authors of this chapter. 'Horses for courses' derives its title from the observation that a racehorse may do well at one track but not another because, say, one goes in a clockwise direction rather than an anti-clockwise one. It is a situation–and–issue method of doing political economy.

DOI: 10.4324/9781003105558-11

Post-Keynesians view the economy as a historical process, with the unchangeable past influencing the present, in other words, a concern with historical time in which the future is uncertain and expectations have a significant and unavoidable impact on economic events. Associated with this is a scepticism of the validity of equilibrium methods associated with a rejection of comparative static equilibrium analysis based on logical time and an emphasis on cumulative causation, which reinforces the denial of the validity or usefulness of general theories. Rather than elaborating a general theory with modifications to allow some role for institutions and social phenomena, post-Keynesians incorporate these into the essence of their models.

This gives us the defining features of post-Keynesian economics. In addition, this chapter considers the importance of institutions, economic and political forces in shaping economic events. According to Kalecki, 'the institutional framework of a social system is a basic element of its economic dynamics' (Kalecki, 1968). Of course, all of these evolve with the economy, with important feedback between all the components.

The central role of effective demand and of money/finance results from output and employment being determined by the level of aggregate demand in a monetary economy where money and finance have important influences on the level of economic activity in both the short and long run – so that the neutrality of money is always denied.

These key features of post-Keynesian analysis will be discussed later.

2 The economy as a historical process

Post-Keynesian emphasis on historical time is strongly related to a commitment to understand how dynamic economic processes function in the real world. Post-Keynesians have a very clear definition of what historical time is and the role it plays in economic theory. The essence of historical time is that events occur in a unidirectional sequence, as a result of which events need to be defined in the context of what has gone on before. This means that history, particularly the sequence of events leading to the current one, will play an important role in shaping that event. Any current event has traces of its past which cannot be removed. As a result, future outcomes cannot be predestined, for this would make the past totally irrelevant. If we accept that history does matter, then the future cannot be based on theories of perfect foresight such as we find in the Rational Expectations models. The acceptance of historical time is a major feature of post-Keynesian economics, and it is one of the major points of difference with the general equilibrium analysis of mainstream economics.

Important aspects of the economy that are profoundly influenced by the past include expectations and the stock of capital – both physical and human – and the set of economic, social and political institutions. The current state of these is determined by the history of the economy, and they play a vital role in determining the potential paths the economy can take.

Part of the reason for the stress on path determinacy is that cumulative causation processes are much more likely to be found at work in key markets, indeed, whole systems, than are equilibrating processes.[1] One of the present authors (GCH) has illustrated the difference between the two by a wolf pack analogy.[2] The mainstream view may be illustrated by a wolf pack running steadily along. If one or more wolves become detached from the pack, strong forces come into play to return them to it. We hope the similarities with existence, local and global stability and the independence of the factors responsible for them, are obvious.

The alternative scenario is that if some are detached, they get further and further away from the pack in either an upward or downward direction, at least for long periods of time. The first possibility is a virtuous cumulative causation process; the second is a vile one. That cumulative causation processes both catch and illustrate what is observed in the real world much more successfully than equilibrating processes seems to us an undeniable proposition. This is not a surprising observation, as its origins are to be found in the writings of Adam Smith, Thorstein Veblen, Allyn Young, Gunnar Myrdal and Nicky Kaldor.[3]

The crucial role for expectations is the result of the key observation, coming from the real world, associated especially with Maynard Keynes's insight, that all important economic decisions have to be made within an environment of inescapable and fundamental uncertainty. All analysis under the post-Keynesian rubric must incorporate this insight from the start. This puts post-Keynesianism completely outside orthodox analysis starting with rational expectations models. In other words, what Keynes is suggesting is that given that the future is unknowable, people rely on convention as a way of dealing with radical uncertainty. In order to deal with such uncertainty, conventions, rules of thumb, 'satisficing' behaviour and institutions have developed – and these are all vital parts of economic behaviour. These rules and institutions will vary between economies and over time. The fact that most agents follow these conventions minimises individual losses. However, conventions will break down outside normal times, and expectations will fluctuate wildly.

When faced with radical uncertainty and the inability to process complex amounts of information, economic agents form rules to follow, and institutions arise. In other words, institutions serve the function of allowing people to make decisions in a world which has too much information to process, and where uncertainty runs riot. Because these procedures do not rely on optimising in any definite way, they are usually considered, in the mainstream, as examples of market failure. In fact, in a complex world of ignorance, these procedures and rules of thumb are quite rational. There are many examples of such rules of thumb in the real world, such as mark-up pricing, financial ratios of various sorts and bureaucratic rules.

The fact that these rules of thumb and institutions will vary between economies and over time reinforces the denial of most post-Keynesian economists of the usefulness of a general theory. However, we must point out that beneath the wide rubric of post-Keynesian economics are two pro-minent and competing methodologies: 'horses for courses' vs a 'compleat system', in which rigorous theory is confined within the bounds of the long-period position.[4] The latter is especially associated with the writings of Pierangelo Garegnani, John Eatwell, Murray Milgate, Heinz Kurz, Neri Salvador and Carlo Panico. Heinrich Bortis's contribution (Bortis, 1997) is something of a half-way house, in which analysis of the long period is a base on which analysis of the trade cycle and the short period are placed.

3 Scepticism with respect to the validity of equilibrium methods

The importance of expectations underlies the rejection by post-Keynesian economists of equilibrium methods. They argue either that equilibrium, if it exists is path determined, or that the economy is never in equilibrium and does not tend towards it.

In spite of its usefulness and widespread appearance over almost two cen-turies of economic discourse, the concept of equilibrium has little place in the work of post-Keynesians. According to Joan Robinson:

> The neo-classical economist thinks of a position of equilibrium as a position towards which an economy is tending to move as time goes by. But it is impossible for a system to get into a position of equilibrium, for the very nature of equilibrium is that the system is already in it and has been in it for a certain length of past time.

> Time is unlike space in two very striking respects. In space, bodies moving from A to B may pass bodies moving from B to A, but in time the strictest possible rule of one-way traffic is always in force. And in space the distance from A to B is of the same order of magnitude (whatever allowance you like to make for the Trade Winds) as the distance from B to A; but in time the distance from today to tomorrow is twenty-four hours, while the distance from today to yesterday is infinite, as the poets have often remarked. (Robinson, 1953–54: 120)

'To move from one point to another we would have either to rewrite past history or to embark upon a long future' (Robinson, 1971: 104).

Robinson is arguing that when we do static comparative analysis of com-paring equilibria as the result of a change in one of the exogenous variables, we cannot pretend that this is the same as moving from one equilibrium to an-other. To do this, given that each equilibrium has a unique history with a unique capital stock and set of expectations, we would need to tell a dynamic story of how the economy moved from one equilibrium to another. In other words, we would have to analyse the path of the economy outside equili-brium, which is sometimes called the traverse.

In historical models, causal relations and social relations are important.

In a historical model, causal relations have to be specified. Today is a break in time between an unknown future and an irrevocable past. What happens next will result from the interactions of the behaviour of human beings within the economy. Movement can only be forward (Robinson, 1962: 26)

As a result of these considerations, most post-Keynesian economists reject both the comparative static method and the use of equilibrium for analysing real-world situations. While equilibrium may be useful for thought experiments and analysing the implications of systemic forces in models, it is limited in its ability to illuminate more practical problems.

4 The role of institutions, social and political forces in shaping economic events

Economic, social and political institutions are important in determining output, employment and money prices in the real world. These institutions include the money and banking system, various (future and spot markets) for goods and financial assets, social relations and most aspects of the labour/capital relation. Institutions arise as ways of dealing with an uncertain future. Rules of thumb are an example of such institutions, as are stock markets which provide valuations and reduce the costs to individuals of uncertainty by herding investors in the same direction.

Economies will have different economic, social, legal and other institutions, reflecting their historical paths and evolutions. This means that a major determinant of their economic dynamics will diverge from that of other economies, and even will change profoundly within an economy over time. Again this mitigates against the efficacy of general theories. These frameworks are the starting points of post-Keynesian analysis – with differences reflecting the different economies being considered.

5 Marxian/Kaleckian influence

More and more the starting point of post-Keynesian analysis is set within Marxian and Kaleckian structures, particularly Marx's schemas of reproduction, rather than Marshallian and Keynesian structures of supply and demand. This implies that the state of the class war observed in the sphere of production, together with the inherited stock of capital goods and methods of production, dominate the environment, the room to manoeuvre, in the sphere of distribution and exchange. There, the characteristics of Keynes's and Kalecki's investment and saving functions tackle the potential realisation problem set up in the sphere of production.

The clearest account of this is to be found in Donald Harris's writings, themselves inspired by those of Marx, Keynes, Kalecki and particularly Joan Robinson (Harris, 1975, 1976; Harcourt, 2006: 119–21). The analysis predicts that modern capitalism contains within itself both the possibility of advance as analysed initially by Keynes's shifting equilibrium model (Keynes, 1936, *CW*, vol. VII; 1973, 93–94) and of crisis.

Allied with this is the stress on cyclical growth processes rather than trends and cycles, the causes of which are independent of each other, as characterising the development of capitalist economic and social systems over time. These developments are especially associated with the contributions of Richard Goodwin, whose 1967 chapter, 'A growth cycle', in the Dobb *Festschrift*, edited by Charles Feinstein, continues to spawn a large and growing literature, and with Michal Kalecki's final view, 'Trend and cycle reconsidered', published in the *Economic Journal* in 1968.

The core insight of the approach is captured in a typically succinct Kaleckian statement: 'the long-run trend is only a slowly changing component of a chain of short-period situations; *it has no independent entity*' (Kalecki, 1968, *CW*, vol. II; 1991, 435, emphasis added). Kalecki's statement reflects the view that in historical-time process analysis, actions must always be, by definition, in the short period, though the importance of relative long period and short-period factors will vary according to the economic decisions being considered. Thus, long-term considerations will dominate investment decisions, short-term factors, the determination of current rates of output and, sometimes to a lesser extent, employment in considering price-setting (as opposed to price-taking, where short-term considerations rule). Movements over time in the economy are thus the result of one short period giving way to another, handing over in the process inherited stocks of capital goods and the ingredients on which to build new sets of expectations, both short-term and long-term. This method underlies both Kalecki's contributions and those independently and much earlier of Goodwin.

Because of his understanding especially of the role of the reserve army of labour and of the sack as disciplinary devices on the factory floor, including restraining increases in money-wages, and of the fight over the distribution of income associated with class war, Goodwin was drawn more and more to an analysis of the symbiotic relationship between populations – 'the Volterra case of prey and predator' (Goodwin, 1967, 1982: 167).

In Goodwin's case, the relationship was between wages and profits, workers and capitalists, bringing about cyclical developments. His masterpiece, 'A growth cycle' (Goodwin, 1967) has the application of Volterra's model bringing about alternating periods of fast and slow, sometimes even negative, growth – 'the symbiosis of two populations – partly complementary, partly hostile" – is helpful in understanding … the dynamical contradictions of capitalism especially when stated in a Marxian form. Joan Robinson criticised him for 'falling' for Say's law. Goodwin responded by integrating effective demand considerations into the analysis as part of his synthesis of aggregative models and production – inter-dependent ones which constitute the centrepiece of his major book with Lionello Punzo, *The Dynamics of a Capitalist Economy: A Multi-Sectoral Approach* (1987).

Post-Keynesian theory incorporates analysis of the increasing dominance of financial capital over industrial and commercial capital, combined with the rise of multi-national oligopolies as the dominant decision-makers in developed economies. These real-world happenings are associated with increasing instability and often crisis. Parallel with these developments is the rise of market structures dominated by oligopolistic price-making.

An outgrowth of cyclical growth models was analysis of the interrelationships between Keynesian and Kaleckian aggregate expenditure – investment, consumption, net exports and government expenditure less taxation – with production interdependence models of Piero Sraffa and (but only in a formal sense) Wassily Leontief, which reflect the fact that much of production is of intermediate as opposed to final goods.

6 Effective demand, money and finance

A core ingredient of post-Keynesian analysis, directly resulting from the work of Keynes and Kalecki, is the pivotal role of effective demand in determining the level of employment and output. They reject the notion that prices can determine outputs, or that prices equate demand and supply. This is because prices are determined in different ways and reflect the strategic decisions of firms rather than acting as scarcity indices. In any case, they do not influence demand in the manner in which conventional theory suggests. The key insight of both Keynes and Kalecki is that there is no mechanism in capitalist economies that guarantees full employment of all resources – especially of labour. Rather than being determined by the wage rate, the demand for labour is a derived demand depending on the demand for goods and services. As a result, analysis of the components of effective demand is the key to understanding employment and growth. Importantly, there is a major role for distribution and class analysis reflecting the different consumption and investment behaviour of different groups in society. Linked to this is their differential access to finance, which also influences their expenditures.

The main variability of effective demand, which is, therefore, the major determinant of cyclical behaviour, is investment, due to the important role of expectations and animal spirits. In a world of inherent uncertainty, expectations are subject to a herd mentality and can vary substantially as a result of very little. The key role of investment is reinforced by the insight that causality runs from investment to saving. Provided investment is able to obtain finance, changes in investment decisions will be realised and, via the multiplier, will generate changes in income, which in turn will induce sufficient saving to 'finance' that investment. In other words, total saving is determined by investment expenditure, and not vice versa.

Keynes's crucial insight that money and finance must be integrated with real factors right from the start of the analysis represents the essence of the post-Keynesian view. Importantly, money is not seen as neutral in either the short or the long run so that it always both affects real economic activity and is affected by it. With this goes the view that money and finance are principally endogenous, and can cause crises independently of the real factors – this particularly emerges from the work of Hyman Minsky.

Rejecting the idea that unemployment is due to price/wage rigidity, post-Keynesians see an important role for government macroeconomic policy to maintain both price stability and full employment.

7 Philosophical underpinnings

Post-Keynesianism has increasingly absorbed the impact that Keynes's philosophical contributions had on his analysis, most importantly in *The General Theory*. By the time Keynes was writing *The General Theory*, he was arguing that in a subject like economics, there was a spectrum of languages which were relevant to economic analysis, running all the way from poetry and intuition through lawyer-akin arguments to formal logic and mathematics, all of which were consistent with arguments being made and knowledge being acquired (Sardoni, 1992, Ch. 11). The literature most associated with this element contains the contributions of Meeks (1991, 2013), O'Donnell (1989), Carabelli (1988) and Coates (1996).

In addition, post-Keynesians have adopted the contributions of Sheila Dow with her argument of the appropriateness of the Babylonian mode of reasoning, which is an open and organic system encouraging pluralism (Dow, 2012, 2013).

8 Inflation

A key approach of post-Keynesianism is associated with conflict inflation processes whereby post-Keynesian theories of distribution and growth are brought together with the concept of conflict inflation. This process concentrates on the political and industrial strife between capital and labour; it suggests that a tendency to sustained but constant rates of inflation may bring about an uneasy truce between inconsistencies in total claims on shares in the national product/income whereby neither class attains their claims but their non-fulfilment does not worsen over time. The theory is especially associated with the contributions of Rowthorn (1977, 1980) and Marglin (1984a, 1984b); see Harcourt (2006, Ch. 6) for our interpretation of these issues and theories.

9 Policy

Rejecting the idea that unemployment is due to price/wage rigidity, post-Keynesians see an important role for government macroeconomic policy to maintain both price stability and full employment. This also reflects the view that markets are limited in their ability to achieve efficient and fair outcomes.

Post-Keynesian policy differs at almost all levels from the suggestions of orthodox economists. At the micro-level, they favour strategic trade and interventionist policies as well as regulation to curb the excess market power of corporations and to encourage prudential supervision including the financial system. To influence conflict inflation, incomes policy is the suggested tool, in line with a commitment to full employment to reduce conflict tensions.

Fiscal policy is seen as being particularly important due to the high multipliers resulting from changes in direct government expenditure, as well as the importance of infrastructure for productivity throughout the economy. Rather than seeing government deficits as being detrimental to the economy, they follow Abba Lerner's emphasis on functional finance that sees the goals of fiscal policy as being full employment and price stability – rather than any relation between government expenditures, government debt and the sale of securities (Lerner, 1943; Hart, 2011). In other words, fiscal policy is seen as a tool of policy, rather than a goal.

Monetary policy, in contrast, is seen as a blunt instrument whose main role is to help facilitate fiscal policy. Most of the components of aggregate demand either are not very responsive to interest rate changes or only respond after long and variable lags. As a result, the ability of monetary policy to influence the macroeconomy is seen as usually being extremely limited, with its efficacy being greatest during boom periods and most limited during downturns.

Notes

1 Carlo has an interesting discussion of cumulative causation and equilibrium in Panico and Rizza (2008).
2 GCH stresses that since he is not a zoologist, he may be completely wrong about how wolf packs behave, but, added, that as an economist, let us assume that he is right.
3 Kaldor's stress on the importance of cumulative causation in the link between manufacturing, exports and economic growth has become an important feature of many post-Keynesian models. See, for example, Thirlwall (2011) and Panico (2012).
4 Luigi Pasinetti, probably the last great system builder of our trade, distinguishes between a fundamental 'natural' system independent of institutions but on which a particular institutional set up may be imposed (Pasinetti, 1981; Harcourt, 2006: 123–5).

References

Bortis, H. (1997). *Institutions, Behaviour and Economic Theory: A Contribution to Classical-Keynesian Political Economy*. Cambridge: Cambridge University Press.

Carabelli, A. (1988). *On Keynes's Method*. London: Macmillan.

Coates, J. (1996). *The Claims of Common Sense: Moore, Wittgenstein, Keynes and the Social Sciences*. Cambridge: Cambridge University Press.

Dow, S. (2012). Babylonian thought. In J. King, (ed.), *The Elgar Companion to Post Keynesian Economics*. Cheltenham: Edward Elgar, pp. 15–18.

Dow, S. (2013). *Methodology and Post-Keynesian Economics*. Edited by Harcourt, G. C. and Kriesler, P. New York: Oxford University Press, pp. 80–99.

Feinstein, C. H. (ed.) (1967). *Socialism, Capitalism and Economic Growth: Essays Presented to Maurice Dobb*. Cambridge: Cambridge University Press.

Goodwin, R. M. (1967). A growth cycle. In Feinstein (ed.), 54–58. Reprinted in Goodwin (1982), 165–70.

Goodwin, R. M. (1982). *Essays in Economic Dynamics*. London: Macmillan.

Goodwin, R. M. and Punzo, L. F. (1987). *The Dynamics of a Capitalist System: A Multi-Sectoral Approach*. Cambridge: Polity Press.

Harcourt, G. C. (2006). *The Structure of Post-Keynesian Economics: The Core Contributions of the Pioneers*. Cambridge: Cambridge University Press.

Harcourt, G. C. and Kriesler, P. (eds) (2013). *The Oxford Handbook of Post-Keynesian Economics, Volume 2, Critiques and Methodology*. Oxford: Oxford University Press.

Harris, D. J. (1975). The theory of economic growth: a critique and reformulation. *American Economic Review, Papers and Proceedings* 65: 329–337.

Harris, D. J. (1978). *Capital Accumulation and Income Distribution*. Stanford, California: Stanford University Press.

Hart, N. (2011). Macroeconomic policy and Abba Lerner's system of functional finance. *Economic Papers* 30: 208–217.

Kalecki, M. (1968). Trend and business cycles reconsidered. *Economic Journal* 78: 263–276. Reprinted in *CW, vol. II: Capitalism: Economic Dynamics*, 1991, 435–450.

Kalecki, M. (1970). Theories of growth in different social systems. *Scientia* 105: 1–6. Reprinted in *CW vol. IV* 1993, 111–118.

Kalecki, M. (1991). *Collected Works of Michal Kalecki, Vol. II*. Edited by J. Osiatynski. Oxford: Oxford University Press.

Kalecki, M. (1993). *Collected Works of Michal Kalecki, Vol. IV: Socialism: Economic Growth and Efficiency of Investment*. Edited by J. Osiatynski. Oxford: Oxford University Press.

Keynes, J. M. (1936). *The General Theory of Employment, Interest and Money*. London: Macmillan. CW, vol. VII, 1973.

Keynes, J. M. (1922). *Introduction to the Cambridge Economic Handbooks*. London: Macmillan. CW, vol. XII, 1983, 856–857.

Lerner, A. P. (1943). Functional finance and the federal debt. *Social Research* 10: 38–51.

Marglin, S. A. (1984a). Growth, distribution and inflation. *Cambridge Journal of Economics* 8: 115–144.

Marglin, S. A. (1984b). *Growth, Distribution and Prices*. Cambridge, MA: Harvard University Press.

Meeks, J. G. T. (ed.) (1991). *Thoughtful Economic Man: Essays on Rationality, Moral Rules and Benevolence*. Cambridge: Cambridge University Press.

Meeks, J. G. T. (2013). The Oxford Handbook of Post-Keynesian Economics. In Harcourt, G.C. and Kriesler, P. (eds), Vol. 2, *Critiques and Methodology*. Oxford: Oxford University Press.

O'Donnell, R. M. (1989). *Keynes: Philosophy, Economics and Politics: The Philosophical Foundation of Keynes's Thought and Their Influence on His Economics and Politics*. London: Macmillan; New York: St. Martin's Press.

Panico, C. (2012). Growth and income distribution. In J. King (ed.), *The Elgar Companion to Post Keynesian Economics*. Cheltenham: Edward Elgar, pp. 264–270.

Panico, C. and Rizza, M. O. (2008). Myrdal, growth processes and equilibrium theories. In N. Salvadori, P. Commendatore and M. Tamberi, (eds), *Geography, Structural Change and Economic Development: Theory and Empirics*. Aldershot: Elgar, pp. 183–202.

Pasinetti, L. L. (1981). *Structural Change and Economic Growth: A Theoretical Essay on the Dynamics of the Wealth of Nations*. Cambridge: Cambridge University Press.

Robinson, J. (1953–54). The production function and the theory of capital. *Review of Economic Studies* 21: 81–106. Reprinted in Robinson, J. (1975). *Collected Economic Papers Volume II*. Basil Blackwell: Oxford, pp. 114–131.

Robinson, J. (1962). *Essays in the Theory of Economic Growth*. New York: St. Martin's Press.

Robinson, J. (1971). *Economic Heresies: Some Old-Fashioned Questions in Economic Theory*. London: Macmillan.

Rowthorn, B. (1977). Conflict, inflation and money. *Cambridge Journal of Economics* I: 215–239. Reprinted in Rowthorn (1980), 148–181.

Rowthorn, B. (1980). *Capitalism, Conflict and Inflation: Essays in Political Economy*. London: Lawrence and Wishart.

Sardoni, C. (ed.) (1992). *On Political Economists and Modern Political Economy. Selected Essays of G. C. Harcourt*. London: Routledge. Reprinted in 2003.

Thirlwall, A. P. (2011). Balance of payments constrained growth models: history and overview. *PSL Quarterly Review* 64: 307–351.

10 Classical theories of wages and heterodox models of distribution

Amitava Krishna Dutt

1 Introduction

The wage in heterodox theories of growth and income distribution and older classical theories is often treated as exogenous by most contemporary interpreters.[1] This is often criticised, mostly by neoclassical economists and even by some heterodox economists with the argument that the real wage, in fact, is not fixed but changes quite frequently and has increased significantly over time. Neoclassical economists usually take the real wage to be flexible and as clearing the labour market, and rely on the marginal productivity theory of wages, although there are numerous examples of such economists allowing the wage to be rigid (especially in what they call the short run), and even explain them using optimising underpinnings.[2]

The purpose of this chapter is to compare newer heterodox theories of wages to earlier classical theories to locate similarities and differences between and within them, to see what, if anything, the newer theories can learn from classical theories. This is done to clarify, and possibly improve, our understanding of what determines the wage and income distribution.

Much has been written on this topic. To narrow the scope of this chapter, it will: provide a brief review of some newer heterodox theories and models (Section 2); review some models that attempt to formalise the theories of wages of some key classical economists (Section 3); discuss briefly some ideas and interpretation of the classical economists (rather than attempting to provide an exegesis of their writing) (Section 4); identify some issues discussed by classical economists, which can enrich new heterodox theories (Section 5); and, finally, summarise and conclude (Section 6).

2 Some heterodox models

Heterodox models of growth and distribution come in several versions. We briefly review some well-known ones under the simplifying assumptions of one sector, a closed economy and absence of explicit government policy. Also, we assume output is produced with capital and labour with fixed coefficients, and there is no depreciation of capital.

DOI: 10.4324/9781003105558-12

In the classical-Marxian (CM) tradition, Marglin (1984), Dutt (1990), Foley, Michl and Tavani (2019) and others assume that the real wage is given in what they call the neo-Marxian or the classical-Marxian model in which growth is driven by the savings of capitalists. This model typically assumes that output, Y, is produced with capital and labour, that there is full capacity of capital, K, so that

$$Y = BK, \tag{10.1}$$

where B is the fixed output–capital ratio, interpreted variously as representing 'full', normal or desired levels of capital utilisation.[3] Labour employed in capitalist production, L, is determined by

$$L = Y/A, \tag{10.2}$$

where A is the given productivity of labour. There is an 'unlimited' supply of labour or a reserve army of the unemployed, and the real wage is given by

$$w = \overline{w}, \tag{10.3}$$

which depends on subsistence levels (taking into account norms and conventions), the state of class struggle and on earnings in the non–capitalist or subsistence sector.[4] Since profit is given by $Y - wL$, if we assume that a constant fraction of profits, s, is saved, and that workers consume all their income, total saving is

$$S = s(Y - wL). \tag{10.4}$$

Assuming that all saving is invested by capitalists (abstracting from borrowing and finance), investment is given by

$$I = S. \tag{10.5}$$

Since investment adds to the stock of capital, the growth rate (shown by the over-hat from now on) of capital (as well as that of labour employed and output) using Equations (10.1) through (10.5) is given by

$$\widehat{K} = s\left(1 - \frac{\overline{w}}{A}\right)B. \tag{10.6}$$

The model assumes the real wage to be exogenous and that an increase in the wage reduces the rate of growth of the economy. If A exceeds $\overline{w}$ capital will grow indefinitely at a constant rate, as does output and capitalist employment.

There are a number of variants of the CM model. Duménil and Lévy's (1999) model assumes that the real wage is given both in the short run, in which the characterised as being Keynesian because the rate of capacity utilisation is determined by aggregate demand, and in the long run, when the rate of capacity utilisation attains a given rate of normal or desired capacity utilisation, in which growth is determined by saving, so it is called classical. It should be noted that all these models take the real wage to be given as a simplification, and do not commit to any particular theory of what determines it, but implicitly they assume that there is unemployed labour or labour supply is endogenous. Some models in the CM tradition also introduce wage changes by introducing an exogenously given rate of growth of labour supply and making the wage depend on labour market conditions. For instance, in Goodwin's (1967) classic model, the employment rate affects the rate of growth of the real wage positively, implying cyclical growth. Another model assumes that the wage change depends on the rate of growth of the demand for labour in relation to that of the supply of labour and implies that long-run equilibrium growth is determined by the rate of growth of labour supply (Dutt, 1990: 50).

Many heterodox models following what has been called the post-Keynesian-Kaleckian (PKK) tradition also take distribution and the wage to be given (if there is no technical change) when growth is determined by aggregate demand rather than by saving as in the CM model.[5] For instance, when the price of the good is given, determined as a markup on variable or labour costs, as in Kalecki (1971), according to

$$P = (1 + z)W/A \tag{10.7}$$

where W is the money wage and z is the exogenously given markup rate, the real wage is given by

$$w = A/(1 + z). \tag{10.8}$$

According to Kalecki, the markup (in a simple one-sector economy) depends on the factors such as the level of industrial concentration, and the relative power of workers and firms. Models that take the real wage (or the distribution of income) to be given in this tradition include those in Dutt (1984, 1990), in which capacity utilisation is endogenously determined, and Serrano (1995), in which capacity utilisation attains its exogenously given 'normal' rate in the long run and the growth rate of the economy is determined by an exogenously given rate of growth of an 'autonomous' non-capacity building element of aggregate demand, such as an exogenously growing component of capitalist consumption.

To be sure, not all models in which aggregate demand has a major role assume that the real wage or income distribution is exogenously given. In Kaldor's (1955–56) version of what he calls the Keynesian theory, the real wage is determined by aggregate demand, at least within limits: if investment demand is high and the economy is at full capacity, and there is an excess demand for goods, the price level increases, and if the money wage is constant (or increases less than the price level), the real wage falls, and equilibrium in the goods market is restored by the fall in the real wage, which distributes income to profits out of which the propensity to save is higher, from wages, which are largely consumed. What Marglin (1984) calls the neo-Keynesian model, which can be attributed to Robinson (1962), assumes that capitalists, who receive profits, save a fraction of their income, and workers, who receive wages, determines the real wage in the same way, but explicitly for capitalists and workers than from the functional categories of labour and profit income. Marglin (1984) also discusses a hybrid neo-Marxian and neo-Keynesian model in which the money wage adjusts to the gap between an exogenously given (target) real wage and the actual real wage and the price level adjusts to the excess demand in the goods market, which implies that the real wage is a variable in the model, but equilibrium occurs in which the rate of growth of the money wage is equal to the inflation rate, so that the real wage becomes constant. The equilibrium real wage therefore depends negatively on autonomous investment and positively on the targeted real wage. Another model developed by Skott (1989), which combines aggregate demand with employment dynamics that depend on profits and the tightness of the labour market, also allows the real wage to change in the Kaldorian manner in the short run to clear the goods market with given capacity, but also in the longer run, when capital accumulates in a cyclical manner.

Models in the PKK tradition that take the real wage to be given (if labour productivity is constant), as shown by Equation (10.8) have sometimes been extended to allow for changes in the real wage, often following the lead of Kalecki's (1971) discussion of the determinants of the markup, or the degree of monopoly power. While Kalecki informally discussed these issues, Dutt (2012) reviews a series of formal models in which changes in the real wage depend on capacity utilisation, industry characteristics (as affected by government policies, conditions of economic growth, technological change, and the level of per capita income), overhead costs (such costs of research and development, the amount of fixed costs required in the form of overhead labour and capital equipment, and the cost of financing investment) and labour market conditions. Such an analysis needs to distinguish changes of a relatively short-term nature (which reflects business cycles) or long-term ones (which reflects longer-run trends or cycles).

A cursory discussion of neoclassical theories of wage allows a comparison with the heterodox theories that take the real wage and the distribution of income as given. In the simplest neoclassical model with smooth substitution of capital and labour and diminishing returns to each input, perfect competition and profit maximisation and an exogenously fixed labour supply, the real wage (in terms of the produced good) is equal to the marginal product of labour, with the demand for labour schedule being downward sloping (as shown by the marginal productivity of labour schedule) and the wage varying to clear the labour market. Of course, there are neoclassical models (in the sense of using the optimising agent) that try to explain rigid wages and prices and introduce involuntary unemployment, from efficiency wages to insider-outsider models, monopsony, and wage bargaining. However, several of the problems caused by such 'distortions', are argued by some to be solved with appropriate contracts and mechanism designs, or are taken not to last beyond the short run, or treated as theoretical curiosa rather than as being empirically widespread. Some neoclassical scholars even argue (incorrectly) that the marginal productivity theory provides an ethical justification of the distribution of income: people receive what they contribute to society, forgetting, among other things, that the marginal product of labour refers not to each worker's contribution to production but the last worker's contribution, and that real economies are unlikely to conform to the assumptions of marginal productivity theory.

We end this section with the justifications provided by those who assume a given exogenous distribution or real wage and whether they take the real wage to be actually 'fixed'. The implicit assumption is that unemployment or underemployment (in the sense that workers are employed outside the capitalist sector for a wage or productivity lower than the real wage in the capitalist sector) is usually a permanent feature of the economy. Marglin (1984: 75) argues that if the growth rates of capital, employment and output in the capitalist sector are less than the growth of population and labour supply, there will never be any labour shortage for the capitalist sector, so that there need be no upward pressure on the wage. However, if the growth rate of output outstrips the growth rate of labour supply, and a shortage of labour eventually occurs, thereby tending the raise the wage, several factors that can prevent this: one is that labour could come from the non-capitalist or petty-production sector which can release labour in part because of the sector's competition with the capitalist sector in selling goods, by new workers joining the labour force, such as women in earlier times, who previously worked at home, or due to the export of capital abroad and thereby using foreign labour, or through immigration. In addition to all this, there may be labour-saving technical change, especially in response to an increase in the wage or due to a labour shortage, which increases the effective labour supply (Dutt, 2006).

None of the models in which the real wage is taken to be exogenously given argue that the real wage in the real world is actually fixed, but it depends on a host of factors that may not systematically depend on other variables included in the models. As discussed earlier, these factors include the tightness of the labour market, government policies, the nature of technology and technical change, power of labour organisations, the degree of industrial concentration, the level of aggregate demand (which may well affect each other), and there have even been attempts to formally endogenise some of these factors.

3 Some classical models

Since our interest lies in amending heterodox models of distribution by incorporating some neglected classical ideas on wages, a convenient place to start is with a brief discussion of some models based on classical ideas. For simplicity, we use a one-sector approach which allows us to interpret that wage as the real wage in terms of the produced good.

A simple Smithian model of growth and distribution assumes that,[6] instead of there being fixed capital as in the models discussed earlier, capital stock takes the form of a wages fund (a fund used to employ labour expressed in terms of the good), so that

$$K = wL, \tag{10.9}$$

and as in the CM model of the previous section, production is given by $Y = AL$, the profit or surplus is given by $Y - wL$, and that capitalists save and invest a fraction s of their profits (and workers do not save), we get

$$\widehat{K} = s\left(\frac{A}{w} - 1\right). \tag{10.10}$$

This is very much like the expression for the growth rate in the CM model of the previous section adjusted for the different way of treating capital, and the model has similar implications.

While this model assumes that A and w are given, Smith argues, as is well known, that labour productivity grows with the division of labour, and that greater division of labour occurs due to an increase in the size of the market, and he emphasises that the wage is higher for economies that grow faster. While formalisations of these ideas may be useful exercises, they need not detain us here (and can be pursued on another occasion or by the interested reader), except to note that an extended model along these lines does not take the real wage as given, but allows it to depend on the economy's growth rate.

Turning next to Malthus, we introduce Malthus's (1798) population principle into the model just discussed. To do so in a simple manner, with some violence to Malthus,[7] we continue assuming that A is constant. Since the rate of population growth is given by the difference between the birth rate (β) and the death rate (δ),

$$\widehat{N} = \beta - \delta \tag{10.11}$$

where N is the total population. We assume that the population is equal to the size of the labour force, the number of capitalists being so small that they can be ignored from the population. The birth rate increases with the real wage, because high wages make workers procreate more rapidly while low wages make workers decide to have fewer children, so that

$$\beta = \beta(w) \tag{10.12}$$

where $\beta' > 0$. Malthus referred to checks on population due to a lower birth rate as preventive checks. The death rate falls with the real wage because more comfortable lives improve nutrition and living conditions and reduce mortality, so that

$$\delta = \delta(w) \tag{10.13}$$

where $\delta' < 0$. Malthus saw these as positive checks, which operate through illness, malnutrition, and other problems due to low wages and incomes.

We examine the dynamics of the economy in two runs. For the short run, the population and the wage fund, N and K, are given and that the real wages is flexible, changing to clear the labour market. In short-run equilibrium the entire labour force or population, N, is employed, implying

$$L = N. \tag{10.14}$$

The short-run equilibrium real wage is therefore

$$w = K/N. \tag{10.15}$$

In the long run N, changes according to Equation (10.11), while K changes according to Equation (10.10) using the same assumptions as those of Smithian model regarding capital accumulation. The dynamics of w are given by

$$\widehat{w} = \widehat{K} - \widehat{N}. \tag{10.16}$$

Using this equation and Equations (10.10) through (10.13) we get

$$\widehat{w} = s\left[\frac{A}{w} - 1\right] - \beta(w) + \delta(w). \tag{10.17}$$

Figure 10.1 shows the dynamics and long-run equilibrium of w. The $\widehat{K}$ and $\widehat{N}$ curves show the growth rates of capital (or wages fund) and population (the difference between the birth rate and the death rate, where w_s is the subsistence wage level at which population growth is zero, and $\widehat{w}$ curve shows the vertical difference between the $\widehat{K}$ and $\widehat{N}$ curves and g denotes growth rates. The long-run equilibrium wage is shown by w_L, when $\widehat{w} = 0$ and $\widehat{K} = \widehat{N}$. As shown in the figure, the equilibrium real wage exceeds the subsistence wage as long as $w_s < A$, so that capitalist have a positive profit at that wage. It is interesting to note that as A increases due to the increasing size of the market as the economy grows, the growth rates of capital (or the wage fund) and output increase. Furthermore, if the rate of capital accumulation increases due to an increase in s or A, the $\widehat{K}$ curve shifts upwards, implying that a higher rate of growth (of capital, employment and population) is associated with a higher level of long-run equilibrium wage. Adding Malthusian population dynamics therefore produces a Smithian conclusion.

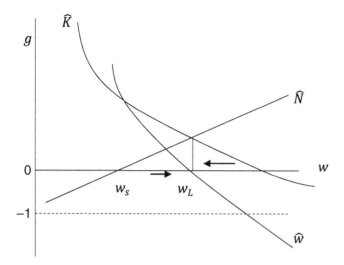

Figure 10.1 Simple Malthusian model without diminishing returns.

Turning to Ricardo (1817) next, Kaldor (1955–56) presents a Ricardian model with a wage that is exogenously given at subsistence in some sense. This is not inconsistent with the Smithian model just discussed with a given wage if we assume that the wage is also determined by subsistence (a wage that is discussed by Smith, although without assuming that the wage is always or even normally at that level). The main difference between the Ricardian model and the earlier Smithian one is that the former assumes that the economy (which is agricultural)[8] uses land owned by landowners. A single good is produced with labour and land, using the production function

$$Y = F(L), \tag{10.18}$$

which exhibits diminishing returns due to declining land quality as employment of labour is extended to less fertile land, so that $F'(L) > 0$ and $F''(L) < 0$. With marginal land accruing no profits since it represents land on the margin between land that is cultivated (because it yields positive profit) and land which is not (because it yields no positive profit), we have rent given by

$$R = Y - LF'(L), \tag{10.19}$$

where the marginal land (for any amount of labour employed) exhausts all the produce after the payment of wages, which are equalised for all workers, and profit rate is also equalised between all units of capital-as-wage-bill. Total profit, Π, the residual output and income, after payment of wages and rent, is given by

$$\Pi = Y - R - w_s L, \tag{10.20}$$

where w_s is the fixed subsistence wage. Capitalists have a wage fund W in real terms from past saving (and investment), which we denote by K for capital, so that

$$K = w_s L. \tag{10.21}$$

Capitalists save a constant fraction of their profits, s, and add it to the wage fund, so that we have

$$\dot{K} = s\Pi, \tag{10.22}$$

where $0 < s \leq 1$ and where the over-dot denotes the time derivative of the variable under the dot. The dynamics of this model involves starting with a given wage fund, K at a point in time and examining how it changes over time. Given K, Equation (10.21) determines L, Equation (10.18) determines Y, which then, using Equation (10.19) determines R, after which Equation (10.20) determines profits and Equation (10.22) determines the change in K over time. We may use these equations to obtain

$$\widehat{K} = s \left[\frac{1}{w_s} F'\left(\frac{K}{w_s}\right) - 1 \right], \tag{10.23}$$

which shows the relation between K and how it grows over time. The dynamics are shown graphically using Kaldor's diagram, in Figure 10.2, slightly amended to show the relation between K and L shown by Equation (10.21) in the lower part of the figure with its slope given by w_S, and with linear average and marginal product curves for labour, shown by Y/L and $F'(L)$, for simplicity and without loss of generality. Starting with any level of capital, say K_1, employment is given by L_1, and total wages, profit and rent are as shown. With positive profit, capitalists accumulate capital as a wages fund, and capital increases as shown by the upward-pointing arrow. According to this model, the stationary state is reached when capital and employment go to the levels denoted by K_{ss} and L_{ss}.

It has often been pointed out (Hicks and Hollander, 1977) that a close reading of Ricardo (1817) suggest he did not, in fact, assume that the wage is always given at the subsistence level. The analysis of wage dynamics in a Ricardian model is presented by Casarosa (1978) and less formally by Hicks and Hollander (1977). The presentation here uses a simple dynamic approach, with two state variables, one being population, N, and the other, capital as wages fund, K.[9] The model distinguishes between labour supply, and employment as in the earlier Malthusian model. In the short run K and N are taken as given and in short-run equilibrium the wage is determined by the

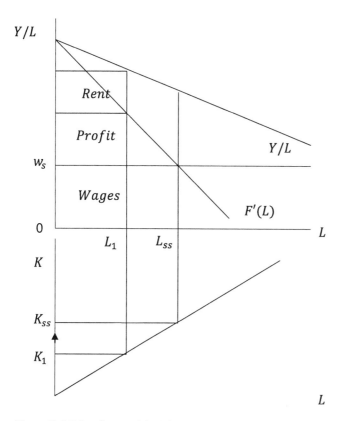

Figure 10.2 Ricardian model with a given wage.

labour market-clearing condition Equation (10.14), so we have $L = N$ and $w = K/N$. In the long run K adjusts according to

$$\dot{K} = s[LF'(L) - wL], \tag{10.24}$$

which is obtained from Equations (10.18), (10.19) and (10.22) and the defi nition of profits, $\Pi = Y - R - wL$. Since in the long run, short-run equilibrium, shown by Equation (10.14), always holds, and the wage is determined by Equation (10.15), this implies

$$\dot{K} = s[NF'(N) - K]. \tag{10.25}$$

The supply of labour adjusts according to

$$\dot{N} = \Theta[w - w_S] \tag{10.26}$$

where Θ is a positive constant and w_S is the subsistence wage as defined by Ricardo, which is not necessarily the same as Malthus's subsistence wage. The equation is a simple reduced form and linear version of the Malthusian principle and implies that if w exceeds (is less than) the subsistence level, population and labour supply increases, and population becomes stationary if the wage is at its subsistence level. This labour market clearing, shown by Equation (10.18), thus implies

$$\dot{N} = \Theta\left[\frac{K}{N} - w_S\right]. \tag{10.27}$$

The long-run dynamics of the model are shown in Figure 10.3. Setting $\dot{N} = 0$ in Equation (10.27) we get $K/N = w_S$, that is, the real wage is equal to the subsistence wage. The slope of this line, shown as $\dot{N} = 0$ is given by w_S. Starting from a position on the line an increase in K increases K/N, or the wage, which makes $w > w_S$, implying N increases, and conversely for a fall in in K; this explains the direction of the horizontal arrows. Setting $\dot{K} = 0$ in Equation (10.25) we find the relation between K and N that brings accumulation to a halt; it is shown by the $\dot{K} = 0$ curve. The slope of this curve is given by

$$\frac{dK}{dN} = F'(N) + NF''(N)$$

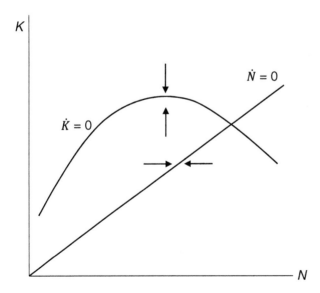

Figure 10.3 Ricardian model with a flexible wage.

Since $F'(N) > 0$ and, with diminishing returns, $F''(N) < 0$, for a typical production function the slope is likely be positive at low values of N, reach its maximum when $-\frac{NF''(N)}{F'(N)} = 1$, that is, the absolute value of the elasticity of the marginal product of labour with respect to labour is unity, and likely to be negative for higher values of N. Starting from a point on the curve, an increase in K makes the profit negative and slows down accumulation so that a rise (fall) in N will be required if the elasticity of the marginal product of labour with respect to N is greater (less) than unity to restore profits back to zero.[10]

The economy converges to long-run equilibrium either along a monotonic path or in a circular manner, converging to the stationary state with $\Pi = 0$,[11] so capitalist profit is zero, and $w = w_S$.[12] For any point in the quadrant, the slope of the line joining that point to the origin shows the real wage. This implies that the real wage can move monotonically or cyclically to the subsistence level.

Finally, a simple Marxian model was called the neo-Marxian or classical-Marxian one in Section 2, for which the growth rate is given by Equation (10.6). This is very similar to the Smithian model of Section 3 with the difference that the latter treats capital as a wage fund and Marxian one treats capital as fixed, non-depreciating, capital.[13] This model clearly does not do justice to much of Marx's analysis of the capitalist economy, for instance by ignoring different types of capital, different sectors, the dependence of the wage on conditions on the labour market, realisation crises and technical change, but has proved to be useful as a simple starting point of some central aspects of Marx's theory.

4 Classical and Marxian theories of wages

The last two sections have briefly reviewed some popular contemporary heterodox models and some models developed to represent the earlier analyses of the classical economists. An important feature of many of them is that the real wage is fixed exogenously, and even when not fixed, it either converges to some exogenous level, often labeled a subsistence level (as in the Ricardian model with a flexible wage), or is related to an exogenous level but converging to it only in the special case in which accumulation stops (as in what was called the Malthusian model), or oscillates indefinitely around some exogenous level (as in the Goodwin model). This section briefly discusses the ideas of the classical economists.

In discussing doing so, it is necessary to examine the differences between the models presented in the previous section with the writings of the classical writers. But in doing so, especially because the classical writers did not provide mathematical formalisations or even precise expositions of their method of analyses, we will quote directly from some of their works, but also take care to avoid taking words out of context. For instance, in discussing the method employed by Ricardo, Kurz (2015: 824) argues that:

[i]n a first step of the analysis Ricardo typically studied in abstract terms the situation of an economy in *a given place and time*. In a second step he then studied the path the economy would take in the case in which it followed the "natural course of things". By this he meant a course of events in which capital accumulates, the population grows, etc., but in which ... there are no further "improvements" in the methods of production ... It is only in a third step that he takes technical progress into account and expounds the different effects different types of it have. ... The focus of much of Ricardo's analysis is on steps one and two. Understandably, he was keen to get the foundations of his analysis right. Setting aside technical progress was also motivated by the fact that little can be known today about future technical breakthroughs.

The Ricardian model of Section 3 with the flexible real wage focuses on Ricardo's first and second steps, and ignored the third. However, that the stationary state can be prevented indefinitely by technical changes, which have not been examined either in Ricardo's first and second steps or in the model. If technical change is examined, there is no reason why the stationary state will ever be reached and why the wage is driven to its subsistence level. Moreover, once this is taken into account, it is possible to incorporate the effects of changes in the subsistence wage using Ricardo's own ideas, to show that the actual wage is not 'stuck' at a given subsistence level, and how factors relevant for one step (for instance, the first and second) can affect what is taken into account in a later step.

The classical economists, including Smith, Ricardo and Marx, all distinguish between 'market' prices at which commodities are actually bought and sold and 'natural' prices which are objects of theoretical analysis (Vianello, 1989). Although the different writers have different theories of natural prices the concept is similar for them all. For Smith (1776, ch. 7), the natural price is

> the central price, to which the prices of all commodities are continually gravitating. Different accidents may sometimes keep them suspended a good deal above it, and sometimes force them down even somewhat below it. But whatever may be the obstacles which hinder them from settling in this centre of repose and continuance, they are constantly tending towards it.

In the same chapter, Smith provides an explanation of why such gravitation occurs: if the effectual demand for a good, the quantity people are prepared to pay for it at its natural price, is more (less) than the quantity brought to the market, the price will tend to rise (fall), and in that case more (less) labour, land and capital are used to produce that good, so that its price will tend gravitate to its natural price. Smith states that the natural price is the price at which 'is sufficient to pay the rent of the land, the wages of the labour, and the profits of the stock employed in raising, preparing, and bringing it to market, according to their natural rates'. Ricardo (1817, ch. 4) also argues that the actual price tends to move towards its natural price due to the mobility of capital caused by different profit rates in different sectors which increases production for goods for which demand exceeds production by drawing in more capital (and labour), and decreases production for sector where the opposite is true. The natural price of a good is generally referred to as the quantity of labour necessary for its production, but also depends on profits being at their normal profit. Marx also distinguishes between the market price of labour from its natural price, where the former is determined by transitory configurations of supply and demand and which tend to the latter, which was the subsistence wage necessary to maintain and reproduce the existing workforce.

Rather than reviewing the writings of the classical economists and Marx individually, and also discussing the vast secondary literature and debates about them, it is useful for present purposes to examine three issues concerning the wage: first, what factors determine the 'natural' wage; second, what explains the convergence of the actual wage to it; and third, on whether the natural wage is fixed or changes over time. It should be made clear that the classical writers did not define the 'natural' wage with any degree of precision. As far as I am aware, Smith never defines what he means by the term natural wage and the words do not even appear in the *Wealth of Nations*. But it seems, as Stirati (1994: 45–53) argues, that he believes that (since it is mentioned in the definition of the natural price of any commodity) it is the 'ordinary' or 'average' wage observable in the circumstances of a particular society, or even a centre of gravitation. The relation between subsistence and natural wages is also not very clear.

On the first issue, the classical writers discuss a number of determinants of the 'natural' wage. Smith (1776, ch. 8) starts with a discussion of the relative bargaining power of workers and capitalists. Although he emphasises the stronger bargaining power of the latter (more on which below), he points out that if workers take collective action (which seldom works) they can increase their bargaining power, they can increase their wage above the subsistence level of the wage which they can only buy necessary goods. He argues that in places where capital stock grows more rapidly (as in the USA), the wage tends to be high; this is not the case when the stock is high but is not growing (as in the UK). In places where accumulation is low or there is economic decline, the existence of unemployed worker puts downward pressure on the wage. While some earlier writers, such as Turgot and Steuart, argued that the wage was at or near subsistence, because of competition between many workers and the weak bargaining power of workers vis-à-vis employers, Smith saw the subsistence level as merely providing a general floor. Thus, according to Smith, the natural price of labour is best seen as being determined by subsistence, the relative bargaining power of workers and labour market conditions as reflected by the rate of accumulation (Stirati, 1994: 45–53).

For Ricardo (1817, ch. 5), the natural wage or natural price of labour 'is that price which is necessary to enable the labourers, one with another, to subsist and to perpetuate their race, without either increase or diminution'. Ricardo (1815) makes the simplifying assumption that the wage is always at this natural level as is represented in the Ricardian model with a fixed wage, as in Kaldor's formulation.[14] However, in Ricardo (1817), he argues that adjustments in the actual level of the wage is the result of increases and decreases in the amount of labour available resulting from changes in population and if capital accumulates takes at a high rate, the wage may be above its natural level for long periods of time. These ideas are captured in the Ricardian model of the previous section with a flexible wage, although using precise assumptions that depart from Ricardo's own views. For instance, he does not take the actual wage to be a theoretical variable determined by market clearing within a supply-demand framework since he recognised that unemployment can exist, does not take the wage fund to be given, and is cautious about treating the population mechanism as a general law (Stirati, 1994: 119, 136–7). For the sake of analytical precision, however, the variable-wage model can be taken to provide a harmless formulation of Ricardo's wage dynamics.

In his earlier writings on the wage,[15] Marx argues that the natural wage is the subsistence wage necessary to maintain and reproduce the workforce, and the market wage is influenced by the more transitory forces related to the demand for labour (which is affected positively by the pace of accumulation and negatively the adoption of machinery) and the supply of labour (which, although affected by population growth, had more to do with the reserve army of the unemployed and those working in the non-capitalist sector). In these early writings Marx mentions the role of organised power of labour on wages, but argues that they only had a temporary effect on wages, given the weaknesses of trade unions and the strong bargaining power of capitalist employers. In his later writings, including especially the first volume of *Capital*, and *Wages, Price and Profits*, Marx provides a clearer analysis of the value of labour power in terms of the mechanism of the reserve army of the unemployed, which provides a floor level of wages. Although he recognises the role of population in affecting labour supply and in influencing wages, he focuses mostly on the non-capitalist subsistence sector and the rest of the reserve army of the unemployed, depending on capitalist accumulation and labour-saving mechanisation and technical change (to which he gives a much more important role than Ricardo), and on the loss of income in the subsistence due to competition from the capitalist sector. He views the value of labour power partly in demographic terms (what is necessary to reproduce the family), but also as something which provides a living according to traditional standard of life, and as the minimum required for workers to offer their labour rather than remaining in the non-capitalist sector, although these may be logically different (Rowthorn, 1980: 206–10). Wages do not fall below the value of labour power because of worker resistance and because of harmful consequences for population growth and worker quality, but can rise well above it, not just temporarily, but for longer periods of time, especially during booms (as formalised in the Goodwin model). Marx (1865) also gives labour organisation and trade unions a larger role in wage determination (in addition to hours and working conditions), examining how worker organisations can help to make the wage increase more rapidly when employment grows, to resist wage declines when employment growth falters, and to obtain higher wages in response to labour productivity growth. He allows the state of class struggle between capitalists and workers to be affected by the state of the economy, that is, on the size of the reserve army, and also on the degree of concentration of firms as employers (anticipating Kalecki in this regard), since this determines whether and how much producers can increase prices and therefore influence the real wage.

On the second issue, of convergence, the population mechanism is a central idea for Smith, Malthus and Ricardo: if the wage is high (low), population tends to increase (decrease), which increases (decreases) labour supply, which reduces (increases) the wage. Smith (1776, ch. 8) also states that even if workers are able to increase their wage, the overwhelming advantages of the capitalists made the wage likely to fall. Although workers may be necessary for capitalists to produce, it is

> not difficult to foresee which of the two parties must, upon all ordinary occasions, have the advantage in the dispute, and force the other into a compliance with their terms. The masters, being fewer in number, can combine much more easily: and the law, besides, authorises, or at least does not prohibit, their combinations, while it prohibits those of the workmen. A landlord, a farmer, a master manufacturer, or merchant, though they did not employ a single workman, could generally live a year or two upon the stocks, which they have already acquired. Many workmen could not subsist a week, few could subsist a month, and scarce any a year, without employment.

The higher level of education of the capitalists and their connections with people wielding political power, is also likely to be a major advantage not only in influencing laws but also in their application and implementation.[16] Malthus and Ricardo and, to some extent, Mill, mostly stress the role of the population mechanism, although the latter famously states that while the laws of production of wealth have the character of physical truths, the laws of the distribution of wealth are matters solely of human social institutions, and are therefore changed by social conditions (Mill, 1848: 199). Marx, although continuing in the classical tradition in many ways, shifts his focus away from population dynamics and although not jettisoning it altogether, relies more on the existence of the reserve army of the unemployed, its replenishment by the possible decline in non-capitalist production sectors, the power of capitalists, and mechanisation and technical change in pushing the wage downwards, as mentioned earlier.

Finally, on the third issue, the classical writers were all very clear that what they referred to either a natural wage or a subsistence wage is not fixed. Thus, Smith (1776, Book 5, ch. 2, part II, p. 4) states that

> [b]y necessaries I understand, not only the commodities which are indispensably necessary for the support of life, but whatever the custom of the country renders it indecent for creditable people, even of the lowest order, to be without. A linen shirt, for example, is, strictly speaking, not a necessary of life. The Greeks and Romans lived, I suppose, very comfortably, though they had no linen. But in the present times, through the greater part of Europe, a creditable day-labourer would be ashamed to appear in public without a linen shirt, the want of which would be supposed to denote that disgraceful degree of poverty, which, it is presumed, nobody can well fall into without extreme bad conduct.

Smith argues that 'common humanity' prevents the wage from falling below the subsistence level that will buy these necessities (Stirati, 1994: 59).[17] Even Malthus (1798) recognises that in some countries population growth can slow down despite there being high wages and incomes, by postponing marriages and having fewer children after marriage. In the first edition he writes that

> [this] check appears to operate in some degree through all the ranks of society in England. There are some men, even in the highest rank, who are prevented from marrying by the idea of the expenses that they must retrench, and the fancied pleasures that they must deprive themselves of, on the supposition of having a family. These considerations are certainly trivial, but a preventive foresight of this kind has objects of much greater weight for its contemplation as we go lower. (Malthus, 1798: 20)

Malthus does not foresee the results of this for a generalised increase in the 'subsistence' wage – which is not surprising because the so-called demographic transition had not really taken hold among most social classes during his time – and he may have been driven to ignore it to support his idea that social efforts to increase the lot of the poor would fail. But it is quite clear from the Malthusian model of the previous section, in which an increase in w_s reduces the birth rate, pushes the population growth line down, and thereby increases the long-run equilibrium wage while lowering long-run growth. Ricardo (1817, ch. 5) stated that

> [i]t is not to be understood that the natural price of labour, estimated even in food and necessaries, is absolutely fixed and constant. It varies at different times in the same country, and very materially differs in different countries. It essentially depends on the habits and customs of the people.

Mill (1848, and later editions), while adopting some form of the population principle, argues that as workers receive higher wages, their proclivity to obtain higher levels of comforts for themselves and their families slow down population growth and result in a higher level of the wage at the stationary state.[18] Marx also argues that the natural price of labour and the value of labour power change over time (which sets a minimum for the wage), and there is an upward shift because a rise (rather than a fall) in the value of labour power is more difficult to reverse. It is worth quoting from Marx's later writing to emphasise these points. Marx (1865: 50–1, italics in original) states:

> [b]esides [the] mere physical element, the value of labour is in every country determined by a *traditional standard of life* … the satisfaction of certain wants springing from the social conditions in which people are placed and reared up … This historical or social element, entering into the value of labour, may be expanded, or contracted, or altogether extinguished … .

Marx (1869, *Capital*, I, 190) writes that:

> the number and extent of [the workers'] so-called necessary wants, as also the modes of satisfying them, are themselves the product of historical development, and depend therefore to a great extent on the degree of civilization of a country, more particularly on the conditions under which, and consequently on the habits and degree of comfort in which, the class of free labourers has been formed.

5 Classical and heterodox theories of the wage and a formulation of wage dynamics

We now examine what, if anything, newer heterodox wage theories can learn from classical theories, and how these features can be incorporated into the former. Some of the *differences* between the theories – particularly in view of current real-world characteristics – are the use of the wages fund theory in the latter, which is made irrelevant by developments in financing, the emphasis on investment to finance wage rather than fixed capital, the Malthusian population mechanism, and the absence of technical change in some of the classical models. In any case, the criticisms of wages fund theory, particularly in the form that leads to a market-clearing wage given labour supply (as in some of Malthusian and Ricardian models), the inclusion of Ricardo (1817), in later editions, of machinery, and especially Marx, the criticism of Malthusian population theory by Marx, and the role of technical change in Smith and Marx and, even Ricardo in his 'third step', raise doubts about the extent to which classical theory insisted upon them.

Of more importance are the *similarities* between them in their treatment of the wage as exogenously given, at least as a first approximation. Of course, there are several examples in both classical theories and models and heterodox theories which do not make this assumption. There are two aspects to this issue, both discussed earlier. First, why the wage can be taken as given and second, what explains the given value of that wage. Regarding the first issue, what makes labour supply expand when output grows, so that there is no upward pressure on the wage, which allows the wage to remain constant, several answers are possible, all of which were discussed in some of the classical analysis or in discussion of newer heterodox models. First, labour supply can expand endogenously due to immigration (both documented and undocumented, despite the presence of restrictions on international migration) from abroad when labour scarcity emerges, people entering or staying in the labour force, like younger people who leave school earlier, and older people, as people live longer and remain in the labour force. 'Natural' population dynamics are less likely to play a role given demographic transitions, government provision of welfare income needs and food, as well as health-care, although with low wages more people can be expected to die due to pandemics (such as COVID-19), so a return to it cannot be ruled out, especially in lower-income countries without effective government safety nets. Second, technical change, especially the spread of artificial intelligence, robotics, improvements in information technology to new tasks and new sectors allow increases in the effective supply of labour or reduce labour demand growth for a given rate of output growth. Indeed, the rise of the informal sector and the use of informal labour in formal sectors, as well as subcontracting and the gig economy, are all signs of an increase in the reserve army. Third, labour demand within countries can be adjusted by international factors, such as international trade policy changes, international capital flows including foreign direct investment.

On the second issue, the classical and more recent heterodox economists have discussed a range of influences, such as the rate of growth of the economy, conditions of labour supply and demand (which influence the rate of unemployment and underemployment), the relative power of workers vis-à-vis capitalists (which depends on a host of factors, including legal institutions, the adoption of labour-saving technologies, the strength of labour unions, and the nature of government policies), and social norms about what is considered to be a basic standard of living and about fairness. While some of these things can be analysed as general tendencies, others can depend on factors that depend on specific and conjunctural forces that may, however, have long-term effects. As a first pass, therefore, the real wage (or income distribution) can be taken as exogenous, not because the wage is actually the same across time and space, but because it is hazardous to theorise about them in terms of systematic relationships between different variables.[19]

That does not mean it is not possible or desirable to model how the wage can change in a more systematic manner to understand some partial aspects of how the wage changes at least in what can be called the formal sector (a sector which may tell us less about the conditions of labour as the formal sector contracts). Not doing so would increase the tendency to believe, as many do, that heterodox theories do not have a theory of wages, just like that what Kurz (2015) calls Ricardo's first and second steps, more systematically examined by Ricardo, has led to belief in the inevitability of the stationary state. Such formalisations, however, should be treated with more caution than other formalisations, and should not be confused with the real world since they all involve abstractions made for particular theoretical purposes to understand some aspects of real-world phenomena.

Two sets of factors can be mentioned as examples, one of which, the power of workers and entrepreneurs and capitalists, is emphasised by the classical economists and heterodox theorists, and the other, changes in social norms regarding wages, as extensively discussed by the classical economists, but not emphasised in heterodox theories.

Power affects the laws that govern the operation of labour unions, labour laws about conditions of firing, immigration, and welfare programs, including unemployment benefits, all of which affect distribution and the real wage. It also affects and depends on what are called labour market outcomes, such as unemployment and underemployment rates, and rates of growth. Dutt (2021) develops a model involving power and class struggle in two sites – markets and the state – and the interdependence between them. Models such as these only capture some aspects of power relations and power structures, since power is very a widely discussed issue in the social sciences. It encompasses many more issues than market power as examined in monopoly and monopsony and imperfect information models for specific markets, or bargaining models in game theory, which use the neoclassical optimising approaches that go beyond the world of perfect competition which, using the notion of atomistic agents attempts to exclude all reference to power.

Regarding social norms and historical forces there are a number of ways of formalising some of the ideas of the classical political economists and Marx on what has been called the natural wage and the actual wage. Although the classical economists took the actual wage as what prevails in reality, we distinguish between a theoretical model and reality, and refer to all variables of a model as theoretical ones. We can therefore interpret the wage as being determined by factors such as the rate of unemployment and underemployment, the growth rate of the economy, government policy, and other factors that affect the power of workers vis-à-vis firms and capitalists, and distinguish between the wage and a 'reference' wage. Although the classical economists and Marx had different names and concepts for what this reference wage refers to, it is simplest to refer to one such wage rather than distinguish between subsistence wage and the natural wage, and avoid terms like 'natural', 'subsistence' and 'value of labor power' to avoid misleading connotations.[20]

The idea that the reference wage is a centre of gravitation of the (theoretical) actual wage can be formalised as

$$\dot{w} = \lambda \left[w_r - w \right], \tag{10.28}$$

where $\lambda > 0$ is a speed of adjustment constant. If w_r is taken to be given, if the real wage is subjected to some 'shock', like an increase in the growth rate of employment, it will tend to return to w_r. If the positive and negative shocks are roughly of equal magnitude and cancel each other out in terms of frequency, the reference wage can be interpreted as the average wage and, if it is constant or changes independently of what happens in the model, and dependent on what can be called 'natural' forces, it can be referred to as the natural wage. If positive shocks predominate in frequency and/or magnitude (for instance, if the output and employment are growing) in a period, the average wage will be above the reference wage, so that the centre of gravitation is not equal to the average wage in that period, unlike some interpretations of Smith's analysis.

Now suppose that the reference wage also changes due to the difference between the actual wage and the reference wage, since what is considered to be the reference wage, which reflects habits and social norms, changes with actual changes in the wage, so that

$$\dot{w}_r = \nu[w - w_r]. \tag{10.29}$$

Here $\nu > 0$ is a speed of adjustment constant. To underscore that the wage adjusts to the reference wage as a centre of gravity, but the reference wage adjusts relatively slowly, we may assume that $\lambda > \nu$. This dependence can be explained by, as the classical economists and many later scholars pointed out, habits, and shared norms and values, that is, consumption habits, objective circumstance such as what is provided by the government instead of requiring private purchase, socio-economic changes that require more income to satisfy the same needs, and a sense of what is called fair, which depends on what people are used to (Duesenberry, 1949; Frank, 1999; Dutt, 2009).

These equations imply that the wage dynamics are shown by a zero-root model given by equations with a continuum of equilibria as shown by the upper part of Figure 10.4. This model implies that starting from an equilibrium at E, if there is a positive shock to the wage, which is followed by a negative shock of the same magnitude, the economy will return to the original equilibrium at E as shown in the upper part of the figure. If positive (or negative) shocks predominate in frequency and/or magnitude, the average wage will be higher (or lower) than the higher (or lower) reference wage.

To add another complication, Equation (10.29) is replaced by

$$\begin{aligned} \dot{w}_r &= \nu_1[w - w_r] \text{ for } w \geq w_r \\ \dot{w}_r &= \nu_2[w - w_r] \text{ for } w \leq w_r \end{aligned} \tag{10.30}$$

with $\nu_1 > \nu_2$. This represents a ratchet effect in the reference wage and produces hysteresis. If the wage is higher than the reference wage, changes increasing the reference wage occur more rapidly than the rate which such changes occur in the downward direction when the wage is lower than the reference wage. Upward adjustments in habits and social norms are likely to more rapid than downward ones, because of resistance to lower consumption norms or what is considered to be a fair wage.[21] In this case, even with positive and negative shocks cancelling each other, there will be an upward movement in the wage and the reference wage as shown in the lower part of the figure. If, moreover, positive shocks are more numerous than negative ones, there will

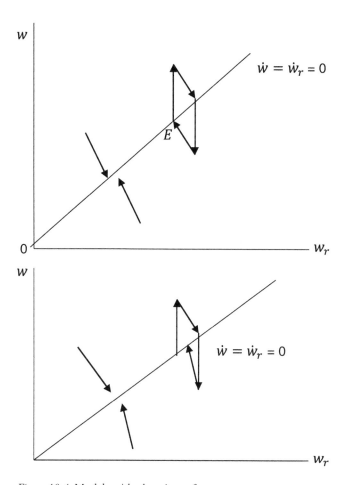

Figure 10.4 Models with changing reference wage.

be a more pronounced upward trend. Of course, even with slower downward adjustment in the reference wage, sufficiently strong and more frequent downward shocks can make the wage go down. Further complications can be added to this by taking into account the amount of time the economy stays at a particular wage that is different from the reference wage: the longer the period of time in which the wage is at a high (or low) level, the more will the reference wage rise (or fall). This captures the notion that longer-lasting changes imply a larger change in habits and social norms in response to a difference between the wage and the reference wage.

The implications of the dynamics of the wage and reference can be examined by embedding them in models of growth and distribution along CM and PKK lines. Since this chapter is about the theory of wages and distribution, and not about a model of the entire economy, that analysis, which also examines other determinants of wage change, and of technological change, can be left for another occasion.[22]

There are many relevant issues that are abstracted from for simplicity, that can and should be incorporated into this framework. One important issue is incorporating different kinds of labour each with possibly different wages. This is already implicit in the analysis of the models discussed above to the extent that the wage considered is that in the capitalist sector and/or what can be called the formal labour. However, it may be useful to explicitly analyse the cases of two or more kinds of workers, perhaps distinguishing between those with different skills levels, those in different sectors which produce different goods and services, those of different genders, race or ethnic groups, or other social differences and those with different kinds of social relations such as capitalist wage labour, the self-employed and state-owned enterprises.

6 Conclusion

The main conclusions of the chapter are:

1   Several, though not all, classical economists and Marx can be interpreted, with some justification, as assuming that distribution or the real wage is exogenous as a first approximation.

2   The fixed-wage assumption, as a starting point, does not imply that the wage does not change over time and space. Our discussion of the writings of Smith, Ricardo and Malthus and even some models formalising Malthus and Ricardo have allowed the wage to change over time.

3   Many heterodox models along classical-Marxian and post-Keynesian-Kaleckian lines also take the real wage or distribution to be exogenously given. However, several such models have endogenised the wage, and some theories have provided reasons for the fixity assumption, which explain changes more informally.

4   These approaches are quite consistent with the enormous rise in the wage that has occurred in many countries, and with large differences between the wages in different countries and regions.

5   Some reasons for changes in the wage have already been explained using formal models and additional issues can be formalised. The last was illustrated using the interaction of the actual (although theoretical) wage and the 'reference' wage, which draws on the ideas emphasised by the classical writers.

6   Differences in the duration of changes in the wage and the reasons for them need to be kept in mind for their different consequences. For instance, changes in the wage over business cycles can depend on some forces representing periodic changes in the tightness of labour market, as represented by the change in the unemployment rate, and longer cycles or secular trends representing changes in norms, power and technology (especially artificial intelligence and robotics), are more likely to

accompany changes in self-employment, the subsistence sector and the gig economy, rather than open unemployment. The appropriate societal responses to them may also be different.

We conclude by recognising that increases in wages, especially for workers who are already well-paid, and higher rates of growth of the economy, are not necessarily ethically desirable. Ever-increasing wages may reflect no improvements in need-fulfilment, but instead lead to conspicuous consumption and the keeping-up with the Joneses phenomenon, which does not improve the wellbeing of workers and lower-income people and even that of higher-income people who are likely to be more affected by (and concerned with) relative, rather than absolute, levels of income. Beyond a point changes social norms that increase consumption and wages are difficult to justify ethically. Moreover, they can lead to greater desire to increase private consumption at the expense of public provisioning and safety nets to reduce financial insecurities, which may be more beneficial and reduce the need for higher wages to maintain the same level of wellbeing. High levels of output and its growth and high and growing levels of consumption are also detrimental for the environment. Reductions in inequality between different classes and countries, between high income and low-income workers and the self-employed, and reductions in 'top' incomes are more desirable. Moreover, paradoxically, higher levels of wages and consumption are less likely to induce workers to collectively reduce inequality and improve their own conditions through political and social movements and by voting for appropriate government policy changes, since they have more to lose than their chains.

Acknowledgement

My friend Carlo Panico has made many important contributions to the history of economic thought and the theory of growth and distribution. I am very pleased to contribute this chapter, which lies at the intersection of these topics, to this volume honouring him. I am grateful to an anonymous referee and to Neri Salvadori for useful comments on an earlier draft.

Notes

1 Some theories take the wage share rather than the wage rate as exogenous. This implies that in them the rate of change of the wage is equal to the rate of growth of labour productivity. Since in most of this chapter we assume that techniques are fixed, the fixed wage and fixed wage share assumptions are equivalent. So, except where explicitly noted, we will refer to the fixed wage.

2 There is some debate about the definitions of neoclassical economics and heterodox economics. For the purposes of this chapter, we define the former as the approach that insists on using the optimising agent as the starting point (or an organising principle) of all analysis, and heterodox economics in the negative sense as comprising approaches that do not use such a starting point. Other definitions of neoclassical economics are also

possible, including those that assume that all agents are self-interested, there is perfect competition and no 'distortions' such as price and wage rigidities, or externalities or 'imperfect' information. Such an economy is seen as resulting in the full employment of all resources, including labour.

3 Although these are different concepts, for present purposes these differences need not detain us.

4 Lewis's (1954) model of the dual economy assumes that the capitalist sector's real wage is held constant at a low level by earnings in the subsistence sector.

5 Panico and his coauthors (Commendatore et al., 2003) provide a discussion and comparison of this and other models in which aggregate demand plays a major role.

6 This model is based on what Hicks (1985) call the original model based on the simplest version of Smith.

7 Malthus's own model is usually interpreted as introducing diminishing returns to labour (Dutt, 2016). This model reproduces another model in Dutt (2016), which is related to some other presentations of Malthus cited therein.

8 Ricardo's discussion actually involves two sectors – an agricultural and an industrial one – and is analysed by Pasinetti (1960) formally. Such multi-sector complications are not directly relevant to the focus of our analysis, that is, wages.

9 This model draws on Casarosa's model but analyses the dynamics graphically in the way that is done here, instead using shifting curves over time in growth rate of capital and labour and the wage space. Hicks and Hollander take the wage to be state variable, which our analysis does not, since the wage depends on K and N.

10 For a log-linear production function of the form $Y = BL^{\alpha}$, the elasticity of the marginal product of labour with respect to employment is equal to $(1 - \alpha)$ which is always less than one, so the line will always be negatively sloped.

11 It is straightforward to introduce a minimum profit rate below which capitalists will not save, in which case the stationary state occurs with a positive rate of profit equal to the minimum rate of profit.

12 The Jacobian matrix of the dynamic system is given by

$$\begin{bmatrix} -s & s[NF''(N) + F'(N)] \\ \frac{\theta}{N} & -K/N^2 \end{bmatrix}.$$

The trace is negative and the sign of the determinant depends on

$$\frac{K}{N} - NF''(N) + F'(N).$$

Since in long-run equilibrium or stationary state $w = \frac{K}{N} = F'(N)$ with $F''(N) < 0$, this expression is positive. Hence, the determinant is positive (in the neighbourhood of long-run equilibrium), the equilibrium is stable.

13 Various other cases can be considered. Marglin treats capital goods as goods that are used up in production, that is, an intermediate good. Some Sraffian models assume that workers are provided wage prior to production, so that capitalists have also to include wages as a part of capital. An interesting possibility is to combine the classical wage fund theory and the new approach with fixed capital which, for simplicity is non-depreciating. In this case with $Y = AL$, $K_C = Y/B$, $K_V = wL$ and $K = K_C + K_V$, where interpreting Marx's terminology loosely, K_C is constant or fixed capital and K_V is variable capital or the wage fund, we get

$$\widehat{K} = s\frac{A - w}{\dfrac{A}{B} + w}$$

in which the real wage is fixed. It has implications similar to both the neo-Marxian model of Section 2 and the Smithian model of Section 3.

14 Sometimes Ricardo mentions that the natural wage may change if the natural price of the necessary goods that workers buy increases, but for our purposes we ignore this complication in our one-good framework.

15 As noted by Rowthorn (1980), Marx's theory of the determination of wages, voluminous and scattered as they are went through two main stages: the first in his writings before the publication of the first volume of *Capital*, and the second after it.

16 For a more detailed analysis of Smith's analysis of the relative power of capitalists and workers, see Kurz (2018). Kurz also discusses some of Ricardo's views, although the latter's analysis of power is arguably more indirect and tenuous.

17 This is an issue discussed at greater length in Smith's (1759) discussion of sympathy or fellow-feeling.

18 See Opocher (2010) for a review of Mill's ideas and a mathematical formulation.

19 Our analysis therefore suggests that the surplus approach championed by Garegnani (1984) and others, which takes wages to be exogenously given, and interprets non-wage income, especially profits, as a surplus above wages, provides a better interpretation of the approach of the classical economists, which extends to Marx and many subsequent heterodox theories than does the supply-demand market-clearing interpretation which sees grater continuity between the later marginalists and neoclassical economists (see Hollander, 1987, which draws on his detailed studies of Smith, Malthus, Ricardo, Mill and Marx). This is irrespective of whether the wage is taken to be constant or variable.

20 Terms like 'natural' prices or wage, frequently used by the classical economists, are misleading and carry undesirable baggage. They are terminologically connected with the idea of natural law which, as Veblen (1898: 387) argues is connected with something that is related to the natural sciences or religion, suggests a law-like objective quality, or being ethically desirable.

21 We could add a similar ratchet effect to the wage change equation, with similar consequences.

22 For discussions of models of technical change along heterodox lines, see, for instance, Dutt (2013, 2017).

References

Casarosa, C. (1978). A new formulation of the Ricardian system. *Oxford Economic Papers* 30(1): 31–68.

Commendatore, P., D'Acunto, S., Panico, C. and Pinto, A. (2003). Keynesian theories of growth. In N. Salvadori (ed.), *The Theory of Economic Growth: A 'Classical' Perspective*, Cheltenham, UK: Edward Elgar.

Duesenberry, J. S. (1949). *Income, Saving, and the Theory of Consumer Behavior*. Cambridge, MA: Harvard University Press.

Duménil, G. and Lévy, D. (1999). Being Keynesian in the short term and classical in the long term: the traverse to classical long-term equilibrium. *Manchester School* 67(6): 684–716.

Dutt, A. K. (1984). Stagnation, income distribution and monopoly power. *Cambridge Journal of Economics* 8(1): 25–40.

Dutt, A. K. (1990). *Growth, Distribution and Uneven Development*. Cambridge, UK: Cambridge University Press.

Dutt, A. K. (2006). Aggregate demand, aggregate supply and economic growth. *International Review of Applied Economics* 20(3): 319–336.

Dutt, A. K. (2009). Happiness and the relative consumption effect. In A. K. Dutt and B. Radcliff (eds), *Happiness, Economics and Politics*. Cheltenham, UK: Edward Elgar.

Dutt, A. K. (2012). Distributional dynamics in post Keynesian models. *Journal of Post Keynesian Economics* 34(3): 431–451.

Dutt, A. K. (2013). Endogenous technological change in classical-Marxian models of growth and distribution. In T. Michl, A. Rezai and L. Taylor (eds), *Social Fairness and Economics. Economic Essays in the Spirit of Duncan Foley*. Abingdon, UK and New York: Routledge, pp. 264–285.

Dutt, A. K. (2016). What's left of Malthus? In G. Freni, H. D. Kurz, A. M. Lavezzi and R. Signorino (eds), *Economic Theory and Its History: Essays in Honour of Neri Salvadori*. London: Routledge, pp. 339–356.

Dutt, A. K. (2017). Heterodox theories of growth and distribution: a partial view. *Journal of Economic Surveys* 31(5): 335–351.

Dutt, A. K. (2021). Growth, inequality and power. In D. Basu and D. Das (eds), *Conflict, Demand and Economic Development, Essays in Honor of Amit Bhaduri*. London and New York: Routledge, pp. 25–43.

Foley, D., Michl, T. and Tavani, D. (2019). *Growth and Distribution*. 2nd ed. Cambridge, MA: Harvard University Press.

Frank, R. (1999). *Luxury Fever. Why Money Fails to Satisfy in an Era of Excess*. New York: The Free Press.

Garegnani, P. (1984). Value and distribution in the classical economists and Marx. *Oxford Economic Papers* 36: 291–325.

Goodwin, R. M. (1967). A growth cycle. In C. H. Feinstein (ed.), *Socialism, Capitalism and Growth*. Cambridge: Cambridge University Press, pp. 54–58.

Hicks, J. R. (1985). *Methods of Dynamic Economics*. Oxford, UK: The Clarendon Press.

Hicks, J. and Hollander, S. (1977). Mr. Ricardo and the moderns. *Quarterly Journal of Economics* 91(3): 351–369.

Hollander, S. (1987). *Classical Economics*. Oxford, UK: Basil Blackwell.

Kaldor, N. (1955–56). Alternative theories of distribution. *Review of Economic Studies* 23(2): 83–100.

Kalecki, M. (1971). *Selected Essays on the Dynamics of the Capitalist Economy*. Cambridge, UK: Cambridge University Press.

Kurz, H. (2015). David Ricardo: on the art of 'elucidating economic principles' in the fact of a 'labyrinth of difficulties'. *European Journal of the History of Economic Thought* 22(5): 818–851.

Kurz, H. (2018). Elements of a science of power: Hobbes, Smith and Ricardo. In M. Mosca (ed.), *Power in Economic Thought*. Cham, Switzerland: Palgrave.

Lewis, W. A. (1954). Economic development with unlimited supplies of labour. *Manchester School* 22(2): 139–191.

Malthus, T. R. (1798). *An Essay on the Principle of Population*. London: J. Johnson, St. Paul's Churchyard.

Marglin, S. A. (1984). *Growth, Distribution, and Prices*. Cambridge, USA: Harvard University Press.

Marx, K. (1865). *Wages, Price and Profit*. Peking: Foreign Languages Press, 1965.

Marx, K. (1869). *Capital*, Vol. 1. Eng. Tr. New York: Vintage Books, 1977.

Mill, J. S. (1848). *Principles of Political Economy with Some of Their Applications to Social Philosophy*. London: John W. Parker.

Opocher, A. (2010). Does economic growth ultimately lead to a nobler life? A mathematical formulation of Mill's stationary state. In J. Vint et al. (eds), *Economic Theory and Economic Thought: Essays in Honour of Ian Steedman*. Abingdon, UK: Routledge.

Pasinetti, L. (1960). A mathematical formulation of the Ricardian system. *Review of Economic Studies* 27(2): 78–98.

Ricardo, D. (1815). *An Essay on Profits*. London: John Murray.

Ricardo, D. (1817). On the principles of political economy and taxation. In P. Sraffa (ed.), *The Works and Correspondence of David Ricardo*, Vol. 1. Cambridge: Cambridge University Press, 1951.

Robinson, J. (1962). *Essays in the Theory of Economic Growth*. London: Macmillan.

Rowthorn, R. E. (1980). Marx's theory of wages. In R. E. Rowthorn (ed.), *Capitalism, Conflict and Inflation: Essays in Political Economy*. London: Lawrence and Wishart, pp. 182–230.

Skott, P. (1989). *Conflict and Effective Demand in Economic Growth*. Cambridge, UK:Cambridge University Press.

Serrano, F. (1995). Long period effective demand and the Sraffian supermultiplier. *Contributions to Political Economy* 14: 67–90.

Smith, A. (1776). *An Inquiry into the Nature and Causes of the Wealth of Nations*. W. B. Todd (ed.), Vol. 2 of *The Glasgow Edition of the Works and Correspondences of Adam Smith*, general editors, D. D. Raphael and A. Skinner. Oxford: Clarendon Press, 1976.

Smith, A. (1759). *The Theory of Moral Sentiments*. D. D. Raphael and A. L. Macfie (eds), Vol. 1 of *The Glasgow Edition of the Works and Correspondences of Adam Smith*, general editors, D. D. Raphael and A. Skinner. Oxford: Clarendon Press, 1976.

Stirati, A. (1994). *The Theory of Wages in Classical Economics: A Study of Adam Smith, David Ricardo, and Their Contemporaries*. Aldershot, UK: Edward Elgar.

Veblen, T. (1898). Why is economics not an evolutionary science? *Quarterly Journal of Economics* 12(4): 373–397.

Vianello, F. (1989). Natural (or normal) prices: some pointers. *Political Economy. Studies in the Surplus Approach* 5(2): 89–105.

11 On changes and differences

Joan Robinson vs Sraffa

Maria Cristina Marcuzzo

1 What is the question

Joan Robinson's possibly best-known *piéce de résistance* in her fierce opposition to orthodox economics, and to some respects, also to her allies in the battle against the neoclassicals, is her rejection of equilibrium economics. Her attack on the notion of equilibrium was long-dated. It can be traced back to the booklet she published in 1953, a collection of three short essays, *On Re-reading Marx*, which, she said, were 'written in a hilarious mood after reading Piero Sraffa's Introduction to Ricardo's Principles' (Robinson [1953] 1973a: 247). In fact, far from being in a hilarious mood, Robinson was in the midst of one of her manic-depressive crises, for which she was hospitalised for several weeks, when she wrote these essays. She explained to Kahn, who tried to persuade her not to publish them: 'I want to have the family joke about Piero. I cannot pinch 20 years of his life's work without acknowledgement and acknowledgement in a joke is the only way I can do it' (Joan Robinson to Richard Kahn, 28 October 1952; Marcuzzo, 2003, 2005).

The second step is her famous article Robinson ([1954] 1978c), which is widely regarded as the starting point of the capital theory controversies. She pointed to the neoclassical failure to distinguish between changes in the conditions of producing a given output, when the quantity of capital is altered, from changes in the value of that capital due to variations in wages and profits. The implication she drew was that 'different factor ratios cannot be used to analyse changes in the factor ratio taking place through time', because in time the value of the quantity of capital may change as a consequence of a change in distribution and we will not be comparing the same quantities. She concluded that 'it is impossible to discuss changes (as opposed to differences) in neo-classical terms' ([1954] 1978: 89). It follows that equilibrium positions could only be compared as differences and never described as changes from one position to another.

However, at the time of the 1954 article, Robinson still considered comparisons between two equilibrium positions, as opposed to movement from one position to another, a legitimate exercise, which she later repudiated in her attack on the equilibrium method, rejecting it *tout court*. It was the critique

DOI: 10.4324/9781003105558-13

of the concept of equilibrium itself, and not only of neoclassical equilibrium, which she took as the main line of attack on the neoclassical theory, and which led her to insist that the point was the distinction between historical time and logical time (Robinson, 1979a: xiv), not between two alternative explanations of prices and distribution.

The publication of *Production of Commodities by Means of Commodities* left most people baffled on the nature of its message, but found Robinson readier than others to grasp some important aspects, albeit in her own way. An un-published letter to Piero Sraffa shows that she was aware that her under-standing of it was not shared by Sraffa:

> When I went off my head I thought that the idea that I had seen in a blinding flash was yours, because it came to me in terms of Ricardo's corn economy; but it was connected with TIME and it now appears is very much alien to your point of view (though to me it seems to fit perfectly well). (Joan Robinson to Piero Sraffa, 18 June 1960; Marcuzzo, 2004)

However, she came to believe that also Sraffa's system was vitiated by falling into the equilibrium method, because it was also set in logical time, unlike Keynes's system which was set in historical time thanks to the short-period approach.

Sraffa never took up this argument. But both Garegnani and Bharadwaj, who were very close to Sraffa, did. Garegnani retorted to Robinson that the assumption of irreversibility in time is implicit only in the method of supply and demand analysis, whereby the tendency towards equilibrium is described as movements along those curves, while the same assumption is not made when comparing two long-run positions determined by a 'classical' theory of prices and distribution (Garegnani, 1979). Bharadwaj agreed with Robinson that history, namely the process involving actual and irreversible as opposed to potential and reversible changes, has to be rescued from neoclassical theory and brought back into economic analysis (Marcuzzo, 2014). She defended the method of comparison between long-term positions as legitimate method of analysis of change, arguing that, on the contrary, the role of change in supply-and-demand theories is to guarantee convergence towards equilibrium and must therefore be conceived as following a well-specified path. Thus, the direction of change required (i.e. the assumption that demand and supply are well-behaved functions) imposes 'constraints which operate against an effec-tive handling of problems of change' (Bharadwaj, 1986: 3).

The question revolves around how change is handled in a framework of equilibrium – as in neoclassical theories – and in long-run positions in the classical political economy approach. While Sraffa and his followers claimed that there is a profound difference between the two, Robinson was of the opposite view, objecting to the method of comparisons in classical political economy and Sraffa because they showed no substantial difference from the neoclassical equilibrium method in their neglect of 'historical' time. These two opposite views are at the core of the dispute between Neo-Ricardians and Post-Keynesians and while I personally side with Garegnani and Bharadwaj in claiming the difference between neoclassical equilibrium and long-run positions, I admit that Robinson has point on the need to better specify the mechanism which may prevent the system end up in a fully adjusted position.

2 Sraffa on the notion of change in economics

Thus, the crux of the matter is whether long-period *positions*, unlike long-period *equilibria*, are equipped to deal with the question of changes in time and not just differences at a given moment of time. As we know, Sraffa never wrote that his production prices were attractors of market prices, nor described the actual mechanism which enforces the equalisation of the rate of profit. On the other hand, many interpreters now agree that what *Production of Commodities* offers is just a photograph[1] that captures the system as it actually is at a given instant in time, while there is no analysis of change or time analysis.

This interpretation – suggested by Sraffa's himself – is that his entire research project is a struggle to escape from 'mechanical', i.e. causal theory, and to develop a 'geometrical' representation of the economic system. In fact, he dedicated a lot of hard thinking to the question of how change is conceptualised in economics.[2] Sraffa was early convinced that in economics there is the need to distinguish between situations in which change is necessary to construct the elements of the theory and those in which it is not required, because the analysis is conducted in terms of differences that co-exist in the same instant. There are in fact two types of change, those which involve the passage time and those which do not. See the annotation by Sraffa dated October 1929:

> [The following] notion of time is important: it really substitutes 'instantaneous photographs' as opposed to ordinary time. It is only a part of ordinary time, it has only some of its connotations: it includes events, also different events, but no change of events. It enables us to compare two simultaneous, but not instantaneous, events – just as if they were 'things'. (Sraffa Paper D3/12/13: 1.3, emphasis added)

This analysis remained buried in Sraffa's manuscripts, but it surfaced – in a different context and much later – in the Introduction to Ricardo's *Principles* which as, we have seen, caught Robinson's attention. Sraffa explicitly referred to 'the two points of view of difference and of change' (Sraffa, 1951: xlix) to distinguish between real and apparent change. The distinction lies behind the question of how to measure 'the magnitude of aggregate of commodities' in order to study the distribution of surplus: there *seems* to be a change in the quantity of output to be distributed whenever there is a change in its value due to a change either in wages or in profits. However, this is an *apparent* change, since the conditions of production of the commodities and the quantities produced remain the same. It is the kind of change studied in *Production of Commodities* when analysing the effects on prices of a change in distribution, not to be confused with effects deriving from the introduction of the time factor, which in fact are not considered in the book.

In the Introduction to Ricardo's *Principles*, the distinction between difference and change is employed by Sraffa to distinguish two different aspects of the effects on the relative value of two commodities of different proportions or capital goods characterised by different durability employed in their production:

> [the first aspect] is that of occasioning a *difference* in the relative values of two commodities which are produced by equal quantities of labour. Second, that of the effect which a rise of wages has in producing a *change* in their relative value. (Sraffa, 1951: xlvii)

Summing up, while for Sraffa all questions relating to change imply the passage of time, there are questions that can be discussed in a timeless framework, as differences existing in a given moment of time.

3 The false analogy with mechanics

Interestingly, both Robinson and Sraffa were against adoption of the method of classical mechanics in economics, although their arguments differed and, more importantly, led them to draw different implications. Robinson wrote:

> the mechanical analogy is inappropriate in economic analysis. For mechanical movements in space, there is no distinction between approaching equilibrium from an arbitrary position and a perturbation due to displacement from an equilibrium that has long been established. In economic life, in which decisions are guided by expectations about the future, these two types of movement are totally different. (Robinson [1974] 1979b: 49)

When a change occurs 'to find a new equilibrium (if there is one) we have to fill in a whole story about the behaviour of the economy when it is out of equilibrium' (Robinson [1974] 1979b: 52).

The false analogy lies in assuming that comparing two equilibrium positions is equivalent to describing the movement from one position to the other; the changes necessary to reach another equilibrium cannot be assumed to occur by default; they require a whole set of behavioural assumptions, for Robinson mainly the state of expectations, but more generally the assumption of existence of a well-defined path.

On the other hand, Sraffa's point was that while the geometrical theory refers to an instant in time, the mechanical theory refers to processes that happen in real time, in which causality is involved (Marcuzzo and Rosselli, 2021). Sraffa wrote:

... in mechanics if the experiment is repeated in similar circumstances (say, on the elasticity of a metal) the same results will be obtained. But with supply and demand, even if the external circumstances were the same, the result would be different because man learns from experience, or at any rate is changed by it, forms and transforms habits, etc. (D3/12/42: 11 recto)

See also his comment in a note of Summer 1927:

... the main stream of modern economic thought proceeds to analyse the ways in which change takes place, without being hindered by the fact that little is known of the ultimate causes of change. (D3/12/3: 14)

Here Sraffa is making a distinction between the notions of 'ultimate cause' and 'mechanical cause', by associating the Classical with the notion of 'ultimate cause' and the Modern with the 'mechanical cause'.

Sraffa's objections to the notion of causality in economics, or at least the notion of causality borrowed from classical mechanics, concerned the time-change-cause nexus. Observed phenomena could be traced back to a given cause only if we could observe the 'forces' that produced that effect, but this presupposes going back in time to produce a change in the existing situation. However, this would mean that we could never be sure that we would be observing the same phenomena because when time is involved, the *ceteris paribus* clause does not apply. However, this does not mean that we cannot study situations following a change, for instance in a given variable (wage or profit), although we can only do so as long as these changes have no time dimension, and are merely a logical derivation.

4 Short-period analysis

Robinson championed the short-period method as more suitable to address issues set in historical time; it may be useful to review the origin and nature of this concept in the Cambridge tradition.

Its origin is certainly in Marshall, but it was revived by Kahn and adopted by Keynes in the *General Theory*, prompting Dennis Robertson, in a letter to Keynes, to refer to it as 'your and Kahn's s[hort] p[eriod] method' (CWK XXIX: 17).

Marshall's distinction between short period and long period is based on the *nature of the decisions* involved, which reflects what individuals take as given and what they expect in different periods of time. See the following passage:

For short periods people take the stocks of appliances of production as practically fixed; and they are governed by their expectations of demand in considering how actively they shall set themselves to work those appliances. In long periods they set themselves to adjust the flow of these appliances to their expectations of demand for the goods which the appliances help to produce. (Marshall [1920] 1961: 310–11)

It is the nature of the *decisions* involved, characterised by the time horizon to which they apply, that sets the boundary between the long and the short period. Accordingly, economic theory can take as constant those factors over which decision can be postponed and take them as variables only when describing situations in which they are a matter of decision by economic agents.

From Marshall's definition of short period, Kahn drew a further implication. He noticed that the possibility of considering machinery and the organisation of production as constant from the point of view of the short period arises from the fact that in both cases the decision to alter them is the same and depends on whether demand conditions are or are not considered 'normal'. Accordingly, depending upon whether changes in demand are *believed* by entrepreneurs to be transitory or permanent, as compared with the level considered as normal, the decisions to modify the plant or the organisation will or will not be taken. Although the short period cannot be 'shorter' than the length of the productive process or longer than the time necessary to modify productive capacity, the time necessary to modify productive capacity depends not only on technological factors but also on the prevailing conditions – depression or boom – which mould expectations regarding the return to 'normal' conditions of demand. Thus, for Kahn, the nature of the short period is seen not as a conceptual experiment but as a matter of fact, namely that the life of fixed capital is considerably longer than the period of production (Kahn, 1932: ch. 2, p. 2; 1989: xiii).

According to Kahn, in fact, the 'ideal' short period is defined as a situation where 'any change that occurs is not expected to be permanent' (Kahn, 1932: ch. 2, p. 10). What matters are expectations regarding the normal value of the level of demand which will induce entrepreneurs to change the level of capacity (a long-period configuration) rather than its degree of utilisation (a short-period configuration). The conditions prevailing in the economy – depression or boom – mould expectations of return to normal conditions of demand and introduce an asymmetry in the length of the short period. In a boom, short-period equilibrium implies that expectations are such that increasing production, at higher costs, is preferred to building up capacity until the increase in demand is confidently perceived as 'permanent'; the short period, however, can be very short and innovations are introduced rapidly. In a depression, short-period equilibrium implies expectations that demand will return to its normal level; in this case, the short period can last decades if the firm survives (at a loss) while its physical capital is decaying.

It follows that the short period need not be a 'short' time interval, nor is it a transitory state before the long-period forces work out their effects. It is, rather, a position which is maintained as long as the set of decisions depending upon the expected level of demand does not change.

It was in fact Keynes who further developed short-period analysis with the more general purpose of accounting for decisions taken under different conditions of knowledge; These different conditions are manifested in what individuals expect in any given situation, and such expectations typically differ from individual to individual. The role assigned to expectations in *The General Theory* is to account for the possibility of an equilibrium at less than full employment. This equilibrium is not described as a situation characterised by 'wrong' expectations since 'the theory of effective demand is substantially the same if we assume that short-period expectations are always fulfilled' (CWK VII: 181). Thus, the short period is not a situation where expectations are not fulfilled, but a situation in which expectations generate 'a state of things' which conforms to them.

This was Robinson's verdict: 'The Keynesian revolution destroyed the basis of [the] concept of long-period equilibrium and put nothing in its place' (Robinson, 1980a: 130).

5 The debate against and in defence of long-period analysis

Robinson fully endorsed the point about short period analysis in the Marshall-Kahn-Keynes line of thought, namely that 'decisions are being taken today on the basis of expectations about the future' (Robinson [1971] 1973b: 96).

In a short period, there is no correct foresight:

> there are individual expectations which need not be consistent with each other and which may turn out later to have been mistaken ... The consequent interaction of individual decisions is seen in the total composition and prices of the total flow of output and its distribution. (Robinson, 1980b: 89–90)

On the contrary, a long-period approach – in which correct foresight regarding output composition and the pattern of prices which maximise profits is the fundamental assumption – is timeless analysis in total disregard of uncertainty and expectations, which are the guiding forces of economic behaviour.

However, Robinson's praise of the short-period approach contrasts sharply with her concern with issues relating to accumulation and technical progress, to which she was drawn very early in the development of her thought in the many attempts to extend the *General Theory* to the long period. Actually, she always claimed that by setting the conditions under which long-period equilibrium would obtain, she did not imply that the system has an inbuilt mechanism to return there after it has been displaced by an external shock. In other words, with this type of analysis we can tell nothing about the effects of unanticipated changes taking place in actual historical time. Robinson's s point was that under conditions of uncertainty, the price-forming process typical of capitalism does not maintain equilibrium and any model which shows that equilibrium could be maintained under the assumption of perfect foresight 'deprives [the] exercise of application and reduces it to a mere pastime' (Robinson [1959] 1964: 141). She wrote:

long-period equilibrium is not at some date in the future; it is an imaginary state of affairs in which there are no incompatibilities in the existing situation, here and now. (Robinson [1962] 1965: 101)

The point came up again during the capital controversy, when she again rejected the notion that in the face of change – which means that expectations are falsified – equilibrium can be maintained. In conclusion, As Gram and Walsh reminded us:

> For Robinson, long run-equilibrium is significant, not as the outcome of a process of getting into equilibrium, but rather as a concept defining a class of models in which it is conceivable that expectations could be realized and therefore continually renewed as the driving force behind the behaviour whose outcome the model depicts. Thus, in a steady state the future is sufficiently simple, relative to the past, to suppose that consistent, realizable expectations exist without assuming perfect foresight (or its stochastic counterpart) and "without being obliged to deprive [anyone] of Free Will". (Robinson, 1979a: 129; Gram and Walsh, 1983: 531)

A related issue is the absence in Sraffa of any role given to expectations, which are seen by Robinson as highly relevant to the question of long-run equilibrium and lay at the centre of debate with Bharadwaj, who made two objections to Robinson's criticism of the equilibrium (in the sense of the long-term position) method. First, a meaningful conceptualisation of the equilibrium concept does not entail that the corresponding prices and the uniform rate of profit actually rule at any particular moment in time. It is rather the tendency towards it, driven by the forces believed to be 'persistent', that is argued for.

Second, it is not denied that uncertainty of expectations has a role to play, but rather that:

> We need to discover [the] objective basis of different states of expectations and we need to know what systematic objective outcomes arise from these different states of expectations. (Bharadwaj, 1991: 95–6)

The point being made by Bharadwaj is that since expectations work in patterns, because imitation and mutuality play an important role, 'broadly uniform behaviour' (ibid.) can be detected and should be made part of the analysis. Thus, the emphasis on the 'objective basis' is to be interpreted as refusal to appeal to non-observable entities, and instead to look to custom, social norms and the like.

This debate on expectations is revealing of a fundamental methodological difference between the approach taken by Joan Robinson (following Kahn and Keynes) and Garegnani and Bharadwaj (following in the footsteps of Sraffa).

Sraffa rejected the idea that unobservable entities like utility, expectations and beliefs could be modelled *as if* they were observable quantities. He went so far as to expunge them from analysis, while Marshall, Keynes, Kahn and Robinson thought they should be part of it. This reflects the different sources their theories were drawn from, which explains why they lead to irreconcilable views on how to account for prices and distribution. Marshall, Kahn and Keynes thought subjective elements – identified with unbounded maximising rationality – need to be part of the *explanans* of the decision-making mechanism that lies behind market outcomes. Sraffa did not deem it necessary as far the price mechanism was concerned, but left open the possibility that norms and customs, embodying non-observable entities, exercise their influence in other parts of the analysis. However, it may be not entirely true that in Sraffa there is no role given to expectations, since an economy able to reproduce itself, year after years, as that analysed by Sraffa in the first chapters of *Production of Commodities* is likely to be a good environment for individual expectations to generate 'a state of things' which conforms to them.

Although in the 'Cambridge' approach decision-making under uncertainty, opinion formation and subjective evaluation of future events are said to be essential elements while Sraffa placed the emphasis on the 'objective basis' of price and distribution determination, the two approaches seem far less distant from one another when it comes to the role attributed to routines, customs and socially given constraints (Marcuzzo, 2020).

6 Concluding remarks

Very early in her work, Robinson had exposed the inadequacy of equilibrium in dealing with the passing of time – which is irreversible – as if it were a movement in space. As she made clearer later on:

> The concept of equilibrium is incompatible with history. It is a metaphor based on movements in space applied to processes taking place in time. In space, it is possible to go to and fro and remedy misdirection, but in time, every day, the past is irrevocable and the future unknown. (Robinson, 1979b: xiv)

She saw the main line of attack on the neoclassical theory as lying not between two alternative explanations of prices and distribution, as Sraffa's followers had it. In fact, she objected that in Sraffa:

> there is no room here for short-period "Keynesian" movements in the level of utilisation of stocks of inputs or employment of labour. The language of change may be used, for it is difficult to describe a map without using the language of moving about on it, but essentially the argument is conducted strictly in terms of comparisons of logically possible positions. (Robinson, 1980a: 132)

There are two separate issues here: one is the legitimacy of comparison of two positions, (neoclassical) equilibrium or (classical) long-run; and the other which of these two approaches is better equipped to study the movement or the change from one resting point to another. Moreover, there is also the question of how 'historical' as opposed 'logical' time to use Robinson's favourite expression can be brought in the analysis.

Her distinction is based on the assumption that there are two types of economic argument in one, the procedure is to specify 'a sufficient number of equations to determine its unknowns, and so [find] values for them that are compatible with each other' (Robinson, 1964: 23). The other is to specify 'a particular set of values [of the variables] obtaining at a moment in time which are not, in general, in equilibrium with each other, and [to show] that their interactions may be expected to play themselves out' (ibid). These two procedures lead to two different types of models. As Gram and Walsh (1983: 531) pointed out:

> The first type of model, if it moves at all, moves in logical time: the effect of differences in the underlying data can be analysed, but change cannot. The second type of model moves in historical time since it is capable of getting out of equilibrium and can therefore be used to analyse the effect of change taking place in a given short period.

The distinction between changes and differences had different meanings and implications for Sraffa and Robinson. For Robinson, it implied rejection of the concept of equilibrium itself, while for Sraffa it meant abandonment of the neoclassical equilibrium. However, since in the system presented in *Production of Commodities* there is no room for change, so that only differences can be made the object of analysis, Robinson's argument about the impossibility of 'moving' from any equilibrium, of whatever type, to another may not be entirely beside the point.

The reasons why this is so, are of course, different in the case of neoclassical equilibrium and Sraffa's snapshot of the economic system. In the neoclassical case it has to do with the difficulties arising from the theory of distribution, based on supply and demand of factors of production, while in the case of Sraffa there is no specified path which the economy will necessarily follow when the configuration of input–output and the distributive variables change. We will be comparing two different snapshots side by side, not the sequence of events leading from one configuration to another.

In her timely review of *Production of Commodities* ([1961] 1965: 9) she got it right:

> The main problem [is] the effect upon process of changes in the division of the surplus between wages and profits ... The wages 'changes' only in the sense that the value of x changes as we run our eye up and down a curve ... we need not to take the word 'change' literally. We are only *to compare* the effects of having different rates of profit, with the same technical conditions and the same composition of output.

However, she went on to believe that Sraffa's analysis was not free from the problems (mainly disregard of expectations) of any long-period approach. This may or may not be a shared opinion among scholars, but it bears witness to Pasinetti's conclusion that 'Joan Robinson tried very hard to assimilate the most important propositions of *Production of Commodities*, but I believe she has not been quite successful' (Pasinetti [1985] 1998: 79).

Notes

1 The first to employ the 'snapshot' metaphor was Roncaglia in his 1975 Italian book, translated into English as Roncaglia (1978). For a more recent restatement of his interpretation of Sraffa's approach, see Roncaglia (2009). On the evidence of Sraffa's reference to the snapshot, see Kurz and Salvadori (2018).
2 In one of the manuscripts of the period 1927–28, possibly where mention of the 'Difference (simultaneous) versus Change (succession in time)' first occurs, Sraffa wrote:

> The general confusion in all theories of value [...] must be explained by the failure to distinguish between two entirely distinct types of questions and the universal attempt of solving them both by one single theory. The two questions are:

> 1. what determines the [difference in the?] values at which various commodities are exchanged in a given market on a given instant?
> 2. what determines the changes in the values of commodities at different times? (e.g. of one commodity). (D3/ 12/ 7: 115; emphasis in the original)

And he continues:

> The first problem gives rise to a geometrical theory, the second to a mechanical one. The first is so much timeless that it cannot even be called statical. It does not represent an ideal stationary state in which it is assumed that no change takes place: but it represents a situation at one instant of time, that is to say something indistinguishable from a real state of things in such a short period of time that no visible movement takes place. Its object is, as it were, the photograph of a market place ... Marshall's theory of value, with its increasing and diminishing costs and marg[inal] utility, scissors, pillars and forces, can only be understood as an attempt to solve the first question in terms of the second. (D3/12/7:117)

The same point, but related to the theory of distribution, was reiterated more than 30 years later in one of the many extant drafts of the Preface to *Production of Commodities* (D3/12/13: 23.2).

References

Bharadwaj, K. (1986). *Classical Political Economy and the Rise to Dominance of Supply and Demand Theories*. 2nd ed. Calcutta: Orient Longmans.

Bharadwaj, K. (1991). History versus equilibrium. In I. Rima (ed.), *The Joan Robinson Legacy*. Armok: Sharpe, pp. 80–103.

Garegnani, P. A. (1979). Notes on consumption, investment and effective demand: a reply to Joan Robinson. *Cambridge Journal of Economics* 3: 181–187.

Gram, H. and Walsh, V. (1983). Joan Robinson's economics in retrospect. *Journal of Economic Literature* 21(2): 518–550.

Kahn, R. F. (1932). The economics of the short period. Unpublished manuscript in Kahn papers. Cambridge: King's College.

Kahn, R. F. (1989). *The Economics of the Short Period*. London: Macmillan.

Keynes, J. M. (1971–89). *The Collected Writings of John Maynard Keynes* (CWK). Edited by D. E. Moggridge. London: Macmillan.

Keynes, J. M. (1971 [1936]). *The General Theory of Employment, Interest, and Money*. CWK VII, London: Macmillan.

Keynes J. M. (1979). *The General Theory and After. A Supplement*. CWK XXIX, London: Macmillan.

Kurz, H. and Salvadori, N. (2018). On the "photograph" interpretation of Piero Sraffa's production equations: a view from the Sraffa archive. In J. Kregel, M. Corsi and C. D'Ippoliti (eds), *Classical Economics Today*. London and New York: Anthem Press, pp. 113–128.

Marcuzzo, M. C. (2003). Joan Robinson and the three Cambridge revolutions. *Review of Political Economy* 15(4): 545–560.

Marcuzzo, M. C. (2005). Robinson and Sraffa. In B. Gibson (ed.), *The Economic Legacy of Joan Robinson*. Cheltenham: Elgar, pp. 29–42.

Marcuzzo, M. C. (2014). On alternative notions of change and choice. Krishna Bharadwaj's legacy. *Cambridge Journal of Economics* 38(1): 49–62.

Marcuzzo, M. C. (2020), Expectations, conjectures and beliefs: the legacy of Marshall, Kahn and Keynes. In A. Arnon, W. Young and K. Van Der Beek (eds), *Expectations: Theory and Applications from Historical Perspectives*. Springer, pp. 53–67, Switzerland AG.

Marcuzzo, M-C. and Rosselli, A. (2021). On Sraffa's challenge to causality in economics. In A. Sinha (ed.), *A Reflection on Sraffa's Revolution in Economic Theory*. Palgrave Macmillan, London, UK, pp. 91–109.

Marshall, A. ([1920] 1961). *Principles of Economics*. 9th ed. London: Macmillan.

Pasinetti, L. ([1985] 1998). Piero Sraffa: an Italian economist at Cambridge. In L. Pasinetti (ed.), *Italian Economic Papers, Vol III*. Bologna: Il Mulino and Oxford University Press, pp. 365–382.

Robinson, J. V. ([1953] 1973a). Essays 1953: introduction. In *Collected Economic Papers*, Vol. IV. Oxford, Blackwell, pp. 247–248.

Robinson, J. V. ([1954] 1978c). The production function and the theory of capital. In *Contributions to Modern Economics*. Oxford: Blackwell, pp. 76–90.

Robinson, J. V. ([1959] 1964). Accumulation and the production function. In *Collected Economic Papers*, Vol. II. Oxford: Blackwell, pp. 132–144.

Robinson, J. V. ([1961] 1965). Prelude to a critique of economic theory. In *Collected Economic Papers*, Vol. III. Oxford: Blackwell, pp. 7–14.

Robinson, J. V. ([1962] 1965). The general theory after twenty-five years. In *Collected Economic Papers*, Vol. III. Oxford: Blackwell, pp. 100–102.

Robinson, J. V. (1964). *Essays in the Theory of Economic Growth*. London: Macmillan.

Robinson, J. V. ([1971] 1973b). The second crisis of economic theory. In *Collected Economic Papers*, Vol. IV. Oxford: Blackwell, pp. 92–105.

Robinson, J. V. (1978). *Contributions to Modern Economics*. Oxford: Blackwell.

Robinson, J. V. (1979a). *The Generalization of the General Theory and other Essays*. London: Macmillan.

Robinson, J. V. (1979b). *Collected Economic Papers*, Vol V. Oxford: Blackwell, pp. 48–58.

Robinson, J. V. (1980a). Retrospect: 1980. In *Further Contributions to Modern Economics*. Oxford: Blackwell, pp. 131–134.

Robinson, J. V. (1980b). Time in economic theory. In *Further Contributions to Modern Economics*. Oxford: Blackwell, pp. 86–95.

Roncaglia, A. (1978). *Sraffa and the Theory of Prices*. Chichester: Wiley.

Roncaglia, A. (2009). *Piero Sraffa and His Life, Thought and Cultural Heritage*. London: Routledge.

Sraffa, P. (1951). Introduction to D. Ricardo. In P. Sraffa (ed.) with the collaboration of M. Dobb, *The Works and Correspondence of David Ricardo, Vol. I. Principles of Political Economy and Taxation*. Cambridge: Cambridge University Press.

12 Behavioural changes and distribution effects in a Pasinetti-Solow model

Pasquale Commendatore, Ingrid Kubin, and Iryna Sushko

1 Introduction

Following Piketty's (2014), issues of distribution have regained centre stage, with a particular emphasis on the long-run evolution of wealth distribution. This seminal contribution triggered many empirical papers, corroborating and extending its findings.

At the same time, a stream of papers developed theoretical arguments, among them recent contributions by Stiglitz (2015a, 2015b, 2015c, 2015d) assuming a preminent position. Stiglitz investigates how standard growth models in the Solow tradition can (or cannot) account for Piketty's (2014) findings. His main conclusion actually is that Piketty's new stylised facts can only be accounted for when acknowledging that his notion of wealth goes beyond that of productive capital used in a textbook Solow model. Stiglitz's most important suggestion is to extend the Solow growth model to account for (possibly increasing) monopoly rents (coming from various sources).

Nevertheless, Stiglitz (2015c; and similarly Mattauch et al., 2016, 2018) also evaluates the explanatory power of the Solow model, reducing the notion of wealth again to productive capital and using a Solow growth model with class-specific savings behaviour as workhorse. In that model, workers follow a life cycle savings motive, whereas capitalists follow a dynastic savings motive. Interestingly, Stiglitz (2015c), extending the model to account for behavioural changes in savings motive, mentions that: If sufficiently rich, workers might start to imitate capitalists' behaviour. However, he does not elaborate this idea. In addition, all his analysis focuses on stationary states.

This is where our chapter kicks in: We show how shifts in the saving behaviour of workers affect long-term capital accumulation and wealth distribution in an economy inhabited by different social classes. Indeed, the issue of how the saving choices of separate social classes and different institutional settings may affect long-run distribution and growth has been one of the main themes in the research program of Carlo Panico, whose work has inspired the early career of two of the authors. In our analysis, we pay special attention to the dynamic analysis, since the stability of the fixed points cannot be taken as granted and more complex attractors have to be accounted for.

DOI: 10.4324/9781003105558-14

The introduction of heterogeneous saving behaviour in a model of growth has a long tradition. It was first proposed by Kaldor (1955–56) in order to solve the Harrod-Domar dilemma (Harrod, 1939; Domar, 1946) concerning the 'knife edge' stability condition of their model of capital accumulation. Put it simply, stability in the Harrod-Domar growth model requires that the rate of growth of population, the 'natural' rate of growth, is equal to the average saving propensity of the economy divided by the capital/output ratio, the 'warranted' rate of growth. Being all three parameters fixed, this equality only occurs by chance. According to Kaldor (1955–56), because of institutional and behavioural aspects, households saving behaviour may differ depending on the income source.[1] As a consequence, they may attach different saving propensities to wages and profits. Changes in income distribution, thus, modify the average propensity to save of the economy allowing the adjustment of the warranted to the natural rate of growth. Solow (1956) proposes an alternative solution to the Harrod-Domar dilemma by introducing a neoclassical technology (exemplified by a Cobb-Douglas production function) and a flexible capital/output ratio. Pasinetti (1962) reformulates Kaldor's analysis by modifying the socioeconomic set-up. Differences in saving behaviour are motivated by individuals belonging to different social classes, workers and capitalists. In this two-class economy, different saving propensities are attached to different groups of agents. Both Kaldor (1955-56) and Pasinetti's (1962) results downplayed the importance of technology and stressed that of institutional and socioeconomic factors in determining income distribution between classes (Pasinetti, 1962) or categories of income (Kaldor, 1955–56).

These contributions originated an intense debate, taking place during the sixties and the seventies of the last century, on the theory of growth and distribution between neoclassical and post-Keynesian authors. The main dispute was on the role of heterogeneous saving behaviour and of technology in shaping wealth distribution along the stationary path of the economy. Samuelson and Modigliani (1966) and other neoclassical economists reacted by extending the Solow (1956) model along Pasinettian lines providing also a more complete analysis of the long-run stationary solutions. They showed that Pasinetti-Solow models can generate two different sustainable long-run outcomes. In a Pasinetti equilibrium, post-Keynesian results prevail: both social classes, workers and capitalists, own capital; the stationary rate of profit does not depend on technology and on workers' propensity to save; the distribution between wages and profits is completely governed by capitalists' propensity to save. Workers' decisions concerning savings only affect the distribution between classes. In the alternative outcome, the dual equilibrium, neoclassical results prevail: it is not possible to distinguish a separate capitalist class – that is, we are back to a one-class economy as in Solow (1956) – and technology regains centrality in the determination of the rate of profit and of the income distribution between wages and profits. An important upshot of the discussion is that the long-run configuration of the economy crucially depends on the saving propensities of the two classes. A sufficiently high saving propensity of workers not only could lead to redistribution in favour of that class but also to the prevalence of a dual equilibrium.

The subsequent literature extended two-class growth models in several directions: for example, by allowing workers saving behaviour to be influenced by the type of income, combining the approaches of Kaldor and Pasinetti (Chiang, 1973; Fazi and Salvadori, 1981, 1985; Pasinetti, 1983; Salvadori, 1991); by introducing a government sector and public debt (Steedman, 1972; Fleck and Domenghino, 1987; Panico, 1993, 1997; Commendatore, 1993); by including a monetary sector and financial activities (Ramanathan, 1976; Panico, 1993; Palley, 1996, 2002; Commendatore, 2002; Park, 2006) and so on.[2]

These models have also been extended to incorporate optimising behaviour in order to explain the saving decisions of the two classes. Broadly, two are the approaches that can be found in the literature. According to some authors (Foley and Michl, 1999; Michl, 2009), following a Classical approach, workers and capitalists behave differently due to socioeconomic factors. Workers may save according to a life-cycle hypothesis – taking decisions according to a temporal structure similar to Diamond (1965) – and capitalists choices are driven by some legacy principle – an individual capitalist being modelled as an infinitely lived dynasty as in Ramsey (1928) or, following Barro (1974), as driven by an altruistic motive. According to others (Baranzini, 1991), there is not a qualitative difference between workers and capitalists saving behaviour, both following the same intertemporal consumption optimisation scheme characterised by some form of altruism.[3]

Quite recently, some contributions have explored, in a discrete-time framework, the long-term properties of Pasinetti-Solow models outside the stationary equilibrium path. For the case of exogenous saving propensities, Böhm and Kaas (2000) assume a Kaldorian saving function, with different propensities to save out of profits and wages, and a concave production function with general properties (satisfying the weak Inada conditions), but limit their analysis to a one-class economy. Commendatore (2008) considers, instead, a two-class economy and a production function with constant elasticity of substitution. For the case of optimising saving behaviour, Commendatore and Palmisani (2009) describe workers and capitalists saving choices on the basis of a Classical approach according to which saving behaviour of individuals is highly influenced by the social class to which they belong; in Agliari, Böhm and Pecora (2020) altruism and the bequest motive play a role for both workers and capitalists. Finally, in Sushko, Commendatore and Kubin (2020), capitalists always take their saving decisions on the basis of a legacy motive, behaving altruistically and leaving bequests; while workers follow two behavioural patterns: if their wealth is low, their saving behaviour follows a life-cycle pattern; instead, if their wealth rises above some threshold, they change their behaviour in two directions: when old they begin imitating capitalists social class behaviour leaving bequests to the young generation, the latter as beneficiary may also alter how to discount present and future consumption.

Some interesting results, achieved by this literature, are worth mentioning: i. the distinction between Pasinetti and a dual regimes holds also for long-run attractors that are not stationary states (or fixed points); ii. low factor substitutability may lead to unstable stationary states, periodic and aperiodic fluctuations and chaos; iii. finally, allowing for changes in workers' behaviour enriches the set of complex dynamic features adding a discontinuity to the dynamics. As a consequence, the number of possible growth regimes increases, instances of multistability are more frequent and complexity could emerge also with a high degree of factor substitutability.

These analyses are mainly confined to the different characterisations of the long-term patterns (attractors) into which the economic system settles down, but do not cover other relevant issues. Specifically, they do not investigate how the introduction of behavioural aspects, related to changes in social class behaviour, may affect the long-term wealth distribution.

In this chapter, we modify Sushko, Commendatore and Kubin (2020) analysis in several directions:

i   we maintain the assumption that young workers do not modify their approach to intertemporal choice, the only shift in behaviour involves the willingness of the old workers of leaving bequests;
ii we allow for consumption in the old age, this translates into workers applying different propensities to save out of wage and profit income (a possibility neglected in Sushko, Commendatore and Kubin, 2020);
iii we focus on the case of low factor substitutability, which, very partly, takes on board the post-Keynesian objection concerning the excessive flexibility of factor substitution of the neoclassical technology;
iv more importantly, we highlight the distributive consequences of workers' behavioural changes.

We would like to give a brief preview of our results. For that, we focus on the Pasinetti equilibria, in which both social classes own capital. As a consequence of workers' behavioural changes, the model has two such equilibria: one, in which workers own only little capital and they do not leave any bequests; and another one, in which workers own a sufficient high amount of capital, such that they change behaviour and leave bequests. In both these steady states, a higher savings propensity of workers leads to an increase in the share of total capital they own. Investigating their dynamic properties, we show that for certain parameter values the steady states lose stability and give rise to cyclical/chaotic time paths, over which the capital shares owned by the two classes fluctuate and the behaviour of workers switches between leaving and not leaving bequests. It is illustrative to investigate the average value of capital shares over these cycles; this average turns out to lie in between the values corresponding to the two Pasinetti equilibria, which reflect the fact that the two equilibria correspond to the two possible behavioural patterns of workers.

We thus show that a comparative static analysis of only stationary equilibrium values does not closely reflect the average behaviour over a cycle, in particular, if the cycle involves switches in workers' behaviour.

In what follows, we introduce the economic model (Section 2); we deal with the stationary states and dynamic properties of the model (Sections 3 and 4); we discuss the relationship between workers' saving behaviour and wealth distribution (Section 5); and we provide a few final remarks (Section 6).

2 The model

The model is framed in discrete time. We denote by t the time unit and let t running from 0 to infinity. In the economy there is only one commodity, which can be used for consumption and production. Capital and labour are the only factors of production. For simplicity, we assume that capital does not depreciate and that labour is constant through time and it is normalised to one.

We assume a neoclassical production technology with general properties, that is, for $k_t > 0$, it holds $f(k_t) > 0$, $f'(k_t) > 0$ and $f(k_t)'' < 0$, where k_t is the capital/labour ratio. This implies that the Inada conditions are not necessarily satisfied. As a working example, we use a constant elasticity of substitution (CES) production function:

$$f(k_t) = \begin{cases} (1 - \alpha + \alpha k_t^\rho)^{\frac{1}{\rho}} & \text{for } \rho \leq 1, \rho \neq 0 \\ k_t^\alpha & \text{for } \rho = 0 \end{cases}, \qquad (12.1)$$

where $0 < \alpha < 1$ is the distribution coefficient, $-\infty < \rho < 1$, the substitution coefficient and $(1 - \rho)^{-1}$ the elasticity of substitution. Notice that when $\rho \to 0$, we have a Cobb-Douglas production function – i.e. intermediate factor substitutability and flexible factor coefficients – which is the only case that satisfies the Inada conditions; instead, we have the case of a Leontief technology – i.e. no substitutability and fixed production factor coefficients –, if $\rho \to -\infty$; finally, factors are perfect substitutes and the technology is linear, if $\rho = 1$.

Capital is the only asset in the economy; and wages and profits are the only sources of income. In a short-run equilibrium, with perfectly competitive labour and capital markets, the rate of profit r_t is equal to the marginal product of capital $f'(k_t)$; and the wage rate w_t is equal to the marginal product of labour $f(k_t) - f'(k_t)k_t$. Considering the CES technology:

$$r_t = f'(k_t) = \begin{cases} [\alpha(1-\alpha)k_t^{-\rho} + \alpha]^{\frac{1-\rho}{\rho}} & \text{for } \rho \leq 1, \rho \neq 0 \\ \alpha k_t^{\alpha-1} & \text{for } \rho = 0 \end{cases} \qquad (12.2)$$

$$w_t = f(k_t) - f'(k_t)k$$

$$= \begin{cases} (1-\alpha)[(1-\alpha)k_t^{-\rho} + \alpha]^{\frac{1-\rho}{\rho}}k_t^{1-\rho} & \text{for } \rho \le 1, \rho \ne 0 \\ (1-\alpha)k_t^{\alpha-1} & \text{for } \rho = 0 \end{cases} \qquad (12.3)$$

The economy is inhabited by two types of agents grouped into social classes, workers (denoted by the subscript w) and capitalists (denoted by the subscript c). Both classes have the same (constant) population size and for both classes the size of each generation is set equal to one. Capitalists earn only income out of capital. They behave according to a pure legacy motive (Michl, 2009) – i.e. they value the wealth they leave to their descendants. A capitalist lives only one period: in her period of life, she decides how much to consume out of her wealth and leaves what is left to her descendants. Workers, instead, live two periods according to an overlapping generations structure. Each worker supplies inelastically one unit of labour when young and retires when old. For old workers, we allow for a possible switch in behaviour. If an old worker's capital is small, she consumes all her wealth and does not leave any bequest to her offspring. If her capital is sufficiently high, she behaves like a capitalist. She consumes only a fraction of her wealth and bequeaths what is left to her children.[4]

In order to determine workers and capitalists savings and accumulation choices, we assume that each individual, worker or capitalist, is endowed with logarithmic preferences and proceed as follows.

Starting from the generation of time t, a capitalist maximises

$$(1 - d_c)\ln c_{c,t} + d_c \ln b_{c,t}$$

subject to the following budget constraint

$$c_{c,t} + b_{c,t} = (1 + r_t)k_{c,t},$$

where $c_{c,t}$ is consumption of a capitalist at time t, $b_{c,t}$ her bequests at time t, d_c her consumption discounting factor and $k_{c,t}$ her capital, corresponding also to the overall capitalists' capital.

The solutions of a capitalist utility maximisation problem are:

$$c_{c,t}^o = (1 - d_c)(1 + r_t)k_{c,t}$$

$$b_{c,t} = d_c(1 + r_t)k_{c,t}.$$

Given that $s_{c,t} = b_{c,t}$, the solution of a capitalist maximisation problem corresponds to[5]

$$s_{c,t} = d_c(1 + r_t)k_{c,t}.$$

Considering workers, we start from the old generation of time t: if her capital is below a certain threshold, $k_{w,t} < \bar{k}$, an old worker consumes all her wealth (income plus capital), where $k_{w,t}$ denotes both the old worker capital and the overall workers' capital. Instead, if her capital reaches that threshold, $k_{w,t} \geq \bar{k}$, an old worker introduces in her utility function also bequests, imitating capitalists' behaviour:

$$(1 - d_w)\ln c^o_{w,t} + d_w \ln b_{w,t}$$

subject to the following budget constraint:

$$c^o_{w,t} + b_{w,t} = (1 + r_t)k_{w,t},$$

where $c^o_{w,t}$ is consumption of an old worker at time t, $b_{w,t}$ her bequests at time t and d_w her consumption discounting factor. In this case, the solutions of the old worker utility maximisation problem are:

$$c^o_{w,t} = (1 - d_w)(1 + r_t)k_{w,t}$$

$$b_{w,t} = d_w(1 + r_t)k_{w,t}.$$

Therefore, at time t an individual of the old generation leaves $b_{w,t}$ to her offspring. This implies that an individual of the young generation gets $b_{w,t}$.

If at time t a young worker does not receive any bequest, her maximisation problem corresponds to:

$$(1 - \beta_w)\ln c^y_{w,t} + \beta_w \ln c^o_{w,t+1}$$

subject to

$$c^y_{w,t} + \frac{c^o_{w,t+1}}{1 + r^e_{t+1}} = w_t,$$

where β_w is the consumption discount factor of a young worker and r^e_{t+1} is her expected rate of return on capital.

In this case, given that $s_{w,t} = w_t - c^y_{w,t}$, the solution of a young worker utility maximisation problem is:

$$s_{w,t} = \beta_w w_t.$$

If at time t a young workers receives a bequest,[6] her maximisation problem corresponds to:

$$(1 - \beta_w) \ln c_{w,t}^y + \beta_w \ln c_{w,t+1}^o$$

subject to

$$c_{w,t}^y + \frac{c_{w,t+1}^o}{1 + r_{t+1}^e} = w_t + b_{w,t},$$

where r_{t+1}^e is the young worker expected rate of return on capital. Considering that $s_{w,t} = w_t + b_{w,t} - c_{w,t}^y$ and that $b_{w,t} = d_w(1 + r_t)k_{w,t}$, the solution of a young worker maximisation problem can be expressed as:

$$s_{w,t} = \beta_w [w_t + d_w(1 + r_t)]k_{w,t}.$$

In our set-up, a young worker at time t does not know the future rate of profit r_{t+1}, so she does not know beforehand her effective consumption when old. And she has not enough resources to make an accurate prediction. We justify in this way why a worker does not decide everything at time t. Since her saving does not depend on r_{t+1}, given the shape of the utility function, even if in principle she could know $k_{w,t+1}$, she postpones her decisions because she would like to adjust her future consumption depending on the realised r_{t+1}.

In some sense, it is a consequence of the special features of the Cobb-Douglas/logarithmic utility function: a change in the 'price' of future consumption $\frac{1}{1 + r_{t+1}}$ leaves the decision on how to use the income at t unchanged, because income and substitution effects cancel out. Therefore, in our set-up, a worker does not know r_{t+1}; nevertheless, in t she splits her income in fixed proportions into consumption and saving for future consumption. In $t + 1$, she can indeed be surprised by her wealth $(1 + r_{t+1})s_{w,t}$ and may change behaviour accordingly: reassessing her consumption and including bequests into her utility function. We believe this is a plausible optimising behaviour of workers not knowing the future rate of return.[7]

By setting $s_c = d_c$, $s_{ww} = \beta_w$, $s_{up} = \beta_w d_w$, and considering that saving translates into capital available for production in the next period, the main dynamic equations governing capitalists and workers accumulation are expressed as

$$\begin{cases} k_{c,t+1} = s_{c,t} = s_c(1 + r_t)k_{c,t} \\ k_{w,t+1} = s_{w,t} = \begin{cases} s_{ww} w_t & \text{for } k_{w,t} < \bar{k} \\ s_{ww} w_t + s_{up}(1 + r_t)k_{w,t} & \text{for } k_{w,t} \geq \bar{k} \end{cases} \end{cases} \quad (12.4)$$

with

$$k_{t+1} = k_{c,t+1} + k_{w,t+1}.$$

We assume $0 \le d_w$, $\beta_w < d_c < 1$, and $\bar{k} > 0$. It follows $0 \le s_{wp} \le s_{ww} < s_c < 1$, with $s_{ww} \ne 0$.

Our model is only one possible way of determining the saving propensities of workers out of wages and profits. Indeed, in the literature, it is possible to find other justifications on why workers change their saving behaviour depending on the source of income, not always based on an explicit micro-foundation (for example, in the context of a corporate economy, because shareholders may not be indifferent between consuming dividends or capital gains, given the more uncertain nature of the latter; see, among others, Odagiri, 1981; Commendatore, 1999). In accordance with the literature and in order to facilitate the comparison, in the simulations below, we will consider s_{wp} and s_{ww} as non-related parameters.[8]

3 Stationary states

Dropping the time subscripts, the system (12.4) can be reformulated as a two-dimensional (2D) discontinuous F map with (k_c, k_w) as state variables:

$$F: (k_c, k_w) \rightarrow F(k_c, k_w) = \begin{cases} F_L(k_c, k_w) & \text{for } k_w < \bar{k} \\ F_R(k_c, k_w) & \text{for } k_w \ge \bar{k} \end{cases}, \qquad (12.5)$$

where

$$F_L(k_c, k_w) = \begin{cases} s_c(1 + f'(k))k_c \\ s_{ww}(f(k) - f'(k)k) \end{cases}$$

$$F_R(k_c, k_w) = \begin{cases} s_c(1 + f'(k))k_c \\ s_{ww}(f(k) - f'(k)k) + s_{wp}(1 + f'(k))k_w \end{cases}$$

and where $k = k_c + k_w$.

There are three types of long-run equilibria or stationary states (corresponding to the fixed points of the map (12.5)). In a Pasinetti equilibrium $P = (k_c^*, k_w^*)$, where $P = P_L = (k_{cL}^*, k_{wL}^*)$, if $k_w^* < \bar{k}$ and $P = P_R = (k_{cR}^*, k_{wR}^*)$, if $k_w^* \ge \bar{k}$, both capitalists and workers own capital. This type of equilibrium is characterised by:

$$r^* = f'(k^*) = \frac{1 - s_c}{s_c} \quad \text{and} \quad k^* = f'^{-1}\left(\frac{1 - s_c}{s_c}\right)$$

$$k_c^* = \begin{cases} k_{cL}^* = \left[1 - \frac{s_{ww}}{s_c}(1 - s_c)\left(\frac{1 - e_f(k^*)}{e_f(k^*)}\right)\right]k^* & \text{for } k_w^* < \bar{k} \\ \\ k_{cR}^* = \left[1 - \frac{s_{ww}}{s_c - s_{wp}}(1 - s_c)\left(\frac{1 - e_f(k^*)}{e_f(k^*)}\right)\right]k^* & \text{for } k_w^* \geq \bar{k} \end{cases}$$

$$k_w^* = \begin{cases} k_{wL}^* = \frac{s_{ww}}{s_c}(1 - s_c)\left(\frac{1 - e_f(k^*)}{e_f(k^*)}\right)k^* & \text{for } k_w^* < \bar{k} \\ \\ k_{wR}^* = \frac{s_{ww}}{s_c - s_{wp}}(1 - s_c)\left(\frac{1 - e_f(k^*)}{e_f(k^*)}\right)k^* & \text{for } k_w^* \geq \bar{k} \end{cases},$$

where $e_f(k) = \frac{f'(k)k}{f(k)}$.

A Pasinetti equilibrium exists and it is unique when the production function $f(k)$ satisfies:

$$\lim_{k \to 0} f'(k) > \frac{1 - s_c}{s_c} \quad \text{and} \quad \lim_{k \to \infty} f'(k) < \frac{1 - s_c}{s_c}. \tag{12.6}$$

Moreover, $0 < k_w^* < k^*$ when

$$\frac{s_{ww}(1 - s_c)}{s_{ww}(1 - s_c) + s_c} < e_f(k^*) < 1 \qquad \text{for } k_w^* < \bar{k}$$

$$\frac{s_{ww}(1 - s_c)}{s_{ww}(1 - s_c) + s_c - s_{wp}} < e_f(k^*) < 1 \quad \text{for } k_w^* \geq \bar{k}.$$

In a Pasinetti equilibrium, a switch in workers behaviour, leading to bequests, has no effect on the overall capital, but only on the distribution between workers and capitalists. After the switch in behaviour (when k_w^* crosses the threshold $\bar{k}$), workers' capital increases, $k_{wR}^* > k_{wL}^*$, and capitalists' capital decreases, $k_{cR}^* < k_{cL}^*$. Moreover, the condition for a positive k_c^* becomes more stringent.

In a Solow or dual equilibrium, $D = (k_c^{**}, k_w^{**}) = (0, k^{**})$, where $D = D_L = (0, k_L^{**})$, if $k^{**} < \bar{k}$ and $D = D_R = (0, k_R^{**})$, if $k^{**} \geq \bar{k}$, only workers own capital and a sufficient condition for $k^{**} > 0$ is $e_f(k^{**}) < 1$. This type of equilibrium is characterised by:

$$\frac{f(k_L^{**})}{k_L^{**}} = \frac{1}{s_{ww}(1 - e_f(k_L^{**}))} \qquad \text{for } k^{**} < \bar{k}$$

$$\frac{f(k_R^{**})}{k_R^{**}} = \frac{1 - s_{wp}}{s_{ww}(1 - e_f(k_R^{**})) + s_{wp}e_f(k_R^{**})} \qquad \text{for } k^{**} \geq \bar{k}$$

$$k_w^{**} = k_L^{**} \qquad \text{for } k^{**} < \bar{k}$$

$$k_w^{**} = k_R^{**} \qquad \text{for } k^{**} \geq \bar{k}$$

$$k_c^{**} = 0.$$

Let $e_f(k) < 1$, if

$$(1 - e_f(k) + e_{f'}(k))(s_{ww} - s_{up}) \geq 0, \tag{12.7}$$

where $e_{f'}(k) = \frac{f''(k)k}{f'(k)}$, a dual equilibrium exists and it is unique when $f(k)$ satisfies

$$l_0^l > l_0^r \text{ and } l_\infty^l < l_\infty^r, \tag{12.8}$$

where $l_0^l = \lim\limits_{k \to 0} \frac{f(k)}{k}$, $l_\infty^l = \lim\limits_{k \to \infty} \frac{f(k)}{k}$, $l_0^r = \lim\limits_{k \to 0} \frac{1 - s_{up}}{s_{uw}(1 - e_f(k)) + s_{up}e_f(k)}$ and $l_\infty^r = \lim\limits_{k \to \infty} \frac{1 - s_{up}}{s_{uw}(1 - e_f(k)) + s_{up}e_f(k)}$.[9]

Instead, if

$$(1 - e_f(k) + e_{f'}(k))(s_{ww} - s_{up}) < 0, \tag{12.9}$$

one equilibrium exists when $f(k)$ satisfies:

$$(l_0^l - l_0^r)(l_\infty^l - l_\infty^r) < 0. \tag{12.10}$$

Otherwise, one, two or no dual equilibrium exists depending on the shape of the production function.[10]

Note that the conditions of existence for a dual equilibrium, (12.7)–(12.10), apply to k_{wL}^{**} when $s_{up} = 0$ and to k_{wR}^{**} when $s_{up} \geq 0$.[11]

Moreover, for $s_{up} > 0$, $\frac{f(k_R^{**})}{k_R^{**}} < \frac{f(k_L^{**})}{k_L^{**}}$ and therefore $k_R^{**} > k_L^{**}$. Consequently, in a dual equilibrium, after the switch in workers' behaviour, capital increases.

Finally, in the trivial equilibrium $O = (k_c^0, k_w^0) = (0, 0)$ there is no capital:

$$k_w^0 + k_c^0 = k^0 = 0.$$

A trivial equilibrium exists when $w(0) = f(0) = 0$.

We now explicit the neoclassical technology as in Equation (12.1) and after inserting the Equations (12.1), (12.2) and (12.3) into the map (12.5), we solve for the stationary states of the economy (the fixed points of this map). Let $\rho \neq 0$, the Pasinetti equilibrium corresponds to

$$r^* = [\alpha(1 - \alpha)k_r^{-\rho} + \alpha]^{\frac{1-\rho}{\rho}} = \frac{1 - s_c}{s_c}$$

$$k^* = \left(\frac{1 - \alpha}{b - \alpha}\right)^{\frac{1}{\rho}} \text{ where } b = \left(\frac{1 - s_c}{\alpha s_c}\right)^{\frac{\rho}{1-\rho}}$$

$$k_w^* = \begin{cases} k_{wL}^* = \frac{s_{ww}}{s_c}(1 - s_c)\left(\frac{b-\alpha}{\alpha}\right)k^* & \text{for } k_w^* < \bar{k} \\ k_{wR}^* = \frac{s_{ww}}{s_c - s_{wp}}(1 - s_c)\left(\frac{b-\alpha}{\alpha}\right)k^* & \text{for } k_w^* \geq \bar{k} \end{cases}$$

$$k_c^* = k^* - k_w^*.$$

Applying condition (12.6), a Pasinetti equilibrium exists when $b - \alpha > 0$, that is, when $s_c < \frac{1}{1 + \alpha^{\frac{1}{\rho}}}$, if $0 < \rho < 1$ or when $s_c > \frac{1}{1 + \alpha^{\frac{1}{\rho}}}$ if $\rho < 0$.

Moreover, since $e_f(k) = \frac{\alpha}{\alpha + (1 - \alpha)k^{-\rho}} < 1$, it is also true that $k_w^* > 0$; whereas $k_w^* < k^*$ when

$$s_{ww} < \frac{\alpha}{b - \alpha}\frac{s_c}{1 - s_c} \quad \text{for } k_w^* < \bar{k}$$

$$s_{ww} < \frac{\alpha}{b - \alpha}\frac{s_c - s_{wp}}{1 - s_c} \quad \text{for } k_w^* \geq \bar{k}.$$

The dual equilibrium corresponds to:

$$[(1 - \alpha)(k_L^{**})^{-\rho} + \alpha]^{\frac{1}{\rho}} = \frac{1}{s_{ww}(1 - \alpha)(k_L^{**})^{-\rho}}[(1 - \alpha)(k_L^{**})^{-\rho} + \alpha] \quad \text{for } k^{**} < \bar{k}$$

$$[(1 - \alpha)(k_R^{**})^{-\rho} + \alpha]^{\frac{1}{\rho}} = \frac{1 - s_{wp}}{s_{ww}(1 - \alpha)(k_R^{**})^{-\rho} + s_{wp}\alpha}[(1 - \alpha)(k_R^{**})^{-\rho} \quad \text{for } k^{**} \geq \bar{k}$$

$$+ \alpha]$$

$$k_w^{**} = k_L^{**} \qquad\qquad\qquad\qquad \text{for } k^{**} < \bar{k}$$

$$k_w^{**} = k_R^{**} \qquad\qquad\qquad\qquad \text{for } k^{**} \geq \bar{k}$$

$$k_c^{**} = 0.$$

Recalling that $e_f(k) < 1$, the conditions for the existence of a dual equilibrium are summarised in Proposition 1:

Proposition 1. *When $\rho(s_{ww} - s_{wp}) \geq 0$, one and only one dual equilibrium exists iff $s_{wp} < \frac{1}{1 + \alpha^{\frac{1}{\rho}}}$. Instead, when $\rho(s_{ww} - s_{wp}) < 0$, one and only one equilibrium exists iff $s_{wp} > \frac{1}{1 + \alpha^{\frac{1}{\rho}}}$. Otherwise, when $s_{wp} < \frac{1}{1 + \alpha^{\frac{1}{\rho}}}$, one, two or no dual equilibria may exist.*

Proof: Considering the CES production function (12.1): the inequality (12.7) corresponds to $\rho(s_{ww} - s_{wp}) \geq 0$; and the condition (12.8) holds as long as $s_{wp} < \frac{1}{1 + \alpha^{\frac{1}{\rho}}}$. Thus, one and only one equilibrium, D_L or D_R, exists. Instead, the inequality (12.9) corresponds to $\rho(s_{ww} - s_{wp}) < 0$ and the condition (12.10) holds as long as $s_{wp} > \frac{1}{1 + \alpha^{\frac{1}{\rho}}}$, again one and only one equilibrium,

D_L or D_R, exists. Instead, condition (12.10) is not satisfied when $s_{wp} < \dfrac{1}{1+\alpha^{\frac{1}{\rho}}}$. In this case one, two or no equilibria may exist. When two equilibria exist, we label them (D_L^1 and D_L^2; or D_R^1 and D_R^2). This completes the proof. □

Note that, when $s_{wp} = 0$, condition (12.10) never holds. For this case, which applies specifically to k_w^{**}, one equilibrium exists if $s_{ww} = s_{ww}^f = \dfrac{1}{-\rho\,(1-\rho)^{\frac{1}{\rho}-1}\alpha^{\frac{1}{\rho}}}$, two when $s_{ww} > s_{ww}^f$, and none when $s_{ww} < s_{ww}^f$.[12]

Now let $\rho = 0$, the production function is Cobb-Douglas. For this special case, the Pasinetti equilibrium corresponds to:

$$r^* = \alpha\,(k^*)^{\alpha-1} = \frac{1-s_c}{s_c} \quad \text{and} \quad k^* = \left(\frac{\alpha s_c}{1-s_c}\right)^{\frac{1}{1-\alpha}}$$

$$k_w^* = \begin{cases} k_{wL}^* = \dfrac{s_{ww}}{s_c}(1-s_c)\left(\dfrac{1-\alpha}{\alpha}\right)k^* & \text{for } k_w^* < \bar{k} \\[3mm] k_{wR}^* = \dfrac{s_{ww}}{s_c-s_{wp}}(1-s_c)\left(\dfrac{1-\alpha}{\alpha}\right)k^* & \text{for } k_w^* \geq \bar{k} \end{cases}$$

$$k_c^* = k^* - k_w^*.$$

We have that, given the shape of the production function, the unique Pasinetti equilibrium k^* necessarily exists (i.e. condition (12.6) is always satisfied). Moreover, since $e_f(k) = \alpha$ and $0 < \alpha < 1$, $k_w^* > 0$; whereas $k_w^* < k^*$ when

$$s_{ww} < \frac{\alpha}{1-\alpha}\frac{s_c}{1-s_c} \quad \text{for } k_w^* < \bar{k}$$
$$s_{ww} < \frac{\alpha}{1-\alpha}\frac{s_c-s_{wp}}{1-s_c} \quad \text{for } k_w^* \geq \bar{k}\;.$$

Indeed, the dual equilibrium is

$$k_w^{**} = k_w^{**} = \begin{cases} k_L^{**} = ((1-\alpha)s_{ww})^{\frac{1}{1-\alpha}} & \text{for } k_w^* < \bar{k} \\[3mm] k_R^{**} = \left(\dfrac{(1-\alpha)s_{ww}+\alpha s_{wp}}{1-s_{wp}}\right)^{\frac{1}{1-\alpha}} & \text{for } k_w^* \geq \bar{k} \end{cases}$$

$$k_c^{**} = 0$$

Given the shape of the production function (for which (12.7) applies and condition (12.8) is always satisfied), it necessarily exists.

Finally, the trivial equilibrium (in which $k_c^0 = k_w^0 = k^0 = 0$) exists when $\rho \leq 0$, since $w(0) = 0$, and it does not exist when $\rho > 0$, since $w(0) = f(0) > 0$.

4 Dynamics

4.1 Local stability analysis

In this section, we briefly explore the local stability properties of the stationary equilibria reported above.

When

$$s_{ww} < s_L^{BC} = \frac{\bar{k}s_c\,e_f{}'(k^*)\,k^*}{(1 - s_c)(1 - e_f{}'(k^*))}, \tag{12.11}$$

the inequality $k_w^* < \bar{k}$ holds and the Pasinetti equilibrium corresponds to P_L. The local stability conditions are:

$$s_L^{Fl} < s_{ww} < \min(s_L^T, s_L^{NS}), \tag{12.12}$$

where $s_L^{Fl} = \frac{s_c}{1 - s_c}\frac{e_f{}'(k^*)(1 - s_c) + 2}{1 + e_f(k^*) - (1 - e_f(k^*))s_c}\frac{e_f(k^*)}{e_f{}'(k^*)}$, $\quad s_L^T = \frac{s_c}{1 - s_c}\frac{e_f(k^*)}{1 - e_f(k^*)}$ $\quad$ and $\quad s_L^{NS} = -\frac{s_c}{e_f{}'(k^*)(1 - s_c)}$.

When s_{ww} is decreased below s_L^{Fl}, the stationary equilibrium P_L loses stability via a flip bifurcation (Fl_L). Instead, when it is increased above s_L^{NS} it loses stability via a Neimark-Sacker (NS) bifurcation (NS_L). Finally, P_L may lose stability via a transcritical bifurcation when the threshold s_L^T is crossed (T_L). The condition related to the transcritical bifurcation corresponds to condition $k_{cL}^* > 0$ – equivalent to impose $k^* > k_L^{**}$ – that guarantees the existence of a Pasinetti equilibrium. Finally, when s_{ww} crosses s_L^{BC}, P_L undergoes a border collision (BC) bifurcation involving the equilibrium hitting a boundary, i.e. the discontinuity line $k_w = \bar{k}$ (BC_L).

Instead, when

$$s_{ww} \geq s_R^{BC} = \frac{\bar{k}(s_c - s_{wp})e_f{}'(k^*)\,k^*}{(1 - s_c)(1 - e_f{}'(k^*))}, \tag{12.13}$$

the inequality $k_w^* \geq \bar{k}$ holds and the Pasinetti equilibrium corresponds to P_R. In this case, the local stability conditions are:

$$s_R^{Fl} < s_{ww} < \min(s_R^T, s_R^{NS}), \tag{12.14}$$

where $s_R^{Fl} = \dfrac{s_c + s_{wp}}{1 - s_c} \dfrac{e_{f'}(k^*)(1 - s_c) + 2}{1 + e_f(k^*) - (1 - e_f(k^*))s_c \, e_{f'}(k^*)}, \quad s_R^T = \dfrac{s_c - s_{wp}}{1 - s_c} \dfrac{e_f(k^*)}{1 - e_f(k^*)}$ and $s_R^{NS} =$

$s_{wp} - \dfrac{s_c - s_{wp}}{e_{f'}(k^*)(1 - s_c)}.$

As before, these inequalities are related to how P_R may lose stability: via a flip bifurcation, when s_{wu} crosses s_R^{Fl} (Fl_R); via a NS bifurcation, when s_{wu} crosses s_R^{NS} (noticing that this type of bifurcation cannot occur when s_{wp} is sufficiently close to s_{wu})(NS_R); or via a transcritical bifurcation, when the threshold s_R^T is crossed (T_R). Again, this last condition − corresponding to $k_{cR}^* > 0$ (or to $k^* > k_R^{**}$) − guarantees the existence of a Pasinetti equilibrium. Finally, a BC bifurcation, involving P_R hitting a boundary, occurs when s_{wu} crosses s_L^{BC} (BC_R).

Considering the CES production function in Equation (12.1), we have that $e_f(k^*) = \alpha b^{-1}$ for $\rho \neq 0$ and $e_f(k^*) = \alpha$ for $\rho \neq 0$, $e_{f'}(k^*) = (1 - \rho)(\alpha b^{-1} - 1)$ for $\rho \neq 0$ and $e_{f'}(k^*) = \alpha - 1$ for $\rho = 0$.

Below we present a more detailed discussion on dynamics based on $\rho \neq 0$.

Regarding the specific case $\rho = 0$, not all bifurcations presented above may occur (in particular, only transcritical and border collision bifurcations may occur when the production function is Cobb-Douglas).

Turning to the dual equilibrium, when $k^{**} < \bar{k}$, $D = D_L$ and the local stability properties for this type of equilibrium correspond to:

If

$$s_{wu} < -\frac{s_c}{e_{f'}(k_L^{**}) + \dfrac{1 - e_f(k_L^{**})}{e_f(k_L^{**})}s_c},$$

the stability condition is

$$s_{wu} > s_L^T = \frac{s_c}{1 - s_c} \frac{e_f(k_L^{**})}{1 - e_f(k_L^{**})},$$

corresponding to $k^* < k_L^{**}$. The unique dual equilibrium exchange stability with the Pasinetti equilibrium when the threshold s_L^T is crossed.

If

$$s_{wu} > -\frac{s_c}{e_{f'}(k_L^{**}) + \dfrac{1 - e_f(k_L^{**})}{e_f(k_L^{**})}s_c},$$

the stability condition corresponds to

$$e_{f'}(k_L^{**}) > -\frac{1 - e_f(k_L^{**})}{e_f(k_L^{**})}.$$

If this condition does not hold, D_L loses stability via a fold bifurcation: two equilibria D_L^1 and D_L^2 merge into one and after the bifurcation they disappear. Notice that this condition does not depend on s_{ww}.

Instead, when $k^{**} \geq \bar{k}$, the local stability properties for the dual equilibrium correspond to:

If

$$s_{ww} < -\frac{(s_c - s_{wp}) - s_{wp}(1 - s_{wp})e_{f'}(k_R^{**})}{(1 - s_{wp})e_{f'}(k_R^{**}) + \frac{1 - e_f(k_R^{**})}{e_f(k_R^{**})}(s_c - s_{wp})},$$

the stability condition is

$$s_{ww} > s_R^T = \frac{s_c - s_{wp}}{1 - s_c}\frac{e_f(k_R^{**})}{1 - e_f(k_R^{**})},$$

corresponding to $k^* < k_R^{**}$. The unique dual equilibrium exchange stability with the Pasinetti equilibrium when the threshold s_R^T is crossed and a transcritical bifurcation occurs.

If

$$s_{ww} > -\frac{(s_c - s_{wp}) - s_{wp}(1 - s_{wp})e_{f'}(k_R^{**})}{(1 - s_{wp})e_{f'}(k_R^{**}) + \frac{1 - e_f(k_R^{**})}{e_f(k_R^{**})}(s_c - s_{wp})},$$

the stability condition corresponds to

$$s_{ww} > s_R^{Fo} = \frac{e_f(k_R^{**})e_{f'}(k_R^{**})}{1 - (1 - e_{f'}(k_R^{**}))e_f(k_R^{**})}s_{wp}.$$

If this condition does not hold, stability is lost via a fold bifurcation. The two existing dual equilibria, D_R^1 and D_R^2, collapse to one at $s_{ww} = s_R^{Fo}$, then disappear as s_{ww} is reduced below this threshold.

Finally, concerning the trivial equilibrium, letting $k_c^* > 0$, it is stable when $\frac{1 - s_c}{s_c} > f'(0)$. This condition is violated via a transcritical bifurcation and it corresponds to $s_c < \frac{1}{1 + \alpha^{\frac{1}{\rho}}}$ (or to $k^* < 0$) when $\rho \neq 0$. This condition never holds when $\rho = 0$. Instead, letting $k_c^* \leq 0$, the trivial equilibrium is stable when $\frac{1 - s_{wp}}{s_{wp}} > f'(0)$, corresponding to $s_{wp} < \frac{1}{1 + \alpha^{\frac{1}{\rho}}}$ for $\rho \neq 0$, the violation of this condition also involving a transcritical bifurcation. Again this condition never holds for $\rho = 0$.

4.2 Global dynamics

In this section, we discuss some of the dynamic properties of our model when the production function is of the CES type and factor substitutability is very weak ($\rho \ll 0$). In particular, we present several bifurcation structures observed in the parameter space of the map F (12.5), when (12.1) holds, and give a few examples of its attractors. We consider the (s_{wp}, s_{ww})-parameter plane and fix the other parameters as follows

$$\alpha = 0.2, \quad s_c = 0.65, \quad \rho = -15, \quad \bar{k} = 0.2 \text{ or } \bar{k} = 0.3 \qquad (12.15)$$

We denote by S_L the parameter region related to the attracting fixed point P_L. As shown in the previous section, this region is confined by the boundaries BC_L, T_L, Fl_L and NS_L, which are associated with bifurcations — border collision, transcritical, flip and NS bifurcations, respectively — of this fixed point. Given that these boundaries do not depend on s_{wp}, in the (s_{wp}, s_{ww})-parameter plane they are represented by horizontal straight lines. The same occurs for any other bifurcation boundary in this parameter plane, which only involves the map F_L. Similarly, we denote by S_R the region related to the attracting fixed point P_R, confined by the boundaries BC_R, T_R, Fl_R and NS_R, associated with the corresponding bifurcations related to this other fixed point. Since for $s_{wp} = 0$, the maps F_L and F_R coincide, each pair of bifurcation boundaries, associated with these maps intersect at $s_{wp} = 0$ in the (s_{wp}, s_{ww})-parameter plane.

In Figure 12.1 (the coloured pictures, present in the e-book version, are also available upon request from the authors), we present a 2D bifurcation diagram in the (s_{wp}, s_{ww})-parameter plane, where the other parameters are fixed as in Equation (12.15), with $\bar{k} = 0.2$ in Figure 12.1a and $\bar{k} = 0.3$ in Figure 12.1b. Here different colors are related to attracting n-cycles of different periods, $n \leq 29$ (the colours corresponding to each periodicity are reported in the palette on the right of the Figure). Moreover, we colored in gray the region Σ_R, associated to the attracting dual fixed point D_R; and in white the regions associated to higher periodicity, $n > 29$, quasiperiodicity or chaos. Of special importance, in Figure 12.1, are the regions S_L and S_R which we colored in red and pink, respectively, where hatched subregions are related to overlapping parts involving coexistence of attractors. Specifically, the fixed points P_L and P_R can coexist with each other and with attracting cycles of various periods. Note that, for the considered parameter values, the boundary T_L is defined by $s_{ww} = s_L^T \approx 1.9$ and lies outside the feasible range of parameters. A detailed description of the dynamics of the map F and, in particular, of the bifurcation structure presented in Figure 12.1, is left for future work, while here we only comment on a few bifurcations illustrated by the 1D bifurcation diagram in Figure 12.2a. This diagram corresponds to a cross-section of Figure 12.1a, obtained by fixing $s_{wp} = 0.2$ and increasing s_{ww}, where $0.2 < s_{ww} < 0.43$. It shows the changes in the dynamics — and therefore in the time evolution of the state variables (k_c, k_w) — due to standard and nonstandard local and global

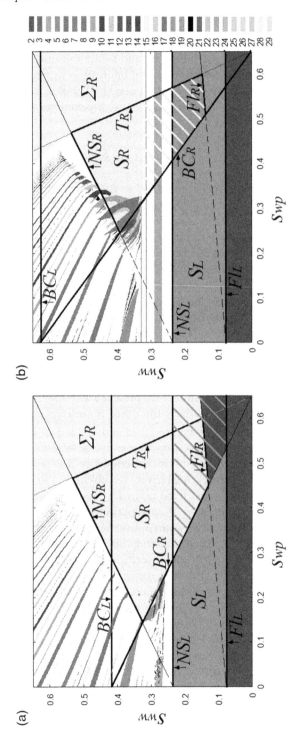

Figure 12.1 2D bifurcation diagram of map F in the (s_{wp}, s_{uw})–parameter plane for other parameters fixed as in (12.15), with (a) $\bar{k} = 0.2$ and (b) $\bar{k} = 0.3$.

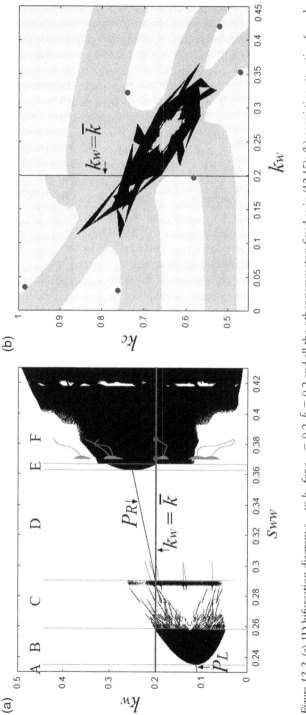

Figure 12.2 (a) 1D bifurcation diagram s_{uw} vs k_w for $s_{up} = 0.2$, $\bar{k} = 0.2$ and all the other parameters fixed as in (12.15); (b) coexisting attracting 6-cycle and a chaotic attractor, together with their basins at $s_{uw} = 0.383$.

bifurcations, occurring in varying the parameter s_{ww}; the distinction of the overall variation of this parameter into different ranges, from A to F, will be very useful in the economic interpretation of Figure 12.2 below Figure 12.1. In particular, for increasing s_{ww}, at $s_{ww} = s_L^{NS} \approx 0.23503$, violating (12.12), the fixed point P_L undergoes a NS bifurcation leading to an attracting closed invariant curve, C_L. It is clear that as long as such a curve has no contact with the discontinuity line $k_w = \bar{k}$ and only one branch of map F, i.e., map F_L, is involved, a standard sequence of 'smooth' bifurcations may occur under variation of a parameter, leading eventually to the destruction of the closed invariant curve and to chaos. A nonstandard mechanism of destruction can be observed, instead, if this curve has a contact with the discontinuity line, as it occurs at $s_{ww} \approx 0.2585$ when C_L collides with the discontinuity line $k_w = \bar{k}$. The fixed point P_R for decreasing s_{ww} undergoes a BC bifurcation at $s_{ww} = s_R^{BC} \approx 0.28952$, violating (12.13), and disappears, while for increasing s_{ww}, at $s_{ww} = s_R^{NS} \approx 0.36271$, violating (12.14), a NS bifurcation occurs leading to a closed invariant attracting curve C_R. This curve in its turn also undergoes a BC bifurcation, at $s_{ww} \approx 0.3668$, leading to the destruction of C_R.

Figure 12.2a illustrates also coexistence of various attractors, shown in black and red. In particular, there is a range of values of s_{ww} (this range is indicated by two blue circles in Figure 12.2a), for which chaotic attractors, in black, coexist at first, for decreasing s_{ww}, with an attracting 6-cycle (see an example in Figure 12.2b where $s_{ww} = 0.383$) born due to a BC bifurcation, and then with 6-cyclic closed invariant attracting curves born after an NS bifurcation of the 6-cycle. Similar to the curves C_L and C_R, the 6-cyclic closed invariant curves disappear also due to a contact with the discontinuity line $k_w = \bar{k}$.

5 Economic interpretation

We now turn to an economic interpretation of the processes underlying the dynamics shown in Figure 12.2. For this section, we neglect the possibility of coexistence and focus on the attractors shown black. It is interesting to analyse the development of the *average* capital and *average* distributive shares on these attractors and their relationship to the corresponding equilibrium values. The range of s_{ww} is subdivided into six intervals, labelled A to F, according to differences in the long-run dynamic behaviour, as discussed in the previous section.

Figure 12.3a shows total capital and capitalists's capital, the difference between these two is the workers' capital. For comparison, we also include the Pasinetti equilibrium values k^*, k_{cR}^* and k_{cL}^*, which show the to be expected propreties: higher values of s_{ww} do not affect total capital, but reduce capitalists' capital (and increase workers' capital). Note that there exist two Pasinetti equilibria, in P_L workers capital is too low and they do not leave any bequests, in P_R workers capital is sufficiently high and they do leave bequests. However, these Pasinetti equilibria are stable only for particular parameter ranges and give way to cyclical or complex attractors otherwise. The Pasinetti equilibrium

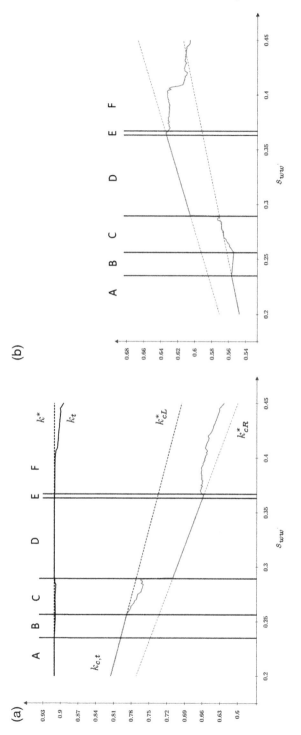

Figure 12.3 Averages on attractor: (a) capital stocks; (b) income share of workers.

P_L, in which workers do not leave any bequests, is stable for low values of s_{ww} in the range A, corresponding to $s_{wp} \leq s_{ww} < s_L^{NS} \approx 0.23503$ (Equation (12.12)).

Capitalists' (workers') capital declines (increases) with an increasing s_{ww}; total capital remains constant. Note that the adjustment time path is cyclical even before the NS bifurcation occurs. The economic rationale is the following: A high value of total capital reduces the rate of profit and increases the wage rate; this is an advantage for workers, who increase k_w, whereas k_c decreases, as well as total capital. The lower value of total capital reverses this process, leading to a cyclical time path. Higher values of s_{ww} deepens the cyclicity and the fixed point loses stability via a NS bifurcation, at the transition between range A and range B (the latter corresponding approx. to $s_L^{NS} \leq s_{ww} \lesssim 0.2583$). For s_{ww} values in the range B, the dynamics shows permanent fluctuations. The threshold $\bar{k}$ does not yet impinge, workers do not yet leave any bequests. The *average* capital stocks of workers and capitalists over the cycles continue to follow the trend given by the Pasinetti equilibrium. Overall capital declines a bit. Increasing s_{ww} increases the amplitude of the fluctuations. Once the capital of workers fluctuates sufficiently to hit the $\bar{k}$ threshold, at the transition between the ranges B and C (the latter corresponding to approx. $0.2583 \lesssim s_{ww} < s_R^{BC} \lesssim 0.2892$, see (12.13)), workers change their behaviour and start to leave bequests in some periods over the cycle. The invariant curve undergoes a border collision bifurcation giving rise to more complex attractors. The *average* of workers' capital starts to increase with an increase in s_{ww} and the *average* of k_c declines. For our parameters, the *average* total capital declines.

The decline in the *average* total capital increases the profit rate and reduces the wage rate (both evaluated as *averages* over the cycle). For capitalists, the increase in the profit rate does not compensate the reduction in the capital stock – their average income declines. Workers gain from the increased rate of profit, that compensates for the reduction in the wage rate. Their *average* income markedly increases, once they start leaving bequests (once $\bar{k}$ impinges on the attractor).

Figure 12.3b shows the *average* income share of workers (consisting of wage and profit income, *averaged* over the cycle); of course, the complement to one of the *average* income share of workers is the capitalists' *average* income share. For comparison, the dotted lines represent the corresponding values on the Pasinetti equilibria. Also in this panel, the two Pasinetti equilibria are visible; in both cases, an increase in s_{ww} increases workers' income share; in the Pasinetti equilibrium P_L, in which workers do not leave any bequests, workers' income share is lower than in P_R, in which workers do leave bequests. Before the NS bifurcation, in the range A, the *average* income share of workers increases with an increase in s_{ww}. After the NS bifurcation, once permanent fluctuations have started – in the range B – a slight decrease is visible. Workers' *average* income share starts to increase again and capitalists' *average* income share declines correspondingly in the range C, i.e. once $\bar{k}$ impinges on the attractor and thus workers start to *leave bequests*.

For higher values of s_{uw}, the dynamics is dominated by the Pasinetti equilibrium P_R, in which workers always leave bequests. In the range D of s_{uw}, corresponding to $s_R^{BC} \leq s_{uw} < s_R^{NS}$ (Equations (12.14) and (12.13)), it is an attracting fixed point. Again, the *average* capitalists' (workers') capital declines (increases) with an increasing s_{uw}; and the *average* total capital remains constant. Also P_R undergoes a NS bifurcation, which does not modify markedly the *average* capital stocks of workers and capitalists; the *average* total capital declines a bit after the NS (see the narrow range E of s_{uw}, corresponding to $s_R^{NS} \leq s_{uw} \lesssim 0.3663$).

With an increase in s_{uw} the fluctuations become stronger; once $\bar{k}$ is hit, at the transition between ranges E and F (the latter corresponding to $0.3663 \lesssim s_{uw} \leq s_c$), workers change their behaviour and in some periods they no longer leave bequests. The higher s_{uw}, the stronger the fluctuations and the more often workers do not leave bequests. Thus, in the range F, workers' *average* capital is reduced, and capitalists' *average* capital increases. For our parameters, *average* total capital declines.

The decline in the *average* total capital increases the profit rate and reduces the wage rate (again measured as *averages* over the cycle). Capitalists gain both form a higher capital stock and a higher profit rate (measured as *averages* over the cycle). For workers, the increase in the *average* profit rate does not compensate the reduction in the capital stock – their profit income declines, once $\bar{k}$ impinges on the attractor (and they no longer always leave bequests).

Turning to the *average* income shares (Figure 12.3b), note that before the NS bifurcation (in the range D), the *average* income share of workers increases with an increase in s_{uw} (reflecting their higher capital stock). After the NS bifurcation in range E and range F, the share remains constant; it sharply declines once workers frequently *leave no bequests*.

Our discussion shows that the behavioural component, which we introduced into the (intertemporal) savings decision of workers, may profoundly change the growth regime, not only its cyclicity, but in particular also the implied *average* wealth and income distribution.

The underlying Pasinetti equilibria appear to govern the behaviour over the cycle: if bequest behaviour of workers changes over the cycle, then the *averages* appear to be in between the two Pasinetti equilibria. Looking only at the equlibria may be misleading: Moving along the equilibrium in which workers leave bequests, increasing s_{uw} should increase workers income share. However, if due to fluctuations sufficiently wide workers start to leave no bequests in some periods over the cycle (Figure 12.3b, range F), then the *average* income share might actually decrease.

Finally note, that the discussion in this section neglected possible coexisting attractors and focused on the attractors shown in black in Figure 12.2a. Allowing for this multistabilty would make abrupt changes in the growth regime much more likely.

6 Final remarks

Piketty's (2014) recent book has revived the interest in the literature on the themes of wealth distribution and income inequality. The issue of distribution, especially between social classes, has also been at the core of the post-Keynesian research program of which Carlo Panico has been an important contributor. This Chapter moves along this line of research by developing a Pasinetti-Solow model of growth and distribution which has neoclassical features but allows for low factor substitutability and introduces behavioural features into the (intertemporal) saving decisions.

The model, framed in discrete time, has been able to produce a large variety of complex behaviour. Especially, for a large set of parameter values, multi-stability (i.e. the coexistence of attractors of various periodicity) has been detected. The economic interpretation of our results highlight that not necessarily an increase in the saving propensities of workers (esp. out of wages) brings about an increase in their capital or in their income share. This conclusion follows immediately from: (i) a dynamics with ample fluctuations favoured by low factor substitutability; (ii) the presence of coexisting attractors and, therefore, of different growth regimes; (iii) the possibility that workers may switch between different intertemporal optimisation plans – characterised or not by some form of intertemporal altruism, imitating or not capitalists – depending on their level of wealth. The shift between growth regimes, induced by workers' behavioural change – involving workers different decisions concerning inter-generational transfers of wealth – has a profound impact on the income and wealth distribution between the social classes.

Notes

1 Indeed, one may consider that, in the context of an economy where capital ownership and control are separated, shareholders may not be indifferent between dividends and capital gains. Thus, they may save out of capital gains in a different proportion compared with distributed profits. Therefore, even allowing for the long-run convergence of capital gains to firms' retained profits, the overall saving propensity out of profits is affected by shareholders precautionary behaviour. This also implies that firms' self-financing decisions may also affect that saving propensity. A post-Keynesian theory of institutional distribution has been proposed in Kaldor (1966). See also, among others, Moss (1978), Skott (1981), Panico (1997), Commendatore (1999, 2003) and Bernardo, Stockhammer and Martinez (2016).
2 For much more detailed reviews, see Baranzini (1991) and Baranzini and Mirante (2018).
3 Baranzini (1991) also explores the case of no workers' inter-generetional transfers but only as a special case.
4 Given the assumption of constant population, the offspring of a capitalist and of a worker corresponds in both cases to one child.
5 Note that this same result applies by representing capitalists as an infinitely lived dynasty as in Barro (1974); see also Michl (2009).
6 We could assume that bequests may affect the young worker behaviour. As a consequence, she might attach a different time discount factor β'_w to her preferences compared to the case when she does not receive bequests, with $\beta'_w \neq \beta_w$. The impact

of this effect could have opposite directions: by getting a bequest, the young worker could feel richer and therefore consume immediately more ($\beta'_w < \beta_w$) or she could care more of her offspring, postponing consumption into the future ($\beta'_w > \beta_w$). In Sushko, Commendatore and Kubin (2020), in a slightly different model, we show that setting $\beta'_w \neq \beta_w$ has interesting implications for the dynamics (see also below).

7 By assuming that young workers decide how much to bequeath when young would increase the complexity of the analysis, since we have to take track also of bequest as a further state variable. Thus, the analysis would depart substantially from that of the standard Kaldor-Pasinetti-Solow model.

8 This implies that a change in s_{uw}, i.e. in β_w, is exactly compensated by a proportional change of d_w in the opposite direction, leaving $s_{wp} = \beta_w d_w$ unaffected.

9 This result follows from the fact that, for $k > 0$, $f(k)/k$ is strictly monotonically decreasing and, if condition (12.7) holds, $\dfrac{1 - s_{up}}{s_{uw}(1 - e_f(k)) + s_{up}e_f(k)}$ is monotonically increasing.

10 This result follows from the fact that, for $k > 0$, if condition (12.9) holds, $\dfrac{1 - s_{up}}{s_{uw}(1 - e_f(k)) + s_{up}e_f(k)}$ is strictly monotonically decreasing.

11 In Sushko, Commendatore and Kubin (2020), the condition $s_{uw} = s_{up}$ applies to k_R^{**}. When $s_{uw} = s_{up}$, $\dfrac{f(k_R^{*})}{k_R^{*}} = \dfrac{1 - s_{uw}}{s_{uw}}$. So, a solution k_R^{**} exists and it is unique, if $\lim\limits_{k \to 0} \dfrac{f(k)}{k} > \dfrac{1 - s_{uw}}{s_{uw}}$ and $\lim\limits_{k \to \infty} \dfrac{f(k)}{k} < \dfrac{1 - s_{uw}}{s_{uw}}$.

12 When $s_{uw} = s_{wp}$ (and $\rho \neq 0$), as in Sushko, Commendatore and Kubin (2020), one and only one dual equilibrium k_R^{**} exists as long as $s_{uw} > \dfrac{1}{1 + \alpha^{\frac{1}{\rho}}}$ and it can be derived explicitly, corresponding to $k_R^{**} = \left(\dfrac{1 - \alpha}{b' - a}\right)^{\frac{1}{\rho}}$, where $b' = \left(\dfrac{1 - s_{uw}}{s_{uw}}\right)^{\rho}$.

References

Agliari, A., Böhm, V. and Pecora, N. (2020). Endogenous cycles from income diversity, capital ownership, and differential savings. *Chaos, Solitons & Fractals* 130: 109435.

Baranzini, M. (1991). *A theory of wealth distribution and accumulation*. Oxford University Press.

Baranzini, M. L. and Mirante, A. (2018). Pasinetti on post-Keynesian income distribution and growth theory: the basic issues. In *Luigi L. Pasinetti: An Intellectual Biography*. Cham: Palgrave Macmillan, pp. 131–176.

Barro, R. J. (1974). Are government bonds net wealth? *Journal of political economy* 82(6): 1095–1117.

Bernardo, J. L., Stockhammer, E. and Martinez, F. L. (2016). A post Keynesian theory for Tobin's q in a stock-flow consistent framework. *Journal of Post Keynesian Economics* 39(2): 256–285.

Böhm, V. and Kaas, L. (2000). Differential savings, factor shares, and endogenous growth cycles. *Journal of Economic Dynamics and Control* 24(5–7): 965–980.

Chiang, A. C. (1973). A simple generalization of the Kaldor-Pasinetti theory of profit rate and income distribution. *Economica* 40(159): 311–313.

Commendatore, P. (1993). Sulla esistenza di una economia a due classi in un modello post-keynesiano di crescita e distribuzione con settore pubblico ed attività finanziarie. *Studi Economici* 51: 5–38.

Commendatore, P. (1999). Pasinetti and dual equilibria in a post Keynesian model of growth and institutional distribution. *Oxford Economic Papers* 51(1): 223–236.

Commendatore, P. (2002). Inside debt, aggregate demand and the Cambridge theory of distribution: a note. *Cambridge Journal of Economics* 26(2): 269–274.

Commendatore, P. (2003). On the post Keynesian theory of growth and 'institutional' distribution. *Review of Political Economy* 15(2): 193–209.

Commendatore, P. (2008). Complex dynamics in a Pasinetti–Solow model of growth and distribution. *Economics & Complexity* 3(1), Summer 2006: 33–55.

Commendatore, P. and Palmisani, C. (2009). The Pasinetti-Solow growth model with optimal saving behaviour: a local bifurcation analysis. In Skiadas C.H., Dimotikalis I. and Skiadas C. (eds) Topics on Chaotic Systems: Selected Papers from CHAOS 2008 International Conference,World Scientific: Singapore, 87–95.

Diamond, P. A. (1965). National debt in a neoclassical growth model. *The American Economic Review* 55(5): 1126–1150.

Domar, E. D. (1946). Capital expansion, rate of growth, and employment. *Econometrica, Journal of the Econometric Society* 14(2),137–147.

Fazi, E. and Salvadori, N. (1981). The existence of a two-class economy in the Kaldor model of growth and distribution. *Kyklos* 34(4): 582–592.

Fazi, E. and Salvadori, N. (1985). The existence of a two-class economy in a general Cambridge model of growth and distribution. *Cambridge Journal of Economics* 9(2): 155–164.

Fleck, F. H. and Domenghino, C. M. (1987). Cambridge (UK) versus Cambridge (Mass.): a Keynesian solution of "Pasinetti's paradox". *Journal of Post Keynesian Economics* 10(1): 22–36.

Foley, D.K. and Michl, T.R. (1999). *Growth and Distribution.* Cambridge: Harvard University Press.

Harrod, R. F. (1939). An essay in dynamic theory. *The Economic Journal* 49(193): 14–33.

Kaldor, N. (1955–56). Alternative theories of distribution. *The Review of Economic Studies* 23(2): 83–100.

Kaldor, N. (1966). Marginal productivity and the macro-economic theories of distribution: comment on Samuelson and Modigliani. *The Review of Economic Studies* 33(4): 309–319.

Mattauch, L., Edenhofer, O., Klenert, D. and Benard, S. (2016). Distributional effects of public investments when wealth and classes are back. *Metroeconomica* 67(3): 603–629.

Mattauch, L., Klenert, D., Stiglitz, J. E. and Edenhofer, O. (2018). Overcoming wealth inequality by capital taxes that finance public investment. *NBER Working Paper*, No. 25126.

Michl, T. R. (2009). *Capitalists, Workers, and Fiscal Policy: A Classical Model of Growth and Distribution.* Cambridge: Harvard University Press.

Moss, S. J. (1978). The Post-Keynesian theory of income distribution in the corporate economy. *Australian Economic Papers* 17(31): 303–322.

Odagiri, H. (1981). *The Theory of Growth in a Corporate Economy: Management, Preference, Research and Development, and Economic Growth.* Cambridge; New York: Cambridge University Press.

Palley, T. I. (1996). Inside debt, aggregate demand, and the Cambridge theory of distribution. *Cambridge Journal of Economics* 20(4): 465–474.

Palley, T. I. (2002). Financial institutions and the Cambridge theory of distribution. *Cambridge Journal of Economics* 26(2): 275–277.

Panico, C. (1993). Two alternative approaches to financial model building. *Metroeconomica* 44(2): 93–133.

Panico, C. (1997). Government deficits in Post-Keynesian theories of growth and distribution. *Contributions to Political Economy* 16(1): 61–86.

Park, M. S. (2006). The financial system and the Pasinetti theorem. *Cambridge Journal of Economics* 30(2): 201–217.

Pasinetti, L. L. (1962). Rate of profit and income distribution in relation to the rate of economic growth. *The Review of Economic Studies* 29(4): 267–279.

Pasinetti, L. L. (1983). Conditions of existence of a two class economy in the Kaldor and more general models of growth and income distribution. *Kyklos* 36(1): 91–102.

Piketty, T. (2014). *Capital in the Twenty-First Century*. Translated by A. Goldhammer. Cambridge: Belknap.

Ramanathan, R. (1976). The Pasinetti paradox in a two-class monetary growth model. *Journal of Monetary Economics* 2(3): 389–397.

Ramsey, F. P. (1928). A mathematical theory of saving. *The Economic Journal* 38(152): 543–559.

Salvadori, N. (1991). Post-Keynesian theory of distribution in the long run. In *Nicholas Kaldor and Mainstream Economics*. London: Palgrave Macmillan, pp. 164–189.

Samuelson, P. A. and Modigliani, F. (1966). The Pasinetti paradox in neoclassical and more general models. *The Review of Economic Studies* 33(4): 269–301.

Skott, P. (1981). On the 'Kaldorian' saving function. *Kyklos* 34(4): 563–581.

Solow, R. M. (1956). A contribution to the theory of economic growth. *The Quarterly Journal of Economics* 70(1): 65–94.

Steedman, I. (1972). The state and the outcome of the Pasinetti process. *The Economic Journal* 82(328): 1387–1395.

Stiglitz, J. E. (2015a). New theoretical perspectives on the distribution of income and wealth among individuals: Part I. The wealth residual. *NBER Working Paper*, No. 21189.

Stiglitz, J. E. (2015b). New theoretical perspectives on the distribution of income and wealth among individuals: Part II: Equilibrium wealth distributions. *NBER Working Paper*, No. 21190.

Stiglitz, J. E. (2015c). New theoretical perspectives on the distribution of income and wealth among individuals: Part III: Life cycle savings vs. inherited savings. *NBER Working Paper*, No. 21191.

Stiglitz, J. E. (2015d). New theoretical perspectives on the distribution of income and wealth among individuals: Part IV: Land and credit. *NBER Working Paper*, No. 21192.

Sushko, I., Commendatore, P. and Kubin, I. (2020). Codimension-two border collision bifurcation in a two-class growth model with optimal saving and switch in behavior. *Nonlinear Dynamics* 102(2), 1071–1095.

Part III

Monetary and fiscal policies and the role of institutions

13 The underground economy and the financial market

A two-sided relationship

Salvatore Capasso and Salvatore Ciucci

1 Introduction

Despite recent years have witnessed a great research effort around the globe, followed by a significant body of informative studies, much of the questions on the causes, consequences and, even the real dimension, of the underground economy[1] remain open. As it occurs for many phenomena in economics, the interplay between the size of the underground sector and other variables in the economy is complex and difficult to disentangle because of the relevant number of factors involved. And often, to complicate matter, much of these relationships are uncertain in the direction of causality.

Research has identified different major causes of the underground economy: an excessive pressure of taxation, the inefficiency of the justice system, an inadequate system of provision of public goods and services, the extent of corruption and the general poor quality of institutions (Friedman et al., 2000; Johnson, Kaufmann and Zoido-Lobaton, 1998; Schneider and Enste, 2000; Schneider, 2005). Yet the full picture of why firms and individuals operate underground and the impact of this sector on the economy are still fuzzy and open to further investigation. It is really not clear, for instance, what is the cost of informality for the economic system, in particular over the long term, and what are the best policy recipes to curb informality. Analogously, other hypotheses on the determinants of informality are under scrutiny and one issue, in particular, remains under the research spotlight for its importance in shaping the economy growth potential over the long term: the interplay between the working of the financial system and the level of underground economy.

Easy access to credit and a relatively low cost of obtaining external financial resources are vital not only for firms' investments but also for individuals' long-term consumption. Hence, the working of the financial system influences firms' investment plans and individuals' long-term consumption and savings choice. At the same time, the working of the financial system represents the opportunity cost for being informal and can influence agents' decision to operate underground. In fact, by choosing to stay underground firms and individuals display a lower ability to signal their profitability and credit worthiness and can access credit at a higher cost and with more

DOI: 10.4324/9781003105558-16

difficulty. Hence, if the average probability of obtaining credit is low and the average cost of credit is high, the opportunity cost of being underground is low. The opposite occurs when the financial system develops: the interest rates go down, and so does the overall cost of credit with the result that being underground becomes costlier. On these grounds, the most recent literature (Antunes and Cavalcanti, 2007; Capasso and Jappelli, 2013; Straub, 2005) have first argued, and then empirically found, a general inverse relationship between financial development and the underground economy: economies with more developed financial system also display lower levels of informality. In turn, by influencing firms' investment plans and individuals' long-term saving/consumption choice, the interplay between the financial system and the underground economy may affect the growth potential of the economy.

Yet, things might be more complicated than this account may suggest, and one can also argue that it is the level of underground economy to influence the working of the financial system. One hypothesis is the following. Since banks issue credit by applying different lending technologies with different monitoring and screening costs (Berger and Udell, 1995), by increasing the average degree of opacity in the system the level of the underground economy may force banks to choose one lending procedure over the other and, by this way, may influence the working of the financial system.

To highlight the main channels of interaction between the financial system and the informal economy, we present two simple models in which the borrowers in need of external funding, approach a lender (the bank) to run a project. In these frameworks, the borrowers can reduce the degree of information asymmetries, and the cost of financing, by supplying some collateral. Agents who do not have sufficient resources to offer as collateral, unable to access the credit market, decide to operate in the underground economy. Hence, the financial contract determines whether access to credit and investing is optimal and, in turn, the number of entrepreneurs choosing to go underground. In the first model (Section 3), the financial system and the level of financial development determine the level of underground economy; in the second model (Section 4), it is the level of underground economy to influence bank's lending procedure and, hence, the working of the financial system.

More specifically, in the first model, based on Capasso and Jappelli (2013), agents choose between a low-return technology and a more advanced and rewarding technology. Investing in the low-return technology does not require a loan, while the high-return technology requires external funding. Firms can reduce the cost of credit by pledging more collateral. Since contracts are not completely enforceable, part of the pledged resources can be lost in case of dispute, for example, because of judicial costs and inefficiencies. Pledging more collateral is costly because firms must disclose their revenues and assets not only to financial intermediaries but also to tax officials. Hence, agents choose how much to invest in the two technologies by trading off the reduced financial cost of supplying more collateral with the benefit of hiding revenues and operating with the low-return technology. The choice between the two technologies is therefore also a choice between the underground and the official economy. Financial development reduces the cost of credit and the incentives to operate underground and renders more profitable to reveal revenues of high-tech (HT) projects.

In the second model, banks can apply two different lending technologies: one which involves the use of hard information and lower monitoring costs; the other which uses more in-depth information on borrowers and entails higher monitoring/screening costs. By using a consolidated terminology in the literature (Berger and Udell, 2002, 2006), we could refer to the first lending strategy as *transaction lending* and the second *relationship lending*. Transaction lending is less costly since it involves the use of hard information and less monitoring, but may not be always optimal.

In fact, entrepreneurs going underground hide revenues and fabricate their financial accounts primarily to escape the tax burden and social security contributions. Yet by doing so, they become opaquer to potential lenders, and their ability to signal income returns and endowments decreases. The result of this action is an increase in the probability of being credit rationed. Indeed, financial accounts and tax statements are among the primary sources of information needed by banks to grant credit. Hence, if the bank operates in a market plagued by informal firms, which can provide very little information regarding their real economic and financial situation, and about their ability to generate future income, standardised lending procedures might decrease the banks' revenue to the extent that they cannot be profitable. In fact, when facing a large number of underground opaque firms and more intense informational problems, banks may find it optimal to mitigate these informational frictions through more intense monitoring. Specifically, more intense monitoring allows bank to access private information (namely *soft information*) and, consequently, to measure firm's real business and profitability. Hence, the model predicts that an increase in the aggregate level of underground economy shapes the working of the financial system.

The chapter proceeds as follows: Section 2 briefly illustrates the most relevant literature on the interrelationship between financial development and the underground economy. Section 3 presents a model in which it is the financial sector to influence the shadow economy sector, and the government's incentive to invest towards financial development. In Section 4, we present a model of optimal lending technology to study the nexus between shadow economy and banks' lending choices, and Section 5 summarises the results and concludes.

2 The related literature

Straub (2005) provides one of the first accounts on the role of financial market in determining informality. In a continuous investment model with moral hazard, he argues that financial institutions allow entrepreneurs and firms greater access to capital to undertake productive investments. The model assumes that entrepreneurs have to be endowed with a minimum level of initial capital to access the financial system. The combination of registration costs and the level of credit rationing makes the formal credit market unattractive, and entrepreneurs who are incapable to obtain credit choose to operate underground. The minimum level of collateral required to access credit is relaxed as interest rates decrease.

Amaral and Quintin (2006) focus on the labour market to build a link between the financial system and the level of informality. The main point is that those who work in the shadow economy earn a lower wage, are less educated and younger than those who work in the formal sector, for this reason managers in the informal sector employ less physical capital and tend to self-finance more investment than those operating formally.

Along similar assumptions, Antunes and Cavalcanti (2007) and Quintin (2008) develop general equilibrium models with credit-constrained heterogeneous agents and a labour market in which informal workers have lower skill endowment than workers employed in the formal sector. The conclusion is that those who work in the formal sector have better access to outside finance and show that regulation costs and the enforcement of financial contracts affect the size of the informal sector; Quintin (2008) also argues that because of regulation costs only the most talented managers choose to operate formally and gain access to more external funds.

Dabla-Norris, Gradstein and Inchauste (2008) posit the idea that the quality of the legal enforcement plays a crucial role in determining the size of the informal sector. In their model, each agent in the economy can choose to become a worker or an entrepreneur in the formal or informal sector. Agents with the lowest managerial ability choose to be a worker, agents with an intermediate level of managerial ability choose to be an informal entrepreneur, and agents endowed with higher managerial ability choose to be formal entrepreneurs. They show that the managerial ability and the quality of the legal system affects negatively the size of the informal sector, while the regulatory burden affects positively informality.

More recently, Blackburn et al. (2012) develop a model of tax evasion and financial intermediation in which individuals may choose to conceal their true wealth status for the purpose of tax evasion. The amount of wealth disclosure and the collateral offered to secure a loan affects the terms and conditions of the financial contract made available to individuals. Hence, financial development negatively affects the level of the underground economy because it reduces the cost of credit and pushes firms to disclose more collateral. Capasso and Jappelli (2013) reach similar conclusion by building a model in which agents choose the optimal amount of tax evasion. In the next section, we provide a detailed and simplified account of this model.

Different works provide an empirical account of the inverse relationship between the level of underground economy and financial development (Bose, Capasso and Wurm, 2012; Capasso and Jappelli, 2013; Dabla-Norris and Feltenstein, 2005; Straub, 2005). These studies employ different measures of the underground sector and many proxies of financial development and all converge by showing that financial development curbs the underground economy.

3 The impact of financial development on the underground economy

We now employ a simple model, based on Capasso and Jappelli[2] (2013), to discuss the channels through which financial development can affect the underground economy.

Consider an economy consisting of risk-neutral entrepreneurs, endowed with an initial wealth A, which can be cash or some kind of productive assets pledgeable as collateral. Assets in the economy, are uniformly distributed among entrepreneurs over the range $[0, \bar{A}]$. Each entrepreneur, indicated by i, can choose to undertake a risky or HT project, which requires an initial investment L_i higher than individual endowment, which must be financed by a bank, yielding QL_i in case of success, with probability p, and 0 in case of failure, with probability $(1 - p)$. By accessing the credit market to borrow L_i, the entrepreneurs can use a fraction $\gamma_i \in [0,1]$ of the initial asset, as collateral which is invested by the bank at an interbank interest rate R_L, yielding the borrower an amount equal to $R_D \gamma_i A_i$, where R_D is the deposit interest rate, and $R_L \geq R_D$. The fraction of undisclosed asset $(1 - \gamma_i) A_i$ can be, instead, invested in a safe or low-tech (LT) project, gaining with certainty an amount $\Phi[(1 - \gamma_i) A_i]^\alpha$, and $\alpha < 1$. The credit market is competitive, banks that finance HT projects, in turn, finance themselves at a rate $\bar{R}$, and face an intermediation cost δ, which can be interpreted as a proxy of financial development. A decrease in δ is associated with a higher level of financial development, since the more developed is the financial system, the lower is the cost of financing. Therefore, the total cost for each unit of loan issued is $\tilde{R} = \bar{R} + \delta$. Banks and government observe only the declared value of the initial endowment $\gamma_i A_i$, and the returns on the HT project. On observable incomes government levies a tax rate t. The amount of the undeclared wealth invested in the LT project is, instead, private information; thus, to avoid tax payments, an entrepreneur may choose to misbehave, declaring only the percentage γ_i of the real value of initial asset. Hence, in this framework, the amount invested by each entrepreneur in the LT projects can be interpreted as the size of the informal sector or underground economy. In case of a defaulting borrower, lenders can get back at most a percentage θ on the HT project return, a percentage σ on the collateral, and can avoid paying the interest on the deposit by withholding the amount $R_D \gamma_i A_i$; therefore, $(1 - \theta)$ and $(1 - \sigma)$ can be interpreted as the cost of judicial efficiency, namely the amount of resources required by the judicial system for its functioning.

Denoting R_i as the ex ante repayment rate charged to an entrepreneur for each unit of capital externally financed, the bank's zero-profit condition is:

$$\tilde{R}L_i - (R_L - R_D)\gamma_i A_i = p \cdot \min\left[R_i L_i, (\theta Q L_i + \sigma\gamma_i A_i + R_D\gamma_i A_i)\right]$$
$$+ (1 - p)\min\left[R_i L_i, (\sigma\gamma_i A_i + R_D\gamma_i A_i)\right]$$

Suppose that the collateral is sufficient to repay the loan,[3] only in the case of success, i.e. $R_i L_i \leq \theta Q L_i + \sigma\gamma_i A_i + R_D\gamma_i A_i$, but not in case of failure, i.e. $R_i L_i > \sigma\gamma_i A_i + R_D\gamma_i A_i$, then bank's zero-profit condition can be rewritten as:

$$\tilde{R}L_i - (R_L - R_D)\gamma_i A_i = pR_i L_i + (1 - p)(\sigma\gamma_i A_i + R_D\gamma_i A_i) \qquad (13.1)$$

Solving Equation (13.1) for R_i, the required interest rate is:

$$R_i^* = \frac{\tilde{R}}{p} - \frac{[(1 - p)\sigma + R_L - pR_D]\gamma_i A_i}{pL_i} \qquad (13.2)$$

Instead, supposing that the collateral is not sufficient to repay the lender even if the project is successful, i.e. $R_i L_i \geq \theta Q L_i + \sigma\gamma_i A_i + R_D\gamma_i A_i$, we can rewrite the bank's zero-profit condition as:

$$\tilde{R}L_i - (R_L - R_D)\gamma_i A_i = p \cdot [\theta Q L_i + \sigma\gamma_i A_i + R_D\gamma_i A_i]$$
$$+ (1 - p)[\sigma\gamma_i A_i + R_D\gamma_i A_i]$$

and simplifying

$$\tilde{R}L_i - R_L\gamma_i A_i = p\theta Q L_i + \sigma\gamma_i A_i$$

Solving for the initial asset, one gets the minimum value of declared endowment, $A_{\min}$, below which the borrower cannot access the financial contract:

$$A_{\min} = \frac{(\tilde{R} + \delta)L_i - p\theta Q L_i}{\sigma + R_L} \qquad (13.3)$$

A borrower can get a bank loan only if $\gamma_i A_i \geq A_{\min}$, and chooses to declare the value of the initial asset which maximises his expected utility. Each entrepreneur solves the following maximisation problem:

$$\max_{\gamma_i} E(u) = p(1 - t)[(Q - R_i^*)L_i + (1 + R_D)\gamma_i A_i] + \Phi[(1 - \gamma_i)A_i]^\alpha \qquad (13.4)$$

Using Equation (13.2), the solution of the above problem is:

$$\gamma_i^* = 1 - \left[\frac{\alpha\Phi}{(1 - t)[(1 - p)\sigma + p + R_L]} \right]^{\frac{1}{1-\alpha}} \cdot \frac{1}{A_i} \qquad (13.5)$$

Since $\partial\gamma_i^*/\partial A_i > 0$ and $\partial^2\gamma_i^*/\partial A_i^2 < 0$, higher collateral increases disclosure, thus, borrowers with higher initial endowment prefer to invest a higher share of their initial capital in the HT project.

Most importantly, Equation (13.3) clearly states that the minimum level of collateral to access credit, $A_{\min}$, depends negatively on the level of financial development (positively on δ). In turn, this implies that as financial markets develop, the number of entrepreneurs that can access credit increases and the level of underground economy decreases. It is also possible to show that the effect of financial development on the size of the underground economy is stronger at low levels of financial development. The effect of financial development on the underground economy is also higher with a more efficient judicial system (higher levels of θ and σ).

It is also interesting to note that since the LT project (operated by informal entrepreneurs) shows decreasing returns to scale, financial market development can never eliminate credit rationing, because for very low levels of assets, entrepreneurs will prefer LT project to HT project.

Using Equation (13.5) and setting $\gamma_i^* = 0$, it is possible to identify the minimum level of asset:

$$A_{LT} = \left[\frac{\alpha\Phi}{(1 - t)[(1 - p)\sigma + p + R_L]} \right]^{\frac{1}{1-\alpha}} \qquad (13.6)$$

below A_{LT}, the LT project dominates HT project.

3.1 The government incentive to invest in financial development

From what discussed earlier, it is quite natural to think that governments or tax authorities would have greater benefits in combating tax evasion through investments directed to improve financial development, rather than through fines and penalties. In this section, we show that, it is not always convenient or feasible, in particular, for financial constrained governments, to invest and promote financial development with the objective to neutralise the shadow economy. Moreover, the model also underlines that the interrelationship between financial development and the underground economy also depends on the wealth distribution among the population, as well as on the minimum level of the initial asset.

Suppose that β_A is the percentage of population endowed with an initial asset A, and β_{LT} the percentage of individuals with an initial capital A_{LT}, and $A_{LT} < A < A_{\min}$. As in Roubini and Sala-i-Martin (1992, 1995), we assume that the cost of financial intermediation in the economy is proportional to the size of underground economy, formally $\delta = a\{\beta_{LT}\Phi[(1 - \gamma_{LT})A_{LT}]^\alpha + \beta_A\Phi[(1 - \gamma_A)A]^\alpha\}$; note that who is endowed with A_{LT}, chooses to invest only in the LT project and therefore γ_{LT} is equal to zero. With the objective to reduce the level of shadow economy, the government finances the residual part of the necessary collateral to allow the β_A percentage of individuals to access the credit market and start investing in the HT project. Therefore, the government has to invest an amount $I = \beta_A(A_{min} - A)$ so that the cost of financial intermediation becomes $\delta = a[\beta_{LT}\Phi[A_{LT}]^\alpha]$. This investment to spur financial development is feasible, in particular for a financially constrained government, only if the amount of resources invested does not exceed the extra tax revenue, generated by the reduction of the size of underground economy. Formally, the following condition must hold:

$$I \leq pt\beta_A[(Q - R^*_{A_{min}})L_{A_{min}} + (1 + R_D)\gamma_{A_{min}}A_{min}]$$

Entrepreneurs initially endowed with A are now able to reach the minimum level of initial wealth, which allows them to obtain external funding. Hence, $L_{A_{min}}$ is the borrowed amount, $\gamma_{A_{min}}$ is the part of initial wealth disclosed, and $R^*_{A_{min}}$ is the repayment rate paid by those individuals.

Using Equations (13.2), (13.5) and (13.6), we can rewrite the above condition in the following way:

$$\beta_A(A_{min} - A)$$
$$\leq pt\beta_A\left[\left(Q - \left[\frac{(\bar{R} + \delta)}{p} - \frac{[(1 - p)\sigma + R_L - pR_D]\gamma_{A_{min}}A_{min}}{pL_{A_{min}}}\right]\right)L_{A_{min}}\right.$$
$$\left. + (1 + R_D)\gamma_{A_{min}}A_{min}\right],$$

and rearranging,

$$A_{min} - A \leq t[pQ - (\bar{R} + \delta)]L_{A_{min}}$$
$$+ t[(1 - p)\sigma + R_L - pR_D + p(1 + R_D)]\gamma_{A_{min}}A_{min}.$$

Recalling that all entrepreneurs previously credit rationed will now be able to access credit by disclosing all their collateral, we obtain

$$A_{min} - A \leq t[pQ - (\bar{R} + a[\beta_{LT}\Phi[A_{LT}]^\alpha])]L_{A_{min}}$$
$$+ t[(1 - p)\sigma + p + R_L][A_{min} - A_{LT}]$$

and finally

$$A_{\min} \leq \frac{t\left[(pQ - \bar{R} - a\beta_{LT}\Phi[A_{LT}]^{\alpha})L_{A_{\min}} - [(1-p)\sigma + p + R_L]A_{LT}\right] + \underline{A}}{1 - t[(1-p)\sigma + p + R_L]} = A^* \quad (13.7)$$

Since $\partial A_{\min}/\partial\delta > 0$, the higher the level of financial development (the lower is δ), the more relaxed is condition (13.7), and vice versa. This implies that it is more difficult to reduce the size of the shadow economy, by investing in financial development, when the pre-existing level of financial development is very low. Moreover $\partial A^*/\partial\beta_{LT}A_{LT} < 0$ and $\partial A^*/\partial\underline{A} > 0$, which it makes clear that the choice of a government to shrink tax evasion, through financial development is strongly affected by the wealth distribution among the population.

4 The impact of the underground economy on the financial system

Following Capasso, Monferrà and Sampagnaro (2015), we now build a simple model in which it is the level of underground economy that influences the financial system.

Consider an economy populated by a large number of firms and a monopolistic bank. Firms are endowed with an initial level of capital, A_i, which is uniformly distributed on [0,1], and with two investment projects: an HT project and an LT project.

We will assume that the HT project requires a capital outlay, $L > A_i$, so that, given the initial endowment A_i, no entrepreneur can finance the project without accessing credit, i.e. $L - A_i > 0 \; \forall \; A_i \in [0, 1]$, which may or may not be supplied by the monopolistic bank. The return on HT project depends on entrepreneur's effort: following the initial investment, L, at time t, the project will deliver Q units of output next period with probability p_s and 0 units of output with probability $1 - p_s$, where $s = h, l$ denotes a high level of effort, h, or a low level of effort, l. By supplying a low level of effort, the entrepreneur obtains a private non-contractible benefit, $B > 0$. We assume (Holmstrom and Tirole, 1997) that the HT project has a positive expected value only if the entrepreneur exerts a high level of effort:

$$p_h Q - RL > 0 > p_l Q - RL, \quad (13.8)$$

where R is the market return on capital.

The LT project does not require a minimum level of investment and grants higher returns when it runs in conjunction with the HT project. Suppose that working on two projects can allow the entrepreneur to acquire more skills and be more productive, or take advantage of economies of scale, then A_i units of capital invested at time t, will deliver, at time $t + 1$, ΦA_i units of output when the LT project runs jointly with the HT project, and ϕA_i otherwise, where $\Phi > \phi$.

We assume that entrepreneurs can hide their income and evade taxes only if they do not access credit. The underlying idea is that when an entrepreneur asks for a bank loan, he becomes immediately visible to the government and is forced to pay taxes. Though it is not a necessary condition for the model to function, this assumption simplifies the matter since it implies that only entrepreneurs not accessing credit (and running only the LT projects) can hide and operate underground.

4.1 The optimal financial contract

We now determine the optimal financial contract. As in the previous model, the borrower can deposit collateral A_i, since the bank is a monopolist, sets a zero deposit rate ($R_D = 0$); the bank then grants a loan of amount L and receives A_i, which can be invested at the market rate R_L (henceforth, we denote it only with R), the loan's opportunity cost is therefore $R(L - A_i)$, because the bank on the market invests only A_i, when instead it could have invested L. It is like each entrepreneur undertaking the HT project will ask for a minimum loan size $L - A_i$. The bank decides whether to grant credit or not, and the financial conditions. The financial contract entails three components: the loan size, the interest rate and the decision on credit rationing. Given Equation (13.8), the bank ensures that each entrepreneur exerts effort h. To achieve this objective, the financial intermediary screens borrowers' abilities and monitors their behavior by acquiring information. We allow the bank to implement two alternative screening/monitoring procedures (lending technologies): (1) a procedure involving a standardised process to access and extract information from formal documentations of any sources (hard information), and which from now on we will refer to as 'transaction lending'; and (2) one involving an in-depth inquiry into firm's profitability, for which the bank will use all available informative channels to investigate the business (soft information), and which from now on we will call it 'relationship lending'. Since retrieving information from easily accessible documents is less costly, we argue that transaction lending entails lower per loan monitoring costs but it is also less efficient than relationship lending at detecting non-profitable loans and reducing moral hazard.

Different lending procedures will obviously deliver different financial contracts and, interestingly, bank's most profitable lending procedure is not the less costly. In fact, the return from lending activity depends on the amount of available hard information: as the number of firms going underground increases and, as a consequence, the aggregate level of hard information decreases, transaction lending becomes less and less profitable.

Assume that all agents are risk neutral. Under the assumption that the bank applies standardised procedures (transaction lending), entrepreneur applying for a loan size, $L - A_i$, will obtain

$$R_f = \frac{B}{p_H - p_L} \tag{13.9}$$

while the bank will retain $R_b = Q - R_f$; therefore, Equation (13.9) is an incentive compatibility constraint, which allows bank to extract all the surplus, ensuring that borrower exerts high effort. The bank will grant credit only if the expected return on the loan covers the market return on capital R, i.e.

$$p_H R_b = p_H \left(Q - \frac{B}{p_H - p_L} \right) \geq R(L - A_i) \tag{13.10}$$

Recalling that the initial level of capital is uniformly distributed on $[0,1]$, constraint (13.10) implicitly defines the minimum level of capital below which firms are credit rationed:

$$\hat{A}(R, B, Q) = L - \frac{p_H}{R} \left(Q - \frac{B}{p_H - p_L} \right) \tag{13.11}$$

In other words, only firms with a sufficient level of initial capital endowment, $A_i \geq \hat{A}$, will be able to obtain a loan to run the HT project, while firms with $A_i < \hat{A}$ will be credit rationed. Since $A_i \in [0, 1]$, $\hat{A}$ is the share of credit constraint firms while $1 - \hat{A}$ is the share of firms undertaking the HT project.

Alternatively, the bank can implement stricter monitoring (relationship lending) and push entrepreneurs to choose effort h. We formally model this idea by assuming that under relationship lending the private benefit to entrepreneurs from supplying low effort l, is reduced to $b < B$. However, relationship lending also requires a higher level of per loan monitoring cost, $C > 0$.[4] In this case, the financial contract entails a payment to the entrepreneur of

$$R_f = \frac{b}{p_H - p_L} \tag{13.12}$$

while the bank will retain $R_b = Q - \frac{b}{p_H - p_L}$ and will grant credit only if

$$p_H \left(Q - \frac{b}{p_H - p_L} \right) - C \geq R(L - A_i) \tag{13.13}$$

In this case, the minimum level of capital below which we have credit rationing is:

$$\tilde{A}(R, b, Q) = L - \frac{p_H}{R}\left(Q - \frac{b}{p_H - p_L}\right) + \frac{C}{R} \tag{13.14}$$

Therefore, only firms with an initial level of capital endowment, $A_i \geq \tilde{A}$, will obtain credit, while firms with insufficient initial resources, i.e. $A_i < \tilde{A}$ will be credit constrained and will only run the LT project.

4.2 Firms and bank's optimal choice

Given the financial contract, firms choose whether to access credit and run the HT project or to operate underground by running the LT project on its own. To simplify matter, we assume that the first option always dominates the second. Project HT requires an initial capital outlay L, which each firm can self-finance up to $A_i \geq \hat{A}$ in case of transaction lending and $A_i \geq \tilde{A}$, in case of relationship lending. Since the repayment does not depend on the loan size (Equations (13.9) and (13.12)), each firm will find it optimal to maximise the loan size by borrowing $L - \hat{A}$ or $L - \tilde{A}$. The remaining resources will be invested in the LT project.

Hence, under transaction lending, firm i's expected utility, after paying the proportional tax rate t, is

$$(1 - t)[p_H R_f + \Phi(A_i - \hat{A})] = (1 - t)\left[p_H \frac{B}{p_H - p_L} + \Phi(A_i - \hat{A})\right], \tag{13.15}$$

while firm i's expected utility under relationship lending is

$$(1 - t)[p_H R_f + \Phi(A_i - \tilde{A})] = (1 - t)\left[p_H \frac{b}{p_H - p_L} + \Phi(A_i - \tilde{A})\right]. \tag{13.16}$$

Credit rationed firms will instead invest all their endowment in the LT project and obtain ϕA_i which can be hidden to the government.

The bank's lending strategy depends on the level of underground economy: indeed, whether it is optimal to apply transaction or relationship lending depends on bank's expected net profits, which in turn depends on lending costs and hence on the aggregate level of issued credit.

Transaction lending entails fixed costs, K, which are independent of the number of loans the bank issues. Very simply, one may think of these costs as sunk costs required to organise the filing and processing formal documents. Hence, under transaction lending bank's expected profit is

$$\Pi_{TL} = (1 - \hat{A}) p_H R_b - K = (1 - \hat{A}) p_H \left(Q - \frac{B}{p_H - p_L} \right) - K \quad (13.17)$$

Since under relationship lending, only $1 - \tilde{A}$ firms access credit and recalling that the intermediary sustains a per loan monitoring cost, C, the bank's expected profit is

$$\Pi_{RL} = (1 - \tilde{A})(p_H R_b - C) = (1 - \tilde{A}) \left[p_H \left(Q - \frac{b}{p_H - p_L} \right) - C \right] \quad (13.18)$$

By combining (13.11) and (13.14), we obtain:

$$\tilde{A} = \hat{A} + \frac{C}{R} - \frac{p_H}{R} \left(\frac{B - b}{p_H - p_L} \right) \quad (13.19)$$

The latter expresses the minimum level of capital below which there is credit rationing (or similarly the percentage of credit rationed firms) under relationship lending, in terms of the equivalent threshold under transaction lending. Equivalently, because firms that do not access credit go underground, Equation (13.19) links the levels of the underground economy under the two intermediation regimes.

By using Equation (13.19), we can rewrite Equation (13.18) in the following way:

$$\Pi_{RL} = \left[p_H \left(Q - \frac{b}{p_H - p_L} \right) - C \right] \left[1 - \frac{C}{R} + \frac{p_H}{R} \left(\frac{B - b}{p_H - p_L} \right) \right]$$
$$- \left[p_H \left(Q - \frac{b}{p_H - p_L} \right) - C \right] \hat{A} \quad (13.20)$$

Transaction lending is more profitable if:

$$\left[C - p_H \left(\frac{B - b}{p_H - p_L} \right) \right] + \frac{1}{R} \left[C - p_H \left(\frac{B - b}{p_H - p_L} \right) \right] \left[p_H \left(Q - \frac{b}{p_H - p_L} \right) - C \right]$$
$$- K > \left[C - p_H \left(\frac{B - b}{p_H - p_L} \right) \right] \hat{A} \quad (13.21)$$

By using the inequality (13.21) it is easy to draw the following conclusions:

$$\Pi_{TL}(\hat{A} = 1) > \Pi_{RL}(\hat{A} = 1) \Longleftrightarrow K < \bar{K}$$

$$\Pi_{TL}(\hat{A} = 0) > \Pi_{RL}(\hat{A} = 0) \Longleftrightarrow K < \bar{K} + \alpha$$

$$\Pi_{TL}(\hat{A} = 1) < \Pi_{RL}(\hat{A} = 1) \Longleftrightarrow K > \bar{K}$$

$$\Pi_{TL}(\hat{A} = 0) < \Pi_{RL}(\hat{A} = 0) \Longleftrightarrow K > \bar{K} + \alpha$$

where $\bar{K} = \frac{1}{R}\left[C - p_H\left(\frac{B-b}{p_H - p_L}\right)\right]\left[p_H\left(Q - \frac{b}{p_H - p_L}\right) - C\right]$, and $\alpha = \left[C - p_H\left(\frac{B-b}{p_H - p_L}\right)\right]$.

Now, if $C > p_H\left(\dfrac{B-b}{p_H - p_L}\right)$ then:

1   $K < \bar{K} \Rightarrow$ TL always dominates RL (Figure 13.1b)
2   $\bar{K} < K < \bar{K} + \alpha \Rightarrow$ TL dominates RL if $\hat{A} < 1 + \frac{1}{R}\left[p_H\left(Q - \frac{b}{p_H - p_L}\right) - C\right] - K$
    and vice versa (Figure 13.1c)
3   $K > \bar{K} + \alpha \Rightarrow$ RL always dominates TL (Figure 13.1a)

If instead $C < p_H\left(\dfrac{B-b}{p_H - p_L}\right)$ then:

4   $K < \bar{K} - \alpha \Rightarrow$ TL always dominates RL (Figure 13.1b)
5   $\alpha - \bar{K} < K < \bar{K} \Rightarrow$ TL dominates RL if $\hat{A} > 1 + \frac{1}{R}\left[p_H\left(Q - \frac{b}{p_H - p_L}\right) - C\right] - K$
    and vice versa (Figure 13.1d)
6   $K > \bar{K} \Rightarrow$ RL always dominates TL (Figure 13.1a).

The results show that for high (low) values of monitoring costs, the TL dominates over RL, for a low (high) level of the underground economy $(\hat{A})$ and vice versa. Therefore, it is the level of underground economy that influences the financial system and the way in which banks operate.

5 Concluding remarks

The underground economy is a complex phenomenon and it is rather difficult to pinpoint its major determinants. Many factors interact with each other and can shape the decision of firms and individuals to hide to government and subtract to formality. Among these factors the working of financial system and financial development are very relevant ones, this is particularly true in most advanced economies where new technologies implementation requires high amount of capital outlay and call for access to external financing.

In a world plagued by informational problems, firms and individuals find it difficult to signal their ability to repay a possible loan. Financial intermediaries

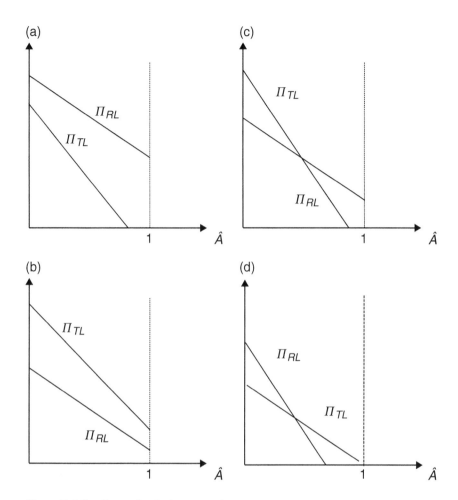

Figure 13.1 Lending technologies comparison.

react by producing financial contracts which penalise agents with low levels of collateral and no guarantees, and by increasing the interest rates and the probability of credit rationing. At the same time, high levels of taxation and regulatory costs push agents to escape in informality and to hide, by decreasing their ability to signal their incomes and profits to financial intermediaries. Hence, the optimal choice to go underground entails the trade off the cost of not being able to access credit with the benefit of lower formality costs.

As financial markets develop, and the cost of credit (for example the interest rates) go down, the choice of informality becomes more and more costly. Hence, the working of the financial system and financial development reduce the level of informality. As we have seen in the first model, financial development reduces the minimum level of collateral which guarantees access to external funding, and, by this way, increasing the number of entrepreneurs that can access the credit market and reducing, accordingly, the underground economy size. We have also shown that when the pre-existing level of financial development is very low, it becomes more difficult to reduce the level of underground economy, by investing in financial development, because of wealth distribution among the population.

The causality nexus may go in the opposite direction: the level of informality may affect the way financial intermediaries work. In principle, it is optimal for banks to reduce as much possible monitoring and screening costs for example by using only hard information to grant credit. However, in an environment overwhelmed by underground firms and individuals, banks may find it impossible to issue credit only by applying lending procedures only based on hard information and evidences. In these circumstances, it could be more rewarding to increase the level of monitoring and screening. Hence, the aggregate level of informality shapes the bank business and influences the working of the financial sector. In the second model, we have shown that the size of the shadow economy affects the bank's choice about the most profitable lending procedure, on which financial contracts depend, this means that the development of the financial system is strongly linked to the size of underground sector.

We hence present two simple stylised models of the interplay between the financial system and the underground economy, each one focusing on one direction of causality. It is interesting to highlight that in both models it emerges a relevant variable linking the financial system to the informal sector: the wealth distribution in the economy. Unequal distributions increase the cost of accessing credit to a larger share of population and feed the underground economy.

Notes

1 Henceforth, we will interchangeably use the terms shadow, informal, hidden or underground economy to designate all of those economic activities, and the income derived thereof, that circumvent or avoid government regulation or taxation.
2 See Capasso and Jappelli (2013).
3 Otherwise, the lender never repays the loan.
4 To simplify, we normalise to zero the per loan monitoring cost under transaction lending.

References

Amaral, P. S. and Quintin, E. (2006). A competitive model of the informal sector. *Journal of Monetary Economics* 53: 1541–1553.

Antunes, A. R. and Cavalcanti, T. V. V. (2007). Start up costs, limited enforcement, and the hidden economy. *European Economic Review* 51(1): 203–224.

Berger, A. N. and Udell, G. F. (1995). Relationship lending and lines of credit in small firm finance. *Journal of Business* 68(3): 351–381.

Berger, A. N. and Udell, G. F. (2002). Small business credit availability and relationship lending: the importance of bank organisational structure. *Economic Journal* 112(477): F32–F53.

Berger, A. N. and Udell, G. F. (2006). A more complete conceptual framework for SME finance. *Journal of Banking & Finance* 30(11): 2945–2966.

Blackburn, K., Bose, N. and Capasso, S. (2012). Tax evasion, the underground economy and financial development. *Journal of Economic Behavior and Organization* 83(2): 243–253.

Bose, N., Capasso, S. and Wurm, M. (2012). The impact of banking development on the size of the shadow economy. *Journal of Economic Studies* 39(6): 620–628.

Capasso, S. and Jappelli, T. (2013). Financial development and the underground economy. *Journal of Development Economics* 101(1): 167–178.

Capasso, S., Monferrà, S. and Sampagnaro, G. (2015). *The Shadow Economy and Banks' Lending Technology*, CSEF WP No. 422.

Dabla-Norris, E. and Feltenstein, A. (2005). The underground economy and its macro-economic consequences. *Journal of Policy Reform* 8(2): 153–174.

Dabla-Norris, E., Gradstein, M. and Inchauste, G. (2008). What causes firms to hide output? The determinants of informality. *Journal of Development Economics* 85(1–2): 1–27.

Friedman, E., Johnson, S., Kaufmann, D. and Zoido-Lobaton, P. (2000). Dodging the grabbing hand: the determinants of unofficial activity in 69 countries. *Journal of Public Economics* 76(3): 459–493.

Holmstrom, B. and Tirole, J. (1997). Financial intermediation, loanable funds, and the real sector. *Quarterly Journal of Economics* 112(3): 663–691.

Johnson, S., Kaufmann, D. and Zoido-Lobaton, P. (1998). Regulatory discretion and the unofficial economy. *American Economic Review* 88(2): 387–392.

Quintin, E. (2008). Contract enforcement and the size of the informal economy. *Economic Theory* 37(3): 395–416.

Roubini, N. and Sala-i-Martin, X. (1992). Financial repression and economic growth. *Journal of Development Economics* 39(1): 5–30.

Roubini, N. and Sala-i-Martin, X. (1995). A growth model of inflation, tax evasion, and financial repression. *Journal of Monetary Economics* 35: 275–301.

Schneider, F. and Enste, D. H. (2000). Shadow economies: size, causes, and consequences. *Journal of Economic Literature* 38(1): 77–114.

Schneider, F. (2005). Shadow economies around the world: what do we really know? *European Journal of Political Economy* 21(3): 598–642.

Straub, S. (2005). Informal sector: the credit market channel. *Journal of Development Economics* 78(2): 299–321.

14 Latin America's macroeconomic policies and growth: An uncoordinated dance

Juan Carlo Moreno Brid, Esteban Pérez Caldentey, and Santiago Capraro Rodríguez

1 Introduction

This chapter is in honour of our friend Carlo Panico, endearing soul, brilliant mind, inspiring mentor, prolific academic writer and splendid economist.[1] Keynes, in his biography of Marshall, established that a good economist, besides having mathematical, historical and philosophical skills,

> must contemplate the particular in terms of the general, and touch abstract and concrete in the same flight of thought. He must study the present in the light of the past for the purposes of the future. No part of man's nature or his institutions must lie entirely outside his regard. He must be purpose fil and disinterested in a simultaneous mood; as aloof and incorruptible as an artist, yet sometimes as near the earth as a politician.[2]

Impossible to describe Carlo, as an economist, in better words. Moreover, his vision, in the Schumpeterian sense of the term,[3] can be considered by the belief that a better future is always possible if one works to build it. That is, in Carlo's by now ample and profound professional trajectory, economic issues are not important per se, as objects of intellectual analysis. They are important because understanding them is a necessary step to generate fair societies; societies that recognise the inherent dignity of everyone, their equal and inalienable rights and freedoms, in full justice and peace.[4]

Carlo's work, impressive in-depth and enormous in scope, has contributions to knowledge in many branches of the discipline, history of economic thought, interest and profit in the theories of value and distribution, central banking, financial regulation, macroeconomic policy coordination, growth and distribution; besides in-depth studies of the works of Keynes Sraffa, Marx, inter alia and the list goes on and on including his very many applied studies of the Italian economy.

However, not so well known yet are his contributions to the analysis of the economic problems of Mexico, and for that matter, Latin America; written in the last seven or eight years since he joined the Faculty of Economics at the Universidad Nacional Autónoma de México. Just as an example of the

DOI: 10.4324/9781003105558-17

relevance of this recent production, in this period Carlo jumpstarted a heated debate on a key issue Banco de Mexico's policies. This is whether the Central Bank has the legal cum regulatory space and the instruments and capacity to directly fund public expenditure. Carlo's analysis of Mexico's central banking and public finance's laws, norms, regulations and practices gives solid ground to answer in the affirmative. As he has argued there are no legal nor technical obstacles to such policy. The obstacles are blatantly ideological or political. The relevance of this issue, in the current situation of dire need of instruments and finance to put in place an effective countercyclical response is immense.

This chapter shines a light on the most recent sphere of his work; to underline the relevance of his analysis to understand the region's – Mexico's in particular – economic growth and distribution challenges. The key objective is to identify the reasons behind Latin America's economic slowdown. An undebatable straightforward answer is not available. Numerous explanations have been offered from diverse economic perspectives. We approach this question through the combined lens of the structuralist school and the Keynesian tradition; in many ways assisted by Carlo's insights to better understand developing economies. In this endeavour, we dig from two major sources of Carlo's intellectual production. The first is his impressive theoretical contributions. The second one comprehends the insights we derived through numerous conversations and discussions on economic matters that the three of us, long-time friends and academic companions, have had with Carlo in many years of friendship and joint collaboration. Actually, while writing this chapter, we had numerous 'Zoom-sessions' with him to discuss Latin America's macro-economic policies and growth challenges. An important part of the analysis we here put forward was nurtured by these conversations. Although Carlo was in the dark on our task to produce this piece – and consequently he didn't write a single word and never saw this manuscript before its publication – we consider him as an intellectual coauthor. We'll see what he says when he reads it!

The chapter has three goals. The first one, as mentioned above, is to show that the mediocre performance of Latin America's economies in terms of growth and income distribution in the last 20 years can be found to a considerable extent in the macroeconomic policies applied in the region, based on inflation targeting and fiscal austerity (see Blinder 2004 on monetary policy). The second one is to highlight that a key obstacle to the region's development is the balance-of-payments constraint; closely linked to its way of insertion in the commercial and financial globalisation processes. The third one discusses and presents an alternative set of macroeconomic policies, in our view, much better geared to trigger the region's economic growth. To accomplish these objectives the chapter is structured in five sections, counting this introduction. The second section presents an overview of the economic performance of Latin America since 1990. The next one shows how the balance-of-payment was a key constraint on the region's growth path. The fourth section analyses the pros and cons of the monetary and fiscal policies implemented in the region. The final section puts forward an alternative set of macroeconomic policies for Latin America. As mentioned above, our work draws on Panico's academic contributions.

2 Latin America's economic growth and development: lights and shadows

As a first approximation to the analysis of Latin America's economic performance since 1990, when it finally left its foreign debt crisis behind, Charles Dickens is a good starting point: 'It was the best of times, it was the worst of times'. Indeed, these years have been full of sharp shifts in the region's fortunes. Stop-go episodes mark its trajectory, having gone through balance of payments and fiscal crisis, commodity booms and busts and pendular swings between right-wing and left-wing governments. On top of it, it is now going through a pandemic that has killed hundreds of thousands and plunged overall trade, output and employment into its worst collapse in a century.

As Table 14.1 shows, its evolution in the last three decades has lights and worrying shadows. On the bright side, there has been progress on the macroeconomic stabilisation front. Indeed, with the conspicuous exceptions of Venezuela, Latin America has managed to bring inflation down significantly. The consumer price index went from a three-digit average annual rise in the 1980s, to two digits in the 1990s and, since then, has remained below 8%. In addition, the public sector's budget has been well under control for decades; with the fiscal balance in surplus or showing a small deficit. On average public debt has not risen excessively relative to Gross Domestic Product (GDP). Low inflation and small fiscal deficits are now standard credentials of Latin America in striking contrast with its not so distant past.

Unfortunately, the results on the stabilisation front are not matched by its economic growth and development. In the 1990s Latin America's economy finally recovered from the dismal performance of the 1980s, the 'lost decade'. Real GDP grew on average at an annual rate of 3.1%. The beginning of the present century seemed promising. Boosted by the improvement in its terms-of-trade, it soon inaugurated a phase of strong expansion. In 2003–2008 its real GDP augmented at an annual average rate of 3.6%. However, the international financial crisis of 2009 turned Latin America's boom into dust. Its real GDP dropped 1.2%, with some national economies experiencing much larger contractions.

In part due to the expansion of external demand and in part to its implementation – for the first time in ages – of swift and most significant countercyclical actions, a 'V'-shaped rebound was soon in force. In 2010 GDP per capita rose on average 5% in real terms. However, its strength was evanescent. As the world economy entered post-2010 the era of 'Great Moderation', characterised by a slowdown of trade and productive activity, Latin America's recovery lost impulse and eventually stalled. By 2019 GDP was stagnant. Most worrying, for the last six years (2013–2019), its real GDP per capita fell at an average annual rate of −0.7%. Figure 14.1 illustrates Latin

Table 14.1 Latin America, key macroeconomic and social indicators, 1980–2019

Table: Latin America, Key Macroeconomic Indicators, 1980–2019

Year	1980s	1990s	2000–2008	2009	2010	2011	2012	2013	2014	2015	2016	2017	2018	2019
GDP growth (%)	1.8	3.1	3.6	-1.8	6.2	4.5	2.8	2.9	1.1	-0.2	-1.2	1.1	0.9	0
GDP growth per capita (%)	-0.4	1.4	2.2	-3	5	3.3	1.7	1.8	0.1	-1.3	-2.2	0.1	0	-0.9
Government revenue (% of GDP)	...	14.5	18.3	19.3	19.4	20.2	20.6	20.3	19.9	19.3	18.2	18.1	18.1	18.1
Government expenditure (% of GDP)	...	16.0	19.9	22.2	21.4	21.6	22.1	22.4	22.5	22.1	21.2	21.1	21.1	21.2
Fiscal balance (% of GDP)	-3.6	-1.6	-1.6	-2.8	-2.0	-1.4	-1.5	-2.1	-2.6	-2.8	-3.0	-3.0	-2.9	..
Debt (% of GDP)	..	35.4	40	44.4	38.9	34.5	37.7	36.5	37	42.3	50.2	48.2	48.5	..
Inflation (%)	126.3	82.7	7.7	3.5	5.4	5.8	4.9	5	6.3	7.9	7.3	5.7	7	8.3
Gini coefficient	0.51	0.53	0.52	0.49	0.49	0.48	0.48	0.48	0.47	0.47	0.47	0.46	0.46	0.46
Poverty rate (%)	41.9	45.4	37.5	32.4	31.6	30.4	28.7	28.5	27.8	29	30	30.1	30	30.5
Extreme poverty rate (%)	19.7	20.3	14.7	8.9	8.6	8.4	8.2	8.3	7.8	8.8	10	10.5	10.7	11.4

Source: CEPALSTAT, CEPAL Cuadernos Estadísticos No. 37, World Bank World Development Indicators and the IMF World Economic Outlook Database (October 2020 Update. For poverty figures from 2009 update based on CEPALSTAT data from Household Surveys Database (BADEHOG). Fiscal data for 1980s includes the average for Argentina Chile, Colombia, Brazil, Venezuela, Peru and Mexico. Gini coefficients for 1980s and 1990s are based on Gasparini et al. (2011) estimations. The figures for fiscal balance are derived as the difference between those of government expenditures and revenues. Data for inflation for 2009 does not include Venezuela.

Note: Average growth for yearly groupings. Growth rates reflect geometric means.

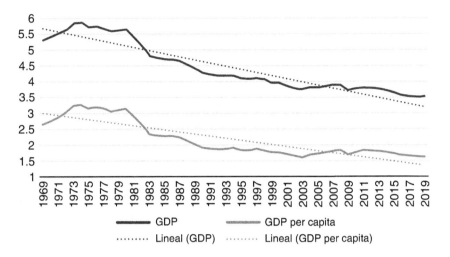

Figure 14.1 Latin America and the Caribbean: real GDP and GDP per capita. Annual average growth rates. Observed and trend values (in percentages, based on constant 2010 dollars) 1969–2019.

Source: Authors' own elaboration based on data from ECLAC.

America's economic growth slowdown. The annual average rate of expansion of its real GDP on average was 6.0% in the 1970s, it declined to 2.7% in 1980–2009 and to 1.9% since then.

Due to its lackluster growth performance, its GDP per capita in real terms lagged behind that of the United States. Indeed, by 2019, it was equivalent to approximately 20% of the US's; a percentage virtually identical to that of 1960.[5] No evidence of catching up, whatsoever![6] In drastic contrast, in this same period, the average GDP per capita of South-East Asian emerging economies went from being equivalent to 12% of the United States to just below 60% of it.

Besides its slow growth, Latin America's economy has been marked by recurrent balance-of-payments crises. Just to name a few, the 'Tequila Crisis' triggered by Mexico in 1994–1995, the 'Corralito Crisis' by Argentina in the early 2000s; the commodity bust in 2009 and, now, the pandemic. Moreover, such performance is reflected in its rather limited social development. There has certainly been social progress in the region. Incidence of poverty registered a regional average of 45% in the 1990s. But, with some ups and downs, it still stood at 30% in 2019. The corresponding figures for extreme poverty are 20.3% and 10.7%. And income distribution is starkly concentrated. On an international comparison, the share of labour in total income in Latin America has been for decades exceptionally low; it stands almost ten percentage points below The Organisation for Economic Co-operation and Development (OECD's) average. Unsurprisingly, Latin America stands as the most unequal region in the world, 'ahead of Sub-Saharan Africa, with an average Gini coefficient that is nearly a third higher than in Europe and Central Asia'.[7] Such inequality is a major obstacle to economic development:

> Equality creat[es] an environment of institutions, policies and efforts for capacity building, speeding up innovation … and the closing of technological gaps, … increased productivity and the opening of sustainable investment opportunities. [A]lso, a better distribution of income fuels demand growth and drives an increasingly diversified and competitive production structure. (ECLAC, 2018b)

As is well known, the situation has worsened in 2020, as the SaRs2-Covid-19 pandemic broke loose, plunged the world commerce and production into a deep contraction and pushed Latin America into its worst recession on the historical record. This massive shock abruptly broke the consensus pro-fiscal consolidation. With few exceptions – distinctively Mexico – all countries in the region applied promptly expansionary fiscal and monetary policy responses. But, in spite of these actions, at the time of writing all forecasts point to a reduction of around 7.7% in Latin America's GDP in real terms; and in real GDP per capita putting it back to its level ten years ago. Most worrying, according to ECLAC's recent estimates for 2020, open unemployment expanded to 13.5%, and inequality – as measured by the Gini coefficient – increased 4.9 points; the poverty rate rose to 37.3%, seven points above its register twelve months ago, and extreme poverty to 15.5% five points above its level in 2019. Repairing this social and economic disaster may take many years. Even if a vaccine is soon discovered, produced and massively distributed, there is consensus that the region is poised to inaugurate a new 'lost decade' in its economic history.

Latin America's 'lights' on stabilisation – i.e. in bringing down inflation and reducing the fiscal deficit – are tightly associated to its 'shadows' on growth and distribution. In fact, its preferred policy mix has prioritised stabilisation, seeing it is a necessary and sufficient condition for the efficient allocation of resources and the expansion of economic activity at its maximum potential. And the consequence has been very costly: a neglect of economic growth and redistribution concerns.[8] In the next section we examine more closely the causes of Latin America's slow growth; causes that were ignored in the region's macroeconomic agenda.

3 The balance–of–payments constraint and macroeconomic policy making in Latin America

Latin America's slow long-run growth is rooted in the semi-industrialised character of its productive structure and, not unrelated, in its form of insertion in world trade and international financial markets. Its economic growth possibilities depend on its capacity to generate sufficient foreign exchange to cover its trade and current account deficits. As the vast empirical literature on the region's trade and growth performance has confirmed, its income elasticity of exports is lower than its corresponding elasticity of imports. In particular, as the income elasticity of its demand for capital equipment and machinery tends to be rather high, a 'domestic push' for strong and persistent expansion of the region's economic activity tends to put excessive pressure on its trade balance.

Thus, unless accompanied by a strong performance of the export sector, any dynamic and persistent economic expansion in Latin America will translate into higher trade deficits and debt to GDP ratios. To the extent that these latter phenomena raise alarm in financial markets and international credit rating agencies, the position will be unsustainable. The picture is too familiar. A rapid economic expansion is accompanied by a loss of international reserves, then gradually by short-term capital flight, and an increasing risk premium on its foreign debt. Pressure builds up on the balance of payments and on the fiscal accounts. And, either the government adopts measures to slow down the expansion or the economy may suddenly be faced with a fully blown crisis.

However, high hopes in the export sector as an engine of growth have been severely tarnished in the region. Its export basket is essentially composed of commodities, products intensive on natural resources, in-bond manufactured goods and tourism. The former two suffer from a long-term decline in their terms-of-trade and acute price fluctuations in the international markets. The latter two have weak backward and forward linkages. These factors help to understand why the region's quest for export-led growth has been doomed. Unless it carries out a profound structural transformation of its productive structure, its long-term economic growth will still be thus constrained.

Let us examine this issue from a somewhat different angle. Given that no country in the region issues a reserve currency, the tendency of the trade deficit to expand as a share of GDP *pari passu* with the rate of expansion of domestic activity sets an upper bound to its long-term economic growth. A major problem for Latin American countries is that the balance-of-payments constrained rate of growth is blatantly insufficient to absorb its working population into decent jobs and to alleviate poverty significantly. The upper bound is, ultimately, determined by the interest, willingness of foreign direct investors, financial organisations, capital markets and -in some small and poor countries- overseas development assistance.

As Table 14.2 shows, in the last two decades the region has funded its current account deficit predominantly with FDI, remittances and short-term capital flows.[9] The figures, however, mask the critical importance of this last source to macroeconomic stability. Indeed, although the annual figure is relatively low compared to the other components, along any year it records sharp fluctuations of much larger magnitude in either direction; in and out of the country. These fluctuations can put acute pressure on the balance-of-payments and subsequently on fiscal and monetary cum exchange rate policy. Direct foreign investment may also pressure the balance of payments through extraordinary episodes of profit repatriation. Note that between 2000–2007

Table 14.2 Latin America and the Caribbean. Financial inflows (in millions of US dollars and percentages of total flows), 2000–2018

	2000–2007	*2008–2009*	*2010–2018*	*2000–2018*
In US$ millions of dollars				
FDI	55,626	85,438	134,628	96,186
Portfolio flows	−725	13,550	74,948	36,623
Other net investment	−17,601	−18,571	−36,993	−26,889
Remittances	41,351	60,321	68,510	56,213
Official development aid	5,959	8,854	10,166	8,151
Total	84,610	149,592	251,260	170,283
As a percentage of the total				
FDI	65.7	57.1	53.6	56.5
Portfolio flow	−0.9	9.1	29.8	21.5
Other net investment	−20.8	−12.4	−14.7	−15.8
Remittances	48.9	40.3	27.3	33.0
Official development aid	7.0	5.9	4.0	4.8

Source: Authors' own elaboration based on official figures from ECLAC.

and 2010–2018 short-term flows increased from 0.9% to roughly 30% of the total capital inflow, while long-term flows declined from 65.7% to 53.6% of the total. Such greater reliance on short-term capital flows comes at the expense of much smaller margins of manoeuvre, of less autonomy in macroeconomic policy making.

The above discussion does not preclude that Latin American countries undergo periods of extraordinary economic dynamism. It states that such periods cannot be sustained. The most recent example occurred in 2003–2008. The commodity boom in world markets brought about a sharp improvement in the terms-of-trade of some economies in the Southern Cone, and somewhat less in Central America. Such favourable shock, accompanied by major inflows of foreign capital, allowed these economies to rapidly expand without deteriorating their trade and current account balances. Moreover, the boom brought about a shift of their export baskets in favour of natural-resource based goods – away from manufactures – in a process described as the 're-primarization' of the region's economy. Such economic dynamism, balanced fiscal budgets and low inflation led some analysts to forecast the region's decoupling from the industrialised world. They believed that it would go on, if not indefinitely, at least for a long time.[10] It didn't. As soon as external demand lost dynamism, the commodity boom collapsed and the external constraint became again painfully binding.

As Figure 14.2 shows, in the absence of the phenomenal improvement in the terms-of-trade, the trade deficit would have soared. And the misperception that the commodity boom would be ever-lasting led these countries to neglect the use of the windfall gain to transform their industrial and foreign trade structure. Failing to reap any long-term benefits, they failed to untangle their economic prospects to the natural resource 'lottery'.

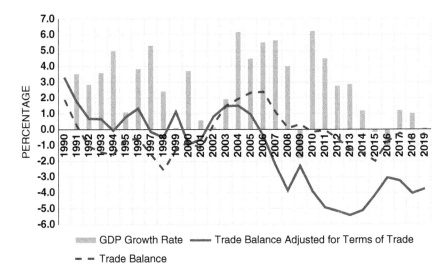

Figure 14.2 Latin America: economic growth and trade balance: as recorded and also adjusted for changes in the terms-of-trade, (annual average in percentages or as a proportion of GDP).

Source: Authors' own elaboration based on official figures.

Having reviewed the stylised facts of Latin America's economic performance and put forward our view that the balance of payments is the binding constraint on its long-term rate of expansion, we now proceed in the following section to analyse the evolution of its macroeconomic policies in its two key areas: monetary and fiscal.

4 Macroeconomic policy in Latin America, a balanced-of-payments constrained region

4.1 Monetary policy in Latin America and the inflation targeting framework

Since the beginning of the 2000s, at the same time, short-term capital flows began to gain more importance, as several Latin American countries (half of the total) adopted inflation targeting regimes apply by independent central banks. These include Brazil (1999), Colombia (1999), Chile (1999), Guatemala (2005), Mexico (2001), Peru (2002) and more, recently, Costa Rica, the Dominican Republic and Paraguay.

Inflation targeting is a monetary policy framework consisting of the public announcement of numerical targets for the inflation rate, bearing in mind that the fundamental objective of monetary policy is low and stable inflation, while maintaining a firm commitment to transparency and accountability. The main instrument of monetary policy is the management of the short-term interest rate through a Taylor type policy rule. A fiscal rule is often invoked to ensure that fiscal policy is aligned with the objectives of monetary policy. In this sense monetary policy dominates over fiscal policy.

The inflation target scheme can be seen as an optimal strategy derived from an explicit objective function of the monetary authority. More precisely, according to the logic of this approach, central banks solve an optimal problem by choosing the price level trajectory that minimises a quadratic loss function subject to the constraints imposed by a linear structure of the economy (Cecchetti and Kim, 2006, p. 176). Formally, the loss function for an open economy can be specified, in general terms, as:

$$L = (y_a - y_n)^2 + \beta (\pi_t - \pi^T)^2 + \gamma (i_t - i_{t-1})^2 + \psi (e_t - e^T)^2 \qquad (14.1)$$

where, y_a, y_p = current and potential output; π_t, π^T = current and target inflation rate, i_t, i_{t-1} = short-term interest rate (i.e. the monetary policy rate) y e_t, e_t^T = current nominal exchange rate and target exchange rate.[11]

The specification of the central bank's loss function has several properties that need to be highlighted. Note first that the choice of a quadratic function, by definition, implies that the central bank attaches the same weight to deviations above and below the inflation target rate and potential output. More precisely, this means that central banks are as concerned about inflation situations as they are about deflation and therefore that the intensity of their reaction is the same in both situations. The same reasoning applies to deviations of current output from its 'natural' level.

Second, it is important to note that the parameter β y the values it takes reflects the degree to which a central bank is averse to inflation. Si $\beta = 0$, (>1) the central bank awards the same (lower) valuation to product fluctuations as to inflation deviations from its target. The higher the parameter β greater will be its aversion to inflation. Both in terms of inflation control, which in this case means reducing the variance of the current inflation rate relative to its target rate (whether from a point inflation rate or a range) is the central bank's priority and hierarchical objective (Svensson, 2004), β is >1 by definition.

Third, the loss function includes an interest rate term $\gamma (i_t - i_{t-1})^2$ reflecting the empirical fact that central banks adjust interest rates according to a *stable path*, which shows that they move in sequences of small changes and that interest rate reversals are rare.[12]

Finally, the nominal (actual) exchange rate and more specifically the deviation of the current exchange rate from its target enters independently into the target function (1). The inclusion of the exchange rate in the objective function is an issue that is subject to debate in the literature.

The loss function (Eq. (14.1)) is minimised subject to the structure of the economy captured by a Phillips New Keynesian curve $(\pi_t = \mu E_t \pi_{t+1} + \alpha (y_a - y_n))$ and a standard aggregate demand curve (IS curve)

$(y_t^g = -\varphi (i_t - E\pi_{t+1}) + Ey_{t+1}^g$). The standard derivation of first-order conditions as a result of the minimisation of the target function subject to restrictions in the first period gives rise to two central properties of inflation targeting.

The first is countercylicality. This implies that when the inflation rate is above its target $(\pi_t > \pi^T)$, the current product will tend to be below its natural level $(y_a < y_n)$. In other words, within the logic of inflation targets, an inflation rate that exceeds the target will lead the authorities to expand demand by increasing the monetary policy interest rate. The second property is the absence of *a trade-off* between the output and inflation gaps, the so-called 'divine coincidence' (Blanchard and Gali, 2005). More specifically, the loss function implies that both inflation and product stabilisation are desirable targets and that in fact there is no conflict between the two.

Due to both the traditional mandate of the central banks and up to the Global Financial Crisis, of the 'divine coincidence' property of the inflation-targeting framework, the reduction of the inflation gap has a hierarchical priority relative to narrowing the real output gap. This is an application of the Tinbergen separation principle which is invoked to argue that the central bank should look after price stability. This also implies that financial stability should be entrusted to a regulatory agency rather than to the central bank (Shin, 2010).

The derivation of both properties is founded upon the idea that the inflation-targeting framework can yield a determinate and stable solution. That is the inflation target is part of equilibrium position that exists and acts as a centre of gravity of a given economy.

4.2 Inflation targeting in an open economy

The constraints to monetary policy derive from the fact that in economies, such as those of Latin America, which are highly integrated with the rest of the world in real and financial terms, the nominal exchange rate which is closely associated to the movement in financial flows plays a key role in the monetary transmission process (see Eatwell and Taylor, 2000). As explained above changes in the exchange rate are a direct channel for the transmission of monetary policy.

Usually, Eq. (14.1) is specified under the condition that $\psi = 0$. Under this hypothesis, the influence of the exchange rate enters the target function through its direct impact on the inflation $(\pi_t - \pi^T)$ and/or output $(y_a - y_n)$ gaps. This presupposes that the authorities act only when the effect of exchange change manifests itself in changes in these gaps (De Gregorio, Tokman and Valdés, 2005).

This view is based on the fact that to assume $\psi > 0$ does not, in principle, have obvious advantages over $\psi = 0$ and that the central bank should worry about the exchange rate, *per se,* only when its variation affects price stability. In fact, $\psi > 0$ presupposes limiting exchange rate variability and, although variability is considered to be harmful, exchange rate movements may in fact act as a buffer for external shocks either through changes in trade volumes or producer profitability. Also $\psi > 0$ may pose inconsistencies in monetary policy management both as it entails, even implicitly, the assumption that the monetary authority has two nominal anchors (the price and exchange rate level).

The counterargument underscores the fact that the exchange rate provides important information on price developments (Svensson, 2000) and the product. Indeed, as Svensson points out Svensson (2000) the exchange rate is a fundamental variable in the mechanism for the transmission of monetary policy in economies with a high degree of openness. In an open economy, transmission mechanisms become more complex than a closed economy.

Variations in the exchange rate are a direct channel for the transmission of monetary policy. On the one hand, they affect the domestic price of final imported goods and therefore the price index. At the same time, the exchange rate affects both the cost of domestically produced goods, through the domestic currency price of imported inputs and via wages. In addition, exchange rate variations act indirectly by strengthening the transmission channel of aggregate demand as the relationship between domestic and imported goods changes.

In addition, the effects of the exchange rate operate through balance sheets. Changes in exchange rates affect the positions on assets and liabilities of companies, households and also of the government.

Depreciation not only raises debt service costs, and thence outgoings, but also swells liabilities by increasing the local-currency value of outstanding debt. If the collateral for the debt is likewise denominated in local currency, depreciation will also cause this asset to lose value. This can give rise to increasing the existing mismatches such that the firm must purchase currency to balance its accounts. Depending on its size and importance in the market and the number of firms behaving in this way, currency purchases can create further pressure for devaluation of the nominal exchange rate, ultimately increasing the external debt of the firms operating in the non-tradable goods sector. Also, a depreciation of the exchange rate will result in capital losses for foreign investors holding titles in domestic currency leading to capital outflows and possibly a further loss in the external value of the national currency.

Contrarily an appreciating currency due to an increase in the monetary policy rate of interest can put downward pressure on prices initially through reduced expenditure and nominal exchange rate appreciation. However, increases in domestic interest rates provide an incentive to attract financial inflows. The consequent increase in international reserves results in an increase in the monetary base and liquidity of the economy which may pose a risk to the achievement of the inflation target. At worst, monetary stability and even financial stability can be jeopardised.

To avoid these risks, central banks tend to sterilise the expansive effect of increased net international reserves. Sterilisation has an upwards effect on the rate of interest which can reinforce the trend of foreign inflows. In the absence of a corrective mechanism, the increase in interest rates within an open economy context can create a cumulative tendency to appreciate. It may also have significant quasi-fiscal consequences when the difference between the domestic and external rates is positive. This mechanism is reinforced by the fact that inflation targeting puts an upward bias on the rate of interest. Even if perfect capital mobility among countries were assumed national currencies and assets are very imperfect substitutes. Holding an asset in domestic currency requires a currency premium. This implies that the divergence between the domestic and the international rates of interest must include a currency premium (Smithin, 2003).

The balance sheet effect of variations in the exchange rate has become particularly important since the Global Financial Crisis (2007–2009) as the evidence shows a widening currency mismatch for the non-financial corporate sector in Latin America, while at the same time, the non-financial corporate sector increased its debt. For Latin America between 2006 and 2014, the net foreign currency assets of non-government as a percentage of exports (a proxy reflecting currency mismatches) increased from 9.7% to 39.7%. For its part, the outstanding debt of the non-financial corporate sector rose from US$50 to US$232 billion for the same period (see Figure 14.3). In 2019, the outstanding debt of the non-financial corporate sector stood at US$327 billion dollars. These effects can be exacerbated by the impact of lower interest rates and a depreciating currency on the expectation of capital losses by foreign investors that hold domestic currency denominated titles.

Finally, the exchange rate operates as a vehicle for transmitting changes in the external context, financial shocks and variations in external aggregate

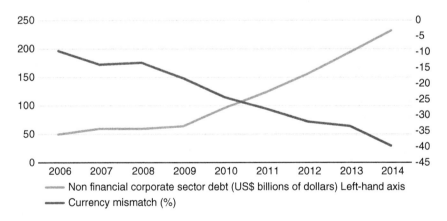

Figure 14.3 Latin America. Non-financial Corporate Debt (US$ billion) and Net foreign currency assets of non-government as a percentage of exports, 2006–2014.

Note: The data is the sum of the aggregate of the following countries, Argentina, Brazil, Chile, Colombia, Mexico, Peru and Venezuela. Source: Chui et al. (2016); FRED (2020).

demand. This transmission channel is highly relevant due to the high degree of international integration between economies and in the case of developing economies due to their high dependency on external markets, especially those of developed economies. This mechanism may be even more important depending on the degree to which the exchange rate rather than behaving as a relative price tends to behave as a financial asset (this is when it meets future expectations of capital gains or losses).

The importance of the exchange rate as a key transmitter of external policy and the challenges it poses to inflation targeting regimes, at the same time, a reflection of domestic policy conditions has been recently underscored by BIS (2019). An accurate assessment of these transmission channels and their importance require an understanding of the institutional components, organisation and operational logic of the financial system. As argued by Panico et al. (2016), the workings of the financial system do not respond to the actions of isolated speculators but rather to the organisation of finance as an industry. Finance is an industry that can, not only influence policy decisions and the public opinion, as was noted by Sraffa (1922) in an article published in the *Economic Journal* on the bank crisis in Italy.

4.3 Fiscal policy

In the aftermath of the international debt crisis in 1981, that inaugurated Latin America's, lost decade, governments in the region made a U-turn in their development agenda. Macroeconomic stabilisation, defined as low inflation and a balanced fiscal budget, was put as the top priority. Fiscal consolidation and, later, inflation targeting became the guidelines for macroeconomic policy.

Public revenues and expenditures, as a percentage of GDP, in spite of their increase in the last three decades are still painfully low. The region's average tax burden (21% of GDP) is way below the OECD's (34%).[13] Moreover, taxes and transfers, as implemented in the region, have scant impact on income distribution.[14] And countercyclical fiscal policies have been more an exception than a rule. Its tax administration is inefficient, with high levels of evasion/avoidance, and a gamut of exemptions whose social benefit remains hard to identify.[15] Another conspicuous weakness is the underreporting and the inexistent direct taxation on the massive informal sector. All these elements open a wide cleavage between the potential and the effective tax base. The consequence is an underfunded State that lacks the resources to meet its basic responsibilities, like social protection and provision of adequate infrastructure. As ECLAC (2018, p. 51) has argued that:

> To aspire to the sustainable financing of public goods and services with a scope and fiscal cost similar to those of the OECD countries, [Latin America] requires much higher levels of tax revenue, not to mention strengthening the efficiency in their collection and in public spending.

The region's fiscal system stands on three sources of revenues: i) taxes on goods and services; mainly on value-added, ii) income taxes and iii) social security contributions. Between 1990 and 2015, taxes on goods and services went from an equivalent of 3.2% of GDP to 7.1% and provided close to a third of total tax revenue. Income taxes climbed from 3% of GDP to 5.4%, and social security contributions averaged 3.9% of GDP. Taxes on property and wealth added up to less than a percentage point. In addition, in several countries, public revenues rely heavily on taxes and levies on the exploitation of non-renewable natural resources. Such 'blessing' goes a long way to explain the perennial postponement of an in-depth fiscal reform. And it introduces a worrying fragility on the State's capacity to implement countercyclical policies as the burst of commodity booms quickly translates into an economic collapse, and a fiscal crisis. Thus, the balance of payments constraint is thus mirrored in a fiscal constraint.

Pari passu with the evolution of revenues, public expenditures also changed, in volume and composition. From being roughly equivalent to 15% of GDP in the mid-1990s, they climbed to 20% in the next decade and recently they stand, on average, around 27% de GDP. The change in its composition reflects the legacy of the neoliberal vision that shifted the State's intervention away from economic affairs to concentrate it on social matters, mainly on poverty alleviation through focalised cash transfers. An additional factor to consider is the reduction of interest payments as the international debt crisis of the 1980s was resolved. In some countries, the re-composition of public sector expenditures mirrors too the end of military regimes.

Another worrying trait of fiscal policy in the region is the declining priority given to public investment. Its share in total public expenditures went from 20% in the early 1990s, to under 18% in the mid-2000s, and has not really augmented since then. The intermittent but steady push towards fiscal consolidation, in the absence of tax reforms, has resulted in a tendency to contain or cut investment. The consequence has been decaying infrastructure, with a widening gap relative both to its domestic needs and to the region's pretenses to compete in the globalised markets. (Serebrisky et al., 2015). On top of this, in Latin America the planning and approval of public projects does not always seem to be in line with a consistent agenda for development. Numerous examples of large-scale public projects abound in the region whose viability rationale and efficiency in terms of long-term social benefits is questionable.

Some analysts point out that the main issue related to public investment in the region is that they consist of inefficient projects rather than their low level. This may be the case for some countries during particularly incompetent administrations. But we find it difficult to generalise this assessment for the while region.

In 2020 the region's fiscal consolidation push came to an end, out of tune with the social and economic challenges posed by the pandemic. The emergency obviated previous debates on the merits and limitations of countercyclical policies. The attention shifted to the more practical issues on its implementation: i) the size of fiscal space, and how to expand it to fund a firm response to meet the sanitary and economic needs of the population and the liquidity needs of private firms, ii) the toolkit of fiscal instruments, and their coordination with monetary and other policies to maximise their impact on income and employment multipliers as well as their impacts on long-term economic growth and iii) the need or possibility of a coordinated response of Latin America and international financial organisations. On a higher level of reflection, the pandemic forced a repositioning of the role of the State in the development agenda, beyond the pandemic emergency.

It's important to point out that since overcoming the financial crisis of 2009, with few exceptions, countercyclical fiscal policies faded away from the agenda of macroeconomic policy in Latin America.[16] Even before 2009, although its performance was full of stop-go cycles, the region, in general, did not put in place effective countercyclical strategies nor automatic stabilisers. Some of the reasons for this are its low and highly volatile public revenues, and very restricted access to foreign capital when in dire need.[17] In addition, on average only 20% of its fiscal budget is not legally tied to previous obligations; a very tight fiscal space. Up to 2019, but for Chile with its rules on maintaining a long-term structural fiscal balance with escape clauses, no country in Latin America had a solid institutional framework to implement countercyclical policies. In practice, the region has opted – a fortiori – to have its stabilisation policies guided less by rules than by discretion.

An important consequence of this fiscal frailty is the reliance on external – more precisely short term – capital flows to accommodate its fiscal needs. Such dependence limits the room of manoeuvre, the autonomy of its macroeconomic policy management. On the fiscal side, expansionary policies which augment the budget deficit and foreign debt are contained by the scrutinous critique of international capital markets and credit rating agencies. As shown in Figure 14.4, there tends to be an inverse relation between country risk and financial inflows.

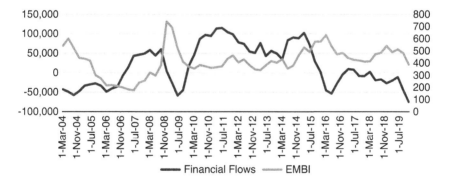

Figure 14.4 Evolution of Latin American 'EMBI' and financial flows net of foreign direct investment (millions of US dollars): March 2004–December 2019.

Note: The Emerging Markets Bond Index (EMBI) measure the difference between the interest rates on dollar-denominated bonds issued by Latin American (Argentina, Brazil, Chile, Colombia, Ecuador, Mexico, Peru, Uruguay and Venezuela) that of United States Treasury Bonds, considered risk-free. Source: On the basis of official information.

Credit rating agencies systematically assess the 'soundness' of macro-economic policy making through very orthodox lenses, that prioritise stability over economic growth and income redistribution, that frown on budget deficits as they, allegedly, create inflationary pressures. Correct or incorrect, a negative assessment on their part raises the nation's cost of external borrowing. Thus, the policy menu of the national authorities is further. Fear of provoking financial markets' mistrust – and by implication an increase in capital flight, loss of investment and higher borrowing costs – tightly conditions the national macroeconomic policy agenda.

The result is that fiscal authorities suffer a 'fear of expanding', much in the same way that monetary ones suffer a 'fear of floating'. Instead of assessing fiscal policy's adequacy based on its long-term impact on economic growth and on social development, it is done based on its short-term impact on the budget deficit and the Debt to GDP ratio. In this process, Austerity becomes the accepted criteria, externally imposed and internally engrained, to gauge fiscal soundness. This incentive to adhere to orthodox fiscal policies has pushed against fiscal discretion and is in favour of rigid rules.[18] In the region a number of countries have adopted different types of fiscal responsibility laws including some sort of transparency rules (Brazil, Colombia, Chile, Ecuador, Panama and Peru) and in several cases, its scope is also both national and subregional (Argentina, Brazil, Colombia and Panama). In the next section, we analyse in-depth the region's monetary policy, paying special attention to its adoption of inflation targeting and the consequences it has had on the growth and development prospects of the region.

5 Final remarks: rethinking macroeconomic policies to trigger economic growth

In this chapter, we show that Latin America suffered a process of stagnation that had its origin at the beginning of the 1990s. We show that the region had episodes of growth characterised by a stop-and-go behaviour. These growth episodes were triggered by an external shock that mitigated the external constrain allowing economic growth (for example, in the 2000s, terms of trade reached a historical level and triggered a period of acceleration of economic growth). In any case, these episodes came to an end when international prices of commodities declined or the countries suffered a balance of payments crisis, and the economy returned to its long-run slow growth trend coupled with high inequality.

We argue the balance of payments constraint is the main stumbling block to boost growth in the region. We show that the set of policies by inflation targeting, fiscal austerity and dependency from international capital financing is an ill strategy to overcome the external constraint, thus we must develop an alternative framework to handle the problems faced by Latin America's economy. An alternative theoretical model can be developed based on Carlo's writings. Mainly through the disentanglement of the equilibrium values of variables to real references based on the neoclassical theory of prices, production and distribution. The key variable in the New Keynesian models (Galí, 2008) that must be criticised is the concept of potential product – or the natural unemployment rate, which is another way to analyse the same theoretical object (Friedman, 1968). This variable indicates the neutrality of monetary (and fiscal) policy in the medium and long term because economic policy actions operate in such a way through the interest rate, that cause the economy to return to its potential level, which does not depend on economic policy in either the short or the long term.

The process of disentanglement starts with Carlo's reinterpretations of the contributions of Keynes and Sraffa. Panico (1988) assumes that Keynes's monetary theory of production (Keynes, 1936) is a long-term theory. Carlo explains that the most significant change between the Treatise on Money and the General Theory is that Keynes realised that the level of economic activity at which the economy tends to (if at all, in the long run) is not independent of monetary policy nor of fiscal policy). This implies that A-priori there are several equilibrium positions, as many as monetary policy decisions. In this way, the concept of natural interest rate vanishes, because if there are as many equilibria as there are interest rates, no level of this variable can be taken as natural.

The traditional response shared by much of the discipline is that the preference for liquidity is a central element of Keynes's General Theory, which can lead to the IS-LM model and hence to the current Neo-Keynesian model (Snowdon and Vane, 2005). Carlo proposes another path, which has recently been highlighted (and expanded) in Shaikh (2016):

> Wray insists on keeping liquidity preference as a foundation, while Panico argues that liquidity preference is insufficient to determine the interest rate because, in the end, this relies on "the common opinion" in the market. … At the other end, Panico's pathbreaking work recovers the classical analysis of the bank interest rate as a cost-based competitive price derived from the equalization of profit rates. It is analyzed in some detail and provides the foundation for my own approach, albeit along somewhat different lines. (p. 25)

Carlo highlights that:

> Two steps can be outlined in Keynes's analysis of the interest rate. The first step deals with the structure of the money market and the different components of demand for and supply or money. The second step deals with the factors that affect the 'common opinion' as to its future value, i.e. it deals with the formation of the convention.
>
> (Panico, 1988, 128)

Panico (1988) does not develop all these aspects, but he has problematised them in different works. For example, Musella and Panico (1995) address the historical determinants of Kaldor's money supply and conclude that while central banks control the interest rate (and not the amount of money) the control is imperfect. As mentioned above in Capraro and Panico (2021), Panico (2014) and Panico and Moreno-Brid (2019) is addressed the issue of money supply money empirically in Latin American countries, in particular Mexico, highlighting the importance of international capital movements on the national monetary policy; which means that the interest rate responds more to the international financial markets evolution than to the national economic conjecture.

Panico (2020b) takes up the issue of the interest rate in Keynes, from a Sraffian[19] perspective, emphasising the structure of the financial market and its consequences on economic development and income distribution. According to Carlo, the structure of the financial sector of an economy reflects the historical evolution of the political power of the society. These ideas are an interpretation of the financial sector based on Sraffa's monetary writings, in particular his vision of the German case. Carlo highlights that:

> In the Lectures Sraffa recalled that, unlike what had happened in Britain, the configuration of the German banking system was the result of a deliberate choice to attribute to the banks the role of promoter of industrial development. The Reichsbank, i.e. the bank of issue that then became central bank, was given the power to establish closer co-operative relations with credit institutions than those existing in England. Since the German unification this form of institutional organization had been allowing the mixed banks to fund the industrial development without running into problems of solvability related to their unbalanced assets-liabilities structure. For Sraffa, the Reichsbank worked as the leading entity of a planned economy in which the mixed or universal banks took a long-term concern in industrial firms by promoting their formation, providing the rating and the certification of their balance sheets, and favoring the sale of their shares in the market. While the banks funded production in strategic sectors of the economy, the Reichsbank assisted them with funds, which were systematically provided to stimulate development, rather than given as an emergency provision, as occurred in Britain. (pp. 7,8)

In the case of Latin America, although it is difficult to develop a homogeneous periodisation for all of all countries, it is possible to consider that from the mid-1930s to the 1980s there was a development financing strategy through public development banks working in coordination with the central banks, guided with the ultimate goal of accelerating economic growth within different industrialisation strategies (Moreno-Brid and Ros, 2009). Private banks (mostly domestic in these years) were also used as growth vectors through central bank-led credit (Cavazos, 1976). The most successful countries in Latin America in terms of growth between 1940 and 1980 were Mexico and Brazil, both countries had development banks that were fundamental instruments to finance investment in their industrialisation processes.

The pursuit of economic development as a target of central banks was set aside from the debt crisis in the early 1980s. After the Lost Decade, central banks were granted independence from political power (Pérez-Caldentey, 2020) and embraced inflation targeting regimes' apothegm, which indicates that monetary policy has no effect on economy's real variables in the long run and therefore cannot be used as an instrument for development (see Section 4.3). Institutional changes in the region were important (Claessens and Van Horen, 2014), we highlighted the rise of foreign banks in the region. However, credit to the private sector as a proportion of the GDP has remained low (50.2% of GDP in 2018–2019, while globally that figure is 129.2% according to the World Bank). Finally, in the last 20 years, Latin America's central banks and governments have been concerned with incorporating their economies into the global financialisation process and this has led to two interesting phenomena: the international financial cycle increasingly has an increased impact on the region's actual economic cycle and a growing indebtedness of non-financial companies through the bonds markets, exposing the region to processes of economic fragility in the face of capital sudden stops (Abeles et al., 2018).

Institutional change is not always beneficial for all members of society. In Panico et al. (2016) it is explained that the redistribution of income that has negatively affected workers in the last 40 years in developed countries is mainly due to the liberalisation of the financial system that have strengthened the companies of the sector in such a way that their managers increase their income more than proportionally respect to the income of the rest of society. In the case of Latin America, the financialisation process that began with the liberalisation of different markets in the 1980s has affected the distribution of income in a negative way for workers. However, it seems that the mechanisms behind the redistributive process are different from those of developed countries. For example, in the case of Mexico, the share of profits from the financial sector has not increased similarly to what has happened in rich countries.

Finally, in order to solve Latin America's major development challenges, macroeconomics policies must consider the following aspects: monetary and fiscal policies affect the long-term equilibrium, international capital movements constraint the autonomy of national policies, institutions can affect economic development and income distribution. Last but not least, industrial policy is key to resolve the external constraint.

Acknowledgements

With valuable assistance from Stefanie Garry and Joaquín Sánchez and thanks to the suggestions of the referees.

Notes

1 'If economists could manage to get themselves thought of as humble, competent people on a level with dentists, that would be splendid' (Keynes, 1933, p. 332).

2 Keynes J.M. (1924). *Essays in Biography*. In Moggridge D.E., ed., *The Collected Writings of J.M. Keynes*, Vol. X, London: Macmillan.

3 Schumpeter, J. A. (1949). Science and Ideology. *The American Economic Review*, Vol. 39, No. 2 (Mar., 1949), pp. 346-359. Schumpeter, J. A. (1954). *History of economic analysis*. New York, Oxford University Press.

4 Panico (2014).

5 IADB (2020)

6 Exceptions include Chile, Perú and Uruguay, which did manage to somewhat reduce that gap from 1990 onwards.

7 See ECLAC (2019).

8 The relations between growth, income distribution and macroeconomic policy design, implementation and coordination are key issues that Carlo has masterfully explored in his many works. See Panico (2011).

9 This pattern goes further back. Data for 1980–2000 shows too that Latin American countries have persistently received both short-term financial flows, remittances and long-term foreign direct investment.

10 There was a debate at that time on whether this apparent decoupling was a consequence of the neoliberal reforms implemented in the 1990s or of the developmentalist agenda put in place by several left-wing governments. For alternative views on this issue see Rojas-Suarez (2009), and on the other hand, Bertola and Ocampo (2012) and Moreno-Brid (2015).

11 In the literature on the subject, the exchange rate usually appears in real terms when it is introduced into the objective function of the central bank (Ainzeman, Hutchinson and Noy, 2008). However, the fluctuations in the real exchange rate are generally due to the movements in the nominal exchange rate.

12 See Sack and Wieland (1999) and Amato and Laubach (2003).

13 Indeed, only Argentina, Brazil and Uruguay have a tax burden in the vicinity of 30% of GDP.

14 The Gini coefficient after transfers and direct taxes falls by more than 33% in the OECD, and by less than 6% in Latin America. This is explained by a prevalence of indirect taxation, a narrow 'base' for income tax collection, and a minimum reliance on taxes on wealth. In 2014, on average in the region, the tax rate paid by richest decile on their income was less than 5%; way below the 21% of the OECD. See Hanni, Martner and Podestá (2015), and Gómez Sabaini, Jiménez and Rossignolo (2012).

15 For the region, fiscal expenditures are close to 2% of GDP, and the revenue forgone due to tax evasion on VAT and income taxes add to more than 6% of GDP (ECLAC, 2020)

16 The exceptions are the creation of some stabilization fund in several countries - Argentina, Chile, Ecuador, Mexico, Paraguay and Peru - to soften downward fluctuations in the economic cycle.

17 Relying on funds from the international private capital markets or multilateral financial organizations is a cursed or blessed? need of Latin America as it can't issue 'hard currency'.

18 Between 1990 and 2005, the following Latin American countries adopted some type of fiscal responsibility law: Argentina (1999 and 2004), Brazil (2000), Chile (2000), Colombia (2003), Ecuador (2002 and 2005), Mexico (2006), Panama (2002 and 2004), Peru (2000 and 2002) and Venezuela (2003).

19 According to Panico (2020b): 'Like Keynes, Sraffa focused on the concept of liquidity and ended up by developing a historical and conventional theory of the interest rate, highlighting the role of the institutional organization of financial markets and monetary policy' (p. 2).

References

Abeles, M., Caldentey, E. P., andValdecantos, V. (2018). Estudios sobre financierización en América Latina, Libros de la CEPAL, N° 152 (LC/PUB.2018/3-P). Santiago de Chile.

Ainzeman, J., Hutchinson, M. and Noy, I. (2008). Inflation targeting and real exchange rates in emerging markets. NBER Working Paper Series. WP 14561.

Amato, J. D. and Laubach, T. (1999). *The Value of Interest Rate Smoothing: How the Private Sector Helps the Federal Reserve*. Economic Review, Federal Reserve Bank of Kansas City. Issue Q III, pp. 47–64.

Bertola, L. and Ocampo, J. A. (2012). *The Economic Development of Latin America since Independence*. New York:Oxford University Press.

BIS (2019). Monetary policy frameworks in EMEs: inflation targeting, the exchange rate and financial stability. *Annual Economic Report II*, 30 June.

Blanchard, O. and Gali, J. (2005). Real Wage Rigidities and the New Keynesian Model. NBER WP 11806.

Blinder, A. S. (2004). *The Quiet Revolution: Central Banking goes Modern*. New Haven:Yale University Press.

Capraro, S. and Panico, C. (2021). Monetary policy in liberalized financial markets: the Mexican case. *Review of Keynesian Economics* 9(1): 129–179.

Cecchetti, S. G. and Kim, J. (2006). Inflation targeting, price path targeting, and output variability, 2005. In B. S. Bernanke, and M. Woodford (eds), *The Inflation Targeting Debate*. NBER. Chicago: University of Chicago Press, pp. 173–195.

Chui, M., Kuruc, E. and Turner, P. H. (2016). A new dimension to currency mismatches in the emerging markets: non-financial companies. BIS Working Paper No. 550.

Claessens, S. and Van Horen, N. (2014). Foreign banks:Trends and impact. *Journal of Money, Credit and Banking* 40(s1): 295–326.

Cavazos, M. (1976). 50 años de política monetaria, in Ernesto Fernández Hurtado (comp.), Cincuenta años de banca central. Ensayos conmemorativos, 1925-1975, EL TRIMES-TRE ECONÓMICO, México, Fondo de Cultura Económica.

De Gregorio, J., Tokman, A. and Valdés, R. (2005). Tipo de Cambio Flexible con Metas de Inflación en Chile: Experiencia y Temas de Interés. *Documento de Política Económica*, No. 14. Banco Central de Chile.

Eatwell, J. and Taylor, L. (2000). *Global Finance at Risk*. New York: The New Press.

ECLAC (2019). *Social Panorama*. Santiago de Chile.

ECLAC (2020). *Fiscal Panorama*. Santiago de Chile.

Federal Reserve Bank of St. Louis (FRED). (2020). Economic data.

Friedman, M. (1968). The role of monetary policy. *American Economic Review* 58(1): 1–17.

Galí, J. (2018). *Monetary Policy, Inflation, and the Business Cycle: An Introduction to the New-Keynesian Framework and Its Applications*. Princeton and Oxford: Princeton University Press.

Gasparini, L., Cruces, G. and Tornarolli, L. (2011). Recent trends in income inequality. *Economia* 11(2): 147–201.

Gómez Sabaini, J. C., Jiménez, J. P. and Rossignolo, D. (2012). Imposición a la renta personal y equidad en América Latina: nuevos desafíos. *Macroeconomics of Development Series*, No. 119 (LC/L.3477-P). Santiago: Economic Commission for Latin America and the Caribbean (ECLAC).

Hanni, M., Martner, R. and Podestá, A. (2015). The redistributive potential of taxation in Latin America. *CEPAL Review*, No. 116 (LC/G.2643-P). Santiago: Economic Commission for Latin America and the Caribbean (ECLAC).

IADB (2020). *Salir del Tunel Pandémico con crecimiento y equidad.* Washington, DC:Inter American Development Bank.

Keynes, J. M. (1936). *The General Theory of Employment, Interest, and Money.* London: Macmillan.

Keynes, J. M. (1933). *Essays in Persuasion.* In Moggridge D.E., ed., *The Collected Writings of J.M. Keynes,* Vol. IX, London: Macmillan.

Moreno-Brid, J. C. and Ros, J. (2009). *Development and Growth in the Mexican Economy. A Historical Perspective.* Oxford:Oxford University Press.

Moreno-Brid, J. C. (2015). Después de la Tormenta: panorama económico de América Latina a cinco años de la crisis financiera internacional. *Foreign Affairs Latinoamérica* 15: 98–104.

Musella, M. and Panico, C. (1995). *The Money Supply in the Economic Process.* Aldershot: Elgar.

Panico, C. and Moreno-Brid, J. C. (2019). El Banco de México y la política monetaria. In L. Ludlow and M. E. Romero Sotelo (coord), *El Banco de México a través de sus constructores: 1917–2017.* Mexico: Faculty of Economics and Institute of History Research, UNAM.

Panico, C. and Piccioni, M. (2016). Keynes on central bank independence. *Studi Economici* 1–3: 190–216.

Panico, C. and Piccioni, M. (2018). Keynes, the Labour Party and central bank independence. In N. Naldi, A. Rosselli and E. Sanfilippo (eds), *Money, Finance and Crises in Economic History: The Long-term Impact of Economic Ideas.* London: Routledge.

Panico, C. (1988). *Interest and Profit in the Theories of Value and Distribution.* London: Macmillan; New York: St. Martin Press.

Panico, C. (2011). Las políticas fiscales y monetarias en un ámbito comunitario. *Problemas de Desarrollo: Revista Latinoamericana de Economía* 42(164): 55–70.

Panico, C. (2014). *Política monetaria y derechos humanos: un enfoque metodológico y su aplicación a Costa Rica, Guatemala y México, ECLAC-Mexico Office.*

Panico, C. (2020a). La coordinación de las políticas económicas en los tiempos del Coronavirus. *ECONOMÍAunam* 17, No. 51, septiembre-diciembre, 2020.

Panico, C. (2020b). *Sraffa's Monetary Writings, Objectivism and the Cambridge Tradition.* London: Palgrave, MacMillan.

Panico, C., Pinto, A., Puchet Anyul, M. and Vázquez Suárez, M. (2016). A Sraffian approach to financial regulation. In G. Freni, H. D. Kurz, M. Lavezzi and R. Signorino (eds), *Economic Theory and Its History: Essays in Honour of Neri Salvadori.* London: Routledge, pp. 249–270.

Panico, C. and Rizza, M. O. (2004). Central bank independence and democracy: a historical perspective. In R. Arena and N. Salvadori (eds), *Money, Credit and the Role of the State: Essays in Honour of Augusto Graziani.* London: Ashgate, pp. 445–465.

Rojas-Suarez, L. (ed), (2009). *Growing Pains in Latin America: An Economic Growth Framework as Applied to Brazil, Colombia, Costa Rica, Mexico and Peru.* Washington, DC: Center for Global Development.

Sack, B. and Wieland, W. (1999). *Interest Rate Smoothing and Optimal Monetary Policy: A Review of Recent Empirical Evidence.* Mimeo.

Serebrisky, T., Suárez-Alemán, A., Margot, D., and Ramirez, M.C. (2015). Financing Infrastructure in Latin America and the Caribbean: How, How Much and by Whom? Banco Interamericano de Desarrollo.

Shaikh, A. (2016). *Capitalism Competition, Conflict, Crises.* New York: Oxford University Press.

Shin, H. S. (2010). *Risk and Liquidity.* New York: Oxford University Press.

Smithin, J. (2003). *Controversies in Monetary Economics.* Northampton: Edward Elgar.

Snowdon, B. and Vane, H. R. (2005). *Modern Macroeconomics: Its Origins, Development and Current State.* Cheltenham, UK; Northhampton, MA: Edward Elgar Pub.

Sraffa, P. (1922). The bank crisis in Italy. *Economic Journal* XXXII (126): 178–197.

Svensson, L. (1997). *Inflation Targeting in an Open Economy: Strict or Flexible Inflation Targeting.* Mimeo.

Svensson, L. (1999). Inflation targeting as a monetary policy rule. *Journal of Monetary Economics* 43: 607–654.

Svensson, L. (2000). Open-economy inflation targeting. *Journal of International Economics* 50: 155–183.

Svensson, L. (2004). Comentary in inflation targeting: prospects and problems. *Federal Reserve Bank of St. Louis* 86(4): 161–164.

Svensson, L. (2007). Inflation targeting. In L. Blum and S. Durlauf (eds). *The New Palgrave Dictionary of Economics,* 2nd ed. London: Palgrave Macmillan.

15 Elections and government deficit spending

Evidence from Italian regions

*Michele Limosani, Emanuele Millemaci, and
Fabio Monteforte*

1 Introduction

Is there evidence of the existence of a political budget cycle,[1] the election
cycle in public spending, taxes and budget deficits, also at intermediate levels
of government? This chapter empirically investigates the hypothesis focusing
on the Italian regional governments' primary deficits in the period between
2000 and 2016.

In the literature, political budget cycles are found to be context-conditional,
i.e. they do not occur in all countries or under all circumstances.[2] The different
competences attributed to different levels of government may determine different opportunities for political budget cycles: some spending items may be
relatively more discretionary and allow politicians easier budget manipulations.
Moreover, the probability of electoral manipulation by incumbents and the
adherence to the budget targets are often found to be related to the distance
between government and voters (Baskaran et al., 2016; Ben-Bassat, Dahan and
Klor, 2016; Köppl Turyna et al., 2016; Pierskalla, 2019).

There are good reasons for selecting the case of the Italian regional governments. First, the President of the Region (sometimes called the governor) is
elected by universal suffrage in almost all regions (the two exceptions are Aosta
Valley and Trentino-Alto Adige). Second, Italy shows highly heterogeneous
levels of regional debt. Third, the Italian regions are almost all subject to the
same legislative, administrative and judicial systems. Fourth, since they were first
established, Italian regions have enjoyed large political and spending powers.
The Titulus V amendment of the Constitutional Law in 2001 widened these
powers allowing Italian regions to establish and impose additional taxes on top of
the national ones. Finally, a methodological advantage is that elections do not
occur in each jurisdiction at the same time and therefore it is possible to dis-
criminate election dates from general time effects.[3]

However, only a few recent contributions focus on the Italian case at the
sub-national level, and most of them concentrate on municipalities rather than
regions. Alesina and Paradisi (2017) show evidence that Italian municipalities
choose lower (real estate) tax rates when close to elections. Alesina, Troiano
and Cassidy (2018) find that younger politicians are more likely to increase

DOI: 10.4324/9781003105558-18

spending in their municipalities and obtain more transfers from higher levels of government in pre-election years, and interpret it as a sign of stronger career concerns incentives. Bonfatti and Forni (2019) provide evidence that subnational fiscal rules can limit the political budget cycle of the municipalities. Repetto (2018) finds that more informed voters reduce political budget cycles in the Italian municipalities.

This study expands the existing literature at least in four aspects. First, to our best knowledge, this is the first attempt to investigate the existence of a political budget cycle in the Italian regional governments, which lay at an intermediate distance from voters, differently from the already studied evidence on the national and municipal level. Second, this chapter indirectly allows to evaluate whether governors have the possibility to manipulate budgets for electoral purposes on subjects where the Italian regional governments benefit from large, if not exclusive, competences, such as health and education, on the same lines as previous evidence showed to happen on different items at the central and municipal levels of government. Third, evaluating regional politicians' budgetary discipline is a valuable exercise also because, during the sample period, two important laws on regional budgets were passed by the Italian parliament: the Domestic Stability Pact and the Balanced Budget Principle. Specifically, the Domestic Stability Pact is a collection of rules introduced for the first time with the 1999 Italian Budget Law (Law No. 488/1998) to make regional and local governments contribute in fulfilling the Maastricht objectives on European countries' debt and deficit ratios. In contrast, the 'Balanced Budget Principle' (Constitutional Law No. 1/2012), enforced since 2015 for regional governments, follows the introduction of the Fiscal Compact for all EU countries. Fourth, the consideration of various panel data estimation methods and a thorough specification analysis can be considered a methodological improvement with respect to most of the related studies.

This chapter finds evidence in support of the political budget cycle hypothesis. The result is somewhat surprising considering that it refers to a period where a strict budgetary discipline should have been assured by the aforementioned policy measures. In contrast, strict budgetary discipline may nevertheless harm the efficacy of counter-cycle policies during downturns, in particular in very deep recessions when extraordinary expansionary fiscal measures are needed and the simple free operation of the automatic stabilisers is not sufficient. This is one reason why the effectiveness of such budgetary discipline measures has been largely criticised, especially in the aftermath of the recent financial and sovereign debt crisis. Several authors argued that fiscal discipline may exacerbate existing imbalances rather than reduce them (Panico and Purificato, 2013) and various possible solutions were proposed, most of them aiming to provide a centralized European fiscal authority, on the same lines of the ECB (Panico and Vazquez Suarez, 2008). Recently, those arguments received a perhaps definitive implicit validation, if considering the EU economic policy response to the current COVID-19 pandemic, which eased existing financial constraints (leading to the activation of the general escape clause in the Stability and Growth Pact) and allowed large primary deficits of member countries (and thus, their regional governments) with the relaxation of state aid rules and pushed towards a more integrated coordination of fiscal policy measures at the European level, both in terms of welfare (the so-called SURE program) and risk-sharing on sovereign bonds. In light of the earlier discussion, a corollary contribution of the results found in the present study may suggest that a stronger focus should be placed in designing better incentives for reducing policymakers' moral hazard problem rather than imposing external constraints which are inevitably sidestepped, hindering the beneficial effects of counter-cyclical policies.

The chapter is structured as follows: Section 2 provides the description of the data used and specifies the empirical model, Section 3 discusses results while Section 4 concludes.

2 Data and empirical model

The empirical analysis is carried out using a panel dataset of the 20 Italian regions over the period 2000–2016. The principal source of data is the Italian Institute of Statistics (Istat), while publicly available information is used to create the political variables. The data source for the EU structural funds is the State General Accounting Department of the Italian Ministry of Economy and Finance. Table 15.1 reports summary statistics of the variables used in the empirical analysis.

Primary deficit is defined as the difference between total expenditures, net of and interest payments on debt and total revenues including transfers from the central government. The following dynamic specification is considered:

$$PD_{i,t} = \alpha + \rho PD_{i,t-1} + \beta' YEARINOF_{i,t} + \delta' X_{i,t} + u_i + \epsilon_{i,t} \qquad (15.1)$$

where the ratio between primary deficit and GDP in the region i and time t, PD_{it}, depends on (i) its own lagged value, $PD_{i,t-1}$, capturing the adjustment process of the dependent variable towards the target ratio; (ii) a vector of dummies for the year of office of the Governor to test for the existence of a political budget cycle, $YEARINOF_{i,t}$; (iii) a vector of controls, $X_{i,t}$; (iv) a time-invariant region-specific component, u_i; (v) and an $i.\,i.\,d.$ error term, $\epsilon_{i,t}$.

When approaching elections, the Governor may be tempted to reduce taxes and/or to increase expenses to maximise the chances of his party or coalition of re-election. Hence, one expects to find a relatively higher deficit in the period before elections with respect to other periods of the legislature.

The model contains a set of demographic and macroeconomic controls, which are selected in accord with both theory and previous empirical findings. Population is included to deal with dimensionality effects. Population density measured as inhabitants per square kilometre may capture higher costs of the

Table 15.1 Summary statistics

Abbreviation (if any)	Variable Name	Mean	Std. Dev.	Min	Max
	Regional primary deficit	−256.472	759.111	−5628.058	1247.167
	Regional GDP	90323.158	81181.826	4956.362	386958.844
	Regional GDP per capita	27330.898	6816.105	11404.486	42093.523
	Total EU structural funds	330.12	558.475	12.417	6007.537
	Population	3.12	2.259	0.312	10.008
deficit	Regional deficit on GDP	−0.003	0.012	−0.073	0.052
yearinof	Year of legislature	2.888	1.391	1	5
pop	Log of population	0.828	0.854	−1.165	2.303
density	Population density	1.942	1.046	0.57	4.294
gdppc	Log of real GDP per capita	10.183	0.263	9.342	10.648
unempl	Unemployment rate	9.735	5.137	2.5	24.1
fund	Structural funds on GDP	0.005	0.005	0	0.032

Notes: Population is expressed in millions of people. All monetary variables are expressed in euros (at constant prices of 2014).

publicly provided good due to congestion (Fenge and Meier, 2002). Income per capita is likely to affect positively public revenues. In contrast, richer regions have easier access to credit and may be allowed to accumulate more debt. The unemployment rate may penalise the budget of the regional government because it reduces tax revenues and increases expenditure on public services and social protection. The EU structural funds variable is the annual reimbursed amounts of the European Regional Development Fund (ERDF) and the European Social Fund (ESF). Importantly, the inclusion of this variable in the model allows to account for the strong cyclicality of this budgetary item, which typically peaks in the second half of the seven years of the European programming period. Given that this funding source is recorded as revenue in the regional budget, it is possible to find, by construction, a negative correlation with primary deficit, as long as these funds substitute for spending that regional governments would do anyway.

To estimate Equation (15.1), the pooled-OLS as well as static and dynamic panel data methods are considered in the empirical analysis: the pooled-OLS, random effects, fixed effects and system-GMM. The pooled-OLS differs from the random and the fixed effects in that it imposes intercepts to be the same for all regions. Consequently, the pooled-OLS estimator is not consistent when there is relevant fixed unobserved heterogeneity across regions. The random effects method does not require such regional effects to be uncorrelated with the independent variables, while estimation via fixed effects does. However, if the dynamic specification is the correct one, the fixed effects method is biased when the time span is limited, even if the number of units is large (Nickell, 1981). This potential problem can be addressed by means of the dynamic panel data method of the system-GMM (Blundell and Bond, 1998), which outperforms all the other possible estimators in terms of accuracy and efficiency also in small samples.

This chapter does not consider the potential heterogeneity in behaviour between incumbent governors who intend and do not intend to run for another term. The attention is on the attempt by incumbent governors of favouring indistinctly themselves, their parties or coalitions.

The regions Trentino-Alto Adige/Südtirol and Aosta Valley are dropped from the analysis because their electoral laws do not contemplate the direct election of the Governor. Moreover, Trentino-Alto Adige/Südtirol is not a unified region but a confederation of two distinct autonomous provinces. In that case, the regional governor who is one of the two provincial commissioners is almost irrelevant, given that most powers are at the provincial level.

As the main endogeneity concern between the year of legislature and primary deficit is related to the possibility of an early election, all data from legislatures ended with early elections are dropped from the sample (37 observations, 12.17%).

3 Findings

Table 15.2 (columns I–VIII) reports the results from four different methodologies – pooled-OLS, random effects, fixed effects and system-GMM – allowing us to compare results. Standard panel tests are employed to choose the more correct methodology. In all specifications, the dependent variable is the ratio between the level of primary deficit of the regional government and its corresponding GDP (*deficit*), while the baseline set of the independent variables includes dummies for each year of office of the Governor (*yearinof*), the log of population (*population*), population density per 100 square kilometres (*density*) and the log of real GDP per capita (*gdppc*). In a more comprehensive specification unemployment rate (*unempl*) and the ratio between structural funds and GDP (*fund*) are included in the set of explanatory variables. To account for serial autocorrelation and heteroscedasticity, robust standard errors are computed for all estimation strategies.

The second year of office is set as the exclusion restriction (or year of reference) and for this reason, the dummy on the second year of office is omitted from the set of explanatory variables. This choice is motivated as follows. The second year of office – the year following the election year – is the most distant year of office, before subsequent elections occur, in which deficit can be certainly attributed to the incumbent governor in the current mandate. If a political budget cycle occurs, the primary deficit is expected to be lower in this

Table 15.2 Estimation results

Regressor	I Pooled-Ols b/(s.e.)	II Pooled-Ols b/(s.e.)	III Random Effect b/(s.e.)	IV Random Effect b/(s.e.)	V Fixed Effects b/(s.e.)	VI Fixed Effects b/(s.e.)	VII SYS-GMM b/(s.e.)	VIII SYS-GMM b/(s.e.)	IX Random Effect b/(s.e.)	X Random Effect b/(s.e.)
election_year	0.007*** (0.002)	0.007*** (0.002)	0.007*** (0.002)	0.007*** (0.002)	0.007*** (0.002)	0.007*** (0.002)	0.005* (0.003)	0.005** (0.002)		
3rd_yearinof	0.009* (0.005)	0.009* (0.005)	0.009* (0.005)	0.009* (0.005)	0.010* (0.005)	0.010* (0.005)	0.012* (0.006)	0.012* (0.006)		
4th_yearinof	0.003 (0.004)	0.003 (0.004)	0.003 (0.004)	0.003 (0.004)	0.004 (0.004)	0.004 (0.004)	0.003 (0.004)	0.002 (0.004)		
5th_yearinof	0.011*** (0.003)	0.011*** (0.004)	0.011*** (0.003)	0.011*** (0.004)	0.012*** (0.004)	0.012*** (0.004)	0.013*** (0.003)	0.013*** (0.004)		
post − election_year									0.008*** (0.002)	0.008*** (0.002)
population	−0.002 (0.002)	−0.001 (0.001)	−0.002 (0.002)	−0.001 (0.001)	−0.058 (0.071)	−0.102 (0.080)	−0.002 (0.001)	−0.001 (0.001)	−0.002 (0.002)	−0.001 (0.001)
density	0.002 (0.002)	0.002 (0.001)	0.002 (0.002)	0.002 (0.001)	−0.023 (0.031)	−0.017 (0.034)	0.002 (0.001)	0.001 (0.001)	0.002 (0.002)	0.002 (0.001)
gdppc	0.004 (0.004)	−0.004 (0.003)	0.004 (0.004)	−0.004 (0.003)	0.0004 (0.003)	0.0003 (0.003)	0.002 (0.003)	−0.007 (0.005)	0.003 (0.003)	0.0001 (0.004)
unempl	−0.041 (0.026)	−0.041 (0.026)		−0.041 (0.026)		0.076 (0.051)		−0.02 (0.024)		−0.02 (0.024)
fund	−0.141 (0.203)	−0.141 (0.203)		−0.141 (0.203)		−0.253 (0.166)		−0.522 (0.406)		−0.099 (0.193)
deficit (−1)							0.153 (0.097)	0.197* (0.094)		

(Continued)

Table 15.2 (Continued)

Regressor	I Pooled-Ols b/(s.e.)	II Pooled-Ols b/(s.e.)	III Random Effect b/(s.e.)	IV Random Effect b/(s.e.)	V Fixed Effects b/(s.e.)	VI Fixed Effects b/(s.e.)	VII SYS-GMM b/(s.e.)	VIII SYS-GMM b/(s.e.)	IX Random Effect b/(s.e.)	X Random Effect b/(s.e.)
Time dummies	YES	YES	YES	YES	YES	YES	YES	YES	YES	YES
N	267	267	267	267	267	267	267	267	238	238

Notes: With respect to the SYS-GMM estimates, *deficit* (−1) is treated as a predetermined variable (GMM-style option in xtabond2), while *population*, *density*, *gdppc*, *unempl* and *fund* are treated as exogenous variables (IV-style option in xtabond2). Only a lag of the GMM-style endogenous variables is used as instrument. Following the suggestion provided by Roodman (2009) for the SYS-GMM, only the moment conditions for the time dummies (and the intercept) in the level equation are considered. Moreover, to better address the unbalanced panel problem, forward orthogonal deviations are used in place of the first-difference transformations. With all methods, standard errors reported in parenthesis are heteroscedasticity robust. For the case of the pooled-OLS estimation, standard errors also account for potential clustering of the same-region observations. ***, ** and * denote coefficients that are significant at 1%, 5% and 10%, respectively.

year than in the others as a governor has less incentive in deviating from fiscal discipline.

In line with the political budget cycle theory, results suggest that, in the last year of office and in the election year, *deficit* is always statistically significantly higher than in the second year of office, at 1% confidence interval in six cases out of eight. Moreover, the effect appears higher in the last year before election (0.011–0.013) than election year (0.005–0.007). This is reasonable, considering that deficit in the election year is a weighted average between deficit produced in the pre-election time and deficit produced in the post-election time. The importance of the political budget cycle effect on deficit is quite large: one standard deviation of the *yearinof* dummies accounts on average for at least 58% of one standard deviation of *deficit*. Somewhat surprisingly, the demographic and economic controls show always statistically not significant coefficients. The lagged dependent variable included in the system-GMM model is also statistically not significant, suggesting that deficit variability across the years is not due to a debt stabilisation strategy, and rather follows a political budget cycle strategy. Moreover, the Hansen test casts some doubts on the reliability of the system-GMM estimates and this fact is probably due to the high number of instruments with respect to the number of regions.

Results are very similar across the four methods and the two specifications under consideration. Nevertheless, a choice between the four methods is possible by means of standard statistical tests for panel data. First, the Breusch-Pagan test for random effects rejects the null hypothesis of zero variance in the estimated regional-specific vector, with the consequence that the pooled-OLS does not provide consistent results. Second, the Hausman test fails to reject the null hypothesis of non-significant differences between fixed and random effects estimates, suggesting selecting the more efficient method between the two (i.e. the random effect model). Finally, the Wooldridge test fails to reject the hypothesis of no serial autocorrelation in the residuals of the static panel data model. This result is coherent with the aforementioned evidence of statistical insignificance of the coefficient associated with the lagged dependent variable. Based on these tests, the better choice appears to be the random effects model.

The last two columns of Table 15.2 show results from a slightly different specification of the model. A dummy on whether the year of office is different from the second replaces the dummies on the year of office. For brevity, only the results obtained from applying the random effect method are reported. As shown in Table 15.3, results are very similar when the sample is restricted to the period where no significant institutional change occurs (2002–2014). Results are also very similar when controlling for ordinary or special statute by adding a dummy variable (*special*) in every specification of the model. The dummy *special* is found to be always negative and statistically significant.[4]

Furthermore, with another set of regressions, whose results are not reported for brevity, *special* and *yearinof* are interacted to check for potential heterogeneity in political budget cycles between the two groups of regions.

Table 15.3 Estimation results – robustness checks

Regressor	I Restricted Sample b/(s.e.)	II Restricted Sample b/(s.e.)	III Ordinary/Special Statute b/(s.e.)	IV Ordinary/Special Statute b/(s.e.)	V Restricted Sample b/(s.e.)	VI Restricted Sample b/(s.e.)	VII Ordinary/Special Statute b/(s.e.)	VIII Ordinary/Special Statute b/(s.e.)
election_year	0.008***	0.008***	0.007***	0.007***				
	(0.003)	(0.003)	(0.002)	(0.002)				
3rd_yearinof	0.01	0.011	0.010*	0.010*				
	(0.008)	(0.009)	(0.005)	(0.005)				
4th_yearinof	0.004	0.004	0.004	0.004				
	(0.004)	(0.004)	(0.004)	(0.004)				
5th_yearinof	0.012***	0.012***	0.012***	0.012***				
	(0.003)	(0.003)	(0.004)	(0.004)				
post − election_year					0.009**	0.009**	0.008***	0.008***
					(0.004)	(0.004)	(0.002)	(0.002)
special_statute			−0.010***	−0.009**			−0.009***	−0.009**
			(0.004)	(0.004)			(0.004)	(0.004)
Additional controls	NO	YES	NO	YES	NO	YES	NO	YES
Time dummies	YES	YES	YES	YES	YES	YES	YES	YES
N	195	195	267	267	195	195	267	267

Notes: Random effects estimates. The restricted sample includes the time period 2002–2014. Controls used in all regressions are *population*, *density* and *gdppc*. Additional controls are *unempl* and *fund*. Standard errors account for heteroscedasticity. ***, ** and * denote coefficients that are significant at 1%, 5% and 10%, respectively.

However, results do not find evidence in favour of the hypothesis of heterogeneity in behaviour between the governors of the two groups of regions.

4 Conclusions

Applying pooled–OLS and panel data methods to Italian regional data for the period between 2000 and 2016, this chapter also provides evidence of a political budget cycle at intermediate levels of government. Interestingly, the primary deficit has been found to be significantly higher in the last year of office and in the election year with respect to the second year of office. Results are robust across the different methods and specification considered, and do not vary even if we restrict the sample time span or distinguish between regional statutes. While some recent studies focus on the Italian municipal and national budgets, this study provides evidence for the case of an intermediate level, as the regional government.

While different competences are attributed to the Italian regional governments with respect to the central and municipal levels of government (e.g. health care and education matters), this chapter indirectly suggests that political budget cycles occur even on these expenditure entries.

The findings of this study may be interpreted as suggesting that, notwithstanding the budget constraints imposed by the Domestic Stability Pact resulting in very low regional deficits in absolute values, the remaining primary deficits variability is still attributable to the political budget cycle. Thus, the Domestic Stability Pact did not provide enough incentives for governors to act more coherently throughout all the legislature in fulfilling the objectives of deficit and debt reduction, and prevented them from implementing effective countercyclical policies when needed. Thus, in light of the earlier discussion, a straightforward implication of the results found in this study is that a stronger focus on structural budget balance exclusively during expansions may be advisable, allowing the implementation of effective counter-cyclical policies during recessions, even at the cost of higher risks of opportunistic behaviour by policymakers (forsaking the underlying principle introduced at European level within the Fiscal Compact).

As already noted, this is a path which, as a matter of fact and notwithstanding the inevitable stop-and-gos within a very heterogeneous Union, the European countries seem to have embarked on, especially in dealing with the consequences of the COVID-19 pandemic. Therefore, a natural extension of the present study may quantify the pros (in terms of countercyclical policies) and cons (in terms of increased policymakers' moral hazard) of such an approach.

Of course, budget manipulations for electoral objectives may take other forms. For instance, if the government is subject to external constraints on its budget, manipulations may affect the composition of government net spending rather than its total amount or, also, may aim to modify spending and revenues levels proportionally and thus keep the current deficit unchanged. Also, this issue deserves further investigations.

Disclaimer

The usual disclaimer applies. All authors contributed equally to each section of the manuscript. This research did not receive any specific grant from funding agencies in the public, commercial or not-for-profit sectors.

Notes

1 Nordhaus (1975), Alesina, Roubini and Cohen (1997) and Rogoff (1990).
2 Alesina and Passalacqua (2016), Bohn and Veiga (2019), Mandon and Cazals (2019) and the references therein.
3 The Italian Constitution guarantees both local self-government and the subsidiarity principle. Moreover, regional governments are granted financial autonomy regarding revenues and expenditure. Since the constitutional reform of 2001, residual competence is assigned to the regions and there is a large number of matters of concurrent legislation for which the State can only set fundamental principles.
4 The regions with special statutes adopted through constitutional laws are Aosta Valley, Friuli-Venezia Giulia, Trentino-Alto Adige, Sicily and Sardinia. The remaining 15 have the ordinary statute.

References

Alesina, A., Roubini, N. and Cohen, G. (1997). *Political Cycles and the Macroeconomy*. MIT Press: Cambridge, MA.

Alesina, A. and Paradisi, M. (2017). Political budget cycles: evidence from Italian cities. *Economics and Politics* 29: 157–177.

Alesina, A. and Passalacqua, A. (2016). The political economy of government debt. *Handbook of Macroeconomics* 2: 2599–2651.

Alesina, A. F., Troiano, U. and Cassidy, T. (2018). Old and young politicians. *Economica* 86: 689–727.

Baskaran, T., Brender, A., Blesse, S. and Reingewertz, Y. (2016). Revenue decentralization, central oversight and the political budget cycle: evidence from Israel. *European Journal of Political Economy* 42: 1–16.

Ben-Bassat, A., Dahan, M. and Klor, E. F. (2016). Is centralization a solution to the soft budget constraint problem? *European Journal of Political Economy*, 45: 57–75.

Blundell, R. and Bond, S. (1998). Initial conditions and moment restrictions in dynamic panel data models. *Journal of econometrics* 87: 115–143.

Bohn, F. and Veiga, F. J. (2019). Political opportunism and countercyclical fiscal policy in election-year recessions. *Economic Inquiry* 57: 2058–2081.

Bonfatti, A. L. and Forni, L. (2019). Fiscal rules to tame the political budget cycle: evidence from Italian municipalities. *European Journal of Political Economy* 60, 101800.

Fenge, R. and Meier, V. (2002). Why cities should not be subsidized. *Journal of Urban Economics* 52: 433–447.

Köppl Turyna, M., Kula, G., Balmas, A. and Waclawska, K. (2016). The effects of fiscal decentralisation on the strength of political budget cycles in local expenditure. *Local Government Studies* 42: 785–820.

Mandon, P. and Cazals, A. (2019). Political budget cycles: manipulation by leaders versus manipulation by researchers? Evidence from a meta-regression analysis. *Journal of Economic Surveys* 33: 274–308.

Nickell, S. (1981). Biases in dynamic models with fixed effects. *Econometrica* 49: 1417–1426.

Nordhaus, W. (1975). The political business cycle. *The Review of Economic Studies* 42: 169–190.

Panico, C. and Purificato, F. (2013). Policy coordination, conflicting national interests and the European debt crisis. *Cambridge Journal of Economics* 37: 585–608.

Panico, C. and Vazquez Suarez, M. (2008). A scheme to coordinate monetary and fiscal policies in the Euro area. In J. Ferreiro, G. Fontana and F. Serrano (eds), *Fiscal Policy in the European Union*. New York: Palgrave Macmillan.

Pierskalla, J. H. (2019). The proliferation of decentralized governing units. In J. A. Rodden and E. Wibbels (eds), *Decentralized Governance and Accountability: Academic Research and the Future of Donor Programming*. Cambridge: Cambridge University Press.

Repetto, L. (2018). Political budget cycles with informed voters: evidence from Italy. *The Economic Journal* 128: 3320–3353.

Rogoff, K. (1990). Equilibrium political budget cycles. *American Economic Review* 80: 21–36.

Roodman, D. (2009). A note on the theme of too many instruments. *Oxford Bulletin of Economics and Statistics* 71: 135–158.

16 Monetary policy and national fiscal policies in the euro area

Erasmo Papagni and Francesco Purificato

1 Introduction

During the last decade, Carlo Panico's research has focused on the problems of coordination between monetary and fiscal policies in the Economic and Monetary Union (EMU). His position has pointed out that the institutional organisation of the policy coordination was inadequate and caused the exacerbation of the sovereign debt crisis. Notably, the European Central Bank (ECB) assumed too late the role of lender of last resort in favour of EMU members, while conflicting national interests pushed governments to adopt overly restrictive fiscal policies, especially for the most distressed countries.

Our paper analyses these issues, taking into account two relevant factors: the reform of the European governance of national fiscal policies, completed in 2015, and the expansionary monetary policy adopted by the ECB since 2015 through the quantitative easing, an asset purchase programme also intended for sovereign bonds. Concerning the first aspect, the Treaty on Stability, Coordination and Governance (TSCG) in the Economic and Monetary Union introduced a numerical benchmark for the process of debt reduction: member countries of the EMU with a debt level exceeding the 60.0% of GDP need reduce the difference at an average rate of one-twentieth per year. Concerning the European quantitative easing, the massive asset purchase by the ECB determined a significant decrease in sovereign bonds' yields, namely, in the debt burden of the EMU states. The paper focuses on the interaction between monetary policy and national fiscal policies, mainly, on how the monetary policy stance has affected the conduct of national fiscal policies taking into account also the role played by the level of public debt.

1.1 Summary of the paper

Based on the framework by Foresti (2015), we present an analytical model of a monetary union to study the strategic interaction between a single central bank and national fiscal authorities. The loss function of the monetary authority considers the standard objectives of price and output stability; instead, fiscal authorities pursue the objective of debt stabilisation, in addition to that of

DOI: 10.4324/9781003105558-19

macroeconomic stability. The model allows us to obtain the optimal reaction function for each fiscal authority, which describes how the primary fiscal balance reacts to the policy rate and the debt level. Given the effectiveness of monetary policy to affect the output level and the exceed of the accumulated debt on the benchmark level, the relationship between the primary fiscal balance and the policy rate depends on the public debt level. The primary fiscal balance is a positive function of the policy rate for EMU countries with higher debt, as a decrease in the interest rate reduces the debt burden, implying a less stringent budget constraint for national fiscal authorities.

From the empirical point of view, we test the previous finding through the methods of nonparametric statistics (Li and Racine, 2007). For the period from 2000 to 2019, these methods allow us to estimate the relationship between primary fiscal balance and policy rate for each broader economy in the EMU and a balanced panel data representing the whole economy of the EMU. Notably, we detect a U-shaped relationship between the Euribor, assumed as a proxy of the policy rate and the ratio of the primary government balance to GDP, and this relationship holds for each level of public debt. At the union level, if the Euribor is lower than the 1.7%, then an expansionary monetary policy pushes national authorities to adopt more restrictive fiscal policies; otherwise, if the interest rate is higher than 1.7%, then a decrease in the Euribor is connected with a reduction in the primary government balance.

Although the econometric analysis does not seem to support the analytical result, we can put forward two possible explanations for this contradiction by considering the following elements. The policy rate has decreased steadily for the whole period from 2000 to 2019, and it has crossed the threshold level of 1.7% approximately during the sovereign debt crisis. Until 2014, the primary tool of the monetary policy has been the refinancing operations; subsequently, the principal instrument has been quantitative easing. In the aftermaths of the sovereign debt crisis, the TSCG has introduced a numerical benchmark for the process of debt reduction. In this context, two possible explanations can reconcile the analytical result with the econometric analysis. The first explanation calls into question the effectiveness of the monetary policy. If the asset purchase programme is assumed to be more effective in supporting the short-term macroeconomic stabilisation in comparison to the refinancing operations, then the optimal policy implies that governments should react with fiscal consolidation to an accommodative monetary policy. The second explanation calls into question the European governance that may have forced national fiscal authorities to implement a sub-optimal policy, namely, an unnecessary fiscal consolidation. According to Panico's analysis, conflicting national interests pushed governments to adopt overly restrictive fiscal policies, especially for the most distressed countries (Panico and Purificato, 2013).

Finally, concerning the relationship between the ratio of the primary fiscal balance to GDP and the ratio of the public debt level to GDP, both the analytical and econometric analysis find a U-shaped relationship. The last shows a benchmark level of the public debt ratio to GDP at around 85%, a value greater than the EMU benchmark of 60%. Hence, we have some evidence that during the years of the financial crisis the rules established by the European institutions on sovereign debt were effective in curbing the fiscal authorities in the EMU countries, notwithstanding the negative effects of the crisis. Indeed, we find that when the ratio Debt/GDP was lower than 85% the crisis was faced with increasing deficits that reached a threshold when public debt overcame 85% of GDP. Then, countries with high debt had to invert the sign of their fiscal policy to avoid a possible risk of default.

1.2 Related literature

The literature has widely analysed the peculiar institutional design of the EMU related to the governance of economic policy, with a single central bank responsible for the monetary policy at the union level and national governments having the role in setting the fiscal policy at the country level (Foresti, 2018). According to Dixit and Lambertini (2001, 2003), if the monetary and fiscal authorities share the same macroeconomic targets, namely, there is symbiosis among institutions, then the optimal policy can always be attained independently of the institutional framework. This finding does not hold if the central bank and the national governments have different targets (Lambertini et al., 2007), as in the case of the EMU where fiscal authorities also have to consider a balanced fiscal budget as an additional objective. In this context, understanding the role of the numerical benchmark for the process of debt reduction introduced by European institutions becomes an interesting issue. Foresti (2015) considers a loss function for the fiscal authorities where they are concerned about the public debt level rather than the primary fiscal balance. As a result, if the monetary authority reduces the policy rate, determining a lower debt burden, then a less stringent budget constraint allows higher debt countries to devote more resources in pursuing the objective of macroeconomic stabilisation. Our contribution extends the previous model by introducing the following elements: an endogenous risk premium on the sovereign bonds' yields; an explicit objective for national fiscal authorities to implement a process of debt reduction towards the benchmark level.

There is an extensive empirical literature on the macroeconomic effects of either monetary policy or fiscal policy (Ramey, 2016); nevertheless, the literature has paid little attention to the issue of the combined impact of both policies. To the best of our knowledge, the paper by Baumann et al. (2019) represents a remarkable and unique exception, and it also analyses the interaction between monetary policy and fiscal policy. Using structural panel vector autoregressions, the authors study the combined role of these policies in reacting to the adverse effects of the financial crisis of 2007–2008; specifically, they compare the policy response in advanced countries to that in emerging countries. Concerning the EMU, the econometric analysis finds that both the monetary and fiscal policies were expansionary in the aftermath of the crisis, promoting the goal of macroeconomic stabilisation. However, following the sovereign debt crisis of 2010–2012, while the monetary policy remained accommodative, the consolidation of public finance negatively affected the growth rate. Thus, our essential contribution to this literature is to extend the analysis at the national level, where the U-shaped relationship between the policy rate and the primary fiscal balance still holds.

The remainder of the essay is organised as follows. Section 2 presents a model to describe the strategic interaction between the monetary authority and the national governments within a monetary union. In Section 3, using methods of nonparametric statistics, we test the previous relationships at the union level and for larger EMU economies. Section 4 discusses both the analytical and econometric findings. Finally, Section 5 presents several conclusions.

2 The model

A simple analytical framework allows modelling the strategic interaction between a central bank responsible for the monetary policy and national governments having the role in setting national fiscal policies. In order to describe the EMU institutional framework, as modified by the TSCG, our focus is on the behaviour of fiscal authorities, which face the short-term trade-off between the objective of output stability and the need to implement a process of debt reduction.[1] Based on Foresti (2015), the analytical model describes a monetary union and also introduces the following elements: an endogenous risk premium on the sovereign bonds' yields; an explicit objective for national fiscal authorities to implement a process of debt reduction towards the benchmark level.

The loss function of the monetary authority describes the standard macroeconomic trade-off between output and price stability:

$$L_M = (\pi - \pi_M)^2 + \beta (y)^2 \tag{16.1}$$

where π is the inflation rate, and π_M is the inflation target; y is the average output gap in the monetary union, with the target for this variable assumed equal to zero. Finally, the parameter $\beta > 0$ defines the weight assigned by the monetary authority to the output gap (y), namely, the deviation of the output gap from the target.

The loss function of the national fiscal authority (i) describes the trade-off between macroeconomic stability and the goal of debt stabilisation:

$$L_{G,i} = (y_i)^2 + \gamma (d_i - d_F)^2 \tag{16.2}$$

where y_i is the output gap in the country (i), with the target for this variable assumed equal to zero; while d_i is the public debt level in this country and d_F its benchmark level. Finally, the parameter $\gamma > 0$ defines the weight assigned by the government to the deviation of the debt level from the target $(d_i - d_F)$, namely, the need to implement a process of debt reduction.

The following equations describe the economy at the union level:

$$\pi = \pi_M + \alpha y + \varepsilon_1 \tag{16.3}$$

$$y = a - b(r - \pi) - kf + \varepsilon_2 \tag{16.4}$$

Equation (16.3) defines the standard Phillips curve, where the parameter $\alpha > 0$ identifies the effect of the average output gap on the inflation rate, and ε_1 is a supply shock. Equation (16.4) defines the standard IS curve, where the parameters b identifies the sensitivity of the average output gap to the monetary policy, namely, to the real interest rate $(r - \pi)$. The variable f defines the primary fiscal balance at the union level, with a primary deficit $(f < 0)$ positively affecting the average output gap, and a primary surplus $(f > 0)$ implying an adverse impact; the parameter $k > 0$ identifies the sensitivity of the average output gap to the fiscal policy stance; finally, ε_2 is a demand shock.

2.1 Monetary authority

The monetary authority decides the optimal monetary policy by minimising Equation (16.1) subject to Equations (03) and (04):

$$\begin{aligned}
&\text{Min}_r \, L_M = (\pi - \pi_M)^2 + \beta(y)^2 \\
&s.\,t.\ \pi = \pi_M + \alpha y + \varepsilon_2; \quad y = a - b(r - \pi) - kf + \varepsilon_1 \\
&r = \pi_M + \frac{a}{b} + \frac{\alpha + \beta b}{\alpha^2 + \beta} \cdot \frac{1}{b} \cdot \varepsilon_2 + \frac{1}{b} \cdot \varepsilon_1 - \frac{k}{b} \cdot f
\end{aligned} \tag{16.5}$$

Equation (16.5) defines the optimal reaction function of the monetary authority, which describes how the central bank set the interest rate taking into account the average fiscal stance and exogenous shocks. Notably, there is a negative relationship between monetary policy and fiscal policy: if the fiscal authorities increase the primary deficit $(-\Delta f)$, then the central bank raises the policy rate $(+\Delta r)$ to offset the positive effect of the output gap on the inflation rate.

2.2 Fiscal authorities

In order to model the behaviour of national fiscal authority, we need to introduce an IS curve that describes the economy at the level of country (i):

$$y_i = a - b(r - \pi) - kf_i + \varepsilon_{i,2} \tag{3'}$$

In this context, both the primary fiscal balance (f_i) and the demand shock $(\varepsilon_{i,2})$ refer to a single EMU country. Moreover, the following equation introduces the budget constraint for the national government of country (i):

$$d_i = [(1 + r - \pi) - \delta_f f_i + \delta_d (\bar{d}_i - d_F)]\bar{d}_i - f_i \tag{16.6}$$

Equation (16.6) shows that the actual level of debt depends on the fiscal stance (f_i), the debt accumulated in the past $(\bar{d}_i)$, the real interest rate $(r - \pi)$ and a risk premium $(\delta_d (\bar{d}_i - d_F) - \delta_f f_i)$. This risk premium is a positive function of the excess of the accumulated debt on the debt target level $(\delta_d (\bar{d}_i - d_F))$; in contrast, it negatively depends on the primary fiscal balance $(\delta_f f_i)$. The parameters δ_f, $\delta_d \geq 0$ identify the sensitivity of the risk premium to these factors, namely, the current fiscal stance (f_i) and the past fiscal stance $(\bar{d}_i - d_F)$, which has determined the level of accumulate debt.

The government of country (i) decides the optimal fiscal policy by minimising Equation (02) subject to Equations (3') and (16.6):

$$
\begin{aligned}
&\text{Min}_{f_i} L_{G,i} = (y_i)^2 + \gamma (d_i - d_F)^2 \\
&s. \ t. \ y_i = a - b(r - \pi) - kf_i + \varepsilon_{i,2}; \qquad d_i \\
&\qquad = [(1 + r - \pi) - \delta_f f_i + \delta_d (\bar{d}_i - d_F)]\bar{d}_i - f_i \\
&\quad f_i = \frac{k \cdot (a - \varepsilon_{i,2})}{[k^2 + \gamma (1 + \delta_f \bar{d}_i)^2]} + \frac{[\gamma (1 + \delta_f \bar{d}_i) \bar{d}_i - bk] \cdot (r - \pi)}{[k^2 + \gamma (1 + \delta_f \bar{d}_i)^2]} \\
&\qquad + \frac{[\gamma (1 + \delta_f \bar{d}_i)(1 + \delta_d \bar{d}_i)] \cdot (\bar{d}_i - d_F)}{[k^2 + \gamma (1 + \delta_f \bar{d}_i)^2]}
\end{aligned}
\tag{16.7}
$$

Equation (16.7) describes the optimal reaction function of the fiscal authority of country (i): how the government sets the primary fiscal balance taking into account the policy rate $(r - \pi)$, the gap between the level of accumulated debt and its target level $(\bar{d}_i - d_F)$ and demand shocks $(\varepsilon_{i,2})$.

The first finding concerns with the relationship between the interest rate and the primary fiscal balance, which is characterised by the following inequality:

$$\frac{\partial f_i}{\partial r} > 0 \quad if \quad \gamma (1 + \delta_f \bar{d}_i)\bar{d}_i - bk > 0 \tag{16.8}$$

Equation (16.8) holds if the effectiveness of monetary policy in affecting the output gap (b) is low enough in comparison to the level of accumulated debt $(\bar{d}_i)$ and the weight assigned by the debt stabilisation in the loss function of the government (γ). Under these circumstances, the primary fiscal balance positively depends on the policy rate: an expansionary monetary policy $(-\Delta r)$

pushes the national government to implement a more accommodative fiscal policy $(-\Delta f_i)$, for instance, increasing the primary deficit. The intuition is that a decrease in the policy rate reduces the debt burden, decreasing the amount of interest to be paid on debt; consequently, the government can devote more resources to pursue the objective of output stability. If the sensitivity of the output gap to the policy rate (b) is high enough in comparison to the accumulated debt $(\bar{d}_i)$ and the weight assigned to the debt stabilisation (γ), then Equation (16.8) does not hold. In this context, the primary fiscal balance negatively reacts to the policy rate: for instance, an increase in interest rate $(+\Delta r)$ determines an increase in the primary deficit $(-\Delta f_i)$. Basically, as the monetary policy can effectively pursue the goal of macroeconomic stability, the government can devote more resources to the process of debt reduction.

The second finding concerns with the relationship between the primary fiscal balance and the accumulated debt level, the last term in Equation (16.7). The primary fiscal balance positively depends on the level of accumulated debt, such that if the accumulated debt level is greater than its target level $(\bar{d}_i > d_F)$, then the government tends to set either a lower primary deficit or a higher primary surplus. The presence of a risk premium on the sovereign bonds' yields $(\delta_f, \delta_d > 0)$ affects the intensity of the debt stabilisation: the higher the risk premium $(+\Delta\delta_f, \delta_d)$, the higher the weight of the process of debt reduction in the implementation of national fiscal policies.

3 Econometric analysis

The model presented in Section 2 highlights the linkages between monetary policy and fiscal policy when both are oriented to control the economy in the short term. In this paper, our interest is on the experience of those European countries that participate in the EMU, sharing the same monetary policy, centrally designed by the ECB. The EMU passed through different macro-economic phases and faced the financial crisis started in 2008. The main question we set in this paper is: How monetary and fiscal policies related during the crisis in the EMU?

3.1 Econometric model and methods

To provide an answer to this question, we specify a very stylised model in which we consider only variables that represent the outcome of policy decisions, like the following:

Government Primary Balance $= f$ (*ECB interest rate*; *Public Debt*).

This model allows us to investigate the interaction between monetary and fiscal policy within the EMU. According to the model presented in Section 2, when the monetary and the fiscal authorities share the same target, as the recovery from a deep macroeconomic crisis like the recent crisis, and the policy rate is closed to the zero lower bound, we expect to observe the complementarity of their interventions. The complementarity implies that $f(\cdot)$ is an increasing function in the interest rate: the lower the ECB interest rates, the lower the government primary balance. Nevertheless, this relation depends on the amount of public debt accumulated by each country in the past, as policymakers may express concern for debt sustainability.

Choosing this function, we leave in the background the variables that approximate the state of the economy (e.g. inflation and GDP). On the one side, this choice allows the clear extrapolation of the relations among the policy variables; on the other side, the model is not structural, in the sense that it does not highlight the decision rules that underlie the policy variables. In the following, it will be apparent that the estimation of a complete structural model would face critical limits in methodology and data availability (the curse of dimensionality).

The basic econometric equation used in our regression analysis is as follows:

$$Y_{i,t} = f(X_{i,t}) + \epsilon_{i,t}, \quad i = 1, 2, \ldots, N; t = 1, 2, \ldots, T, \tag{16.9}$$

where $f(\cdot)$ is a smooth function, i denotes countries, t denotes quarters of years, $X_{i,t}$ is the matrix of data of the regressors, and $\epsilon_{i,t}$ is the error term. This quite general model can be estimated using the methods of nonparametric statistics (Li and Racine, 2007). In this framework, the function $f(X_{i,t})$ is the mean value of $Y_{i,t}$ conditional on $X_{i,t}$ and each point of the function is estimated using observations around the point (X, Y). The local-linear regression method (Fan and Gijbels, 1996) estimates $f(X)$ with a linear regression on data points in the local neighbourhood of X.

We apply this method to the estimation of Equation (16.9) for each of the following main countries in the EMU: France, Germany, Italy and Spain. Quarterly time series provide a sufficient but not large number of observations for local-linear regression. In order to use a larger dataset, more than 500 observations, and obtain more general results, we also estimate Equation (16.9) pooling the data of seven countries in the EMU: Belgium, France, Greece, Italy, Netherlands, Portugal and Spain.[2] Besides, the estimation takes into account possible heterogeneity across countries, that in traditional linear panel data analysis is approximated by individual fixed effects. Indeed, we apply the results of recent research (Li and Racine, 2007) that extends nonparametric regression to discrete explanatory variables. Hence, we include country dummy variables in Equation (16.9) and estimate the following regression model on panel data:

$$Y_{i,t} = g(X_{i,t}, \delta_i) + \varepsilon_{i,t}, \quad i = 1, 2, \ldots, N; t = 1, 2, \ldots, T, \tag{16.10}$$

Where δ_i is a vector of binary variables for countries in the panel dataset. This approach to individual heterogeneity is very general because it does not impose additive linearity of individual effects. Every point of $g(X_{i,t}, \delta_i)$ is estimated distinguishing the effect of the regressors (X) from country-specific factors.

3.2 Data

In our analysis, the dependent variable is the ratio of Primary government balance, namely, government net lending/net borrowing excluding interest payable, to gross domestic product (GDP) (Source ECB), that approximates for fiscal policy; while the explanatory variables are the Euribor 12-month (Source: Eurostat), namely, the euro interbank offered interest rate, and the ratio of Government debt to GDP (Source: Eurostat). We concentrate first on the experience of the four main countries in the EMU: France, Germany, Italy and Spain, estimating Equation (16.10) on the time series of each country. Table 16.1 summarises the essential statistics of the Euribor and the variables specific to those countries. Then, we search for more robust and general results with the estimation of the model on data of a panel of seven countries in the EMU: Belgium, France, Greece, Italy, Netherlands, Portugal, Spain. Table 16.2 presents the main statistics of the variables in this panel data.

Table 16.1 Summary statistics: France, Germany, Italy and Spain

Variable	Quarters	Mean	Std. Dev.	Min	Max
Euribor 12-month	80	1.94	1.74	−0.33	5.37
Government primary balance★					
France	79	−1.14	1.60	−4.67	2.13
Germany	68	1.23	1.55	−2.58	3.09
Italy	79	1.68	1.09	−0.71	4.90
Spain	79	−1.22	4.05	−9.77	4.16
Government debt★					
France	80	79.87	15.73	57.90	100.80
Germany	80	68.36	7.32	57.50	82.40
Italy	80	120.30	12.48	103.90	138.80
Spain	80	68.08	24.48	35.00	100.90

Notes: (★) Ratio to GDP.

Table 16.2 Summary statistics. Panel data of seven countries in the EMU★

Variable	Mean	Std.	Min	Max	Obs.	Quarters
Government primary balance★★	−0.18	3.16	−11.50	6.83	553	79
Government debt★★	94.14	33.94	35	182.3	553	79

Notes: (★) Belgium, France, Greece, Italy, Netherlands, Portugal, Spain. (★★) Ratio to GDP.

Figure 16.1 shows the plot of the quarterly time series of the Euribor 12-month interest rate from 2000:1 to 2019:4. Two phases can be distinguished: before and after the worldwide financial crisis of 2008. During the crisis, the ECB implemented an expansionary monetary policy with a significant decrease in the interest rate, which fell from around 5% to negative values after 2015. The first reaction to the crisis caused a substantial drop in the policy rate, followed by a temporary increase that ended in 2011 when the sovereign debt crisis again induced the ECB to an expansionary monetary policy.

In the same period, each country in the EMU adopted a specific fiscal policy. Focusing on the main four countries, Figure 16.1 allows us to distinguish the first period with positive primary surpluses of Italy and Spain, and a government balance close to zero for France and Germany. The accumulated public debt is higher than 100% of GDP only in the case of Italy. The years after 2008 see in the four countries a first strong attempt to recover the economy with huge deficits, followed by more moderate expansive fiscal policies in France and Spain, while Germany and Italy after 2010 supported debt sustainability with primary surpluses. In the same period, public debt grew substantially in the first years of the crisis and then it remained stable in Italy, France and Spain while the sovereign debt of Germany fell to a low percentage of GDP.

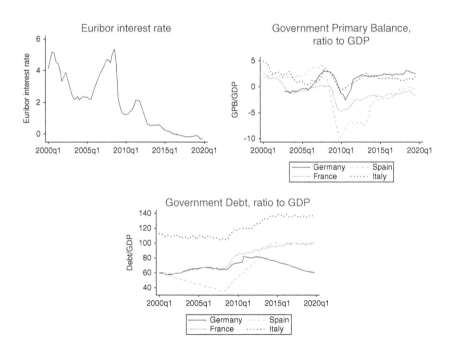

Figure 16.1 The trends of the main macroeconomic variables.

3.3 Results

The application of the methods of local-linear regression to single countries provides the estimation of the function (9) for France, Germany, Italy and Spain. Table 16.3 presents some statistics derived from the estimates. In particular, high values of R^2 suggest that model fitting is quite good in all regression but that of Germany that refers to Government debt. The table also displays the estimated average of derivatives with respect to each explanatory variable, and their test statistic and confidence interval. Figure 16.2 presents the estimated relation between the Euribor interest rate and the government primary balance to GDP ratio for each of the four countries in a selected number of points and at the mean value of Government debt.[3] Statistical significance of the estimate at each point can be gauged from confidence intervals obtained using the method of bootstrap.

In Figure 16.2, the plot of the mean function for Germany, Italy and Spain shows the shape of a U with a decreasing trait when Euribor takes negative or close to zero values, followed by an increasing section. This relation is almost regular and smooth in the case of Germany, with the two branches of the curve quite symmetric around the mean value of Euribor. The graph of Italy and Spain is characterised by a decreasing section only when Euribor is lower than 0.7%, and a positive slope in a larger part of the curve.[4] The same graph obtained from the French data shows a different shape. Although the curve seems well estimated with tight confidence intervals from nonparametric regression, the graph says that government primary balance does not depend on the Euribor interest rate in the whole period that we investigate. The test statistic on the average of derivatives shown in Table 16.3 confirms this result.

Table 16.3 Nonparametric local linear estimates of primary government balance: main countries in the EMU

	Effect Estimate	Std. Err.	z	P>z	Confidence Interval, 95%		R^2
Germany							
Euribor	−0.49	0.16	−3.00	0.00	−0.80	−0.17	0.72
Government debt	0.00	0.03	−0.10	0.92	−0.05	0.06	0.002
France							0.96
Euribor	0.17	0.21	0.82	0.42	−0.32	0.52	
Government debt	−0.05	0.02	−2.49	0.01	−0.10	−0.02	
Italy							0.77
Euribor	0.73	0.19	3.85	0.00	0.30	1.05	
Government debt	0.07	0.03	2.08	0.04	0.00	0.14	
Spain							0.91
Euribor	0.74	0.83	0.90	0.37	−1.06	2.16	
Government debt	−0.01	0.04	−0.23	0.82	−0.12	0.06	

Note: Data refer to quarterly time series of Germany, France, Italy, Spain in the period 2000q1–2019q3. Effect estimates are averages of derivatives of the dependent variable with respect to Euribor and Government Debt. Bootstrapped standard errors and confidence intervals.

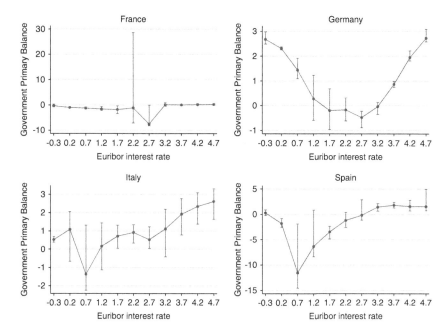

Figure 16.2 Nonparametric local linear kernel estimates of government primary balance. Effect of the Euribor interest rate with confidence intervals. Main countries in the EMU.

The U-shaped relation between Euribor and primary government balance hints at two different possible forms of interaction between monetary and fiscal policies. Apart from a few years before 2008, since the start of the EMU in 1999, we observe a declining trend in Euribor that recently takes negative values. The present analysis suggests that, in the first part of this phase, the expansive monetary policy adopted by ECB has been complementary to expansive fiscal policies of some important countries such as Germany, Italy and Spain. However, in the same countries at low or negative interest rates, a concern for the negative state of public finances seems to prevail, and we consequently observe a positive trend that takes the public balance from primary deficits to surpluses. In this tale, public debt should have a role.

Indeed, Figure 16.3 presents the plots of the estimated relation between primary government balance-GDP ratio and government debt-GDP ratio for the four countries of this regression analysis, setting the Euribor at its mean value in the period. This functional relation is well known in the literature because it has often been parametrically specified and estimated (Bohn, 1998). A positive first derivative suggests that the primary balance varies to ensure the sustainability of public debt. Fiscal policy also depends on the state of the economy,

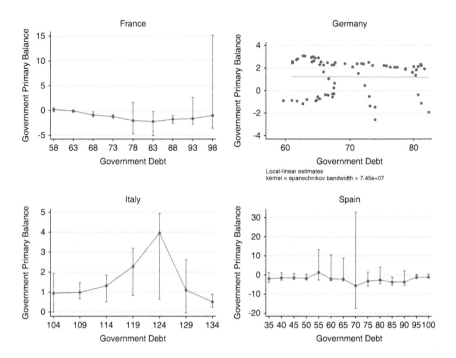

Figure 16.3 Nonparametric local linear kernel estimates of government primary balance. Effect of government debt. Main countries in the EMU.

namely, the macroeconomic stabilisation objectives of the government. Interpretation of the results has to consider that the value of the debt-GPD ratio at the beginning of the period is close or lower than 60% for Germany, France and Spain, but higher than 100% for Italy. Accordingly, the estimated plot for Italy shows an increasing relation between primary balance and debt that becomes decreasing only during the last years of the crisis when the debt-GDP ratio reaches high values. Hence, we find a significant concern of the Italian government for debt sustainability in the period.

Our nonparametric analysis does not detect any relation between primary balance and debt in the case of Germany, as shown in Figure 16.3, and confirmed by the statistics of Table 16.3. The experience of public finance in France tells of a public balance more oriented to short term macroeconomic targets than to debt sustainability. The average of derivatives of the primary balance with respect to the debt-GDP ratio takes a negative and statistically significant value. In the case of Spain, the average of derivatives is not significantly different from zero, although the debt-GDP ratio grows more than three times in the period. This result suggests that the Spanish government tried to balance both objectives: short term economic recovery and debt sustainability. The whole set of results seem to suggest that concern for public debt growth has been present in the policy decisions of the government of the main EMU, but not so strongly to change the strategy for the recovery of the economy.[5]

Given the indications we have got from the data on four important countries in the EMU, we also try to test the model of Equation (16.10) on a panel data of seven EMU countries, which consists of much more observations and provides a test of the model on a larger number of countries: we consider the time series of primary balance and debt of Belgium, France, Greece, Italy, Netherlands, Portugal, Spain from 2000:1 to 2019:3.[6] Table 16.4 presents the results of the nonparametric regression methods exposed in Section 3.1. The regression also includes binary dummy variables for each country but one (Belgium). The effect of these variables is strongly significant, which supports their introduction in the model. The estimated model fits quite well the time series of the ratio of the government primary balance to GDP.

Figure 16.4 presents the plot of the estimated relation between Euribor and primary balance, at the mean value of the debt–GDP ratio, that shows very clearly a U-shape. Each point of the curve is estimated with tight confidence intervals. Two curves with the same shape come from the estimates with the debt–GDP ratio at 60% and 110%. Figure 16.5 presents the estimates of the effect on the dependent variable of a sequence of increases of Euribor by 0.5%, from the minimum to the maximum values over the period. These estimates too display tight confidence intervals and sign consistent with the U-shaped curve in Figure 16.4.

Our nonparametric regressions allow the drawing of the curve relating the ratio of the primary government balance to GDP to the debt–GDP ratio, at the mean value of the Euribor. Figure 16.6 shows the graph where we observe a quite easily interpretable curve. Indeed, the first section is decreasing for low

Table 16.4 Nonparametric local linear estimates of government primary balance. Panel data of seven main countries in the EMU

	Effect Estimate	Std. Err.	z	P>z	Confidence Interval, 95%	
Euribor	−0.118	0.121	−0.98	0.327	−0.349	0.142
Government debt	−0.003	0.008	−0.34	0.733	−0.016	0.014
France	−0.676	0.053	−12.73	0.000	−0.781	−0.583
Greece	−1.462	0.114	−12.84	0.000	−1.719	−1.270
Italy	−1.748	0.184	−9.48	0.000	−2.212	−1.470
Netherlands	−2.260	0.222	−10.18	0.000	−2.774	−1.918
Portugal	−2.821	0.263	−10.73	0.000	−3.473	−2.422
Spain	−3.050	0.298	−10.22	0.000	−3.770	−2.565
R^2	0.706					
Observations	553					

Note. Data refer quarterly time series of Belgium, France, Greece, Italy, Netherlands, Portugal, Spain in the period 2000q1–2019q3. Effect estimates are averages of derivatives for Euribor and Government Debt and averages of contrasts for country dummies. The dummy variable for Belgium is excluded from estimates.

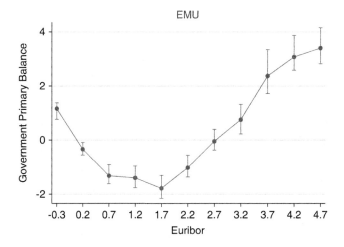

Figure 16.4 Nonparametric local linear kernel estimates of primary government balance: the effect of the Euribor. Panel data of seven main countries in the EMU.

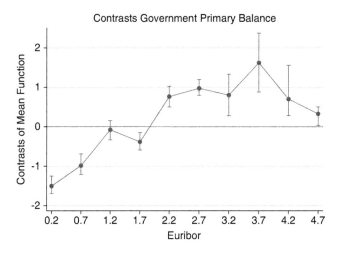

Figure 16.5 Bootstrap estimates of the effect of a discrete change of Euribor on government primary balance. Panel data of seven main countries in the EMU.

debt-GDP ratios: governments take advantage of a good state of the public finance to sustain the aggregate demand with decreasing surpluses. When the public balance becomes negative and debt grows in all countries of EMU, fiscal policy becomes more cautious. It seems interesting to note that the change of policy happens when the average public debt approximates the

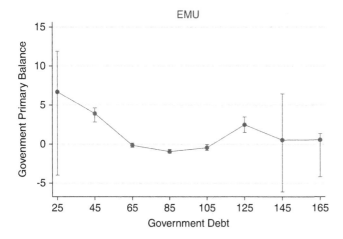

Figure 16.6 Nonparametric local linear kernel estimates of primary government balance: effect of the government debt. Panel data of seven main countries in the EMU.

value of 60% established by the EMU treatises, and the curve becomes increasing for values greater than 85%. Our econometric estimates do not produce a good fit of the relationship between primary balance and debt for those countries with debt greater than 125%. In the period, Greece and Italy were concerned with a very high debt–GDP ratio and committed to important policies of fiscal consolidation.

4 Discussion

In this section, the focus is on the relationship between the primary fiscal balance and the policy rate, as the econometric analysis does not seem to support the analytical result. The first found a U-shaped relationship, independently by the debt level: if the policy rate is low enough, a more expansionary monetary policy implies a more restrictive fiscal policy; otherwise, if the policy rate is high enough, a more expansionary monetary policy pushes also the governments to adopt a more expansionary fiscal policy. Instead, according to the parameter values, particularly, to debt level, the analytical result implies either one or the other of these two possibilities, independently of the policy rate value. Before trying to reconcile the econometric with the analytical finding, we have to notice the following facts. First, the policy rate has decreased steadily for the whole period from 2000 to 2019; probably, it crossed the threshold level after the sovereign debt crisis of 2010–2012. Thus, in the aftermath of the sovereign debt crisis, the decrease in the policy rate pushes governments to tighten the fiscal stance. Second, until 2014, the primary tool of the monetary policy was the refinancing operations, which allow the ECB to provide liquidity to the banking sector; instead, since 2014, the principal instrument was the European quantitative easing, a massive asset purchase programme, also intended for sovereign bonds. Third, during the same period, the reform of the European governance introduced a numerical benchmark for the process of debt reduction: member countries of the EMU with a debt level exceeding 60.0% of GDP need reduce the difference at an average rate of one-twentieth per year.

Now, we can put forward two possible explanations for the apparent contradiction between the econometric and analytical findings. First, if the asset purchase programme is assumed to be more effective in supporting the short-term macroeconomic stabilisation in comparison to the refinancing operations, then an increase in the effectiveness of monetary policy $(+\Delta b)$ may reconcile the analytical result with the econometric finding. Nevertheless, this explanation does not seem convincing. At the EMU level, the public debt to GDP ratio grew from 66.3% in 2007 to 91.3% in 2016 $(+\Delta \bar{d}_i)$, as an effect of the adverse impact of both the financial and sovereign debt crisis. Thus, the net effect is uncertain.

The second explanation is that European governance may have pushed national fiscal authorities to implement a sub-optimal policy, namely, an unnecessary fiscal consolidation.[7] Corsetti et al. (2019) review the literature on DSGE models to analyse the role played within the EMU by the monetary and fiscal policy in the aftermath of the sovereign debt crisis. The authors argue that if a sizeable adverse shock hits the economy and the zero lower bound influences the effectiveness of the monetary policy, then both the monetary and fiscal policy need to be accommodative in order to support the economic activity. Nevertheless, the European institutions were not able to adopt this policy mix since the institutional design was not able to face with the essential problem of the EMU. The ECB cannot take over the role of lender of last resort in favour of EMU member countries since it has to prevent them from running an excessive fiscal deficit. Thus, if national fiscal authorities finance accommodative fiscal policy through the issue of public debt, then they may be vulnerable to market sentiments (De Grauwe, 2012; Jarociński and Maćkowiak, 2018). Even when the ECB implemented the quantitative easing from 2015, also buying sovereign bonds from commercial banks, national governments could not adopt expansive fiscal policies because the European institutions forced them to pursue a process of debt reduction. According to Panico's analysis, conflicting national interests prevented the adjustment of the institutional design and pushed governments to adopt overly restrictive fiscal policies, especially for the most distressed countries (Panico and Purificato, 2012).

5 Conclusions

Concerning the institutional design of the EMU, the paper studies the strategic interaction between a central bank responsible for the monetary policy and national governments having the role in setting national fiscal policies.

We present a simple model to describe the behaviour of national governments that face the short-term trade-off between the objective of output stability and the need to implement a process of debt reduction. Specifically, the focus is on how the primary fiscal balance reacts to changes in the policy rate and the public debt level. As the main finding, we find that higher debt countries should adopt a more expansionary fiscal policy in response to a more accommodative monetary policy, independently of the policy rate level. Instead, based on the methods of nonparametric statistics, we detect a U-shaped relationship, independently of the public debt level. If the policy rate is low enough, then a more expansionary monetary policy implies a more restrictive fiscal policy; otherwise, if the policy rate is high enough, a more accommodative monetary policy pushes also the governments to adopt a more accommodative fiscal policy.

The more reasonable explanation of this apparent contradiction takes into account the following facts. First, the policy rate has decreased steadily for the whole period from 2000 to 2019; probably, it crossed the threshold level after the sovereign debt crisis of 2010–2012. Second, during the same period, the reform of European governance introduced a numerical benchmark for the process of debt reduction. In this context, European institutions may have forced national fiscal authorities to implement a sub-optimal policy, namely, the so-called austerity. These institutions were not able to adopt the optimal policy mix, based on the combined role of an accommodative monetary policy together with expansionary fiscal policies at the national level.

Notes

1 To simplify the analysis, we do not consider the issue of inflation bias or the role of other fiscal rules.
2 This panel data is balanced in both country and time dimensions. We exclude Germany, Ireland and Austria because of several missing values in the time series of Government Primary Balance. In any case, including those countries in the analysis does not change the qualitative results that we obtain with the balanced panel.
3 Because Germany has less data on government primary balance, 68, than the other countries, we estimate two distinct functions of one regressor each time.
4 The estimate of the average of the derivatives synthesises the nonlinearity of the fitted curves in the whole period (Table 16.3). Here, we observe that the sign of the mean of derivatives is negative and significant for Germany, meaning that the decreasing relation between Euribor and Primary balance prevails over the period under investigation. The same statistic shows a significant positive estimate for Italy, while the Spanish results suggest the balance between negative and positive derivatives.
5 Further econometric analysis of the model (9) shows that the U-shaped relation between primary government balance and Euribor does not change significantly at different values of the debt-GDP ratio.
6 The panel dataset consists of 553 observations and is balanced in both country and time dimensions.
7 Notice that a change in the parameter γ does not justify a U-shaped relationship since the condition represented by Equation (8) becomes less binding with an increase in the weight of debt stabilisation.

References

Baumann, U., Lodge, D. and Miescu, M. S. (2019). Global growth on life support? The contributions of fiscal and monetary policy since the global financial crisis. Working Paper Series, European Central Bank, 2248.

Bohn, H. (1998). The behavior of US public debt and deficits. *The Quarterly Journal of Economics* 113(3): 949–963.

Corsetti, G., Dedola, L., Jarociński, M., Maćkowiak, B. and Schmidt, S. (2019). Macroeconomic stabilization, monetary-fiscal interactions, and Europe's monetary union. *European Journal of Political Economy* 57(March): 22–33.

De Grauwe, P. (2012). The governance of a fragile Eurozone. *Australian Economic Review* 45(3): 255–268.

Dixit, A. and Lambertini, L. (2003). Symbiosis of monetary and fiscal policies in a monetary union. *Journal of International Economics* 60(2): 235–247.

Dixit, A. and Lambertini, L. (2001). Monetary–fiscal policy interactions and commitment versus discretion in a monetary union. *European Economic Review* 45(4-6): 977–987.

Fan, J. and Gijbels, I. (1996). *Local Polynomial Modelling and Its Applications: Monographs on Statistics and Applied Probability 66.* Vol. 66. CRC Press, Boca Raton, Florida, USA.

Foresti, P. (2018). Monetary and fiscal policies interaction in monetary unions. *Journal of Economic Surveys* 32(1): 226–248.

Foresti, P. (2015). Monetary and debt-concerned fiscal policies interaction in monetary unions. *International Economics and Economic Policy* 12(4): 541–552.

Jarociński, M. and Maćkowiak, B. (2018). Monetary-fiscal interactions and the euro area's malaise. *Journal of International Economics* 112 (May): 251–266.

Lambertini, L., Levine, P. and Pearlman, J. (2007). Fiscal policy in a monetary union: can fiscal cooperation be counterproductive? School of Economics Discussion Papers, 1707.

Li, Q. and Racine, J. S. (2007). *Nonparametric Econometrics: Theory and Practice.* Princeton University Press, Princeton, New Jersey, USA.

Panico, C. and Purificato, F. (2013). Policy coordination, conflicting national interests and the European debt crisis. *Cambridge Journal of Economics* 37(3): 585–608.

Ramey, V. A. (2016). Macroeconomic shocks and their propagation. In J. B. Taylor and H. Uhlig (eds), *Handbook of Macroeconomics,* Vol. 2A. Elsevier, Amsterdam, The Netherlands, pp. 71–162.

17 Monetary policy and financial stability in the Economic and Monetary Union

Francesco Purificato and Elvira Sapienza

1 Introduction

We feel pleased to contribute a paper to the book in honour of Carlo Panico. In writing about macroeconomic stability and financial stability, it seems right to us start from what Carlo himself has written on this topic. Indeed, based on Sraffa's analysis of money and banking, Carlo has studied the evolution of financial regulation before and after the financial crisis, highlighting how the growth of the financial system can determine an increase in income inequality (Panico et al., 2012). Moreover, based on the experience of the Mexican economy, he has supported the thesis that the process of financial liberalisation can promote both an expansion of the banking sector and a rise in the systemic risk; as a result, this process also affects the conduct of the monetary policy, contributing to generate a lower growth in the Mexican economy (Capraro and Panico, 2021). By moving from the different perspectives of the Economic and Monetary Union (EMU), this chapter also explores these critical factors related to the role of financial regulation. Specifically, the focus will be on how financial stability can influence the conduct of the monetary policy and, in turn, the trade-offs among price stability, output stability and financial stability.

The 2007–2008 financial crisis has shaken the confidence in the macro-economic policy framework: a monetary policy focused primarily on price stability has proven not to be a sufficient condition for financial stability. As a result, a new theoretical framework has emerged, in which monetary policy aims at price stability, and macro-prudential policy aims at financial stability. However, there is a debate about whether the monetary authority should amend the monetary policy framework to include also financial stability objectives along with price stability. According to the Modified Jackson Hole Consensus (MJHC) view, the monetary policy should pursue its relatively narrow mandate of price stability, stabilising the production around a sustainable long-run level; in contrast, macroprudential authorities should pursue financial stability. Instead, the leaning against the wind vindicated (LAWV) view argues that the monetary authority should also consider the objective of financial stability, as the macro-prudential policy cannot address the financial

DOI: 10.4324/9781003105558-20

cycle adequately, and financial instability can imply adverse effects on price stability. Finally, the financial stability is price stability (FSPS) view suggests merging the intertwined objectives of price and financial stability fully, as the financial sector determines the degree of inside money creation and the risk premium in the economy.

In the aftermaths of the sovereign debt crisis of 2010–2012, European institutions have reformed the institutional framework to pursue the objective of financial stability. They have established the Single Supervisory Mechanism (SSM), which introduces the following critical elements. First, under the direct control of the European Central Bank (ECB), centralised micro-prudential supervision aims to promote the soundness and safety of individual credit institutions. Second, under the responsibility of national designed authorities, decentralised macro-prudential supervision aims to prevent the building up of systemic financial risks; however, in this case, the ECB retains the power to tighten the measures adopted by these authorities.

The chapter's main contribution is a thorough assessment of the new institutional design introduced by the SSM. For this purpose, the essay presents a review of the literature and a simple analytical model to clarify the critical motivations behind the reform process and to discuss the actual application of the SSM.

Concerning the literature review, it detects the following elements. Until 2014, the ECB acts as a LAWV-type central bank, which tends to raise the policy rate more than an MJHC-type central bank to face the trade-off between macroeconomic and financial stability (Friedrich et al., 2019). Nevertheless, the benefits of a more restrictive monetary policy, namely, a lower probability for a financial crisis to occur, outweigh its costs, namely, a lower growth rate during normal times (Svensson, 2017; Kockerols and Kok, 2019). Moreover, the macro-prudential and micro-prudential supervision are effective in handling financial risks, promoting both macroeconomic and financial stability (Darracq Pariès et al., 2019); specifically, following asymmetric shocks, national macro-prudential measures can support the single monetary policy, taking into account national differences. Despite a still incomplete reform process, as the decision-making process lacks total transparency and accountability, and the goal of a levelled regulatory field has not yet been achieved (Schoenmaker and Véron, 2016; Fromage and Ibrido, 2019), some empirical findings appear to support the view that the SSM promotes the financial stability of the banking system (Loipersberger, 2018).

Concerning the analytical model, it describes the decision-making process of a central bank like the ECB. The analytical framework is based on the New Keynesian static macro-model (Bofinger and Mayer, 2007; Dehmej and Gambacorta, 2019; Poutineau and Vermandel, 2015), where we introduce a simplified endogenous mechanism of a financial crisis, as proposed by Woodford (2012). Financial risks depend on endogenous factors, such as the trend of the business cycle, which are affected by the policy rate, and exogenous factors beyond the control of the monetary authority, such as the propensity to take risks by banks or the impact of macro-prudential and micro-prudential policies. If the exogenous component of the systemic risk is high enough compared to the endogenous part, then a monetary policy based on the LAWV view implies larger output costs than a monetary policy based on the MJHC view. This finding exactly mirrors Panico's argument about the role of financial liberalisation: if the deregulation process promotes increasing financial risks, then a monetary policy pursuing the goal of financial stability reduces the investment level and the competitiveness of the economy, determining a lower economic growth (Capraro and Panico, 2021).

Overall, we can express a positive assessment of the new institutional framework implemented by the European institution, as it appears consistent with the critical factors detected by the literature. According to our model, both centralised micro-prudential policy and decentralised macro-prudential policy under the supervision of the ECB aim at increasing the capacity of the monetary authority to face the exogenous factors affecting stability financial risks. Basically, the new institutional design satisfies Tinbergen's principle. Each instrument should be devoted to the objective that it can most efficiently achieve: the monetary policy mainly aiming at macroeconomic stability and the macro-prudential and micro-prudential supervision aiming at financial stability.

The remainder of the essay is organised as follows. Section 2 provides an overview of the EMU institutional framework. Section 3 reviews the literature, focusing on contributions that consider the peculiar features of the EMU and the actual implementation of the SSM. Based on the analytical model and the key elements detected by the literature, Section 4 discusses and assesses the new institutional framework established by the European institutions. Finally, Section 5 presents some conclusions.

2 The institutional framework

The Treaty on the Functioning of the European Union (TFEU) identified in the price stability the primary objective of the ECB. Subsequently, the ECB's Governing Council adopted the following quantitative definition: in pursuing the objective of price stability, the Governing Council aims to maintain in flation rates below, but close to, 2.0% over the medium term.

The ECB defines financial stability as the ability of the financial system, which consists of financial institutions, markets and market infrastructures, to withstand shocks and the onset of financial imbalances. At the macroeconomic level, financial stability is related to the resilience of the financial system as a whole, namely, a condition in which the system can mitigate the effect of systemic shocks on the credit intermediation process, preventing a negative impact on the real economy. At the microeconomic level, financial stability is related to the soundness and safety of individual credit institutions, namely, a condition in which these institutions can resist idiosyncratic shocks (Boissay and Cappiello, 2014).

Within the EMU, the TFEU and the Council Regulation 1024/2013, which established the SSM,[1] define the institutional framework to face and pursue the objectives of price stability and financial stability. Table 17.1 reassumes the critical characteristics of this legal framework, specifying the functions and responsibilities of the monetary authority (Cassola et al., 2019).

In order to pursue the goals of price stability and financial stability, at both macroeconomic and microeconomic level, the European institutions can use three functions: the monetary policy, the macro-prudential policy and the micro-prudential policy. A different degree of centralisation and decentralisation characterises the decision-making and the implementation process connected with these three functions.

In the case of monetary policy, the decision-making process is centralised. Based on the support of the Executive Board and several technical committees,[2] the Governing Council of the ECB, which comprises the president of the ECB, the governors of euro area National Central Banks (NCBs) and the members of the Executive Board, sets the single monetary policy of the EMU. This institutional body adopts all monetary policy measures, taking into account a clear euro area perspective without reference to regional interests. Specifically, it defines the features of the standard measures as the refinancing operations and the non-standard measures as the asset purchase programmes. In contrast, the implementation process of the monetary policy is decentralised, with the NCBs performing almost all the operational tasks.

In the case of macro-prudential policy, the decision-making and implementation processes are mainly decentralised. The SSM assigns the power to decide and apply macro-prudential measures to the National Competent Authorities (NCAs), namely, the national institutions responsible for implementing the micro-prudential supervision. These measures, for instance, counter-cyclical capital buffers or capital requirements, are applied at the national

Table 17.1 Price and financial stability: the EMU's legal framework

Objectives	Functions	Decision-Making Process	Implementation Process
Price stability	Monetary policy	Centralised – ECB	Decentralised – NCBs[1]
Financial stability	Macro-prudential policy	Decentralised – NCAs[2] Centralised – ECB	Decentralised – NCAs Centralised – ECB
	Micro-prudential policy	Centralised – ECB	Centralised for significant institutions – ECB Decentralised for other institutions – NCAs

Notes: (1) National Central Banks (NCBs); (2) National Competent Authorities (NCAs).

level regarding the banking sector of a country. Nevertheless, the Governing Council can comment and object to the planned decisions by the NCAs, but mostly it may tighten macro-prudential measures adopted by the NCAs. This legal framework reflects that the euro area banking sector is highly fragmented, and financial imbalances often arise at the country level. Moreover, it also recognises a vital role to the ECB in mitigating possible cross-border spill-over effects, providing a euro area perspective in the assessment of the systemic risk.

In the case of micro-prudential policy, the decision-making process is centralised: supported by the Supervisory Board,[3] the Governing Council ensures the homogeneity of supervisory practices and regulatory frameworks for individual credit institutions and the banking sector as a whole. About the implementation of the supervisory activity, the ECB directly supervises financial institutions classified as significant, based on their economic relevance at either country or euro area level. Otherwise, the NCAs are responsible for supervising less significant entities, subject to the oversight of the ECB to make sure the homogenous application of supervisory standards.

3 The literature review

Following the newly emerging paradigm (International Monetary Fund IMF, 2013), the policymaker can use both monetary and macro-prudential policies for counter-cyclical management, the first primarily aimed at price stability and the second at financial stability. Otherwise, the micro-prudential policy focuses on the safety and soundness of individual financial institutions. By starting from a different appreciation of the pervasiveness of the interaction among these policies, the literature presents three alternative views about the relationship between price stability and financial stability: the MJHC view, the LAWV view and the FSPS view.[4]

The first view considers as limited the interaction between monetary and macro-prudential policy, and it suggests maintaining these functions separate, as long as there is sufficient information sharing amongst the authorities. The monetary policy should pursue its relatively narrow mandate of price stability, stabilising the production around a sustainable long-run level; in contrast, macroprudential authorities should pursue financial stability (Svensson, 2012; Bernanke, 2015). This framework is an assignment consistent with Tinbergen's principle, which says that each instrument should be devoted to the objective that it can most efficiently achieve (Smets, 2014). The clear separation of objectives, instruments and communication of the two policy domains will increase the transparency and the accountability of policymakers, increasing the effectiveness and efficiency of policies. According to this view, monetary policy is not an appropriate instrument to pursue financial stability on which it has only a weak, indirect, effect and, rarely, might even constitute a threat to financial stability (Svensson, 2017; Ajello et al., 2019). In order to actively and systematically influence financial risks, policymakers need a separate macro-prudential policy. In leaning against the wind for financial stability purpose, the monetary policy implies costs superior to the estimated possible benefits since a tighter monetary policy leads to lower average inflation and growth rates, and consequently a slow decrease in the real value of debt over time (Svensson, 2017; 2018).

The LAWV view considers the strong mutual dependencies between the two policy functions, which can be expected to complement and support each other. Monetary policy should have as secondary objective financial stability, as price stability itself has proven not to be a sufficient condition for financial stability (Borio, 2014; Billi and Vredin, 2014).[5] Besides, the macro-prudential policy cannot address the financial cycle adequately, and the lack of financial stability can, in turn, have considerable adverse effects on price stability. The overall primacy of maintaining a price stability objective over the medium term is not affected. However, taking into account financial stability concerns in the adjustment path allows the central bank to lean against the wind; indeed, the financial cycle interacts with the business cycle in various potentially non-linear ways, with important drivers of financial imbalances, such as credit, liquidity and risk-taking (Smets, 2014). The monetary policy should adopt a flexible inflation targeting framework: the set-up is the same but it becomes more complicated since the policy horizon of the monetary authorities will extend due to the length of the financial cycle compared to that of the business cycle (Woodford, 2012). Thus, central banks may face additional trade-offs, which will require increased credibility of the price stability target.

The FSPS view suggests merging monetary policy and macro-prudential policy objectives fully. The argument is that financial stability and price stability are intimately intertwined, and it is impossible to make a distinction. This close connection comes from the fact that the financial sector determines the degree of inside money creation and the price of risk in the economy (Brunnermeier and Sannikov, 2015). In the case of a negative shock, bank equity declines, assets are sold to reduce the risk exposure, banks' balance sheets deteriorate, and the degree of money creation falls. The overall reduction in the money supply causes a deflationary pressure, and a liquidity spiral affects banks, redistributing wealth away from productive balance sheet-impaired sectors; especially, if fiscal-policy measures cannot be implemented in a timely manner. The monetary policy has to dampen the amplification effects going strictly beyond inflation targeting, figuring out which sectors suffer, redistributing wealth and restoring the flow of funds to productive parts in the economy (Roger, 2009). Essentially, aware of the interactions between price and financial stability, central banks should employ monetary policy tools in such a way as to reduce negative moral-hazard implications in the long run (Brunnermeier and Sannikov, 2014).

In order to assess the adequacy of the EMU institutional framework, a useful starting point would be the stylised facts that emerge from the empirical studies, which analyse the trade-off between macroeconomic and financial stability and the role of macro-prudential policy in the context of a monetary union. For our purposes, the two following sections evaluate these results. Subsequently, Section 3.3 reviews the literature on the SSM implementation.

3.1 The trade-off between macroeconomic and financial stability

The first strand of analysis refers to the interaction between macroeconomic and financial stability. The econometric analysis by Friedrich et al. (2019) studies how the objective of financial stability affects the monetary policy framework and, in turn, the choice of the policy rate during normal times and periods of financial booms, namely, situations where potential systemic risks are building up. The peculiar element of this analysis is the construction of the Financial Stability Orientation (FSO) index,[6] which allows classifying a monetary authority according to its propensity to use the policy rate to prevent the onset of systemic financial risk. At the end of 2014, when the European institutions had not yet fully implemented the reform process, the ECB scored a value for the FSO index, such that the ECB was classified as a LAWN-type monetary authority. Friedrich et al. (2019) detect that a LAWV-type monetary authority tends to raise the policy rate more than a MJHC-type central bank in the presence of a financial stability risk. This differential behaviour is most significant during period of financial booms, namely, a situation where potential systemic risks are building up.[7] Substantially, the LAWN-type central bank faces with a short-run trade-off among price stability, output stability and financial stability, and it tends to assign a lower weight to macroeconomic objectives than a MJHC central bank: the latter responds more aggressively than the forward with respect to inflation and output gaps. As a result, during normal times and financial booms, the operation of the LAVW-type central bank is characterised by a more restrictive monetary policy stance, determining lower growth and inflation rates.

At this point, it is essential to evaluate if the benefits of a more restrictive monetary policy, namely, a lower probability for a financial crisis to occur, outweigh its costs, namely, a lower growth rate during normal times. Both Friedrich et al. (2019) and Svensson (2017) detect that the LAWV-type monetary policy implies higher costs in comparison to its benefits. Kockerols and Kok (2019) also support this finding, by modifying the Svensson (2017) framework and taking into account the spatial and time dimensions of the financial cycle dynamic, the ECB's systemic risk indicator (SRI) and the role of macro-prudential supervision.[8] They find that the LAWV-type monetary policy does not fundamentally alter the structure of the problem and it failed to consider endogenous downturn costs. In such a scenario, an active use of national macro-prudential policies targeting financial stability risks could determine the further benefit of countering the national imbalances, alleviating the burden on monetary policy to lean against the wind.

3.2 The role of macro-prudential and micro-prudential supervision

The second strand of analysis refers to the interaction among monetary policy, macro-prudential policy and micro-prudential policy. Few papers have discussed this issue, all using a DSGE model that introduce a financial and a housing sector and assume strategic cooperation and a joint objective function. Substantially, they find that macro-prudential policies can usefully or partly contribute to macroeconomic welfare although with some costs. Table 17.2 summarises the main features of these papers.

A number of studies find that macro-prudential policies strongly promote macroeconomic welfare acting at the core of the financial system. They support monetary policy in addressing destabilising fluctuations in credit

Table 17.2 The empirical literature on the macro-prudential policy

	Economy (1)	Financial Frictions (2)	Macro-prudential Tools (3)	Effects of Macro-prudential Policy (4)		
				Financial Stability	Output Stability	Distribution of Benefits
						Core Periphery
Results based on model estimation						
Darracq Pariès et al. (2011)	CE	CC	CAR	+++	+++	... ...
Carboni et al. (2013)	CE	CC	CAR	+	+	
Quint and Rabanal (2014)	MU	FA	CAR	+++	+++	− ++
Results based on model calibration						
Brzoza-Brzezina et al. (2013)	MU	CC	LTV	+++	−−	− ++
Poutineau, Vermandel (2017)	MU	FA	CAR	+++	+++	+ +++
Dehmej, Gambacorta (2019)	MU	CC	LTV	++	−−	++ ++
Rubio and Comunale (2017)	MU		LTV, ETR	+++	+++	
Malmierca (2022)	MU	FA	CAR	++	++	++ ++
Darracq Pariès et al. (2019)	MU	FA	LTV	+++	−−−	+ +++
Kockerols and Kok (2019)	MU	CC	LTV-BCR	−−−	−−−	... ...

Notes: (1) Closed economy (CE), Monetary Union (MU); (2) Collateral constraint (CC), Financial accelerator (FA); (3) Capital requirement (CAR), Loan-to-value ratio (LTV), Bank capital requirement (BCR), Extended Taylor Rule (ETR); (4) Positive effect (+), Negative effect (−).

markets and intertemporal wedges between financial costs. Among these studies, Darracq Pariès et al. (2011) estimate a model[9] with financially constrained households, firms and an oligopolistic banking sector. They examine the monetary policy implications of the various financial frictions to credit supply and demand and furthermore the real economic implications of increasing capital requirements. By means of countercyclical regulation (credit and asset prices) macro-prudential policy strongly affect monetary policy determining a superior macroeconomic outcome. Similar results are obtained by Quint and Rabanal (2014) that uses a two-country (core and peripheral) model with two sectors and two types of agents, savers and borrowers. A financial accelerator mechanism is introduced on the household side such that risk shocks in this sector affect conditions in the credit markets and the broader macroeconomy. The findings show that macroprudential regulations affect savers and borrowers differently: e.g. credit-to-GDP ratio improves welfare in the EMU the most but reduces that of borrowers while nominal credit growth improves welfare for all citizens. Since do not appear any adverse spill-over effect of regulation from one-member state to another, the setting macroprudential policies at the national or EMU-wide level does not seem to change the outcome.

The importance of a coordination among the different policy functions emerges also in the results of Kockerols and Kok (2019) who try to understand to what extent macroprudential policy is the right tool to address financial stability risks. They take financial cycle dynamics[10] into account considering longer time horizons and changes in bank capital requirement. It emerges that in the short term, the cumulative costs of macro-prudential policy outweigh the benefits, but in a longer-term, the implementation has cumulated net marginal benefits.[11]

In the sense of a limited impact of macro-prudential policy, Carboni et al. (2013). In their model with financial frictions the banking sector[12] as also households and firms on the real side of the economy, are subject to capital constraints. The assessment presents two dimensions: the transmission mechanism of individual macro-prudential instruments from a system-wide perspective and the strategic complementarities in exceptional crisis circumstances. The impact of alternative macro-prudential configurations on GDP remains contained throughout the regular business cycle overall, while their effects on loans are more pronounced. Instead, during the financial crisis, the macro-prudential response, although effective in leaning against the financial cycle, implies an adverse drop in real GDP.

Other studies find that the effectiveness of the macro-prudential policies as a stabilising tool depends on they being set individually for each region since area-wide policy results ineffective in this respect. Brzoza-Brzezina et al. (2015) provided a model with a housing market and a banking sector, where banks and borrowers face a binding capital constraint. By means a simulation of asymmetric shocks hitting the core and the periphery, they find that a countercyclical application of macro-prudential tools can partly compensate the loss of independent monetary policy in the peripheral economy lowering the output fluctuations and reducing shocks related to monetary policy or to the housing market.

Rubio and Comunale (2017) develop a DSGE new Keynesian model calibrated for Lithuania and the euro area. They consider two different scenarios: one in which the ECB extends (an extended Taylor rule) its goals to also include financial stability and a second one in which a national macroprudential authority uses the LTV ratio as an instrument. The results show that both rules are effective in making the financial system more stable in both countries but the macroprudential Taylor rule comes with a cost in terms of inflation volatility while the LTV rule, less effective, does not compromise the objective of monetary policy. This reinforces the Tinbergen principle, which argues that there should be two different instruments when there are two different policy goals.

Other evidence that macroprudential policy should be adjusted to regional evolutions comes from Poutineau and Vermandel (2017). They consider the link between investors and the banking system as the main channel for the build-up of financial imbalances and introduce in the model a financial accelerator mechanism on the productive side. In comparing the welfare implications of homogenous versus heterogeneous macroprudential rules across regions it emerges that the welfare gains are unequally shared, with the peripheral countries being the main winners and only limited welfare improvements for the core countries.

Similar outcome is provided by the simplified model of Dehmej and Gambacorta (2019) that considers an additional equation incorporating financial frictions. They find that federal and country-targeted macroprudential policies give similar outcomes when both countries and shocks are fully similar. Otherwise, when core and periphery economies are hit by asymmetric shocks country-targeted macroprudential policies are more appropriate in taming financial and economic imbalances. Again, Malmierca (2020) who builds a two-country model with a financial accelerator to analyses, through different macroprudential scenarios, the response to an asymmetric credit risk shock. When national macroprudential policies are implemented, macroeconomic and financial stability is reached in both countries, mainly due to the private-public debt channel. By contrast macroprudential policies federally implemented lead to higher macroeconomic stability in the country hit by the shock but destabilise the other country because of the open economy channel.

A similar outcome emerges from Darracq Pariès et al. (2019) who use a two-country model with financial frictions representing, through calibration, the essential features of the largest euro-area economies, such as Germany, France, Italy and Spain. The model runs various simulations that illustrate how macroprudential policies measures targeting imbalances at the national level can help to achieve better policy outcomes in terms of price and financial stability, especially in presence of asymmetric financial cycles. However, their impact varies across different macroprudential instruments. Furthermore, they find that national macroprudential measures (such as LTV ratio or the portfolio-specific capital requirement) can have also relevant cross-border spill-over effects[13] channelled via international financial and trade linkages. Such outcome provides a rationale for coordinated action among national authorities as well as a co-ordination role for the central monetary and macroprudential authority to help minimise any unintended negative spill-over effects.[14]

What emerges from the theoretical and empirical literature is that there are synergies and trade-offs between monetary and macroprudential policies, and these interactions may become particularly pronounced in a monetary union where there is an area-wide monetary policy. Consequently, macroprudential policies targeting national imbalances can help to achieve better policy outcomes in terms of price and financial stability. This underlines the need for a coordination mechanism.

3.3 The application of the SSM

The SSM is a complex supervisory structure that involves the ECB, the NCBs and the NCAs and relies on a high degree of coordination and communication among them; this complexity is a challenge in terms of governance. In line with its objectives, the SSM should positively affect the control of the leading bank risk-taking and spur economic activity, eliminating financial instability (Vallascas and Keasey, 2013; Creel et al., 2015). However, examining the literature investigating its impact, contrasting results appear with respect to the SSM adequacy.

Concerning the effectiveness of the SSM as a supervisory regime to improve financial stability, some authors find a positive effect in terms of market response. Fiordelisi and Galloppo (2018) detect that financial markets positively reacted to the implementation of the SSM, as signalled by the stock market prices that provide information on the expected effectiveness of the SSM to stabilise the financial system. Fiordelisi et al. (2017) find that banks' response to the first step of the SSM was positive: banks under direct ECB supervision reduced their lending activities, with differences across countries in the variation of reserves for credit losses and capital ratios of the treated banks. Specifically, the reserves of French and Italian banks decreased less than those of the other treated banks; as a result, their capital ratios were less affected by the launch of the SSM. However, the more stringent limits imposed on the banks' activity can entail costs for their shareholders by restricting profitable strategies. From this perspective, the expected effect of the SSM will be positive only when its benefits are sufficient to offset these costs. Analysing the stock market reaction to the creation of the SSM for a sample of EU banks, also Loipersberger (2018) concludes that the SSM improves banking stability, especially for banks with lower capitalisation or located in institutionally weaker countries. Overall, the new institutional framework reduces the propensity of banks to take excessive risks and stabilises the financial sector. Nevertheless, the empirical findings by Abad et al. (2020) do not support this conclusion, highlighting how coordination problems between the ECB and the NCAs may lead to an increase in systemic and idiosyncratic financial risks.

Regarding the SSM architecture, indeed, the literature emphasises some issues. Ferrarini (2015) points out that the SSM represents a semi-strong centralised system: it is still based on supervisory cooperation, although the ECB has direction powers with respect to NCAs. Consequently, it may give rise to agency problems, particularly in the relationships with supervisors of non-euro area countries, affecting the profitability of euro area banks. Concerning the powers conferred to the ECB, Danieli (2020) stresses that the monetary authority mainly focuses on the conduct of the monetary policy; therefore, the fragmentation of the financial system generates the lack of an authority fully responsible for the supervision of the macroprudential policy and the adoption of the micro-prudential policy.

In assessing how the SSM works in practice, Schoenmaker and Véron (2016) find that it is still insufficiently transparent, providing little public information about all supervised banks; specifically, the opacity that characterises the determination of Supervisory Review and the Evaluation Process SREP scores. Moreover, as stressed by the European Court of Auditors (2016), Fromage and Ibrido (2019) and Nicolaides (2019), the SSM does not use a formal set of performance indicators and metrics for monitoring and assessing its effectiveness. Further, Amtenbrink and Markakis (2019) provide a qualitative assessment for the effectiveness of the mechanism of accountability of the ECB and its supervisory board vis-à-vis the European Parliament and national parliaments of the member states. They highlight the lack of a clear yardstick against which to assess the ECB's performance in the area of banking supervision, as well as a gap in terms of political accountability due to the limited sanctioning powers available to the European Parliament as the SSM regulation was not adopted under the ordinary legislative procedure.

Another relevant point concerning the functioning of the SSM is that the goal of a levelled regulatory field has not yet been achieved. Angeloni (2015) observes that the legal fragmentation, the uncertainties surrounding the completion of the banking union and the absence of area-wide deposit insurance limited the extent to which financial resources could be allocated efficiently. Moreover, according to Schoenmaker and Véron (2016), the SSM maintains practices that contribute to cross-border fragmentation: the imposition of entity-level, as opposed to group-level, capital and liquidity requirements, also known as geographical ring-fencing; the omission of geographical risk diversification inside the euro area in stress test scenarios. Going beyond the European perspective and looking closely at nine member states, these authors adopt a two-level perspective that shows how national idiosyncrasies continue to shape the system regarding banking models and structures and of perceptions and politics.

Overall, the ex-post assessment of the SSM reveals positive and negative elements. On the one hand, some empirical findings support the view that the SSM has promoted the financial stability of the banking system, although inefficient coordination may lead to increased systemic and idiosyncratic financial risks over time. On the other hand, the literature also has shown some deficiencies in the institutional framework, such as the difficulty of the ECB to take on the role of supervisor of the NCAs, the lack of transparency and accountability in the decision-making process and the persistence of a legal fragmentation of the euro area financial system across member countries.

4 An analytical analysis of the EMU institutional framework

Section 4.1 presents an analytical model to analyse the conduct of the monetary policy in the presence of financial risks. Subsequently, based on the analytical findings and the literature described in Section 3.3, Section 4.2 discusses and assesses the new institutional framework established by the European institutions.

4.1 A simple analytical framework

This subsection presents a simple model to analyse the decision-making process of a central bank like the ECB. The analytical framework is based on the New Keynesian static macro-model by Bofinger and Mayer (2007). Specifically, we modify this framework as follows. First, as proposed by Woodford (2012), we introduce a simplified endogenous mechanism of a financial crisis. Second, following Dehmej and Gambacorta (2019) and Poutineau and Vermandel (2015), we consider how the business cycle affects credit conditions for the economy. The analytical framework consists of five equations: a) an equation that determines the expected value of an increase in the risk premium caused by a financial crisis; b) an equation that determines the interest rate on loans by taking into account the mechanism of the financial accelerator; c) the IS curve, which describes the relationship between the aggregate demand and the interest rate on loans. d) the Phillips curve, which describes the macroeconomic trade-off between price stability and output stability; e) the objective function of the monetary authority, which describes its preferences concerning the trade-off between macroeconomic stability and financial stability.

The following equation defines the endogenous mechanism for a financial crisis to occur:

$$p\Theta = (\sigma\gamma + F)\Theta = (\sigma\gamma\Theta) + (F\Theta) = \gamma\Theta_\gamma + \Theta_F \tag{17.1}$$

The risk premium is the difference between the interest rate on loans to firms granted by the banking sector and the interest rate on a safe financial asset, namely, the policy rate. The parameter (Θ) identifies the increase in the risk premium determined by the occurrence of a financial crisis, and p is the probability that an economy may face a financial crisis. Thus, their multi-plication ($p\Theta$) denotes the expected increase in the risk premium. The probability (p) depends on two factors. The first is the endogenous mechanism that can lead to a financial crisis, which implies that the output gap (y) posi-tively affects the probability (p), and the parameter ($\sigma > 0$) is the marginal impact of y on p. This parsimonious relation summarises the stylised fact that the growth rate of loans is positively related to the growth rate of output, namely, an increase in the production level raises the leverage of credit in-stitutions. However, the greater the leverage, the smaller the unexpected decline in asset values required to trigger a crisis, such that a positive output gap raises the probability of a financial crisis. The parameter Θ_y synthesises the marginal effect of y on the expected increase in the risk premium ($\sigma\Theta$). The second factor concerns the role of exogenous elements, such as the propensity to take risks by banks or the impact of macro-prudential and micro-prudential policies. These elements, identified by the parameter ($F \geq 0$), can influence the expected increase in the risk premium ($\Theta_F = F\Theta$), independently by the output gap (y). Basically, the monetary authority cannot affect this component of the expected increase in the risk premium through the policy rate; in contrast, it can influence the endogenous component of the expected increase through the police rate since the probability that an economy may face a financial crisis depends on the output gap.

During normal times, when potential financial vulnerabilities are building up, but they have not started to materialise, the credit rate depends on the monetary policy and the mechanism of the financial accelerator:

$$r_c = r - \gamma y \tag{17.2}$$

The interest rate on loans (r_l) is positively related to the policy rate (r) and negatively to the output gap (y); the parameter ($\gamma > 0$) defines the sensitivity of the credit rate to the level of economic activity.[15] As shown in Dehmej and Gambacorta (2019) and Poutineau and Vermandel (2015), Equation (17.2) allows a parsimonious representation of the credit market. On the one hand, the loan supply is a negative function of the policy rate: an increase in r raises the opportunity cost for investing in more remunerated financial activities than deposits, so that their demand decreases, as the amount of financial resources available for loans. On the other hand, the loan supply is a positive function of the output gap: an increase in y raises the value of bank capital since loans are more likely to be repaid, so that also the loan supply increases with the level of economic activity.[16]

The following equation defines the IS curve:

$$y = -\alpha (r_c - r_N) + \varepsilon_D \tag{17.3}$$

The variable (r_N) is the natural interest rate, and the parameter (ε_D) identifies a demand shock, namely, an exogenous shift in the aggregate demand deriving from autonomous changes in consumption or investment. The difference between the interest rate on loans and the natural rate matters for the output gap: favourable financial conditions ($r_c < r_N$) support the aggregate demand, determining a positive output gap ($y > 0$); differently, unfavourable financial conditions ($r_c > r_N$) depress the aggregate demand, determining a negative output gap ($y < 0$). The parameter (α) defines the sensitivity of the output gap to the difference between the credit rate and the natural interest rate.

The following equation defines the Phillips Curve:

$$\pi = \beta y + \varepsilon_S \tag{17.4}$$

The variable (π) is the inflation gap; the parameter (ε_S) represents a supply shock, namely, a cost-push factor like the price of raw materials). The parameter ($\beta > 0$) defines the positive marginal effect of the output gap (y) on the inflation rate (π).

Finally, the following equation identifies the objective function of the monetary authority:

$$L_M = (y)^2 + \lambda_\pi (\pi)^2 + \lambda_\Theta (p\Theta)^2 \tag{17.5}$$

Based on the assumption that the relative weight of output stability in the monetary authority preferences is equal to 1, the parameters ($\lambda_\pi \geq 0$) and ($\lambda_\Theta \geq 0$) identify the relative weight of the goals of price stability and financial stability, respectively.

The monetary authority minimises the loss function represented by Equation (17.5), subject to the constraints defined by Equations (17.1) and (17.4), to handle the trade-off between macroeconomic stability and financial stability. The first-order condition is as follows:

$$\partial L_M/\partial y = 2[y + \lambda_\pi (\beta y + \varepsilon_S)\beta + \lambda_\Theta (\Theta_y y + \Theta_F)\Theta_y] = 0$$

therefore, the optimal output gap is the following:

$$y_{OPT} = -\frac{(\beta\lambda_\pi)\varepsilon_S}{(1 + \lambda_\pi\beta^2 + \lambda_\Theta\Theta_y^2)} - \frac{(\lambda_\Theta\Theta_y)\Theta_F}{(1 + \lambda_\pi\beta^2 + \lambda_\Theta\Theta_y^2)} \tag{17.6}$$

In the case of a positive supply shock and exogenous elements determining the risk of a financial crisis (ε_S, $\Theta_F > 0$), the optimal output gap is lower than zero ($y_{OPT} < 0$). The monetary authority mitigates the negative impact of these two factors through a restrictive monetary policy: however, the lower the relative weight of price and financial stability in the monetary authority preferences (λ_π, λ_Θ), the lower the decrease in the production level. Notice that the derivative of Equation (17.6) with respect to Θ_y is greater than zero ($\partial y_{OPT}/\partial \Theta_y > 0$); an increase in the marginal effect of the output gap on the expected increase in the risk premium reduces the output contraction needed to balance the adverse effects of a positive supply shock and exogenous elements determining the risk of a financial crisis.

By substituting Equation (17.2) in Equation (17.3), it is possible to determine the equilibrium output gap; then, by using this expression and Equation (17.6), and solving for r, we obtain the optimal policy rate, namely, the policy rate adopted by the monetary authority to achieve the optimal output gap. In the case of a LAWV-type central bank ($\lambda_\Theta > 0$), the optimal policy rate is the following:

$$r_{lawn} = r_N + \frac{(1 - \alpha\gamma)\left[(\beta\lambda_\pi)\varepsilon_S + (\lambda_\Theta\Theta_y)\Theta_F\right]}{\alpha(1 + \lambda_\pi\beta^2 + \lambda_\Theta\Theta_y^2)} + \frac{1}{\alpha}\varepsilon_D \qquad (17.7)$$

In the case of a MJHC-type central bank ($\lambda_\Theta = 0$), the optimal policy rate is the following:

$$r_{mjhc} = r_N + \frac{(1 - \alpha\gamma)(\beta\lambda_\pi)\varepsilon_S}{\alpha(1 + \lambda_\pi\beta^2)} + \frac{1}{\alpha}\varepsilon_D \qquad (17.8)$$

In this analytical framework, the LAWV-type central bank conducts the monetary policy to manage macroeconomic stability and financial stability. In contrast, the MJHC-type central bank sets the monetary policy to cope only with the trade-off between output stability and financial stability. The following condition allows us to compare the optimal policy rate under these two alternative monetary policy views.

$$r_{lawv} < r_{mjhc} \quad if \quad \frac{\Theta_F}{\Theta_y} < \frac{(\lambda_\pi\beta)\varepsilon_S}{(1 + \lambda_\pi\beta^2)} \qquad (17.9)$$

Equation (17.9) holds if the expected increase in the risk premium determined by exogenous factors (Θ_F) is low enough compared to the marginal effect of the output gap on the expected increase (Θ_y). Under this condition, the monetary policy based on the LAWV view implies a lower level for the optimal policy rate, namely, lower output costs, than the monetary policy based on the MJHC view.[17] This finding exactly mirrors Panico's view about the role of financial liberalisation: if the deregulation process promotes increasing financial risks, then a monetary policy pursuing the goal of financial stability reduces the investment level and the competitiveness of the economy, determining a lower economic growth (Capraro and Panico, 2021). Thus, reduced efficiency of the macro-prudential and micro-prudential supervision to prevent credit institutions from taking over too many financial risks implies that the monetary authority should not consider the goal of financial stability, but it should focus its action only on the traditional macroeconomic trade-off between output stability and price stability $(+\Delta\Theta_F)$. Otherwise, when the output gap, namely, the policy rate, affects the expected increase in the risk premium decisively, the central bank should take into account the objective of financial stability in conducting the monetary policy $(+\Delta\Theta_y)$.

4.2 Discussion

The Council Regulation 1024/2013 that established the SSM reformed the European institutional framework to pursue the goal of financial stability at the macroeconomic and microeconomic level. Before the reform, centralised monetary policy and decentralised macro-prudential and micro-prudential supervision characterised the institutional design.

The critical implication of the old framework was that the ECB took on the features of a LAWV-type central bank, having to handle the trade-off between macroeconomic and financial stability through only one instrument: the policy rate. As a result, the monetary policy stance generally was more restrictive than that one of an MJHC-type central bank, determining lower growth and in-flation rates but also a lower probability of a financial crisis to occur. However, at the macro-level, the empirical literature has detected this framework in-effective, with its costs outweighing its benefits. Moreover, also at the micro-level, the national authorities responsible for the micro-prudential supervision did not prevent the building up of systemic risks: in 2012, for instance, the Spanish government had to apply for a financial support programme of the European institutions in order to rescue its banking sector from the effect of the international financial crisis. According to the simple model presented in Section 4.1, this context refers to a situation where Equation (17.9) does not hold: the expected increase in the risk premium determined by exogenous factors (Θ_F) is sufficiently high in comparison to the marginal effect of the output gap on the expected increase (Θ_y). The monetary authority cannot affect the expected increase in the risk premium decisively; therefore, a monetary policy based on the LAWV view, which pursues both macro-economic and financial stability, is not optimal.

These problems pushed the European institutions to launch the SSM to handle the trade-off between macroeconomic and financial stability. Specifically, the SSM introduced the following critical elements: a) centralised micro-prudential supervision under the direct control of the ECB; b) de-centralised macro-prudential supervision under the control of the NCAs, with the ECB that retains the power to tighten the measures adopted by the na-tional authorities.

The empirical evidence described in Section 4.2 appears to support this new institutional framework. It finds that the macro-prudential and micro-prudential supervisions are effective in handling financial risks, promoting both financial and macroeconomic stability. The adoption of macro-prudential measures implies a decrease in the probability and severity of the financial crisis, with a moderate adverse effect on output during the business cycle overall: the marginal benefits of these measures outweigh their marginal costs. Moreover, in the presence of asymmetric shocks, national macro-prudential measures can support the single monetary policy, taking into account national differences. In contrast, the monetary policy only reacts to the average conditions at the union level. Through the centralisation of micro-prudential supervision, the European reform process has aimed at reducing the vulnerability of credit institutions to idiosyncratic risks. Similarly, the introduction of macro-prudential supervision has pursued the goal of preventing the building up of systemic risk at the national level. Concerning our model, both these features of the reform process imply a reduction in the expected increase in the risk premium determined by the exogenous factors (Θ_F). In this context, the condition expressed by Equation (17.9) becomes less stringent because of the adoption of the SSM, and the ECB can more effectively manage the trade-off between its institutional objectives, namely, price stability and financial stability.

Overall, analysing the reaction of financial markets, the empirical literature appears to support the view that the new EMU framework reduces the propensity of banks to take excessive risks, stabilising the financial sector. Nevertheless, the implementation of nationally oriented macroprudential policies may lead to several problems. First, unequal distribution of benefits, with peripheral countries that achieve greater economic stability compared to core countries; especially, when asymmetric shocks affect the most disadvantaged countries precisely. Second, a moral hazard problem; indeed, NCAs could adopt softer macro-prudential policies to support national interest, relying on the bailout by the European institutions.

Concerning the first issue, the new institutional design should consider the impact of both trade and financial linkages across countries and the interaction between monetary policy and national macro-prudential policies. Moreover, it should also take into account the growing integration of financial markets since the birth of the EMU, which has increased in magnitude potential cross-border spill-over effects.[18] All of these factors highlight the case for a strong coordination function, as also emerges from Basel III accords. The reform process of banking supervision goes in the direction to coordinate regularly the two domains of monetary and macro-prudential policy. The Supervisory Board performs this function when it proposes to the Governing Council draft decisions concerning the micro-prudential policy and preliminary evaluations related to national macro-prudential measures. Its composition, which comprises representatives of the ECB and NCAs, allows this internal body of the monetary authority to consider cross-countries linkages in the decision-making process of both micro-prudential and macro-prudential policies.[19] Nevertheless, the literature reviewed in Section 3.3 undermines that the goal of a levelled regulatory field has not yet been achieved. Moreover, it does not agree on the actual ability of the ECB to take on the new role designed by the SSM, generating the lack of an authority responsible for the supervision of the macroprudential policy and the adoption of the micro-prudential policy.

Regarding the second issue, Council Regulation 1024/2013 introduces a precautionary tool to prevent moral hazard behaviours by NCAs. According to Art. 5 of this Regulation, the ECB, if deemed necessary, may tighten macro-prudential measures adopted by the NCAs. Thus, only if the national designed authorities underestimate the onset of systemic financial risks and implement too soft measures, the monetary authority may act, taking into account a euro area perspective. In this case, however, despite the legislative provision, the literature reviewed in Section 3.3 raises several issues. This literature stresses the lack of transparency and accountability in the decision-making process through the study of the actual implementation of the new institutional design.

5 Conclusions

In the aftermaths of the sovereign debt crisis of 2010–2012, the European institutions have established the SSM in order to pursue the objectives of price stability and financial stability. The new institutional arrangement provides for a centralised micro-prudential policy, under the direct control of the ECB, and a decentralised macro-prudential policy, under the responsibility of NCAs and the supervision of the ECB.

The chapter contributes to the literature through a comprehensive discussion on the SSM features and the main reasons behind the reform process. On the one hand, we review the recent empirical literature that analyses the role of the macro-prudential and micro-prudential supervision, in the context of a monetary union like the EMU; moreover, we also review the recent literature on the actual implementation of the SSM. On the other hand, we present an analytical model to analyse the conduct of the monetary policy in the presence of financial risks. These risks depend on endogenous factors, such as the business cycle trend, affected by the policy rate, and exogenous factors beyond the control of the monetary authority, such as the propensity to take risks by banks or the impact of macro-prudential and micro-prudential policies. The analytical finding highlights that if the exogenous component of the systemic risk is high enough in comparison to the endogenous part, then the monetary policy based on the LAWV view implies a higher level for the optimal policy rate, namely, higher output costs, than the monetary policy based on the MJHC view. This finding exactly mirrors Panico's view about the role of financial liberalisation: if the deregulation process promotes increasing financial risks, then a monetary policy pursuing the goal of financial stability reduces the investment level and the competitiveness of the economy, determining a lower economic growth (Capraro and Panico, 2021).

Overall, we can express a positive assessment of the new institutional framework implemented by the European institution, as it seems to be coherent with the empirical evidence that detects a positive effect of the macro-prudential and micro-prudential supervision in increasing financial stability. According to our model, both centralised micro-prudential and decentralised macro-prudential policies aim at increasing the capacity of the monetary authority to face the exogenous factors affecting stability financial risks. The new institutional design satisfies Tinbergen's principle, such that each instrument should be devoted to the objective that it can most efficiently achieve: the monetary policy mainly aimed at macroeconomic stability and the macro-prudential and micro-prudential supervision aiming at financial stability. Thus, in spite of several problems concerning transparency and accountability in the decision-making process, it appears reasonable the hypothesis that the increased ability to pursue financial stability allowed the ECB to launch a massive asset purchase programme in 2014: the European quantitative easing. By using the micro-prudential supervision to prevent idiosyncratic risks for individual financial institutions and the power to tighten national macro-prudential measures to prevent national systemic risks, the ECB was able to pursue the objective of macroeconomic stabilisation under fewer constraints.

Notes

1 The SSM and the single resolution mechanism are the two pillars of the European banking union. The first mechanism refers to the institutional design of the supervision on the European financial institutions; instead, the second introduces an orderly resolution procedure of failing banks with minimal costs for the real economy.

2 The Executive Board is an internal body of the ECB; it prepares the meetings of the Governing Council and coordinates the implementation process of the monetary policy.

3 The Supervisory Board is an internal body of the ECB, which comprises the chair, the vice-chair, chosen from the members of the Executive Board, four representatives of the ECB and the representatives of the NCAs. Concerning the supervision of credit institutions, its main task is to propose draft decisions to the Governing Council.

4 For a survey see Smets (2014).

5 Monetary policy can be a source of financial instability, for instance, promoting bank risk-taking concerns, especially in crisis times.

6 The FSO index encompasses the following three elements. A statutory dimension that accounts for the degree to which the legal mandate and its implicit interpretation by the central bank refer to the goal to maintain or promote financial stability. A regulatory dimension that accounts for the degree to which a monetary authority is directly responsible for the adoption and implementation of macro-prudential and micro-prudential policies; notice that the availability of these regulatory instruments reduces the pressure on the policy rate as a tool to pursue the goal of financial stability, implying a decrease in the FSO index. Finally, a discretionary dimension that accounts for the degree to which the public explanations of monetary policy decisions explicitly refer to issues related to the objective of financial stability. The value of the index can run from 0.0 to 3.0, with a lower value identifying a JHC-type central bank and higher value a LAWV-type. At the end of 2014, the ECB scored a value of 1.91 for the FSO index.

7 Specifically, an increase of 1.0 percentage point in the financial stability risk measure determines an increase in the policy rate of 0.054 percentage points for the LAWV-type, against 0.035 percentage points for the JHC-type.

8 The temporal dimension of financial stability explains the build-up of risks related to the functioning of the financial system over time while the spatial dimension refers to the build-up of risks in specific market sectors or segments. The generic composite systemic risk indicator (SRI) created by the European Central Bank (for more details see ECB,

2018, p. 165) is defined as a weighted average of the normalised sub-indicators. Pooled indicator normalisation and constant weights across countries and time implicitly assumes that there are common indicator patterns across the crises experienced by individual European countries at different points in time which, once extracted, are useful in identifying the build-up of systemic risk.

9 Various papers of the European Central Bank (ECB) study optimal monetary policy in the Euro area by assuming it works essentially as a closed economy, since area-specific shocks are more important than country-specific.

10 They examine its temporal and spatial dimensions of financial instability. The temporal dimension explains the build-up of risks related to the functioning of the financial system over time while the spatial dimension refers to the build-up of risks in specific market sectors or segments.

11 In the context of the euro area, the relative effectiveness of macroprudential policy in containing the financial stability risks is higher due to a single monetary policy not well-suited to deal with financial imbalances building up at the national level.

12 The sector faces monopolistic competition. The degree of market power of banks and the costs of financial intermediation determine the banks' interest rate-setting behaviour.

13 The term 'spillovers' is used to describe when regulations in one market have consequences for other markets or other institutions. But spillovers do not necessarily reflect regulatory arbitrage or policy leakages. Spillovers can also occur as a natural response to changing supply or demand for credit in particular locations and by particular institutions.

14 The literature on cross-border macroprudential policy spillovers is grown hand in hand with the use of macro-prudential policy with a mixed evidence suggesting that the effect of macroprudential policy on cross-border bank credit is instrument type specific. However, it is generally not referred to a monetary union. For this reason, we remand for a recent collection of coordinated empirical studies to Buch and Goldberg (2016). A work that attempt to measure cross-border effects of macro-prudential regulation in the euro area is Nocciola and Żochowski (2016). They find the sign of cross-border spillovers is instrument-specific, confirming they play a role in altering the efficacy of macro-prudential policy in containing systemic risk. From this the need for coordination.

15 During financial distress, the materialisation of financial risks implies that Equation (17.2) becomes $r_c = \Theta + r$, determining an extremely large increase in the interest rate on loans. In this context, the monetary policy only focuses on the objective of output stability to mitigate the impact of the economic downturn, without worrying about the trade-offs among price stability, output stability and financial stability. For this reason, we do not analyse the case of financial distress.

16 For a more complete description of the credit market refer to Dehmej and Gambacorta (2019), Poutineau and Vermandel (2015) and Badarau et al. (2020).

17 This result also holds for different assumptions. Specifically, if we consider the difference between the credit rate and the policy rate as an argument of the objective function of the monetary authority, or we introduce in Equation (17.2) the endogenous mechanism for the financial crisis described by Equation (17.1).

18 Notice that differences in inward and outward transmission channels characterise macro-prudential measures (Darracq Paries et al., 2019; Nocciola and Żochowski, 2016). The inward transmission of cross-over spill-over effects refers to how domestic regulation affects the behaviour of branches of foreign banks. In contrast, the outward transmission of cross-over spill-over effects refers to how national regulation affects foreign activities of domestic banks. Concerning these mechanisms, the European Systemic Risk Board recommend the use of the instrument that exerts a less cross-border effect.

19 The ECB Financial Stability Committee (2020) has recently devised a best practice framework for the analysis and assessment of cross-border spill-over effects from the activation of national macro-prudential measures. The framework is meant to serve as a starting point for NCAs when assessing the need for reciprocity in the context of activations of macroprudential measures (European Central Bank ECB, 2018).

References

Abad, P., García-Olalla, M. and Robles, M. D. (2020). Does the single supervisory mechanism reduce overall risk in the European Stock Market? *Global Policy* 11(January 1): 39–51.

Ajello, A., Laubach, T., López-Salido, D. and Nakata, T. (2019). Financial stability and optimal interest rate policy. *International Journal of Central Banking* 15(1): 279–326.

Amtenbrink, F. and Markakis, M. (2019). Towards a meaningful prudential supervision dialogue in the euro area? A study of the interaction between the European Parliament and the European Central Bank in the single supervisory mechanism. *European Law Review* 44(February 1): 3–23.

Angeloni, I. (2015). The single supervisory mechanism. *European Economy* 3: 43–55.

Badarau, C., Carias, M. and Figuet, J. (2020). Cross-border spillovers of macroprudential policy in the Euro area. *The Quarterly Review of Economics and Finance* 77(August): 1–13.

Bernanke, B. S. (2015). Should monetary policy take into account risks to financial stability. https://www.brookings.edu/blog. Downloaded: 27 April 2021.

Billi, R. M. and Vredin, A. (2014). Monetary policy and financial stability – a simple story. *Sveriges Riksbank Economic Review* 2014(2): 7–22.

Bofinger, P. and Mayer, E. (2007). Monetary and fiscal policy interaction in the Euro area with different assumptions on the Phillips curve. *Open Economies Review* 18(3): 291–305.

Boissay, F. and Cappiello, L. (2014). Micro-versus macro-prudential supervision: potential differences, tensions and complementarities. European Central Bank, Financial Stability Review, May, 135–140.

Borio, C. (2014). Monetary policy and financial stability: what role in prevention and recovery? (2014). Bank for International Settlements (BIS) Working Papers, 440.

Brzoza-Brzezina, M., Kolasa, M., and Makarski, K. (2015). Macroprudential policy and imbalances in the euro area. *Journal of International Money and Finance* 51: 137–154.

Brunnermeier, M. K. and Sannikov, Y. (2014). A macroeconomic model with a financial sector. *American Economic Review* 104(2): 379–421.

Brunnermeier, M. and Sannikov, Y. (2015). Reviving money and banking. In 'Is inflation targeting dead?', edited by Lucrezia Reichlin and Richard Baldwin. London: CEPR, 95–101.

Buch, C. and Goldberg, L. (2016). Cross-border prudential policy spillovers: how much? How important? Evidence from the International Banking Research Network. National Bureau of Economic Research Working Paper, 22874.

Capraro, S. and Panico, C. (2021). Monetary policy in liberalized financial markets: the Mexican case. *Review of Keynesian Economics* 9(1): 109–138.

Carboni, G., Darracq Pariès, M., and Kok, C. (2013). Exploring the Nexus between macro-prudential policies and monetary policy Measures. *Financial Stability Review* 1: 99–111.

Cassola, N., Kok, C. and Mongelli, F. P. (2019). The ECB after the crisis: existing synergies among monetary policy, macroprudential policies and banking supervision. European Central Bank, Occasional Paper, November, 237.

Creel, J., Hubert, P. and Labondance, F. (2015). Financial stability and economic performance. *Economic Modelling* 48(August): 25–40.

Danieli, M. (2020). The lack of ECB's conduct supervisory power. An analysis of the architecture and application of supervision. EUDIFIN Research Working Paper, April 8.

Darracq Pariès, M., Kok, C., and Rodriguez-Palenzuela, D. (2011). Macroeconomic propagation under different regulatory regimes: Evidence from an estimated DSGE model for the euro area. *International Journal of Central Banking* 7(4): 49–113.

Darracq Pariès, M., Kok, C. and Rancoita, E. (2019). Macroprudential policy in a monetary union with cross-border banking. European Central Bank, Working Paper Series, March 2260.

Dehmej, S. and Gambacorta, L. (2019). Macroprudential policy in a monetary union. *Comparative Economic Studies* 61(2): 195–212.

European Central Bank (ECB). (2018). Financial stability review, May.

European Central Bank (ECB). (2020). Financial Stability Committee, Framework to assess cross-border spill-over effects of macroprudential policies.

European Court of auditors. (2016). Single Supervisory Mechanism - Good start but further improvements needed. Special Report.

Ferrarini, G. (2015). Single supervision and the governance of banking markets: will the SSM deliver the expected benefits? *European Business Organization Law Review* 16(3): 513–537.

Fiordelisi, F. and Galloppo, G. (2018). Stock market reaction to policy interventions. *The European Journal of Finance* 24(18): 1817–1834.

Fiordelisi, F., Ricci, O., Stentella L. and Francesco S. (2017). The unintended consequences of the launch of the single supervisory mechanism in Europe. *Journal of Financial and Quantitative Analysis* 52(6): 2809–2836.

Friedrich, C., Hess, K. and Cunningham, R. (2019). Monetary policy and financial stability: cross-country evidence. *Journal of Money, Credit and Banking* 51(2-3): 403–453.

Fromage, D., Ibrido, R. (2019). Accountability and democratic oversight in the European Banking Union. In L. S. Gianni (ed), *The European Banking Union and the Role of Law*. Edward Elgar Publishing, Cheltenham UK: 66–86.

International Monetary Fund (IMF). (2013). The interaction of monetary and macroprudential policies.

Kockerols, T. and Kok, C. (2019). Leaning against the wind: macroprudential policy and the financial cycle. European Central Bank, Working Paper Series, January 2223.

Loipersberger, F. (2018). The effect of supranational banking supervision on the financial sector: event study evidence from Europe. *Journal of Banking & Finance*, 91(June): 34–48.

Malmierca, M. (2022). Stabilization and the policy mix in a monetary union. *Quarterly Review of Economics and Finance*. 83(February): 92–118.

Nicolaides, P. (2019). Accountability of the ECB's supervisory activities (SSM): Evolving and responsive. *Maastricht Journal of European and Comparative Law* 26(1): 136–150

Nocciola, L. and Żochowski, D. (2016). Cross-border spillovers from macroprudential policy in the euro area, BIS paper n 86. 16.

Panico, C., Pinto, A. and Puchet Anyul, M. (2012). Income distribution and the size of the financial sector: a Sraffian analysis. *Cambridge Journal of Economics* 36(6): 1455–1477.

Poutineau, J. C. and Vermandel, G. (2017). A welfare analysis of macroprudential policy rules in the Euro area. *Revue d'économie politique* Vol. 127/2.

Poutineau, J. and Vermandel, G. (2015). A primer on macroprudential policy. *The Journal of Economic Education* 46(1): 68–82.

Quint, D., Rabanal, P. (2014). Monetary and macroprudential policy in an estimated DSGE model of the euro area. *International Journal of Central Banking* 10(2):169–236.

Roger, S. (2009). Inflation targeting at 20: Achievements and challenges. International Monetary Fund (IMF) Working Paper, 09/236.

Rubio, M. and Comunale, M. (2017). Lithuania in the euro area: monetary transmission and macroprudential policies. *Eastern European Economics* 55(1): 29–49.

Schoenmaker, D. and Véron, N. (2016). European banking supervision: the first eighteen months. *BRUEGEL Blueprint Series*, 25: 7–52.

Smets, F. (2014). Financial stability and monetary policy: how closely interlinked? *International Journal of Central Banking* 10(2): 263–300.

Svensson, L. E. O. (2012). The relation between monetary policy and financial stability policy. *International Journal of Central Banking* 8(s1): 293–295.

Svensson, L. E. O. (2017). Cost-benefit analysis of leaning against the wind. *Journal of Monetary Economics* 90(October): 193–213.

Svensson, L. E. O. (2018). Monetary policy and macroprudential policy: different and separate? *Canadian Journal of Economics* 51 (3): 802–827.

Vallascas, F. and Keasey, K. (2013). The volatility of European banking systems: a two-decade study. *Journal of Financial Services Research* 43(1): 37–68.

Woodford, M. (2012). Inflation targeting and financial stability. National Bureau of Economic Research (NBER) Working Paper Series, w17967.

Part IV

The problem of rationality in economics

18 Economics situational rationality

Celia Lessa Kerstenetzky

Introduction

A perception generally shared among practitioners of both disciplinary fields is that economics and sociology provide two distinct representations of the social world, the first emphasising individual rationality, the second emphasising social norms, conventions, or habits as drivers of individuals' social actions. Also generally noted is the difficulty in fitting Max Weber's sociology, as well as the economics of, say, Marx or Keynes, into this distinction. Rather than directly arguing how things are in fact fuzzier than prima facie distinctions suggest, the purpose of this paper is, in the first place, to try and identify a common methodological element that allows the inclusion of the economic and sociological explanations under the broader umbrella of the social sciences. This element is the notion of situational logic, originally developed by philosopher Karl Popper, the acclaimed methodologist of economists, very much in line with, and even recognisably under the influence of, the acclaimed sociologist Max Weber. It will be argued, secondly, that this notion, in addition to providing a common analytical element joining together economics and sociology, can also offer an encompassing principle of economic rationality within which the conception of rationality as maximisation of an objective function features only as a particular case. Evidently, the intention is not to reduce all explanation in the realm of the social sciences to the logic of situation – a dismal enterprise – but to explore its methodological fertility.

To carry on these purposes, the essay is organised under the form of five theses, which are steps that progressively work out the twin ideas of the limits of human knowledge and methodological pluralism. In the first section, Popper's solution to Kant's famous question 'what can we know?' is briefly presented. The rejection of both extreme forms of rationalism and positivism makes Popper advocate a form of fallibilism which he calls critical rationalism. This is a form of rationalism that however limited is still committed to the search of the truth. So, the first thesis states that human knowledge is fallible but committed to the search of the truth. In Section 2, we seek to understand what from a Popperian viewpoint is possible to know in the social sciences, whether, in other words, there is a specific problem of knowledge in this

DOI: 10.4324/9781003105558-22

domain, in addition to the general limitation of human knowledge; and in case there is, whether there is a specific solution. It is in this section that the notion of situational logic is presented. So, the second thesis postulates that there is a specific problem of knowledge when it comes to the knowledge of phenomena in the social world and that the solution consists in identifying the 'logic of the situation' in the problems the social scientist is addressing. In Section 3, the effort is to discern the existence of one or more situational logics in the social sciences, and to discuss this issue against the backdrop of the relationship between economics and sociology. The third thesis, then, proposes the existence of multiple and even 'nested' situational logics. In Section 4, a couple of situational logics in economics are discussed. The fourth thesis therefore asserts the co-existence of multiple situational logics in economics. In Section 5, two possible forms of integrating economic and sociological explanations are briefly presented and contrasted: the rational choice and the situational logic approaches. The fifth thesis then proposes an agenda of methodological integration in the social sciences, led by situational logic, within which rational choice has a limited role. Section 6 concludes the essay with a summary of the main ideas.

1 'What can we know?'

In the 1960 essay on 'The origins of knowledge and ignorance', Popper argued that, in order scientifically to validate the knowledge we have, more important than ascertaining its origins are the procedures adopted to get it. In developing this idea, Popper interpreted two philosophical traditions that are central to modern scientific thought – Cartesian rationalism and Baconian empiricism – as proposals for validating knowledge via checking its origins either in 'reason' or 'facts'. The main problem with these traditions, Popper reckoned, is that reason and facts are quite unreliable as sources of knowledge: drawing on them, we often make mistakes, alone or collectively, our theories and evidence are often false or deceiving.

To the epistemological optimism of those traditions, Popper opposed the universal fallibility of human knowledge and the cautious perspective he called critical rationalism. This consists in submitting received knowledge to critical analysis, indicating procedures, not sources, as the distinctive mark of scientific knowledge. Thus, while facts and reasoning are still key, they are now recruited not so much to ascertain the truth content of statements about the world as to submit them to scrutiny – reasonable doubt and counterevidence. The only way to advance scientific knowledge, he asserted, is via conjectures and refutations.[1]

Moreover, the notion that scientific knowledge is acquired via conjectures and refutations has implications for Popper's views on the progress of science and ignorance. While the rationalist-empiricist tradition held the view that the progress of science amounts to the progressive elimination of ignorance, the more skeptical (though not hopeless) Popper thought otherwise: 'Every solution given to a problem raises new problems', 'the more we learn about the world, the deeper our knowledge, more specific, conscious and articulate will be our knowledge of what we ignore - the knowledge of our ignorance' (idem: 57).

From the above, we might conclude that the Popperian answer to the question 'what can we know?' is, therefore, not much. Again, not in the sense of the amount of knowledge, but of the stuff out of which it is made: conjectures that for the moment have resisted critical examination; increasing problems arising from the knowledge we thus far have gotten. This limitation concerns all human knowledge, whether of the natural or the social world; it is a limitation that exists on our side as knowers, on our ability to know, i.e. the limited reach of the tools (senses and reasoning) at our disposal, and not on the other side, on the nature of the objects we investigate.

2 Social world distinct from the natural world?

The contrast between the methodological positions of Hayek and Popper, two philosophers in other respects well attuned, deserves attention. In his 1942–1944 volume The Counter-Revolution of Science (1942–1944), Hayek famously reacted against the then dominant naturalisation of the object of study in the social sciences. For him, this attitude expressed disregard of the fact that in the social world man studies himself in his relations with other men. And while the relations among humans are mediated by mutual expectations and conjectures, the 'fact' which social scientists must investigate are opinions, i.e. the material which expectations and conjectures are made of. Contrastingly, opinions should be taken only as rough approximations that must be progressively eliminated as one approaches the physical-chemical-biological intimacy of natural objects and relations among them. In sum, while the natural scientist tries to get rid of opinions, the social scientist revels in them as they are the facts to be investigated. In Hayek's words:

> The question is here not how far man's picture of the external world fits the facts, but how by his actions, determined by the views and concepts he possesses, man builds up another world of which the individual becomes a part. And by 'the views and concepts people hold' we do not mean merely their knowledge of external world. We mean all they know and believe about themselves, about other people, and about the external world, in short everything which determines their actions, including science itself. (Hayek, 1942–44: 24)

Hayek's position was of great import in the methodological struggle against the behaviourist mainstream in the social sciences of the first decades of the 20th century. True, it was also important, perhaps even more so, to ground his fight against 'scientism'. This is a condition that consists in treating social facts as if they were subject to laws of causation, and which, according to Hayek, has the dangerous implication of strengthening the belief in the possibility of total engineering of the social world, or 'social engineering'. Popper disagreed with Hayek that the premise of a social world unguided by laws of causation, which he shared, should necessarily lead to abstention from social engineering; he actually advanced philosophical grounds for a social engineering of sorts.[2] More to the point, perhaps for not being so intellectually committed with finding grounds for inhibiting deliberate social reforms as Hayek was, Popper, in distinction to Hayek, insisted that the limitation in terms of achieving full-blown objective knowledge is not confined to the social sciences: the limitation for him, as said, is located on our ability to know things given our cognitive apparatus, not on the nature of the object to be known. In all cases, he insisted, human knowledge can only progress with the help of conjectures and refutations, starting from the unstable terrain provided by the knowledge received and animated by the inherently human desire to solve problems and try out solutions.

Disagreements on dualist (Hayek) or monist (Popper) methodologies notwithstanding, both Hayek and Popper agreed that there is something specific about 'social facts' that makes their explanation peculiar, no longer possible in terms of causal laws or natural mechanisms. Equally coincident is their rejection of the suggestion that social facts can be rendered as indisputable 'historical facts', i.e. pure descriptions of sets of events involving human beings at certain places and time. Historical fact for them is still a fact, not a given; it is constructed by conjectures (in Popper's words), or rationally reconstructed (in Hayek's words) by the imposition of a mental pattern that selects elements of the external world, organise them and render them intelligible. In what follows, we will see them both submitting an idea of objectivity peculiar to the knowledge of the social world.

According to Hayek, social fact refers to human action in society, social action. It contains four ingredients: a subject, a purpose, a means or set of means that the subject, supported by the opinions she holds, judges adequate to the purpose that she judges worthwhile. In order to grasp a social fact, the social scientist needs to 'understand it'. This means understanding what the subject is doing. This is only possible because the social scientist is herself a social subject, so that by analogy with what she would have done had she been placed in the others' overall circumstances she can understand what they are doing or intending to do. Of course, the possibility of understanding through empathy is relative, being more intense the closer is the similarity in terms of socialisation among the social scientist and those whose social action she tries to make sense of.

While Hayek thus advanced in the Weberian direction of assuming that social knowledge is 'understanding' (*verstehen*, in German) and, therefore, 'rational reconstruction' of social action, it is Popper who by introducing the analytical tool of 'situational logic' manages to convey a precise meaning of it. To begin with, Popper declares that his adherence to the Weberian interpretation of understanding means the acceptance of an objectivist (i.e. non-psychological) interpretation of it. Popper then proposed the method of situational logic, 'which consists in sufficiently analysing the situation of active men to explain the action with the help of the situation', as the method of explanation in the social world. We reach an explanation as 'understanding' when '[we consider] that the action was objectively appropriate to the situation' (Popper, 1978: 31). The explanation proceeds in three stages: (1) formulation of a situational model (the situation) and its principle of rationality (how it is rational to act in the situation, or logic of the situation); (2) the identification of initial conditions; and (3) the explicandum – that is, the explanation of the event in terms of the model and the principle of rationality. The social researcher in their everyday work always starts from a conjecture, a model of the situation, a hypothesis that fits together with the elements of the social reality she observes and tries to produce an explanation of.[3]

In trying to distinguish objective from subjective ideas of 'understanding', Popper proposed that the situational (objective) manner of explaining social action contrasts with the psychological (subjective) one in that

> the situation is analyzed enough that the elements that initially appear psychological (such as desires, motives, memories and associations) are transformed into elements of the situation. The man with certain desires, therefore, becomes a man whose situation can be characterized by the fact that he pursues certain objective targets; and a man with certain memories or associations becomes a man whose situation can be characterized by the fact that he is equipped, objectively, with other theories or with certain information. (31/32)

And even though the method avoids 'psychological analysis', Popper insisted that it is still an individualist method, only psychological elements are replaced with 'objective situational elements' (32). Here the resemblance with Weber's 'ideal types' seems not to be casual.

Now, 'situation' is defined in terms of purposes and beliefs ('theories') that individuals hold which are relevant to the attainment of their purposes. The 'logic' of the situation is the orientation of the action, and this is supplied by the institutional context. Institutions, Popper suggested, are the social (i.e. non-physical) part of the world in which we act, they 'consist of all the social realities of the social world'. (33). As such, institutions 'determine the peculiar social character of our social environment', they indicate the logic of action, how it is rational to act in that environment: e.g. the logic of power, the logic of the market and so on. But, again, important as institutions are, Popper insisted, action is always of individuals: 'Institutions do not act; instead, only individuals act, within or for or through institutions'.

Social theory, as knowledge of the social world, is then the articulation of those logics. It can also be, Popper believed, a theory of change, of the creation and development of the institutions themselves, or as he put it, of the 'institutional consequences, planned or not, of intentional action' (33).

Through the lens of situational analysis, the interplay between individuals and social institutions is seen as productive. Popper is here navigating through the narrow stretch of sea between the Scylla and Charybdis of subjectivism and holism.

In the end, it is only from the understanding of the whole situation in the sense above that it is possible to adequately formulate a *principle of rationality*, to form an idea about what is rational – adequate, appropriate – to do in the context where the social action is taking place. The principle of rationality is proposed as a normative principle, attached to specific ideal-typical situations:

> The method of applying a situational logic to the social sciences is not based on any psychological assumption concerning the rationality (or otherwise) of 'human nature'. On the contrary: when we speak of 'rational behavior' or of 'irrational behavior' then we mean behavior which is, or which is not, in accordance with the logic of that situation. In fact, the psychological analysis of an action in terms of its (rational or irrational) motives presupposes that we have previously developed some standard of what is to be considered as rational in the situation in question. (Popper, 1971, v.2: 97)

★★★

It must be recognised that the method of situational analysis was followed by some critical discussion which while not the object of this essay is worth a mention. I have in mind the criticism taking issue with the scientific status of the situational logic device. After all, is situational logic an empirical proposition subject to falsification or just a methodological principle to approach social facts? While Popper himself quite controversially reaffirmed the double status of the principle, that it is both an empirically falsifiable contention about how people act and a methodological device whereby social scientists approach social actions, in this essay I work out the rationality principle as the methodological principle of the social sciences proposed by Popper. As such principle, I am mainly interested in its fertility: the range of social scientific problems it helps to shed light on. In particular, as we proceed to the next section, I examine the following claims: (i) the concept of situational logic may be used to nest the economic explanation within the sociological one and in this way clarify motivations, restrictions and beliefs against the backdrop of the social situations that embed the particular economic situation; (ii) the concept of situational logic may support the thesis of the existence of multiple situational logics, and then of multiple (situation-specific) rationalities in economics. Both claims go against the grain of rational choice theory, which assumes that the social sciences can be reduced to economics and economic action admit only one form of rationality: the maximisation of an objective function.

3 Logics of the situation: economics and sociology

Situational logic was presented as a sociological concept and developed by Popper with the explicit purpose of claiming an autonomy of sociology (the analysis of social institutions) in relation to psychology (the analysis of human motivation). But then how to distinguish economics from sociology? Interestingly, this distinction does not appear in Popper's *The Logic of Social Sciences*, where the word 'logic' appears significantly in the singular.

As we have seen, Popper developed the notion of situational logic out of the theoretical framework of the so-called sociology of objective understanding (verstehende soziologie), where the predicate 'objective' was meant to distinguish that interpretation from a subjectivist or psychological one, aimed at motivations not social situations. Moreover, while it is true that human minds are involved in the process of understanding, both as subject and object, the activity of producing scientific propositions requires objectivity also in the sense of the confrontation of hypotheses with criticism – arguments or facts provided by critics. This much sociology shares with economics.

In trying to figure out one possible relation/distinction between sociology and economics, I devise the possibility of applying the methodology of situational logic by means of a two-step approach. In a first approximation, situational analysis requires the existence of a well-defined situation, the actor's purposes and beliefs being the essential part of the picture. Through the exercise of understanding, the social scientist puts himself in the actor's shoes and judge the conformity of the actor's behaviour with the observed situation. It is in fact only in a second approximation that this judgement may form, when, that is, situational analysis helps shed light on the broader framework within which the actor formed purposes and cultivated beliefs that situated himself in that specific context. This is so in such a way as he finds himself practically imprisoned in that context's logic, for he can free himself of it only at the cost of behaving irrationally (i.e. in a way we, the social scientist, cannot understand). Let us call the first situation (s1) and the second, the meta-situation (S1). We can say that s1 is encapsulated in S1.

Think of a simple example: the situation s1 being that of someone trying to sell to others what he produced, aiming at the greatest possible net benefit from his sale and believing it to be possible; the S1 meta-situation being the market framework which establishes among other things that an individual's material survival depends on the success of his sales. The S1 meta-situation focuses on the macro-situational logic, the market situation, within which the actors, in this case the salesman, form purposes and beliefs in order to realise them. Another example could be the following. We observe an individual systematically maintaining his sister's family without leaving any reserves for his own maintenance and that of his family (s2). How to evaluate the rationality of his gesture? It is necessary to expand the focus to the macro-situation that reveals the social rule according to which the norm of generalised reciprocity holds, whereby the survival of the individual is tied to the survival of the group, which in that case requires the individual to support the family of his relative without receiving direct compensation (S2). (Conversely, the salesmen under S2 or the one-way donor in S1 would painfully pay – with ostracism or starvation – for their irrationality.[4])

In a sense, what we did was to encapsulate 'economics' (s1.; s2...), the representation of what someone does to survive materially, in 'sociology' (S1; S2...), the representation of social rules which regulate activities related to material survival, the market (S1) and generalised reciprocity (S2) being two hypothesised social institutions that regulate the economic aspects of social life. We said nothing about how the meta-situation (S1; S2...) itself came about. Still, if the investigation were to deepen further, which it will not, the next question would certainly be: how are social institutions formed and modified within specific societies? This question would shift the focus to what we might call the meta-meta-situation, say, the super-S.

4 Logics of the situation: economics

When flesh and blood economists looked at the economic activity of men and women what logic, the principle of rationality, did they 'find' while trying to make sense of their behaviour?

In the history of modern economic thought, up until the first decades of the 20th century, it was broadly assumed that, in their economic activity within the boundaries of a market economy, individuals behave as *homo economicus*, i.e. moved by the selfish desire to improve their material condition. While Adam Smith's contribution as an economist-moral philosopher, his description of human nature in particular, is rich in complexity, it is the anthropology of the man who wishes simply to improve his material condition that has the upper hand in *Wealth of Nations*. The premise is also there that while material self-interest moves men in a market economy, this economy flourishes as a consequence. In the overmentioned passage which relates the fulfilment of the purposes of all the others to the zeal with which each one pursues his or her own material interests, Smith dismisses benevolence as the situational logic. Material self-interest is the logic of the situation in a market economy, period.

It is fair to say that, celebrated in the *homo economicus* expression coined by John Stuart Mill, this view of economics's situational logic prevailed in the English political economy of the 19th century. It for example conspicuously appeared in John Neville Keynes' famous 1890 methodological opus, *The Scope and Method of Political Economy*, which was written in the intellectual climate of the Marginalist Revolution. There, Neville Keynes argued along similar lines as Smith's that the rational behaviour in a market economy is the ceaseless pursuit of material well-being.

To be sure, Neville Keynes opened up his short treatise with a presentation of two possible meanings of economics, as the study of individual *choice*, i.e. adjustment of scarce means to multiple ends, or, alternatively, the study of human *activity* of production, accumulation and distribution of wealth. The latter implies spatial and historical variation. But, from the start, Neville Keynes makes it clear that the latter definition is his favourite, the one that according to him conveys the true scope of scientific economics. It may be said, without much exaggeration, that Neville Keynes's conviction was shared by economic scholars across the board up until the 1930s. The publication by Lionel Robbins in 1932 of a volume on the nature and meaning of economics would mark an inflection in this respect.

The new vision which would eventually contribute to shape the new economics's mainstream was that the distinctive thing about economic analysis is the explanation of the problems and relations that arise from the sheer existence of scarce means to satisfy a multiplicity of ends. Any human activity, 'material' or otherwise, that involves an 'economic' aspect in that sense should be the object of interest of the economist. Interestingly, the hypothesis of *homo economicus*, in Smith's, Mill's and Keynes's sense, suddenly became unduly restrictive; choices may not be motivated by selfishness, nor do they necessarily relate to accumulation of riches. The logic of the economic situation, instead of the selfish pursuit of material well-being, became the pursuit of the maximum satisfaction of consistently ordered preferences over virtually any matter. As economics morphed into the science of choice, *homo economicus* evolved into *homo 'consistentis'*.

Prima facie, as hinted at above, the option of rendering economic rationality as consistent choice frees it from objections as to the overly restrictive motivational supposition of material selfishness. Yet, from a methodological point of view, such motivational restriction might be an advantage. The correspondence of the *homo oeconomicus* hypothesis with the facts might be checked and even falsified in particular situations in a way that the *homo consistentis* one, even though admitting a plurality of motivations, might not so easily be. In fact, the *homo economicus* hypothesis may seem more cogent in the context of a market economy than elsewhere (Polanyi, 1944), and even in a market economy it may be falsified in an ample array of cases as recent experimental economics has suggested (Steinmo, 2018; Stevens, 2019). The *homo consistentis* hypothesis is certainly more difficult to put to test: an apparent irrationality (for example, a departure from self-interested behaviour) might be rationalised by the ex-post attribution of some other motivation that renders the agent's choice coherent. A person, for example, is observed consistently choosing to destroy his assets and sources of income generation until the total impoverishment of himself and his family, observing well-ordered preferences – complete and transitive – and is still recognised as economically rational in view of his consistent decisions. Another line of methodological objections regards the hardly compelling set of axioms that comes with the consistency requirement, such as full knowledge of alternatives, ranking completeness (which precludes incommensurability or even incomparability between alternatives), and transitive preferences. Other axioms are aggregated to make sense of choice in the context of uncertainty, similarly involving paradoxes that have caught even impeccable logicians and statisticians (for an early review, see Schoemaker, 1982). Panico's (2011) paper provides rich detailing of the troubles haunting this research agenda.

On the side of attempts to get rid of objections related to unrealistic axioms (though not of the non-falsifiability claim mentioned above), we might mention Samuelson's (1938) lighter reading of the principle of rationality as *rational choice*. Focusing on the observed behaviour, Samuelson infers preferences from observed choices, and considers them rational (as well as sufficient grounds on which to base the shape of the demand curve) whenever they are stable, i.e. consistent over time. Yet, critics such as Amartya Sen (1985) have noted that consistency is not sufficient to define rationality (as in the case of behaviour consistently contrary to the declared objective of the agent) and not even necessary (Sen, 1991; Lagueux, 2004), since, for example, the requirement of inter-temporal stability of preferences would exclude learning, forgetfulness and creativity, to name a few of possible drivers of preferences reversal. Lagueux, consequently, proposes the idea of rationality as flexibility, while Sen advocates rationality as acting based on reasons.

While Sen's and Lagueux's alternatives do not directly address the problem of defining a principle of *economic* rationality, a model of economic behaviour (MEB) as rational choice in the sense of Samuelson, suggested by Kirchgässner (2004), is meant to address the objections that both Sen's and Lagueux's alternatives raised to consistency. In the model, the economic situation is still defined as a choice situation involving preferences and restrictions, but the stability of preferences is supposed to obtain only at a certain point in time, not inter-temporally. The only consistency requirement that is retained is the independence between preferences and restrictions.

While to keep assessing the realism or otherwise of that proposal (or of others) in order to test the cogency of *homo consistentis* is a way to go, another one, suggested here, is instead to gauge the fertility of the proposed version of the principle of economic rationality. Fertility refers to the range of situations it helps to shed light upon. On the one hand, MEB consists in an application of the principle of rationality that does not mobilise the notion of situation as *historical* context which refers human activity to particular spatio-temporal circumstances, but as *generic*, a-historical context, recognisable in a diversity of human activities at different points in time. Thus, economics, as the study of the consequences of that behaviour, is believed to contribute to elucidate different spatio-temporal situations. On the other hand, while lack of historical context might suggest an unlimited room for the application of the MEB, it arguably restricts the model's applicability to a range of special cases – the cases in which the model's distinctive features and conditions are present.

So, MEB may seem more appropriate to articulate the logic of the situation of the specific historical context of a *market economy* than that of other economic situations where markets are absent or have a subordinate social role. This is so because in market economies individual *choices* seem to have more weight than for example social norms in shaping economic relations and outcomes. Even in that specific context, it would be necessary to assess the extent to which the workings of the *economic system* as a whole could be in-ferred from the behaviour of individual *homo consistentis* alone, as an aggregate of the many individual optimal decisions, and so to gauge the eventual feedback effects of the system on individual actions. Lagueux, for example, suggests that there is an implicit rationality principle in classical economics, assumed of economic agents, which is that these 'classical' agents do not 'act stupidly'. Capitalists are attracted to higher profits; workers, to higher wages; landowners, to higher rents; in general, it is assumed, man seeks to improve his condition. However, together, these agents' combined actions produce a 'composition effect' which is the (unplanned) coordination of their actions. This coordination is mediated by institutions, which, in turn, are simultaneously the combined results of and preconditions for those actions. The latter consideration by embedding economic decisions in complex institutional settings limits the validity of certain knowledge axioms. For example, the higher the degree of genuine uncertainty involved in the choice situation, both on alternatives and consequences of choices, the less attractive MEB may appear. Part of this un-certainty originates in composition effects that agents do not or even cannot be aware of. Also, and relatedly, the stronger the interaction between preferences and restrictions there is – as, for example, in the case of endogenous preferences which indicates the infiltration of the 'means' into the very 'ends' that are pursued – the less valid MEB appears to be. In the latter cases, the relevance of alternative logics of choice beyond MEB should be assessed.

5 Two forms of integrating economics and sociology

The theory of rational choice, in advanced form as developed in the writings of Gary Becker of the 1980s and 1990s (Becker, 1993), was formulated as *the* situational logic of the social sciences, implying that the economic logic (in the 'means to ends' sense) would explain human behaviour in a wide and virtually unlimited range of social activities. It is however evident that as a pure logic of action, the model of rational choice theory is not the only possibility – there are other logics of human action that do not fit Becker's means-to-ends de-finition, for example, the logic of a certain kind of Dantesque love, 'an ap-petite that grows with what satiates it', or the quite reasonable daily renunciations of optimal decisions in difficult, dilemmatic, crucial or complex situations, which make imitation, following norms, even throwing a dice, much more 'rational' behaviour – rational, again, in the sense of 'not being stupid' and ending up stuck in non-action. It is also likely that the theory of rational choice, despite its original project, does not serve as a reliable re-ference for the integration of economics and sociology because it leaves out situational logics that cannot be expressed in the lexicon of pure choices: individual preferences and restrictions.

Another possibility of integration is provided by the notion of situational logic which not only admits of two readings of 'situation' – the historical and the generic – but recognises the existence of a plurality of logics, rationality principles appropriate to different contexts (Kerstenetzky 2009). Rational choice in the means-to-ends optimal adjustment sense appears as a particular case within a more general set of situational logics which allows us to identify rationality in a broader sphere of human action. The situational logic solution to what may be taken as rationality or rational action safeguards the pluralism inherent in the idea of human rationality, which is particularly dear to the social scientist who tries to grasp social facts by resorting to understanding. Furthermore, in the interpretation suggested in this essay, situational logic is compatible with both an individualistic and a non-strictly individualistic reading of social action, as in a theory of quasi-action of social institutions.

6 Conclusion

In this conclusion, I articulate the main ideas presented in this essay in terms of a sequence of questions and theses:

1   What can we *know*? Human knowledge is fallible and limited to conjectures; it advances through relentless criticism;
2   What can we know in the *social* world? The limitation of knowledge refers to both the natural and the social worlds; the peculiarity of knowledge of the social world is that we can only know what we understand; understanding is possible via the characterisation of the situation, the action that takes place in it, and the articulation of its logic; knowledge in and of the social world delivers the 'rationality principle' of the social situation; ultimately, social institutions provide the logic of the situation;
3   How to distinguish economics from sociology? Economics is a subset (the situational micro-logic) of the sociological explanation (the situational macro-logic), a situation with specific social logics and institutions;
4   What is the model of economic behaviour? Is this model adequate to explain economic problems? In other words, is the model an adequate logic for the situation which economics wants to provide an explanation of? The model explains human action in terms of preferences and restrictions; the model may be a more adequate representation of economic behaviour the stronger the historical context of a market economy and provided the conditions for rational decisions in the sense of the model are present. But even so, there is no way to ensure that the systemic functioning may be deduced from the economic behaviour of individuals alone and does not in turn affect their economic actions;
5   Integrating economics and sociology: rational choice or situational logic? Situational logic seems to be more general a principle of rationality, sensitive to the plurality of contexts, and suited to the fallibilist starting point than rational choice is. For these reasons, it is also a less precise and determined principle. The theory of rational choice turns out to be a special, in fact, a *very* special case of the encompassing concept of situational logic.

7 Postcriptum: Carlo Panico

When in 2012 I invited Carlo to visit the Federal Fluminense University in Niteroi to participate as a keynote speaker in the seminar of my inequality research group, a paper he had previously sent to me in preparation for our first in-person meeting called my attention to the range of our common interests. The topic of that paper was the problem of rationality in Economics (Panico, 2011). The next year, upon Carlo's kind invitation, I was to present a couple of methodological papers before his research group in the University of Naples, and the occasion could not have been more stimulating for me (Kerstenetzky, 2007, 2009). While my own scholarly work has since shifted towards interdisciplinary institutionalist analysis and social policy, whereas that of Carlo kept anchored in macroeconomics and Sraffian scholarship, it pleases me to think that, again, despite different fields and analytical choices we keep sharing the conviction that a position regarding what is to be taken as rational, thus intelligible, human action cannot be avoided in the social scientific work. Especially when the extent of policy leeway is one's ultimate interest. I am glad to add that Carlo enjoyed my Popperian moment, so it is in the spirit of a personal homage to my honourable friend that in this short essay I revisit and extend some ideas I had tried on in that previous work that so pleased him.

Notes

1 While it may appear that fallibilism amounts to falsificationism, implying the elimination for good of falsified conjectures, the interpretation I favor here is of (what I call) 'procedural falsificationism' – do not rest!, always submit your theories to scrutiny – rather than 'substantive falsificationism' – which amounts to the deletion of refuted conjectures. For a discussion, refer to Kerstenetzky (2009).
2 I tackled this disagreement between Hayek and Popper in Kerstenetzky (2007).
3 An entire problématique may ensue regarding the formation of such conjectures via analogy between observers and the observed subjects, and the limitations of such analogies. What happens when certain expected behaviors are not observed, given the initial model? Does this mean that actors behave irrationally or that observers got them wrong? For Popper, the ultimate purpose of the social researcher is to unearth the logic of people's actions, even the mad acts of a mad man with mad beliefs. For further discussion, refer to Kerstenetzky (2009).
4 That situation is reported by Karl Polanyi, in *The Great Transformation*, and it describes the Kula exchange system among the people of the Trobriand Islands in Melanesia. Polanyi offers other less exotic instances of norms of redistribution and reciprocity regulating markets and other economic systems in Europe up to the eve of the Industrial Revolution.

References

Becker, G. (1993). Nobel lecture: The economic ways of looking at behaviour. *Journal of Political Economy* 101: 385–409.
Hayek, F. ([1942–1944], 1979). *The Counter-Revolution of Science: Studies on the Abuse of Reason*. Indianapolis: Liberty Press.

Kerstenetzky, C. L. (2007), Hayek and Popper on Ignorance and Intervention. *Journal of Institutional Economics* 3 (1): 33–53.

Kerstenetzky, C. L. (2009). Plural situational logic: the rationa(lisabi)lity principle. *Cambridge Journal of Economics* 33: 193–209.

Keynes, J. N. and Neville Keynes, J. ([1935] 1955). *The Scope and Method of Political Economy.* New York: Kelley & Millman, Inc.

Kirchgässner, G. (2004). *The Weak Rationality Principle.* Discussion Paper No 13. Switzerland: Universität St. Gallen.

Lagueux, M. (2004). The forgotten role of the rationality principle in economics. *Journal of Economic Methodology* 11(1): 3–51.

Lagueux, M. (2006). Popper and the rationality principle. In I. Jarvie, K. Milford and D. Miller (eds), *Karl Popper: A Centenary Assessment,* Vol. III. Aldershot: Ashgate Publishing Ltd.

Panico, C. (2011). Some thoughts on the concept of rationality in economic theory. *Revista Galega de Economia* 21(1): 313–332.

Polanyi, K. (1944). *The Great Transformation.* New York: Rinehart & Co.

Popper, K., ([1945]1971). *The Open Society and Its Enemies.* Princeton: Princeton University Press.

Popper, K. ([1960], 1972). As origens do conhecimento e da ignorância. *Conjecturas e Refutações.* Brasília: Editora Universidade de Brasília.

Popper, K. (1978). *A Lógica das Ciências Sociais.* Brasília: Editora da UNB.

Robbins, L. (1932). The nature of economic generalizations In *An Essay on the Nature and Significance of Economic Science.* London: Macmillan, chapter IV.

Samuelson, P. (1938). A note on the pure theory of consumer's behaviour. *Economica* 5: 61–71.

Schoemaker, P. (1982). The expected utility model: its variants, purposes, evidence and limitations. *Journal of Economic Literature* XX: 529–563.

Sen, A. (1985). Rationality and uncertainty. *Theory and Decision* 18: 109–127.

Sen, A. (1991). *On Ethics and Economics.* Hoboken, New Jersey: Wiley-Blackwell.

Steinmo, S. (2018). *The Leap of Faith: The Fiscal Foundations of Successful Government in Europe and America.* 1st ed. Oxford: Oxford University Press.

Stevens, D. E. (2019). *Social Norms and the Theory of the Firm: a Foundational Approach.* Cambridge, UK; New York, NY: Cambridge University Press.

19 Rationality, uncertainty and ecological adaptation

Valerio Filoso[1]

1 Introduction

In his contribution to the study of rationality in economics, Panico (2012)[2] elaborates, among other issues, on two key points: (1) Can we consider scientifically sound a theory based on assumptions, like those regarding the utility function, whose validity cannot be empirically verified? (2) Do different versions of the neoclassical theory imply plausible accounts of human psychology? These two questions involve the validity of the neoclassical economics' research program (NEP) as a theoretical and empirical investigation tool, but also raise a number of normative interpretative issues. Panico's (2012)*tour de force* of these fundamental problems blends sharp critical analysis with an extraordinary mastery of economic thought, emphasising the turning points in the debate's intellectual history and providing several insights worth reflecting on.

Panico's (2012) questions still lie at the heart of the debate and continue to ignite interest in the study of rationality by economists, psychologists and biologists; though his article does not take a specific stance in the debate, nevertheless, in what follows, I add my personal perspective on these issues. Along these pages, I will revisit some Panico's (2012) accounts of the historical development of rationality in economics with my specific contribution being adding new views from the most recent literature on uncertainty and ecological adaptation. Moreover, I revive the Austrian school's contribution and show its relevance in today's debate.

I find that an answer to Panico's (2012) first question is a sound yes, while an answer to the second is a qualified no. Regarding the first question, while Panico (2012) states that Myrdal's (1930) radical critique to using utility functions has not received satisfactory answers so far, I show evidence that the constructive part of Myrdal's critique helped advance new enquiries on the nature and possible uses of utility functions. Panico (2012) also describes how Sraffa rejected any reference to subjective constructs in economics, not to mention utility functions. Actually, Sraffa adopted a narrow neopositivist stance expunging altogether any unobservable or unmeasurable variable from scientific discourse: hardly any economist would subscribe his view today. While I show how

DOI: 10.4324/9781003105558-23

Sraffa's approach is methodologically unappealing, nonetheless I save his insistence on objectivity, when properly qualified.

Regarding the second question, both the theoretical and the applied literature on rational choice have blossomed in a wealth of studies showing how the neoclassical paradigm fails applying to many relevant problems, because of unobtainable crucial information or prohibitive computational costs: beyond Simon's (1997) seminal contribution, Gigerenzer and Selten's (2002) work greatly enriched the economist's toolkit, helping economics become more grounded in empirical testing. Moreover, as multiple paradigms do coexist in psychology and no grand unifying theory of action is in sight, as economist, we can hardly appeal to a *single* psychologically-founded reconstruction of choice.

In the course of this essay, I walk in the footprints traced by Panico's (2012) historical reconstruction of rationality's concept in economics starting from Section 2 where I state the role of rationality and entrepreneurship in classical economics. In Section 3 I briefly describe general equilibrium theory along with the often neglected Austrian school's alternative viewpoint; also, I reject Sraffa's methodological extreme stance as too restrictive for applied economic research. Then, in Section 4, I examine a number of critics and defenders of neoclassical choice theory, including Myrdal, while in Section 5 I describe two main attempts to reconcile empirical evidence and theoretical choice theory. Finally, in Section 6, I selectively discuss how new adaptive rationality models fit empirical evidence and match Hayek's (1945) original intuition on how markets work.

2 Classical economics

Classical economics' research program focused mainly on market's supply side and downplayed the demand side: since production drives consumption only through budget constraints (incomes and prices), there remained little room, if any, for studying consumers as rational actors in the marketplace. In a model where the fundamental causal link goes from production to consumption, some remarkable exceptions at a philosophical level can be found in Adam Smith's masterwork (1776) and in his *Theory of Moral Sentiments* (1759), but hardly constitute a systematic attempt at modelling consumers as rational actors interacting with producers through market prices.

Classical economists, nonetheless, took for granted producers' rationality. Virtually, any major classical work in economics hints at producers as rational entrepreneurial actors driven by the desire to maximise profits from industrial or agricultural activities, pursuing rational strategies to allocate productive factors, choosing techniques and marketing the final products. A surprisingly vivid and still relevant depiction of the entrepreneur's psychology and rational action appears in Richard Cantillon's *Essai sur la nature du commerce en général* (1755); furthermore, Cantillon includes *alertness* as a key features of the entrepreneurial mind as emphasised by the Austrian school of economics (Kirzner, 1997).

Classical economics' internal inconsistencies about the value's problem led to a deep rethinking of the fundamental causal link from production to consumption: the debate which followed led to overturn that link and replaced producers with consumers as the ultimate drivers of economic value. William Stanley Jevons, Carl Menger and Léon Walras fully integrated the concept of marginal utility within a general architecture of exchange and production, though the concept had been already formalised in probability theory as an essential tool in the study of choice under risk (Bernoulli, 1738). Most probably, the earliest proponent of marginal utility theory was the Provençal Franciscan friar Pierre de Jean Olivi (1248–1298). The change of perspective sparked by the marginalist revolution put the consumer's subjective evaluation (Horwitz, 1994) on economic theory's forefront and turned economists' attention toward the demand side of the economy and its underlying psychology.

3 General equilibrium economics

While Carl Menger's (1871) radically subjective approach to the value problem retained the classical idea of economic exchange as ruled by the universal law of cause and effect, Walras' approach of mutual causation between economic variables, as modelled through systems of simultaneous equations, obfuscated causal links and ultimately prevailed in the debate, so becoming the standard tool of economic analysis (Menger, 1871, p. 7). This framework expunged the time dimension from choice analysis, especially the temporal irreversibility of human action (O'Driscoll and Rizzo, 1985) and implicitly introduced a Newtonian concept of time conflicting with humans' reality and perception. NEP's emphasis on equilibrium behaviour lead to increasingly generalised existence proofs of a general economic equilibrium price vector $\mathbf{p}^*$ as in the classical Arrow-Debreu-McKenzie model (Debreu, 1959), while solutions to the problem of global dynamic stability of equilibrium still remain much less satisfactory. Even when markets are frictionless, conditions to ensure global stability need introducing strong restrictions foreign to the standard set of economic axioms (Bryant, 2010).

Does the Arrow-Debreu-McKenzie model have empirical implications? The answer remains open to date. Provided that a complete vector of equilibrium prices p^* exists, some markets adjust fast and equilibrium prices acceptably approximate observed trading prices, while other markets are sluggish and slow to adjust. In this last case, out-of-equilibrium behaviour becomes relevant because agents trade at non-equilibrium prices; unfortunately, very few economists have systematically tried to tackle this thorny issue (Fisher, 1989), though recent advances in computation have made this study easier (Arthur, 2006).[3]

Some authors from the Austrian school of economics approach dynamic stability by introducing *entrepreneurial agents* who intentionally take advantage of out-of-equilibrium prices and stabilise markets in doing so (Kirzner, 1997), while other authors reject equilibrium altogether as irrelevant (Lachmann, 1976). The Austrians of Hayekian observance emphasise the notion that the economy continuously moves across equilibria and consider the Samuelsonian analogy between economic equilibrium and physical state of rest as misleading (Bowles, Kirman and Sethi, 2017). For Hayekians, individual rationality plays a limited role as a local phenomenon in large economies with most human institutions resulting from the unintentional consequences of human action: the economy itself is a self-organised emergent property of several complex adaptive systems (Shermer, 2009).

While NEP's approach promoted mathematical consistency and universality, some interpretative issues remained controversial. Panico (2012) notes that since its introduction, the concept of utility raised serious concerns, with very few scholars defending its cardinal interpretation. Sraffa's extreme neopositivist claim[4] that economics should only deal with observable variables and abstain from concepts like subjective utility (Kurz and Salvadori, 2005) received some support also in the NEP field. As an example, revealed preferences theory (Samuelson, 1948a), an alternative approach to consumer's behaviour theory based solely on ranking consumption baskets under given budget sets, free of any reference to utility functions, complies with Sraffa's concerns and is still under active development (Chambers and Echenique, 2016). Though Samuelson himself noted that revealed preferences theory was merely the old utility theory in disguise, nonetheless his statement proves that a priori assumptions on unobservable quantities may well give rise to empirically observable implications. In this sense, Allen's (1932) emphasis on testing underlying *initial assumptions* of consumer theory becomes redundant.

Despite neopositivism's obvious merits for supporting clear terms' definition in scientific discourse and careful analysis of empirical evidence as foundation of science, Sraffa's claim can hardly be stretched up to promoting systematic data collection and statistical analysis in economics: apart from some early articles on the Italian banking system, Sraffa himself devoted all his research in economics exclusively to theoretical issues. Likely, he prescribed the use of visible and measurable variables as a way to revive classical economics' value theory against the emergent neoclassical paradigm. One could further note that scholars from the Neo-Ricardian school have rarely engaged in extensive data collection about objective data supporting empirical evidence to their theories. While we should abandon Sraffa's methodological prescriptions, nonetheless we should save his neopositivist emphasis on objectivity in economic science.

4 Defenders and critics

The adoption of NEP also paved the way to (1) axiomatising consumer's behaviour relying upon the maximisation principle as a unifying tool to model agents interacting in the marketplace (Samuelson, 1948b) and to (2) a strong emphasis on equilibrium behaviour. The problem and the solution to an individual's choice problem according to NEP can be stated as follows:

Scheme 1 (NEP)*In its most basic form, the individual consumption optimisation problem takes the form*

$$\max \quad u(\mathbf{x})$$
$$s.\ t.\quad \mathbf{p}^{\mathsf{T}}\mathbf{x} \leq m \tag{19.1}$$

where $u(\cdot)$*is the utility function,* $\mathbf{p}$*is the price vector,* $\mathbf{x}$*is consuption bundle vector and* m*is the monetary income. Vectors* $\mathbf{p}$*and* $\mathbf{x}$*are* N*-dimensional.*

The first-order conditions for optimality are

$$u'(x_i) = \lambda p_i \text{for each } i = 1,\ldots,N$$
$$\mathbf{p}^{\mathsf{T}}\mathbf{x} = m \tag{19.2}$$

where λ*is the marginal value of relaxing the budget constraint.*

The former scheme is a mathematical axiomatization of choice theory: as such, it has no empirical content and describes an abstract decision-maker. Indeed, the scheme of General Equilibrium Theory (GET) shares the same nature and has no aim at describing reality as it is, leaving discussion on its applicability to alternative interpretations (Debreu, 1959, p. x). The scheme has no empirical implications as it lives in a purely theoretical world; nevertheless, it has its philosophical roots in the Benthamite utilitarianism (Hollis and Sugden, 1993) and is flexible enough to accommodate a large array of non-selfish and social preferences.

Moving beyond Sraffa's radical methodological critique, Panico (2012) notes that early critics of utility functions' use in economic analysis abounded. For example, Keynes (1933) and Labriola (1922) emphasised consumption's social dimension, namely interactions between agents giving rise to new complex behavioural patterns that cannot be captured in the narrow NEP: in this case, the similarity with Hayek's (1945) approach to emerging properties of complex interactions strikes the reader. Far from being a critique to the very concept of utility functions, Keynes' and Labriola's remarks paved the way to new approaches, including agent-based computational economics, network analysis and evolutionary economics.

Myrdal (1930) also was an early critic of NEP, especially of using utility functions because, in his reconstruction, this would imply accepting the discredited Benthamite philosophy of the *pleasures and sorrows* calculus used to justify conservative political views, whereas he himself promoted progressive policies. On the contrary, Savage (1954) demonstrated that is possible to have a rational scheme of choice including utility functions while abandoning the utilitarian psychology. Whereas Myrdal correctly pointed out how inadequate and *passé* was the naive model of rationalist psychology, he went too far rejecting the concept of objectivity itself in economic theory, a self-defeating argument blocking the very possibility of rationally debating the issue at stake. Despite these limitations, he hinted at the role of genuine uncertainty in economic problems and how the human mind tackles these problems by resorting to habits, shortcuts, routines. His vocal suggestion to develop stricter connections with psychology and especially social psychology proved fruitful and has been followed by fellow economists ever since.

The empirical relevance of NEP lies at the core of the Chicago school of economics. Becker (1962) proved that some key theorems in economics – demand curves' negative slope, for example – do not actually rely on well-behaved preferences, but on pressure from *scarcity*, i.e. budget sets; the same argument applies to productive factors demand. More specifically, he showed how markets force irrational individuals (erratic, impulsive or inert) to act *as if* they were genuinely rational to survive changing incomes and prices: actions by rational and irrational agents put under pressure by scarcity are observationally equivalent. Becker's argument implicitly helps distinguish two alternative concepts of rationality: (1) an a priori necessary requirement of consistency between ends and means for economic action and (2) an adaptive response to environmental market forces. Depending on the analytical context, rationality can function either as an assumption for or as an outcome of human action. Most probably, classical economists had the second definition of rationality in mind when discussing producers' behaviour.

The growing dissatisfaction with the cursory treatment of risk and uncertainty in economic theory led economists integrating NEP with classical statistical decision theory. At the theoretical level, the new research program by von Neumann and Morgenstern (1944) (NMP) extended scheme (1) to include the case of risk, so completing the NEP scheme.

Scheme 2 (NMP) *Consider the following objects of choice that are lotteries (L) with finite support, i.e.*

$$L = P\colon X \to [0, 1]$$
$$\text{such that} \quad \#\{x \mid P(x) > 0\} < \infty \tag{19.3}$$
$$\text{and} \quad \Sigma_{x \in X}\, P(x) = 1$$

and the following set of axioms:

1   *Weak Order:* $\succsim$ *is complete and transitive.*
2   Continuity: *for every* $P, Q, R \in L$, *if* $P \succ Q \succ R$, *there exist a function* $\alpha, \beta \in (0, 1)$ *such that* $\alpha P + (1 - \alpha)R \succ Q \succ \beta P + (1 - \beta)R$.
3   Independence: $P \succsim Q$ *iff* $\alpha P + (1 - \alpha)R \succsim \alpha P + (1 - \alpha)R$.

In this context, von Neumann and Morgenstern (1944) *demonstrated that* $\succsim \subset L \times L$ *satisfies former axioms if and only if there exists* $u\colon X \to \mathbb{R}$ *such that, for every* $P, Q \in L$,

$$P \gtrsim Q \text{ iff } \sum_{x \in X} P(x)u(x) \geq \sum_{x \in X} Q(x)u(x). \tag{19.4}$$

Moreover, u is unique up to a positive linear transformation (Gilboa, 2009, p. 80).

Furthermore, any agent maximising the expectation of u complies with the formerly described axioms. The theorem simply states that under some axioms, the behaviour of an agent can be *represented* by an utility function: as such, it has no normative value, i.e. does not represent the benchmark against which actual behaviour must be compared to assess optimality.

NMP treats risk in a novel way accommodating more realistic features of some economic choices. In an NMP world, opportunity costs also encompass information search needed for decision; as an example, informational and stochastic constraints help modelling optimal stopping problems where agents balance at the margin the value of keeping the current option against the value of continuing their search for a better option, as in the case of job search (McCall, 1970; Stigler, 1961). NMP's most mature and accomplished theoretical normative outcome is the *theory of mechanism design* (Hurwicz, 1960), a robust toolbox blending elements from, among others, noncooperative game theory, contract theory and information theory to produce *mechanisms*, namely rules of the game to optimally organise economic institutions while also accounting for information asymmetries and strategic interactions between agents: in this scheme, Walrasian markets, matching markets or auctions represent alternative devices designed to pursue specified goals (Börgers, 2015).

Among critics, Herbert Simon (1997) attacked NEP, but for very different reasons than Myrdal's: starting from a background in administrative science, he focused on practical and especially organisational applications of choice theory. He devoted all his research to developing empirical models of behaviour based on *bounded rationality*, namely the concept that human reason, because of its limitations, often cannot tackle choice problems by following the NEP/NMP scheme.

According to Simon, there exist other problems unfit for NEP even in the NMP enriched version, either because computational costs of extensive search are prohibitive or because crucial data are missing altogether. Starting from the study of game of chess, where an unconstrained search for the optimal move in a set of 10^{120} possibilities is unattainable also for the most powerful computers, Simon emphasised the computational infeasibility of many rational choice algorithms. In these contexts humans do decide upon *satisficing* rules, i.e. consider available options up to the point of meeting or exceeding a predefined threshold, the *aspiration level*, for a minimally acceptable outcome (Wheeler, 2020). In the words of Simon,

> … decision makers can satisfice either by finding optimum solutions for a simplified world, or by finding satisfactory solutions for a more realistic world. Neither approach, in general, dominates the other, and both have continued to co-exist in the world of management science. (Simon, 1979)

Simon was the first prominent economist to understand rationality as a human mind's adaptive feature. Whereas Samuelson's (1948b) research program promoted mathematical generalisability and very general exact decision rules, Simon emphasised how cognitive limitations call for context-dependent decision *procedures*: in his vision, rational action is all about picking the most appropriate choice procedure given the problem at hand by selectively searching for crucial information and adopting stopping rules, i.e. accepting approximate solutions as the best available option. Procedural rationality so becomes the best kind of rationality when problems cannot be tackled by NEP. While not at all dismissive of neoclassical approaches, Simon showed how escaping the Procrustean bed of optimisation–equilibrium analysis in many contexts allows for a richer analytical toolbox, often more expressive and intuitive (Simon, 1978).[5]

Beyond analytical and methodological reflection, studying actual decision procedures requires extensive empirical observation. Since the limited rationality concept became a staple in the economic debate, Simon's auspice of economics as a more empirically-based discipline has become a standard methodological guideline for applied research. Decision psychology now firmly intertwines with the study of any kind of behavioural problems in economics and often economists deliver solutions which become part of decision psychologists' toolkit (Sapolsky, 2017).

5 Cumulative prospect theory

Walking in the footprints first traced by Simon, decision psychologists began studying the brain as an information processing device. Since the 1960s, cognitive psychologists like Amos Tversky and Daniel Kahneman started comparing empirically-based models of decision-making under risk and uncertainty to NMP models of rational behaviour. The Kahneman-Tversky Program (KTP), using controlled experiments, systematically tested, among other things, whether individuals react to risk as predicted by NMP: quite rapidly, new evidence accumulated showing systematic departures from traditional models (Thaler, 2015; Kahneman, 2011).

At first, new theoretical models were advanced to organise empirical evidence, as in the case of *cumulative prospect theory* (Tversky and Kahneman, 1992) where expected utility is written as

$$u\left(\mathbf{p},\ \mathbf{x}\right):\ =\pi\left(\mathbf{p}\right)^{\mathsf{T}}v\left(\mathbf{x}\right). \tag{19.5}$$

The vector $\mathbf{p}$ collects probabilities over each possible outcome, $\mathbf{x}$ is a consumption bundle, π is a vector-valued *probability weighting function* and v is a vector-valued *value function*. The probability weighting function reflects overreaction to small probability events and underreaction to large probabilities, i.e. overweighting the tails of any distribution: for example, Bordalo, Gennaioli and Shleifer (2012), show how salience can give raise to probability weighting. The value function embodies *loss aversion*, namely the idea that people feel more sensitive to losses than gains of the same magnitude (Barberis, 2013).

Economists and choice theorists longed for an alternative analysis of risk capable of substituting the NMP approach. The new theory proved fruitful of new developments and applications, which has been the case, among others, for auction theory (Rosenkranz and Schmitz, 2007), the equity premium puzzle (Benartzi and Thaler, 1995) and asset pricing (Barberis, Huang and Santos, 2001).

Cumulative prospective theory, nevertheless, raises a fundamental question: since the theory measures gains and losses relative to a *reference point*, any application cannot but focus on it; unfortunately, to this regard, there is no universal or intuitive rule to apply. The theory is clearly undetermined and any attempt to find the reference point empirically risks overfitting the problem's data.

Kőszegi and Rabin (2006) traced a remarkable way out of this dilemma by blending elements from standard theory, rational expectations and optimising behaviour, with some fundamental behavioural insights from cumulative prospect theory, namely reference-dependent preferences and loss aversion. The authors posit an overall utility function defined as

$$u(\mathbf{x} \mid \mathbf{r}) := m(\mathbf{x}) + n(\mathbf{x} \mid \mathbf{r}),$$

where $\mathbf{x}$ is a consumption bundle and $\mathbf{r}$ is a reference bundle. The component $m(\mathbf{x})$ is the standard utility function, whereas $n(\mathbf{x} \mid \mathbf{r})$ is a *gain-loss* function reflecting how the consumption bundle compares to a reference point vector $\mathbf{r}$. Critically, these points are not passive habits or cognitive biases as it happens in most behavioural economic literature, but reflect rational expectation *beliefs* on future outcomes constructed on outcomes experienced in the recent past. When certainty prevails, the model predicts standard choice outcomes, but reference-dependent preferences and loss aversion come into play when dealing with risk. Though attractive from a theoretical standpoint, Kőszegi and Rabin's (2006) emphasis on consumption rational expectations hardly fits applications in finance where benchmarks are exogenous and depend on expected costs and returns on specific investments (Barberis, 2013). In sum, Kőszegi and Rabin's (2006) model pictures rational agents as living in an empirically-enriched version of NMP.

Finance offers another example of fertile mixing between NMP and behaviourist approaches. According to Osband (2020a, b), agents in capital markets devise price forecasts combining extrapolations from past trends with future events' speculation. As agents exploit all relevant information, they unceasingly *correct* forecasting errors: in contrast to orthodox finance theory where capital markets deliver full knowledge, Osband (2020a) demonstrates they rather function as efficient *learning* devices. He also shows how a reduced-form modified Bayesian updating rule accounts for many apparent anomalies observed in financial markets; his model includes subjective probability estimates, standard Bayesian learning and new epistemic knowledge inclusion: this mixture contributes bridging the gap between behavioural and orthodox finance theories.

The behavioural approach to rationality has given rise to several objections. For example, Levine (2012) convincingly demonstrates how many apparent behavioural biases can be actually accommodated within KTP using more general choice models; though he acknowledges inaction as a genuine anomaly, he qualifies hyperbolic discounting, loss aversion or framing effects as individual preferences' legitimate variants. The *picoeconomics* approach carried out by Ross et al. (2012) epistemologically rejects the holistic view of the individual economic agent. Observed behaviour would result from multiple heterogeneous selves maximising their returns and interacting with each other: these units, physically localised in the brain, show behavioural anomalies as they coordinate with each other. Though fascinating, the explanation relies on univocal correspondences between specific brain areas and behaviour, a thesis empirically falsified as many decisional functions are actually scattered across the brain (Stimolo, 2016; Van Rooij and Van Orden, 2011).

6 Constructivism vs naturalism

KTP mainly focuses on risk evaluation and its misperceptions: any systematic deviation from the NMP and return–maximising outcomes is inevitably labelled as irrational. Almost invariably, researchers design the lab experiment with a single *correct*, NEP-compliant, way to solve a given choice problem, so that the empirically observed non-conforming behaviour reveals cognitive *biases*. These biases reflect maladaptation of hard-wired primordial ways of thinking to the cognitive complexities of the modern world. At best, behavioural anomalies can be *gently* attenuated or corrected by nudging people picking up *optimal choices* by reframing the problem at hand (Thaler and Sunstein, 2009), though these procedures violate the basic principle of individual autonomy (Beraldo, 2017). This approach's epistemic foundation relies on the implicit normative inter-pretation of VNM, namely *constructivist rationality*.

The constructivist approach fails completely when necessary data are not available: for example, when price knowledge is incomplete, or search strategies are so abundant that an extensive examination of them all is unattainable, or when choice sets change unpredictably. As these circumstances take place, both the prescriptive and the normative value of NEP/NMP approaches become problematic. The radical difference between risk – a situation in which out-comes are unknown in advance but agents have reliable estimates of their oc-curring probabilities – and genuine uncertainty, i.e. when future tastes, prices, technologies are truly unknown in nature and time of occurrence, is all but new in economics as it dates back at least to Frank H. Knight (Langlois and Cosgel, 1993). Though virtually all economists acknowledge the distinction between risk and uncertainty, research on uncertainty has generally produced only vague schemes (like Keynes' famous *animal spirits*) or nihilistic approaches (like G.L.S. Shackle's).

Gigerenzer (2019), on the contrary, has provided a fertile systematisation in the study of uncertainty distinguishing and articulating the notions of *axiomatic* and *ecological* rationality. Axiomatic rationality is the behavioural conformity to an abstract set of axioms and rules, while ecological rationality is a *formalization of means–end instrumentalist rationality, based on Herbert Simon's insight that rational behavior is a function of the mind and its environment* (Gigerenzer, 2019, p. 1). The founder of Bayesianism, Leonard Savage (1954), limited the normative application of axiomatic rationality to *small worlds* (S, C) in which future states (S) and consequences (C) are fully known in advance, but considered it not applicable to *large worlds*, where S or C are unknown. This latter setting implies that the normative interpretation of scheme (1) is irrelevant in large worlds, where genuine uncertainty on key outcomes and probabilities reigns, adaptation to environment prevails and *ecological* rationality is at work: these are the worlds where heuristics replace NEP/NMP optimality rules.

In large worlds, Savage (1954) points out that most choice problems are either *computationally intractable*, like the game of chess and the Travelling Salesperson Problem, or *ill-defined*, like organising a picnic. The picnic problem is ill-defined because constraints and objectives are not clearly defined at the outset: consequences may be unknown due to unexpected events and accidents, or the problem is unfamiliar and decision time is scarce (Gigerenzer, 2019, p. 3). In general, ill-defined problems require using general-purpose heuristic rules, creative integration of a problem's details, or both: these activities enrich the set of behavioural rules and shape information sets taking advantage of the individual agent's features. This choice setting radically departs from NMP which requires full knowledge of probabilities, objectives' function and constraints, leaving out any individual creative contribution.

Whereas many problems are computationally intractable, many *quasi-optimal* solutions are available and commonly used, explicitly in computer science and implicitly by humans. This implies that NEP axioms of completeness and transitivity over choice sets cannot be applied to computationally intensive problems: this makes problematic any normative approach to NEP and, more interestingly, the interpretation of KTP results, since there is no more a normative standard against which comparing behavioural *biases*. The notion itself of bias becomes fuzzy when adaptation to the environment is the key and deviations from axiomatic rationality seem to bear little or no cost (Arkes, Gigerenzer and Hertwig, 2016).

Since in the KTP approach any deviation from the NEP/NMP paradigm is interpreted as a *failure* of the rational mind, this normative conclusion is unfounded in case of uncertainty where efficient heuristics provide frugal and fast solutions to complex choice problems. In other words, we humans are endowed with a system for treating uncertainty which does help getting sufficiently close-to-the-best solutions. This system, probably of evolutionary origins, rather than being a source of cognitive biases, helps humans dealing with the impervious intricacies of choice problems, i.e. cognitive and computational overloads and ill-definiteness. Remarkably, many of these insights already appear in Hayek's (1952) original model of adaptive mind.

Gigerenzer's heuristics are behavioural rules that analytically translate vague notions like *gut feelings, natural spirits, intuitions, experience* and the like into precise recipes. When uncertainty prevails, heuristics can exploit only a subset of available data to produce *less-is-more* effects that work more efficiently than data-intensive algorithms and do not incur the accuracy-effort tradeoff. In the case of prediction problems (Geman, Bienenstock and Doursat, 1992), where

$$\text{Prediction error} = (\text{Bias})^2 + \text{Variance} + \varepsilon \qquad (19.6)$$

variance can be reduced by heuristics dropping explaining variables and avoiding overfitting, as it happens for the LASSO and ridge estimators or the $1/N$ rule for constructing finance portfolios that empirically outperform Markowitz's optimal mean-variance rule (DeMiguel, Garlappi and Uppal, 2009). Excluding redundant predictive variables and simplifying models translates in better predictions. Often, heuristics are based on lexicographic preferences, i.e. orderings defying representations by utility functions: the evidence found in Şimşek (2013) shows that in a large sample of data sets – from biology to business, computer science, ecology, economics, education, engineering and medicine – linear and lexicographic models produce the same predictions.

While Gigerenzer's approach owes more than a lot to Simon's research program on behavioural decision making, the main takeaway from Gigerenzer's studies is that, at the agent's level, when uncertainty prevails, often simplified recipes *win* over more sophisticated NEP rules: this point makes a leap forward compared to Simon's approach. Then, it comes natural to ask: as humans are endowed with efficient heuristics for tackling computationally intensive choices, what does happen at the market level? In several experiments, Smith (2003) has demonstrated that markets transactions work exactly as predicted by theory under less stringent assumptions about rational agency: globally stable price trajectories are observed also when, for example, informational requirements are significantly weakened. Also, in this case, simple (trade) mechanisms provide robust outcomes that in theory require much stronger conditions to work properly.[6]

We find that this evidence, at the individual and the market level, matches with Hayek's (1945) fundamental insight: genuine uncertainty pervades the economic world, but spontaneous institutions like markets find ways to convey the relevant price information relying on adaptive individual behaviour (Horwitz, 2000). How all this collective computation can take place? Most probably, as suggested by Gigerenzer, this happens because we rely on heuristically simplified but efficient methods of choice.

7 Conclusions

In this essay, I have reviewed two main themes touched in Panico's (2012) article on rationality in economics: the acceptability of axioms on which neoclassical choice theory rests and the role of psychology in shaping choices. Choice theory is the object of study of many disciplines, but economics favours explicit statement of assumptions and implications, very often in mathematical terms. While mathematical sophistication of choice models helps analysis and applicability, the interpretation given to models depends on another layer of meaning. I have shown that very often the neoclassical model is given a prescriptive or a normative interpretation, as if it were the only correct way to find a solution to a choice problem. While the neoclassical scheme can accommodate lots of apparently *anomalous* behaviours, the idea that the neoclassical scheme is *always* applicable to any kind of problem stretches the argument too much to prove empirically fruitful. Showing how computationally hard and ill-defined choice problem are actually solved using heuristics, I have asserted that including them in the economist's toolbox would remove the normative interpretation of the neoclassical scheme and enrich our knowledge of how real humans make choices. While the debate on economic rationality remains all but settled, historical accounts like Panico's (2012) still help us reconstruct and clarify one of the key issues in economics.

Notes

1 I personally thank Pasquale Commendatore, John Eatwell and Neri Salvadori. I gratefully acknowledge an anonymous referee who provided extremely enlightening insights on Herbert Simon's economics of choice. My special thanks go to Marco Stimolo for countless enthusiastic discussions on rationality and the philosophy of economics. Leonidas Zelmanowitz provided great feedback on the manuscript and Kent Osband's deep reading and suggestions helped me discover a novel perspective on market learning: I am more than grateful to both of them. I also thank Massimo Salviati for his sharp technical remarks on neurology and brain functioning. All the remaining errors are mine. Last but not least, I thank Luigi Borghero and Nicoletta Piras for the great dinners we had together in Porto Pino during the summer days I was thinking about and writing these pages.

2 On a personale note, I have had (and still have) the privilege to have Carlo Panico as a colleague and interlocutor for almost twenty years to date: with both of us interested in the methodology of economics, we still often discuss the issue of rationality and how it leaks into economic analysis. Needless to say, I hope the present article will help spark new passionate discussion between us.

3 Interestingly, even though he himself championed equilibrium thinking in economics, Kenneth Arrow backed the research program at Santa Fe Institute on out-of-equilibrium economics (Arthur, 2019).
4 Sraffa's epistemological position owes a lot to O. Neurath and to early R. Carnap's works.
5 I thank an anonymous referee for suggesting key corrections and additions to this paragraph.
6 Vernon Smith's work on social interactions at the personal level rather than market's (Smith, 2009) reveals a gamut of results that do not match with the stylised NEP model. Social interactions are also covered, from a sociobiological viewpoint, in Robert Sapolsky's (2017) book *Behave* which, for example, provides an extensive account of how hierarchies and intentions impact on non-market transactions.

References

Allen, R. G. D. (1932). The foundations of a mathematical theory of exchange. *Economica* 36: 197–226.

Arkes, H. R., Gigerenzer, G. and Hertwig, R. (2016). How bad is incoherence? *Decision* 3(1): 20.

Arthur, W. B. (2006). Out-of-equilibrium economics and agent-based modeling. In *Handbook of Computational Economics*, Volume 2, Amsterdam, NL: Elsevier, pp. 1551–1564.

Arthur, W. B. (2019). Kenneth arrow and nonequilibrium economics. *Quantitative Finance* 19(1): 29–31.

Barberis, N. C. (2013). Thirty years of prospect theory in economics: a review and assessment. *Journal of Economic Perspectives* 27(1): 173–196.

Barberis, N. C., Huang, M. and Santos, T. (2001). Prospect theory and asset prices. *The Quarterly Journal of Economics* 116(1): 1–53.

Becker, G. S. (1962). Irrational behavior and economic theory. *Journal of Political Economy* 70(1): 1–13.

Benartzi, S. and Thaler, R. H. (1995). Myopic loss aversion and the equity premium puzzle. *The Quarterly Journal of Economics* 110(1): 73–92.

Beraldo, S. (2017, September). An impossibility result on nudging grounded in the theory of intentional action. Technical Report 485, Naples, IT: Centre for Studies in Economics and Finance (CSEF).

Bernoulli, D. (1954 [1738]). Exposition of a new theory on the measurement. *Econometrica* 22(1): 23–36.

Bordalo, P., Gennaioli, N., and Shleifer, A. (2012). Salience theory of choice under risk. *The Quarterly Journal of Economics* 127(3): 1243–1285.

Börgers, T. (2015). *An Introduction to the Theory of Mechanism Design*. New York, NY: Oxford University Press.

Bowles, S., Kirman, A., and Sethi, R. (2017). Retrospectives: Friedrich Hayek and the market algorithm. *Journal of Economic Perspectives* 31(3): 215–230.

Bryant, W. D. A. (2010). *General Equilibrium: Theory and Evidence*. Singapore, SG: World Scientific Publishing.

Cantillon, R. (2015 [1755]). *Essay on the Nature of Trade in General*. Indianapolis, IN: Liberty Fund.

Chambers, C. P. and Echenique, F. (2016). *Revealed Preference Theory*, Volume 56. Cambridge, MA: Cambridge University Press.

Debreu, G. (1959). *Theory of Value: An Axiomatic Analysis of Economic Equilibrium*. Number 17. New Haven, CT: Yale University Press.

DeMiguel, V., Garlappi, L., and Uppal, R. (2009). Optimal versus naive diversification: how inefficient is the $1/N$ portfolio strategy? *The Review of Financial Studies* 22(5): 1915–1953.

Fisher, F. M. (1989). *Disequilibrium Foundations of Equilibrium Economics*. Cambridge, MA: Cambridge University Press.

Geman, S., Bienenstock, E., and Doursat, R. (1992). Neural networks and the bias/variance dilemma. *Neural Computation* 4(1): 1–58.

Gigerenzer, G. (2019). Axiomatic rationality and ecological rationality. *Synthese* 198 (4), 1–18.

Gigerenzer, G. and Selten, R. (2002). *Bounded Rationality: The Adaptive Toolbox*. Boston, MA: MIT press.

Gilboa, I. (2009). *Theory of Decision Under Uncertainty*, Volume 45 of *Econometric Society Monographs*. Cambridge, MA: Cambridge University Press.

Hayek, F. A. (1945). The use of knowledge in society. *The American Economic Review* 35(4): 519–530.

Hayek, F. A. (1952). *The Sensory Order: An Inquiry Into The Foundations of Theoretical Psychology*. Chicago, IL: University of Chicago Press.

Hollis, M. and Sugden, R. (1993). Rationality in action. *Mind* 102(405): 1–35.

Horwitz, S. (1994). Subjectivism. In P. J. Boettke (ed), *The Elgar Companion to Austrian Economics*, Chapter 3, Cheltenham, UK: Edward Elgar Publishing, pp. 17–22.

Horwitz, S. (2000). From the sensory order to the liberal order: Hayek's non-rationalist liberalism. *The Review of Austrian Economics* 13(1): 23–40.

Hurwicz, L. (1960). Optimality and informational efficiency in resource allocation processes. In K. Arrow, S. Karlin and P. Suppes (eds), *Mathematical Methods in the Social Sciences*. Stanford, CA: Stanford University Press, pp. 27–46.

Kahneman, D. (2011). *Thinking, Fast and Slow*. New York, NY: Farrar, Straus and Giroux.

Keynes, J. (2012 [1933]). *Edgeworth, Francis Ysidro*, Volume 10 of *The Collected Writings of John Maynard Keynes*, Chapter 16. Cambridge, UK: Cambridge University Press.

Kirzner, I. M. (1997). Entrepreneurial discovery and the competitive market process: an Austrian approach. *Journal of Economic Literature* 35(1): 60–85.

Kőszegi, B. and Rabin, M. (2006). A model of reference-dependent preferences. *The Quarterly Journal of Economics* 121(4): 1133–1165.

Kurz, H. D. and Salvadori, N. (2005). Representing the production and circulation of commodities in material terms: on Sraffa's objectivism. *Review of Political Economy* 17(3): 413–441.

Labriola, A. (1922). *Il valore della scienza economica. Introduzione a una critica dell'Economia politica*. Naples, IT: Alberto Morano Editore.

Lachmann, L. M. (1976). From Mises to Shackle: an essay on Austrian economics and the Kaleidic society. *Journal of Economic Literature* 14(1): 54–62.

Langlois, R. N. and Cosgel, M. M. (1993). Frank Knight on risk, uncertainty, and the firm: a new interpretation. *Economic Inquiry* 31(3): 456–465.

Levine, D. K. (2012). *Is Behavioral Economics Doomed? The Ordinary versus the Extraordinary*. Open Book Publishers.

McCall, J. J. (1970). Economics of information and job search. *The Quarterly Journal of Economics*, 84(1), 113–126.

Menger, C. (1950 [1871]). *Principles of Economics [Grundsätze der Volkswirtschaftslehre]*. Auburn, AL: Ludwig von Mises Institute.

Myrdal, G. (2017 [1930]). *The Political Element in the Development of Economic Theory*. New York, NY: Routledge.

O'Driscoll, G. P. and Rizzo, M. J. (2015 [1985]). *The Economics of Time and Ignorance*. New York, NY: Routledge.

Osband, K. (2020a). Bridging the orthodox/behaviorist divide. *Wilmott* 2020(105): 16–28.

Osband, K. (2020b, November). Rationally uncertain expectations. Technical Report 3662920, Social Science Research Network (SSRN).

Panico, C. (2012). Some thoughts on the concept of rationality in economic theory. *Revista Galega de Economía* 21(1): 1–21.

Rosenkranz, S. and Schmitz, P. W. (2007). Reserve prices in auctions as reference points. *The Economic Journal* 117(520): 637–653.

Ross, D., Sharp, C., Vuchinich, R. E., and Spurrett, D. (2012). *Midbrain Mutiny: The Picoeconomics and Neuroeconomics of Disordered Gambling: Economic theory and Cognitive Science*. Boston, MA: MIT Press.

Samuelson, P. A. (1948a). Consumption theory in terms of revealed preference. *Economica* 15(60): 243–253.

Samuelson, P. A. (1948b). *Foundations of Economic Analysis*. Cambridge, MA: Harvard University Press.

Sapolsky, R. M. (2017). *Behave: The Biology of Humans at Our Best and Worst*. New York, NY: Penguin Press.

Savage, L. J. (1954). *The Foundations of Statistics*. John Wiley and Sons, Inc.

Shermer, M. (2009). *The Mind of the Market: How Biology and Psychology Shape Our Economic Lives*. New York, NY: Henry Holt & Company.

Simon, H. A. (1978). Rationality as process and as product of thought. *The American Economic Review* 68(2): 1–16.

Simon, H. A. (1979). Rational decision making in business organizations. *The American Economic Review* 69(4): 493–513.

Simon, H. A. (1997). *Models of Bounded Rationality: Empirically Grounded Economic Reason*, Volume 3. Cambridge, MA: MIT Press.

Şimşek, Ö. (2013). Linear decision rule as aspiration for simple decision heuristics. In C. Burges, L. Bottou, M. Welling, Z. Ghahramani, and K. Weinberger (eds), Advances in Neural Information Processing Systems. Number 26, pp. 2904–2912.

Smith, A. (1981 [1776]). *An Inquiry into the Nature and Causes of the Wealth of Nations*. Indianapolis, IN: Liberty Fund.

Smith, A. (2010 [1759]). *The Theory of Moral Sentiments*. New York, NY: Penguin Press.

Smith, V. L. (2003). Constructivist and ecological rationality in economics. *American Economic Review* 93(3): 465–508.

Smith, V. L. (2009). *Rationality in Economics*. Cambridge, MA: Cambridge University Press.

Stigler, G. J. (1961). The economics of information. *Journal of Political Economy* 69(3): 213–225.

Stimolo, M. (2016). An economic agent in my brain? A critical analysis of multiple-self models in neuroeconomics. *Review of Social Economy* 74(4): 329–348.

Thaler, R. H. (2015). *Misbehaving: The Making of Behavioral Economics*. New York, NY: W. W. Norton.

Thaler, R. H. and Sunstein, C. R. (2009). *Nudge: Improving Decisions About Health, Wealth, and Happiness*. New Haven & London: Yale University Press.

Tversky, A. and Kahneman, D. (1992). Advances in prospect theory: cumulative re-presentation of uncertainty. *Journal of Risk and Uncertainty* 5(4): 297–323.

Van Rooij, M. and Van Orden, G. (2011). It's about Space, It's about Time, Neuroeconomics and the Brain Sublime. *Journal of Economic Perspectives* 25(4): 31–56.

von Neumann, J. and Morgenstern, O. (2007 [1944]). *Theory of Games and Economic Behavior (Commemorative Edition)*. Princeton, NJ: Princeton University Press.

Wheeler, G. (2020). Bounded rationality. In E. N. Zalta (ed), *The Stanford Encyclopedia of Philosophy* (Spring 2020 ed.). Stanford, CA: Metaphysics Research Lab, Stanford University.

Index

Note: Page numbers in bold indicate tables; page numbers in italics indicate figures; page numbers followed by "n" indicate notes.

Printed in the United States
by Baker & Taylor Publisher Services